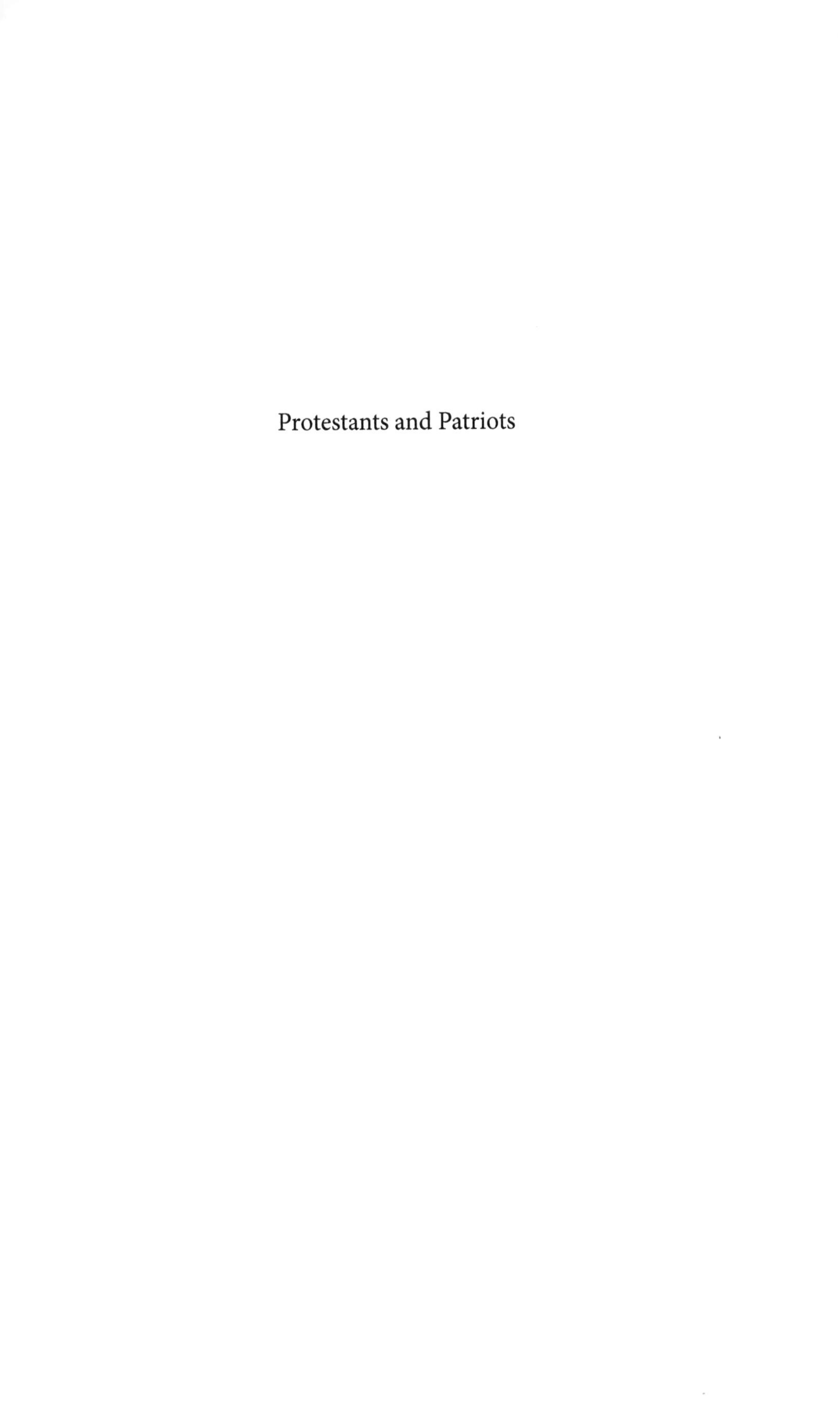

Protestants and Patriots

PROTESTANTS AND PATRIOTS

Presbyterians in the Age of Revolution

D. G. Hart

University of Notre Dame Press

Notre Dame, Indiana

University of Notre Dame Press
Notre Dame, Indiana 46556
undpress.nd.edu

Published in the United States of America

Library of Congress Control Number: 2025948058

ISBN: 978-0-268-21082-3 (Hardback)
ISBN: 978-0-268-21085-4 (WebPDF)
ISBN: 978-0-268-21084-7 (Epub3)

GPSR Compliance Inquiries:
Lightning Source France, 1 Av. Johannes Gutenberg, 78310 Maurepas, France
compliance@lightningsource.fr | Phone: +33 1 30 49 23 42

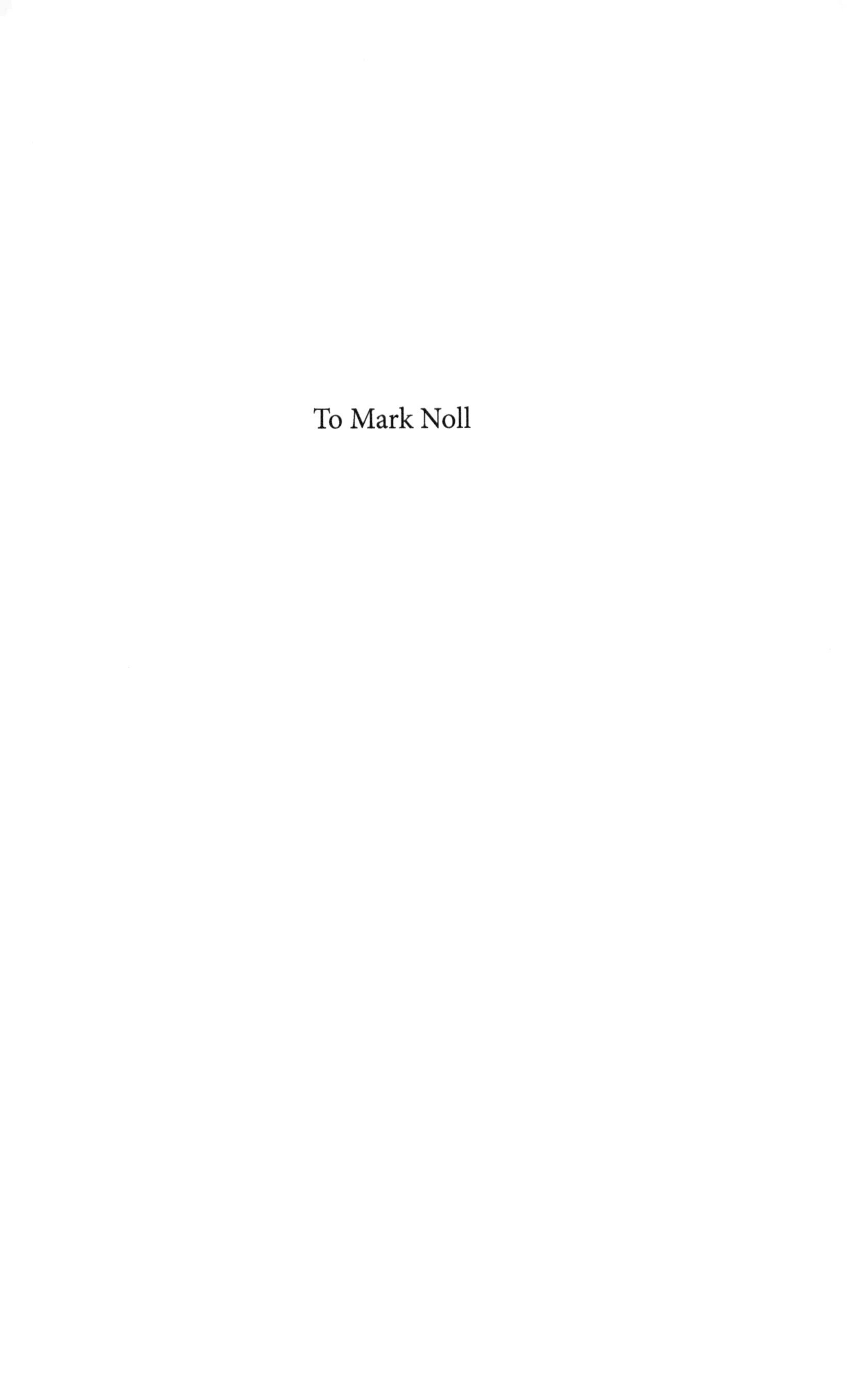

To Mark Noll

CONTENTS

ILLUSTRATIONS

PREFACE

This book began in 2012 over lunch in Dublin with friends and colleagues, Crawford Gribben (then teaching at Trinity College Dublin and now at Queen's University Belfast) and Graeme Murdoch (Trinity College Dublin). We talked about many topics, Dublin's appeal, Irish society, Trinity College, and—yes—Presbyterianism and revolution. Both of these historians write about early modern British and European Christianity. Their perspective added layers of historical depth to the ideas I had about Presbyterians in the American Revolution and Founding. It was also my first time in Ireland and the beginning of my awareness of the island's unusual history within the Anglophone world. My trip included speaking to Presbyterians who belonged to different denominations. Those meetings planted additional seeds about the varieties of Presbyterians and political loyalties in the transatlantic world because Irish Presbyterianism aligned oddly with American Presbyterian history (or vice versa depending on one's perspective). In addition to my impressions of Ireland and its Presbyterian churches was my own newly acquired teaching responsibilities at Hillsdale College. There members of the Department of History teach America and the West from soup to nuts, from Hammurabi's Code and the Hebrew scriptures to the 9/11 attacks on the World Trade Center. No matter a historian's training, he or she needs to acquaint freshmen and sophomores with the ancient world, medieval Christendom, early modern Europe, and American/U.S. history from its colonial to its post–Cold War stages. Having to think and make understandable the big picture involved in these courses was another backdrop to my conversations in Dublin about Presbyterians and political rebellion. This was the context that encouraged me to conceive of the American Revolution, famously called a "Presbyterian rebellion" by King George III, from a wider perspective than the particular circumstances of the American churches and their pastors and members' responses to British imperial policies after the French and Indian War (1756–63).

As grand as this larger awareness of Presbyterian politics may have been, my own pilgrimage as a Presbyterian has likely reduced the big historical picture's frame. In some ways this book began—of course, I did not know it—with a baby boomer fundamentalist's exposure to what seemed like the much grander and more historic world of Presbyterianism. Francis Schaeffer, who may not measure up intellectually these days to his reputation fifty year ago, exposed me to his Presbyterian brand of Reformed theology when I was a student at his study center, L'Abri. Whatever the verdict on Schaeffer, the mountains visible from the Swiss canton of Vaud were glorious. Following on the heals of reading and listening to Schaeffer was exposure to J. Gresham Machen at Harvard Divinity School. He became the eventual subject of my dissertation at Johns Hopkins University. In the world of American conservative Presbyterians, Machen and Schaeffer represent the yin and yang of political postures. Schaeffer wanted a return to America's Christian (Presbyterian) roots; Machen insisted the church of his day stay of clear of politics.

As limited as their understanding of Presbyterianism's political history was (and mine at the time), the Schaeffer and Machen stances on church–state relationships have nevertheless become the backbone of this book. Presbyterians have generally fallen into two camps—those who think government works best when it is upholding God's truth, and those who believe the church is the chief vehicle for Christianity. Consequently, the government should mind its civil business. Throughout most of the modern era, Presbyterians have belonged to both camps. Not until the eighteenth century did these two outlooks sort into two relatively different camps. As a graduate student, I had a slim grasp of where Schaeffer and Machen fit into the migration of Presbyterianism, from Calvin's Geneva to Knox's Edinburgh and eventually to John Witherspoon's Philadelphia. But now with the benefit of hindsight, it turns out that Machen and Schaeffer stand legitimately within the streams of Presbyterian politics mapped in this book. For what it is worth, the author is glad that Presbyterianism developed in ways to make room for Machen's view of the church as a spiritual institution, distinct from the civil government's jurisdiction. At the same time, I do not pretend to think Machen represents the "true" or historic Presbyterian position. The original Presbyterian view of politics was conflicted thanks to the strange categories that Christ left to all his followers: "Render unto Caesar the things that are Caesar's, and to God the things that are God's" (strange if only because Caesar belongs to God?). How to make sense of that evasive reply to Pharisees has bedeviled Christians ever since the ink dried on the Q source's palimpsest. If Presbyterians struggled to sort out God's and Caesar's belongings, they stood in a long line.

An early book on the transatlantic history of Calvinism also helped me prepare for this undertaking. In the case of this book, the subject is one tribe of Reformed Protestants—Presbyterians—whose political origins and developments were bound up with the fortunes of English and Scottish monarchs and Parliaments and those rulers built. Unlike my *Calvinism: A History* (2013), this history, *Protestants and Patriots*, of Presbyterians and British politics in Britain and North America comes closer to a single narrative than trying to fit French, German, Dutch, English, Scottish—and more—Reformed churches into one story. To be sure, differences of national and denominational history prevent the Presbyterian story from being a simple one. It is more a novel than a short story—yet true! But most of contemporary Presbyterian communions belong to a timeline that stretches from Calvin's 1541 *Ecclesiastical Ordinances* to the 1875 union of the Presbyterian Church of Canada.

Trying to tell one story—from 1541 to 1875 and over five nations—covers a lot of pages, maybe too many. At the same time, if Frances Fitzgerald can devote 752 pages to American evangelicals, why can't British and American Presbyterians merit a hefty book? One reason for the book's girth is the aim of bringing together disparate episodes and characters that have lived in isolated monographs and articles. In other words, this is a work of historical synthesis. It builds on the remarkable contributions of political, denominational, and intellectual historians who have explained specific parts of Presbyterian politics. To include all of the details of this subject is obviously impossible. But trying to curate the most relevant chapters of Presbyterian history within the unfolding of Anglo-American politics from 1560 to 1875 is an effort not yet attempted. Readers will judge the book's success.

It goes without saying that readers should not blame the conversation partners upon whom I have relied while writing and presenting parts of this book. Among my colleagues at Hillsdale, Mark Kalthoff, Richard

Gamble, Korey Maas, Matt Gaetano, Miles Smith, Tom Connor, Paul Moreno, Paul Rahe, Brad Birzer, Anna Vincenzi, Bill McClay, and Charles Yost have provided valuable perspectives on the history of politics and the place of Christianity in the West. At the Presbyterian Scholars' Conference, held each year at Wheaton College (Illinois), Jeff McDonald has not only graciously allowed me to present parts of the chapters that follow but has also been a constant source of encouragement. Among the scholars who have attended those conferences, I value especially the comments of George Marsden, Brad Longfield, Brad Gundlach, Mark Valeri, Dan Williams, Don MacLeod, John Muether, William Harrison Taylory, Richard Burnett, John Wiers, Amber Reynolds, Tim Larsen, and Ken Stewart.

The lovely and talented Ann Hart, my dear wife and cat lady, has listened to many, many comments about this book, from that 2012 lunch in Dublin to yesterday's morning walk. Her gifts as an editor have greatly improved the book.

One of the regulars at the previously mentioned Wheaton conferences was Mark Noll, to whom this book is fondly dedicated. Mark has been a reader of my manuscripts for forty years, from my original forays into Presbyterianism via Machen to this book. He first planted the seeds of comparative history and taught me about Canada's Christian past. In the case of this book, his corrections and suggestions have contributed dramatically to sharpening its arguments and staying on point about the most important parts of the story. I have been an intellectual debtor to Mark since I was a young man, and I remain so.

Introduction

Why did Presbyterianism so often emerge as an irritant in British and American politics between 1630 and 1800?A system of church government that favored assemblies and councils over bishops, Presbyterianism was technically a version of church reform. To be sure, in a context of state churches, changing church government could spill over into the affairs of civil magistrates. Even so, outside the English-speaking world in the early modern period, church reforms that replaced bishops with councils did not instigate as many heated political contests, with violent outbursts, that English and Scottish Presbyterians did. A brief chronology of the most stormy episodes of Presbyterian political intrigue establishes a baseline for the relationship between reforming church government and political rebellion.

- In 1606, King James I of England (VI of Scotland) sentenced Scotland's leading advocate for Presbyterianism, Andrew Melville, to prison for four years after luring the Scottish churchman to London for a meeting allegedly about church reform.
- In 1638, the Scottish Parliament adopted the National Covenant, which called upon the king, the church, Parliament, and the people to pledge their support for the true faith of Reformed (and Presbyterian) Protestantism, a declaration that fueled the Bishops' Wars of 1639 and 1640.

- In 1643, an alliance between the English Parliament and Scotland led to the adoption of the Solemn League and Covenant, an act that committed England and Wales to the same terms (with a Presbyterian church government) as Scotland's 1638 National Covenant.
- In 1649, the English (Rump) Parliament executed Charles I for treason.
- In 1690, William III, king of England and king of Scotland after the Glorious Revolution of 1688–89, defeated James II at the Battle of the Boyne (in Ireland) with overwhelming support from Protestants in England, Scotland, and Ireland.
- In 1776, the United States declared independence from Great Britain with Presbyterian and Congregationalist pastors providing the most vigorous support among American clergy.
- In 1798, the United Irishmen, which consisted of Presbyterians and Roman Catholics, led unsuccessful armed rebellions against the British government for its religious and economic policies that favored the Protestant (Anglican) Ascendancy.

This book is about Presbyterian protest, what made Anglophone Reformed Protestants particularly combative and activist, and how political circumstances in England and Scotland colored efforts for ecclesiastical reform. It also completes the story by showing how these committed Protestants became defenders of liberal democracy. The turn from theocratic expectations for a godly society to an embrace of representative government and voluntary churches is an unlikely outcome to Presbyterians' original theological and political ideals. Between 1640 and 1800, Presbyterians remained politically assertive. But over those 160 years, Presbyterians switched from state churches and covenanted monarchs to civil and religious liberties and republican government.

Divine-Right Monarchs Prefer Bishops

"No bishop, no king" was a line attributed to James I, king of England and Scotland, after a 1604 meeting between Puritan ministers and bishops from the Church of England.[1] Whether the Scottish version of Puritanism, Presbyterianism, occupied the same space in the king's mind as the English ministers present is not clear. Both groups objected to vestments, a uniform liturgy (the Book of Common Prayer), and insisted on a strict observance of the Sabbath. Both Puritans and Presbyterians, who drew their initial energy from objections to episcopacy, were a constant and nettlesome presence in British politics for the next two centuries.

So pronounced were the debates' consequences over the proper form of church government for British politics that when colonists in North America declared independence, the unanimous verdict was that the American Revolution was a Presbyterian rebellion. Statements supporting this point are legion. From Andrew Hammond, British commander of the *HMS Roebuck*, who said Presbyterians "have brought this revolt," to Ben Franklin's observation that King George hated the revolutionaries because the king associated them with "whigs and Presbyterians," ample literary evidence supports the claim that the American Revolution was an outworking of Presbyterianism. A letter from a colonist in New York, published in a London newspaper in 1774, was explicit: "Believe me, the Presbyterians have been the chief and principal instruments in all these flaming measures, and they always do and ever will act against Government, from that restless and turbulent anti-monarchical spirit which has always distinguished them everywhere."[2]

More than two centuries later, James Webb, former U.S. secretary of the navy (and U.S. senator from Virginia), employed that same understanding of Presbyterians in *Born Fighting* (2004).For Webb, a descendant of Presbyterian Ulster Scots, the "refusal to be intimidated from above" was not only in the "Scots-Irish DNA" but as old as "the creation of the Presbyterian Kirk."[3]

Although common, it was also a one-sided reading of a Protestant group that in the American colonies had no part in religious establishment the way Anglicans (in New York and Virginia, for instance) or Puritans in New England did. It also misread Presbyterian politics in the United Kingdom, where for many reasons those who promoted Presbyterian church government had repeatedly supported Scottish and then British monarchs. That support did not always seem congenial to the Stuart line of monarchs. But compared to the English Protestants who supported Oliver Cromwell's war with Charles I and Parliament's execution of the king for treason, Presbyterians were conventional and orderly.

A later British monarch's attribution of bad manners to Presbyterians, namely, George III's assertion that the American Revolution was a

"Presbyterian rebellion" (fact-checked by historians as true),[4] has fueled inquiry into Presbyterianism's political implications. In the case of the American War for Independence, assessments of Presbyterian arguments and leadership have generally avoided situating colonial developments within the longer history (two centuries worth) of Protestant and British history. Students of what became the United States have had an outsize place in the study of Presbyterianism and rebellion. Some of that interest owes to the fingerprints colonial Presbyterians left on the debates leading up to war and independence. In 1775, the Presbyterian Synod of New York and Philadelphia, for instance, counseled its churches that despite Parliament's foolish counsel to the king, loyalty to the Crown was still in order and a way to uphold "the revolution principles [of 1689]." The synod also advised congregations to look after the morals of church members, because the Continental Congress was discouraging "luxury in living, public diversions, and gaming of all kinds." John Adams saw such churchly intervention in politics, no matter where it fell on loyalty to the Crown, as possessing a "fervour" that "will produce wonderful Effects." Benjamin Franklin's son, William, governor of New Jersey, disagreed. In 1765, he blamed Presbyterians (and Congregationalists) for stirring up the colonists against the British government.[5]

During the initial stages of the War for Independence, Ambrose Searle, secretary to Admiral Richard Lord Howe, asserted that the conflict was "at the Bottom very much a religious War," with Presbyterianism responsible for "this whole Conspiracy."[6] This explains historian Howard Miller's verdict that "Presbyterians invested much of their group identity in the war for independence and its success."[7] To be sure, Presbyterians were not alone in supporting independence, nor were they unanimous since some remained Loyalists. Other colonial Protestants were no less vigorous members of the patriot cause. Even so, J. C. D. Clark's estimate of the revolution hints at the prominence of Presbyterians: "Under the inspiration of New Light Presbyterians, a highly politicized elite," associated with the founding of the Presbyterian College of New Jersey, gave a religious energy to populist attacks on "privilege and hierarchy, an assertion of divinely-sanctioned popular sovereignty against the divine right of the English monarchy."[8] Connecting a church polity such as Presbyterianism that featured rule by the few (over against episcopacy's rule by one) to the rising tide of support for popular sovereignty in the British American colonies is hardly rocket science. The same point applies to the Puritans' Congregationalism, which was even more democratic than Presbyterianism.

As important as the American Revolution may be for considering Presbyterianism's role in the rise of liberal democracy, historians of Scotland have so much more to explain than their North American counterparts. After all, how Presbyterianism became the church polity of the Church of Scotland, not to mention its involvement in civil war and regicide, is a story fraught with more drama than Presbyterian ministers advocating autonomy from British rule. Much of the Presbyterian energy that fueled Scotland's national church resorted not only to political advocacy but also to armed aggression. The Bishops' Wars of the 1630s and the Scots' alliance with Parliament during England's Civil War (1642–49) possessed explicit religious dimensions, with an established church the prize for political and ecclesiastical victors. In North America, Presbyterians had not insisted on an established church or a national covenant. Instead, American Presbyterians shared political convictions with other Protestants, whether Congregationalist John Adams or Anglican Thomas Jefferson. If anyone wants to conduct an experiment to test the potency of Presbyterian politics, Scotland is the laboratory.

Scottish historians, in turn, have had no trouble measuring the influence of Presbyterianism on national politics or describing its adherents' rebellious tendencies. Roger Mason, for instance, has located John Knox's understanding of the Scottish Reformation in the sort of apocalyptic thinking that generally prevails among revolutionaries trying to understand and justify their actions: "Decoding the sacred books" of biblical prophecy was a means for discovering the meaning of the Scottish church's "struggle with the false and Antichristian church of Rome."[9] Whether for self-interested reasons or not, Presbyterian critics, Collin Kidd adds, attributed at least a dash of radicalism to the claim that Christ, not the king, was head of the church. Episcopalians in particular tied "presbyterian rebels" to regicide and asserted that Scotland's National Covenant made loyalty to the Crown "conditional."[10] Likewise, David Allen recognizes rightly that the Scottish argument for a Reformed church was a direct threat to the Stuart monarchy since the Reformation was the path to a truly Christian nation (and future) and the reign of Charles I was an obstacle to Protestant progress. Because the king was "meddling" with the Kirk's "pristine integrity," advocates of the National Covenant believed they were justified in taking up arms against the Crown (as they did in the Bishops' Wars).[11]

Did Presbyterianism have to come to this? Did its doctrinal assumptions or plans for reforming the church inevitably lead to insurrection and rebellion? The answer this book gives is no. The reason to keep reading, however, is that Presbyterianism, unlike any of the historic Protestant communions emerging during the Reformation (Lutheran, Anglican, and Reformed, which includes Presbyterians), became a significant source of political controversy within Britain and its satellites—Ireland, Canada, and the American colonies. What makes Presbyterianism's rebellious history so remarkable is that it started as a clever and novel reform of church life in small, French-speaking Geneva. English and Scottish exiles, enraptured by John Calvin's reform of church and social life, brought Presbyterian ideals back to their homelands. Their ensuing efforts to reform the Church of England and the Church of Scotland inevitably generated political controversy—sometimes war—owing to church–state relations in explicitly Christian societies. Presbyterians' challenge both to episcopacy and to the English monarch as the head of the national church created space for either reforming monarchy or doing away with the office altogether. Once England adopted a constitutional monarchy during the Glorious Revolution, Presbyterians throughout the Anglophone world also adjusted to liberal political norms of separation of powers, religious pluralism, and religious disestablishment. Over the course of three centuries (1560–1860), the claims of Presbyterians were a reliable indicator of Christendom's status within Anglo-American societies.

Observers watching the launch of Presbyterianism in 1540s Geneva would likely not have predicted its political potency. To be sure, Calvin sparred with Geneva's civil authorities over the power of excommunication (because it concerned spiritual matters, Calvin said it belonged to the church's prerogatives). Yet, as a method of governing the church, despite breaking with the episcopal model reaching back to the ancient church, Presbyterianism was merely a church polity midway between the hierarchical structures of bishops and the democratic ideals of Congregationalism (rule by church members). Presbyters were pastors and elders, clergy and gifted laity, joined in a kind of republican rule both in the local church and working out to regional and national bodies. Calvin's *Ecclesiastical Ordinances* (1541) was part of his condition for returning to Geneva after his earlier reform efforts went further than the city council was prepared to go. His three-year absence, which took him to Strasbourg, where Presbyterian patterns of government were in place, solidified a commitment to what was essentially a conciliar path for rule within the church. Conciliarism, in fact, is one way to undercut the novelty of Presbyterianism. When the Western, Catholic Church needed a resolution to the Great Schism (1378–1415), a period of rival popes, one in Avignon and one in Rome, a council of bishops (Constance) intervened. This body restored a single papacy in Rome and called for a regular council (every ten years) to assist the pope in church administration. (Subsequent popes were not convinced of the wisdom of conciliarism and refused to call assemblies of bishops.)

Whether or not Calvin drew directly on conciliarism, his plan for church government in Geneva did replace bishops with presbyters or elders. *Ecclesiastical Ordinances* called for four offices—pastors (preachers), elders (laymen), deacons (laymen), and teachers (pastors who taught theology). Calvin's teachers worked in the Geneva Academy and both trained pastors and taught citizens in two tiers of curricula, thus demonstrating Protestantism's aid and dependence on literacy. The elevation of qualified laity into church government was novel, even if most Presbyterian apologists argued that this was the pattern of the ancient church (when the Christian administration itself was fluid). Elders were responsible for reviewing and supplementing the teaching and authority of pastors (for starters), and deacons undertook the work of charity—everything from welfare to health care—which was considerable in a city teeming with refugees. Presbyterianism had no direct equivalents to the separate powers of modern governments—the executive, legislative, and judicial branches of civil polity—but the experience of Scottish Presbyterians within the confederal structures of the British Empire was a political lesson that heirs of the Scottish Kirk did learn.[12] What Presbyterianism promised was mechanisms of accountability and improving the quality of pastors that episcopacy lacked.[13]

Presbyterianism even promised greater godliness among the laity and thus appeared to deliver on the demand for ecclesiastical reform that Martin Luther's protests had underscored. If Calvin's system had only applied to church structures, it would not have addressed directly the call by humanist scholars and Protestants for godliness in both clergy and laity. On the one hand, Calvin's ideas promised improvement among clergy (pastors) by establishing clear guidelines (education and tests) for ordination, a contrast to the seeming arbitrariness of bishops' standards for ordaining priests. On the other hand, Presbyterianism emphasized discipline in church life, not only as a method to correct Christians who had veered from holiness, but also to encourage believers through direct oversight by elders who were both neighbors and church officers. Calvin's church order, consequently, provided a clear model for correcting the medieval church, whose reputation for hypocrisy stemmed at least from widely inconsistent standards for priests, bishops, and wealthy patrons of the church. In a sociological sense, Presbyterianism was an early instance of modernity's drive to rationalize human interactions by supplying the church with professional standards and transparent structures of governance.

What impressed visitors to Geneva—especially English and Scottish exiles—was that Geneva practiced what it prescribed. The church there seemed to be a model of a Christian commonwealth. For instance, as early as 1542, the consistory (pastors and elders) insisted that Genevans attend weekly sermons, learn new prayers and the catechism, and abandon Roman Catholic forms of devotion. Minutes of the Geneva churches also reveal that officers heard hundreds of cases of un-Christian behavior, from improper behavior during church services and strained relations between spouses to gambling and dancing.[14] When John Knox traveled to Geneva (1556–59) during his years of exile under the reign of Mary Tudor (1553–58), he marveled that the city was "the most perfect school of Christ that ever was in the earth since the days of the apostles."[15] Presbyterian church government seemed to be responsible for Geneva's success, and it became the ideal for a church to be adequately reformed.

Calvin's reforms had clear political implications and sometimes brought him into conflict with Geneva's city government. As much as historians of political theory have linked Reformed Protestant ideas about government (of which Calvin was a major voice) to an older tradition of resistance theory, such as when subjects or citizens may legitimately disobey civil authority, the route to challenging rulers was relatively straightforward. Instead of conjuring the divine origins of government and the reciprocal duties between magistrates and the people, in the context of an established church Calvin's reforms could (and did) pit the ideals of church officers against the government that supported the city's mandated faith. Calvin's disagreement with Geneva's city council over the power of excommunication forced the pastor to leave the city for three years before authorities recognized they needed Calvin to reform their churches. He was in Strasbourg between 1538 and 1541. There Calvin refined ideas about church reform and learned patience from Martin Bucer before returning to Geneva, where he lived until his death in 1564. An ideal Christian society for Calvin was for church and state to cooperate. In his *Institutes of the Christian Religion*, Calvin insisted that the magistrate had a responsibility to enforce the true religion. This position was largely agreeable to Geneva's city council, but the pastors and magistrates did butt heads. English and Scottish Protestants, inspired by Geneva, took disagreements with political rulers to a different level of opposition.

Because English and Scottish exiles saw the effects of Calvin's efforts during the 1550s, instead of the way those reforms rolled out in the 1540s, Presbyterians may have imagined that importing Geneva's Reformation would be easier than political and ecclesiastical realities in the old country allowed. One of England's most difficult challenges, something that Calvin did not face, was a divine-right monarch. One reason that Anglicanism differed from its Reformation cousins was that Lutheran and Reformed churches did not have to cooperate with a civil magistrate who was head of the church. In 1534, the English Parliament made Henry VIII the head of the Church of England (as opposed to the pope). The Act of Supremacy made the English church Protestant, even if bishops, priests, and members of Parliament were uncertain about where the reforms launched by Luther and Ulrich Zwingli were headed. The English church vacillated between Reformed and Roman Catholic iterations after Henry VIII's death and during the reigns of his children Edward VI (1547–53) and Mary Tudor. But with the reign and long tenure of Elizabeth I (1558–1603), the Church of England came down firmly on the Protestant side, even if the queen herself favored moderation, an ecclesiastical posture that characterized Anglicanism and provoked Puritans and Presbyterians (some of them exiles from Geneva) to seek further reformation.

The politics of both church and state in England and eventually Scotland, thanks to James VI succeeding Elizabeth I in 1603 to be the monarch of both kingdoms, drove Presbyterians to challenge kings, queens, and bishops who prevented reforms designed to return the church to its apostolic order and simplicity. Historians often use resistance theory—theoretical arguments about when political rebellion is legitimate—to explain Presbyterianism's affinity for revolt. Some follow Quentin Skinner, who observed that resistance theory had a long pedigree among Roman Catholics and Lutherans even before Presbyterians embraced it. What is missing from most accounts of Presbyterians and revolution is the unusual set of circumstances Presbyterians in England and Scotland faced because of the relationship between the Crown and national church. John Knox's inflammatory *First Blast Against the Monstrous Regiment of Women* (1558) may look like another instance of Presbyterians challenging monarchical tyranny. But the hero of the Scottish Reformation, whose authority most Presbyterians later invoked, was also faulting English and Scottish monarchs for failing to implement church reforms that would replace bishops with councils.[16]

More than the Dutch, German, or French Reformed churches, Presbyterianism became identified with political rebellion, as this book explains, because church reform in England and Scotland involved challenging two sacred and ancient institutions—the Crown and the episcopate. The other Protestant magisterial traditions did not require such dramatic change.

Other scholars have observed this peculiarity about Presbyterians and written at length about Reformed Protestant zeal and political reform. The major themes include the two kingdoms doctrine (spiritual and temporal, ecclesiastical and civil), natural law, resistance (to tyranny) theory, divine-right monarchy as opposed to the consent of the people, and even the political implications of Christology (how Christ's human and divine natures correspond to temporal political sovereignty).[17] None of these approaches, however, examine specifically the political implications of Presbyterian church government. One reason could be that correlations between ecclesiastical and civil structures throughout the Protestant world were generally secondary to political structures in specific social settings. Yet, as Reformed Protestantism gained momentum in England, Scotland, Ireland, and eventually the New World, Presbyterian church government added a distinct voice to political debates. For that reason, tying Presbyterianism to the American Revolution, a major turn in modern history thanks to what the United States became, is too narrow a frame of reference. The larger and modern political narrative—the decline of sacral monarchy, the dismantling of religious establishments, the growth of constitutional checks on government, and the protections of personal freedoms—is in large measure a Presbyterian story.

Such a claim—the significance of Presbyterian church government for modern Anglo-American political history—sounds odd because running an ecclesiastical institution seems inconsequential to governing a nation, managing diplomacy, and providing social services. For instance, forms of government that relied on councils instead of bishops were relatively common outside England and Scotland. Although sixteenth- and seventeenth-century Reformed and Presbyterian churches by no means had the exact same structures of ecclesiastical administration, they all adopted a system of church assemblies that resembled Calvin's original design (sometimes even with hybrid episcopal arrangements). In addition to the Swiss cities' church orders, Huguenots in France adopted what Philip Benedict called "the most critical independent initiative" of those persecuted churches, namely, a "presbyterian-synodal" system.[18] In Heidelberg, one of the centers of Reformed Protestantism in the German-speaking world, church leaders again followed a Presbyterian model of ecclesiastical authority. The same pattern prevailed in the Dutch provinces, where no matter how weak and ineffective, the Reformed churches relied on consistories (pastors and elders) and synods to regulate ecclesiastical life. For Polish and Hungarian churches, where Reformed Protestantism flowered briefly and faded, church reform also included structural change to ecclesiastical governance. In each of these locales, Reformed church leaders confronted remarkably different political circumstances. Almost everywhere except for the semiautonomous cities in Switzerland, churches cooperated with princes or monarchs (e.g., Heidelberg, Netherlands, England, Scotland) to implement reform. In those cases where the magistrate was hostile, such as France, Reformed Protestants sought legitimate grounds for resisting tyrants, but others went into exile.[19]

Dutch and French examples indicate that Reformed Protestantism could provoke political rebellion the way Presbyterianism did. But only in the Anglophone world did Presbyterianism persist for more than two centuries as an incubator of political agitation that aided the adoption of Anglo-American constitutional arrangements. It might have been the case that Presbyterianism, as it found a footing within British politics, was alone responsible for the process that replaced a divine-right monarch and episcopal establishment with the modern separation of church and state. But within the history of Reformed Protestantism, the Presbyterian controversies within British societies were exceptional in associating one group of Protestants with modern liberal political reforms. Lest anyone conclude that this story is a Whiggish one of Presbyterians taking credit for planting the seeds of liberal democracy, readers should remember, as the following chapters will remind, that the liberalizing consequences of Presbyterian politics only came after—and as a course correction to—these English and Scottish Protestants' initial theocratic impulses.

The crucial period for Presbyterian church history and British politics was not the American Revolution, but the English Civil War, or War of the Three Kingdoms. That military contest between Parliament and the Crown, a conflict with clear theological rivalries over Charles I's religious policies, was the backdrop for the Presbyterian equivalent of the United States' Constitutional Convention of 1787. As part of its alliance with the Scots to fight Charles I, Parliament called an assembly of priests and pastors to reconstitute the Church of England. This body, the Westminster Assembly, met during most of the Civil War, and its documents, chiefly the Westminster Confession of Faith, Larger and Shorter Catechisms, and Directory for Worship, became standards for Presbyterians throughout the English-speaking world and remain to this day. Although those who met at the Westminster Assembly could not agree on church polity—the Congregationalist wing of Puritanism prevented Presbyterians from prevailing in the English church—the Confession of Faith did show the fingerprints of both Presbyterian church polity and Reformed Protestant political theory.

The telling elements were not the Westminster Confession's instruction on the civil magistrate (chapter 23) or the generic guidelines for church government (chapter 31). Granted, both of these chapters suggested harmony over matters that had been contentious among the Westminster Assembly's members. On the question of the civil magistrate's authority in connection to the church, Erastians (named for Thomas Erastus, a sixteenth-century Swiss physician who opposed the introduction of Presbyterian polity at Heidelberg) wanted government to have authority to carry out the spiritual sanction of excommunication. Opponents, who agreed with Geneva, wanted to reserve this power to church officers. The language of chapter 23 might have sounded Erastian by asserting that the civil magistrate, in Constantine-like fashion, had authority to oversee the church so that order, correct doctrine, and true worship were the norm. But chapter 30 reserved to ecclesiastical officials the actual discipline of offending church members and officers, from levels of admonition and suspension to excommunication. Delegates to the Westminster Assembly also disagreed on church government. Presbyterians wanted a system of councils to regulate church affairs, but Independents, who feared a tyrannical church, favored Congregationalist polity, which located church power among members of a congregation. The Confession of Faith recommended synods and councils as a means for resolving controversy but advised flexibility on the frequency and regularity of such assemblies ("as they shall judge expedient").

What was telling in the Westminster Confession about Presbyterian politics was the lengthy chapter 22, "Of Lawful Oaths and Vows." Without mentioning Scottish Presbyterian politics directly, the chapter distinguished the Westminster Confession from all other creedal statements of the Reformation era. For all of the influence that covenant theology—the pattern of vows made throughout scripture, especially the Old Testament, between God and his chosen people—exerted in medieval and early modern conceptions of monarchs, feudal lords, nations, and popular consent,[20] no other Reformed confession included an entire set of affirmations on oaths and vows. (This chapter 22 continues to baffle today's Presbyterians.)[21] To be sure, other Reformed creeds, the affirmations of the Debrecen Synod (1567), for instance, discussed the import of vows and oaths in connection with church membership, ordination, marriage, and citizenship. But devoting an entire chapter, seven paragraphs long, was an anomaly.

Chapter 22 on oaths and vows made sense, however, from the perspective of Scottish commissioners to the English assembly. The terms for an alliance between the English Parliament and Scotland in the former's war with Charles I involved a pledge by Parliament in 1643 to ratify the Solemn League and Covenant. By promising to collaborate with Scotland's Parliament in defending and maintaining the true (Protestant) faith in England, Scotland, and Ireland, the English were able to gain the help of Scotland's army in the war against the Crown. The Solemn League and Covenant, in effect, extended to England and Ireland the Scots' National

Covenant (1638), a declaration that defied Charles I's religious policies in Scotland and justified Scots taking up arms against the Crown in the so-called Bishops' Wars (1639, 1640). In the Scots' opposition to Charles I, Covenanters formed militias to resist religious policies that violated Presbyterian norms. These Scottish convictions became politically useful to the English Parliament in its own conflict with Charles. The Solemn League and Covenant did not use the word "Presbyterian," but the contours of its church polity were obvious. When the National Covenant described a church truly "reformed," it linked "superstition, heresy, schism, profaneness," and anything else contrary to "sound doctrine" and "godliness" to "Church-government by Archbishops, Bishops, their Chancellors, and Commissaries, Deans, Deans and Chapters, Archdeacons, and all other ecclesiastical Officers depending on that hierarchy."[22]

Whatever the National Covenant assumed about church government, it used strenuous language to describe the duties of anyone who signed. The preliminary paragraph of the National Covenant, which described the perilous times facing England, Scotland, and Ireland, ended with a resolution and determination "to enter into a mutual and solemn League and Covenant, wherein we all subscribe, and each one of us for himself, with our hands lifted up to the most High GOD, do swear" to all six articles of the document. Of course, promising and pledging were common in such documents. The United States' Declaration of Independence concluded with the phrase, "we mutually pledge to each other our Lives, our Fortunes and our sacred Honor." The Solemn League and Covenant went beyond the sort of resolve that came with political adversity. Article 6 of the National Covenant described the signers as having formed a "union and conjunction." This was also a lifelong commitment—"all the days of their lives." Signers even acknowledged that they would have to give an account to God on the Day of Judgment: "This Covenant we make in the presence of ALMIGHTY GOD, the Searcher of all hearts, with a true intention to perform the same, as we shall answer at that great day, when the secrets of all hearts shall be disclosed." Such religious and political zeal likely explains why even after the Civil War, Oliver Cromwell's rule as Lord Protector during the Commonwealth (1649–60), and the 1660 return of the monarchy, the ideals of the National Covenant remained a watershed moment in Presbyterian history.

The National Covenant could also well make sense of the Westminster Confession's long chapter on oaths and vows. According to that chapter, a vow was part of a religious ceremony, like the promises a church officer made in an ordination service. An oath, in contrast, was a "promissory oath," to be "voluntarily, out of faith, and conscience of duty, in way of thankfulness for mercy received, or for the obtaining of what we want, whereby we more strictly bind ourselves to necessary duties." Whether the Westminster Assembly's commissioners had the Solemn League and Covenant in mind is a question that few historians have tried to answer. But the political context for the Westminster Assembly makes the Westminster Confession's chapter 22 look more than coincidental, especially since such detail on oaths and vows was absent in other Reformed churches' creeds. Not even the French Reformed, who faced dilemmas over conflicting loyalties to the French Crown and lesser nobles, failed to add guidance to its national creed (the Gallican Confession of 1559) about the religious significance of vows or oaths.

The English Civil War, together with efforts to reform the churches of England and Scotland, is largely responsible for transforming the obscure form of church government in Geneva into a vehicle for political reform that sometimes had dramatic consequences for Britain, its satellites, and modern political ideals. Historians, political theorists, and ecclesiastical leaders have often attempted to link the Reformation, and especially its Calvinistic wing, to the political achievements of classical liberalism—from Calvin, to Milton, Locke, and Jefferson. What follows is the story of that progression without a Whiggish inevitability. Presbyterianism did alter England's and Scotland's political developments, and those changes, in turn, had important consequences for Ireland and the British colonies in North America. But as the history of English, Scottish, Irish, American, and Canadian Presbyterianism shows, the beliefs and polity of these churches did not follow the same lines of development. Nor did the presence of Presbyterian leaders in forming national governments lead to similar outcomes. Most Presbyterians, with the exception of Americans, remained loyal to the British Crown. Despite different trajectories, Presbyterians were united in a belief that their form of church government was the best means for inculcating holiness among God's people. They also recognized that the church needed cooperation from the magistrate to ensure reformation of lives and society. Hopes for a friendly magistrate, however, proved to be Presbyterianism's Achilles' heel. The only way to achieve actual reformation was not through a king who swore a reformed covenant, but through independence from the state. The separation of church and state is a cliché in descriptions of liberal politics. But the difficult lessons that Presbyterians learned in trying to protect the integrity of the church from meddling kings or legislatures were crucial to Protestants abandoning the civil magistrate as an ally forming a Christian society.

What started in England and Scotland around 1560 as efforts to follow biblical standards in civil and ecclesiastical governance, as the following pages will show, over the next three centuries became a lesson in the benefits of liberal politics. Between 1560 and 1700, roughly, Presbyterianism was one part catalyst and another part justification for challenges to existing arrangements in England, Scotland, and Ireland. The Glorious Revolution and the establishment of Presbyterianism within the Church of Scotland more or less tamed the most demanding parts of Calvin's church order. Thanks to the disruptive tendencies of Presbyterianism in seventeenth-century England and Scotland, observers could well regard the American Revolution as a Presbyterian rebellion, even if the colonial clergy's support for political independence drew on considerations far removed from the Scots' National Covenant or Parliament's Solemn League and Covenant. The Irish Rising (or Rebellion) of 1798 also echoed Presbyterian cussedness, but it too (aside from being tiny) drew more on local economic and political grievances than devotion to an ideal Christian church and society. The United Irishmen, those responsible for the rising, were also nonsectarian (see chapter 5 herein).

Once the American and Irish aftershocks of the original Presbyterian revolution of the 1640s calmed, Presbyterians embraced modern political arrangements in the classical liberal sense. Throughout the Anglophone transatlantic world, Presbyterians became champions of free markets, representative government, personal responsibility, national improvement, and religious liberty. That nineteenth-century Presbyterians drew on the zeal and examples of Calvin, Knox, and the seventeenth-century Scottish Covenanter Samuel Rutherford to explain the church's place in modern society was an irony that only few noticed. At the same time, the seemingly progressive results of both the Glorious and American

Revolutions confirmed Presbyterians in their sense that they were indeed on the right side of social advancement.

To capture the fits and starts of Presbyterianism's transformation between 1560 and 1875, this book unfolds in two parts. In part 1, "Presbyterians Aggressive (1560–1700)," chapter 1 traces the origins of Presbyterianism in England and Scotland and locates the occasions of greatest Presbyterian advocacy within the unfolding administration of church life in British society. It follows the original arguments for Presbyterianism by the likes of Thomas Cartwright and John Knox, both in detail and in reception. Complaints about episcopacy and royal supremacy in the church gave Presbyterianism a distinct language that actually persisted across the centuries, even if the consequences for civil government subsided. Chapter 2 follows Presbyterianism under the united monarchy of the Stuarts and the particular challenges that James I and Charles I posed to church reforms in both England and Scotland. It also unearths the intensity of Scottish objections to Charles I's attempts at religious uniformity and the political fallout from it—civil war and even regicide. As revolutionary as Presbyterianism felt in the events leading to Charles I's execution, the Scots themselves remained committed to the monarchy, if only because the theological architecture of a national covenant drew inspiration from the Hebrew kings of the Old Testament. Chapter 3, the last in this part, traces the consequences of the Restoration for Presbyterians in England, Scotland, and Ireland, and of their strategies in the struggles that led to the Glorious Revolution. To claim that their experience between James I and William III had tempered Presbyterian political ideals is an understatement.

Part 2, "Presbyterian Modern, 1700–1875," traces adjustments that these Protestants made to constitutional monarchy and its administration in Britain and North America. In chapter 4, debates about subscription and reckoning with a dissenter status throughout the Anglo-American world (except for the Church of Scotland) show Presbyterians to have been hastily retreating from zeal for the true religion to positions of protecting liberty of conscience. Even in Scotland, where Presbyterians emerged as the ecclesiastical establishment, the Kirk adopted a moderate stance and proved that earlier zealots had not considered the compromises that accompany political victory.

One feature of this new outlook was the recognition that cooperation and coordination between the church and civil magistrate was inadequate for societies with religious diversity beyond a simple Roman Catholic/Protestant binary. This moderation makes Presbyterian involvement in the American War for Independence and the Irish Rising of 1798 the subject of chapter 5, all the more perplexing. Since Presbyterian involvement in those political rebellions had more to do with frustration that mainly liberal governments were not living up to their ideals, late eighteenth-century Presbyterian political agitation was more civil than ecclesiastical in substance. Because those rebellions were more liberal than theocratic, the shift that Presbyterians made to a voluntary (as opposed to established) church in the early nineteenth century, as chapters 6 and 7 show, was largely in keeping with the American and Irish political disturbances. Specifically, the freedoms that religious minorities had advocated against the monopoly of ecclesiastical establishments now became the norm for Presbyterians to escape the state's meddling in religious affairs.

This new and modern Presbyterian attitude to the state did not diminish political activism among Presbyterians. They continued to advocate policies and laws designed to produce a godly society. Chapter 8 explains that Presbyterians were unflinchingly involved in the reforms that accompanied liberal or Whig politics throughout much of the nineteenth century. Specific outlets for these measures depended on the parties available and the opening of suffrage to wider swaths of society in England, Scotland, Ireland, the United States, and Canada. Presbyterian political involvement was also connected to each respective communions' identification with their nation-states. Chapter 9 follows nineteenth-century Presbyterians as they settled into national identities that followed the extension of political liberalism in the transatlantic world. Whether Presbyterians, as in the case of the Scots, could argue that their form of Protestantism was responsible for the rise of national sovereignty, or, in most other cases, was merely a congenial aid to liberal, democratic constitutional arrangements, the descendants of Calvin and Knox continued to identify the Christian ministry with the effective administration of a specific nation.

Many of the episodes recounted here have received due attention in their own right but often stand alone without reference to a larger narrative of Presbyterianism in the transatlantic world between 1560 and 1875. Of course, the attempt to trace broad themes and find coherence in the diversity of time and place misses some of the specificity and richness of focused analysis. At the same time, if we look at Presbyterianism's place in Anglo-American politics, the enduring features of this Protestant tradition emerge even as its leaders needed to abandon what had seemed, in the first flush of Reformation, like crucial elements of serving God, church, and kingdom. In sum, *Presbyterians and Patriots* highlights the degree to which ecclesiastical reform was a catalyst in major political developments within Britain and North America. The same set of developments also shed light on the ways that Western Christians, in this case Presbyterians, adjusted their own desires for church and society to the realities of society after Christendom.

Both of these stories—church reform leading to a godly society and liberal politics protecting churches—give Presbyterianism a sort of double-mindedness. On the one hand, Presbyterians can revel in the significance they once enjoyed in the days of the Scottish Reformation and the wars with Stuart monarchs. On the other, they can praise the democratic and tolerant policies of modern societies and take some credit for systems that figures such as Calvin and Knox could never have contemplated. The explanation for this tension could simply be a bubbly optimism that Presbyterians bring to their changing circumstances. But anyone who knows the original demanding zeal of Presbyterians also understands that these Protestants have seldom been cheerful. More likely is a habit of mind, established early on, that regarded the church as playing an outsize role in national life, either as part of the establishment or a voluntary church. How Presbyterians maintained that outlook even as they moved from the center of political debates to the sidelines is an important dimension of the story that follows.

PART 1

Presbyterians Aggressive, 1560–1700

CHAPTER 1

The French Connection

For most Presbyterians, the road to church government by elders and assemblies rather than bishops ran through Geneva. This was an odd circumstance for English and Scottish Protestants since Geneva was a republic with no real analogy to monarchy. Church reform in Geneva, as in most of the Protestant world, came at the behest of civil magistrates who had various motives—some devout, some earthly—for having a church free from Rome's oversight. But civil government in Geneva was through a city council, a political body that has little hold in the West's political imagination compared to the glories of the Palace of Versailles, Buckingham Palace, the Hofburg, or even the White House. Rarely do members of city councils emerge as national leaders or empire builders. In Geneva's case, Ami Perrin (1500–1561), who functioned as the city's mayor and had a thorny relationship with John Calvin, colored within the lines of urban politics. One of his notable interventions in international affairs came in 1546 amid fears that Charles V would invade the city because of an influx of Protestant refugees. Perrin called on a French garrison to secure Geneva's integrity. That act of foreign policy landed Perrin in a trial for treason. The courts acquitted the mayor. But the incident was part of a larger struggle between Calvin's ideals for a Reformed church and native Genevans' preference for less strict norms in personal and civic righteousness, a position nicknamed "libertine" by the devout.[1]

Friction between church and civil government, Calvin and Perrin, may have resembled remotely what transpired in England and Scotland between Presbyterians and Tudor and Stuart monarchs, but pastors taking mayors to court was not the lesson that Scottish and English Protestant exiles learned in Geneva. John Knox sojourned in the city twice, and this led to his often quoted observation about Geneva's reformed church and godly society, which came during his second stay.[2] His first visit had occurred in 1554, when Knox was forty years old, during a time when many English Protestants were in exile thanks to Mary Tudor's religious policies. Knox was not there long, since a group of English Protestants in Frankfurt called him to be their pastor. There amidst antagonisms over liturgy among English-speaking Protestants, Knox was in the rare position of conciliator. After a return to Scotland for church reform, in 1556 he received a call to Geneva from a congregation of English-speaking exiles. He was pastor at that church with Calvin's blessing for three years before his final return to Scotland and the official start of the Scottish Reformation. In Geneva, Knox paid more attention to texts and orders of worship than he did to church government. He was operating within one congregation of English-speaking refugees, but Calvin's church polity covered the network of churches in Geneva and the surrounding territories. When Knox returned to Scotland and after gaining support from Parliament, he was responsible for a book of discipline that relied on lessons learned in Geneva. Jane Dawson observes that Scotland's First Book of Discipline "probably reflected" Knox's experience of church life with Calvin at the helm of Geneva's company of pastors.[3]

Thomas Cartwright, arguably the most prominent voice for Presbyterianism in England a few years after Knox's successes in Scotland, was also several years behind his Scottish contemporary in visiting and learning from church life in Geneva. Cartwright, eighteen years old when Mary Tudor became queen, had to abandon studies at Cambridge University but found work as a law clerk. When Elizabeth ascended to the throne in 1558, Cartwright completed his studies and became a fellow at Trinity College. After serving as a chaplain in Ireland under the bishop of Armagh, he returned to Cambridge as the Lady Margaret's Professor of Divinity. When the Admonition Controversy broke out in the early

1570s—based on pamphlets surreptitiously published that attacked episcopacy in ways that troubled members of Parliament—Cartwright himself backed the side of the Church of England and called for "thorow [*sic*] Reformation."[4] Lectures that Cartwright gave in 1570 on the polity of the New Testament church—he found no support for bishops—crossed authorities. They denied him his professorship. Only in 1571 did Cartwright leave for what was in effect the capital of Presbyterianism, Geneva. He did not relocate as a refugee or exile. Calvin had been dead for almost a decade, which left another Frenchman, Theodore Beza, the primary force in the city.

Beza, who had originally run the Geneva Academy, invited Cartwright to teach theology, not the most enviable of positions since the city was experiencing another outbreak of plague. Beza also conceded (to Knox) that by 1571 Geneva was no longer the godly city that the Scotsman had experienced fifteen years earlier. Whatever the Englishman learned about Presbyterianism from Beza in Geneva, his experience with episcopacy in 1572 after his return to England put him decisively in the Presbyterian camp. Authorities not only denied Cartwright an opportunity to teach Hebrew at Cambridge but sought his arrest over involvement in the Admonition Controversy. To escape civil proceedings, Cartwright fled to the Low Countries, where he ministered to English-speaking congregations in Antwerp and Middleburg.[5]

Whatever these two early proponents of Presbyterianism learned during their stay in Geneva, the ecclesiastical order that Calvin had drafted in 1541 became the gold standard for a truly Reformed church among a strain of Protestants in Scotland and England. The reasons for Presbyterianism varied. In some cases, it was a basic method for pushing back against bishops who seemed to have overstepped their bounds or were indifferent to strenuous Christian piety. In other cases, Presbyterianism was the best way to implement further reform of church and personal life by giving hands-on authority to church officers overseeing the ministry of the local church and inspecting the lives of church members. For those drawn to Presbyterianism, the record of episcopacy was long with hypocrisy, abuse of ecclesiastical power, and outright failure to do the work of ministry. For others, Presbyterianism was simply what the New Testament church practiced, an argument that set into motion debates about the Constantinian pattern of civil authority, sometimes cooperating, sometimes intervening, in church affairs. The early advocates of Presbyterianism in England and Scotland did not question monarchy as the best form of civil government, only whether the monarch supported the biblical reform of the church. And because bishops invariably curried the favor of the Crown, they were real barriers to ecclesiastical reform. Because of the long history of imperial Christianity that entangled bishops and emperors, proposals for Presbyterianism inevitably led to questions about civil government. That was not the case among most Reformed churches on the Continent. But in the British Isles, Presbyterianism pulled the thread that could unravel the political status quo.

The Reformed Church of England

England's Reformation was hardly the product of Christian devotion or improving the church's ministry. Whatever Henry VIII thought about Christ and the church, his need for a male heir and a divorce from his first wife, Catherine of Aragon, set in motion a reform of England's church that removed the pope as head and filled the void with the king. For the next twenty-five years, under the reigns of Henry, his son, Edward VI, and his daughter Mary Tudor, the Church of England rode the roller coaster of Reformation-era polemics. The person in the front car, Thomas Cranmer, archbishop of Canterbury from 1533 to 1555, had to finesse the Crown, the king's advisors, and factions within church and society. Under Henry, church reforms were uncertain if only because of the political situation and Protestantism was hardly an established form of Christianity. Under Edward, a boy with strongly Calvinistic regents, the Church of England opened numerous ties to the Reformed churches on the Continent (which led to a reduced place for Lutheranism, the original source of reform, among English Protestants). When Edward died and his Roman Catholic half sister ascended to the throne, the Continental influence on the Church of England ran the other way. "Bloody" Mary's efforts to eliminate Protestantism in England not only made Cranmer a martyr but sent many Protestants in England (among them John Knox) to Europe, where they saw how Reformed churches operated free from a mercurial monarchy. When Elizabeth I succeeded Mary in 1558 and reigned for a remarkable forty-five years, English politics achieved a modicum of stability.[6]

Elizabeth's position as head of the church was both stabilizing religiously and a source of frustration for English Protestants who had seen what a Reformed church could be. In the mid-1560s, the church's bishops were generally supportive of further reform along lines drawn by Reformed church leaders. One particular bill from 1566 outlining such reforms received support in both the House of Commons and the House of Lords, where the bishops added their endorsement. But the queen refused to assent, a move that had repercussions both for the church and politics. Elizabeth insisted on uniformity in the church, but one group of English Protestants pushed for the elimination of Roman Catholic vestiges. Initially, dissent from the queen's moderation took the form of not wearing the surplice. Then resistance moved to the liturgy. In 1567, when the archbishop requested all priests to acknowledge the legitimacy of the Book of Common Prayer, many went along, but at a meeting in London, thirty-seven of them still refused. These Nonconformists were also sensitive about rubrics that said worshipers should make the sign of the cross or kneel for the Eucharist.[7]

Whatever the merits of particular forms of devotion or even the wisdom of uniformity in a nation's churches, the subtext of authority to enforce the accidents of liturgy soon became the text of controversy. Was the Crown rightfully the head of the church? Did bishops' power extend all the way to parishes and the particulars of rites and ceremonies? In other words, questions about ecclesiastical practice inevitably led to the enforcement of adopted norms. This was obvious in the case of England, where the Crown was explicitly at the top of an ecclesiastical pyramid. But it was a question that afflicted all Protestants (minus Anabaptists, who renounced a Christian magistracy). Whether in England, Geneva, or Lutheran territories, if Protestants needed the civil magistrate's blessing and protection to achieve independence from Rome, they also opened the door to the government's intervention in church life. Only in the British Isles and English colonies, however, did those difficult questions produce political instability on the order of revolution.

Religiously inspired political rebellion took longer to surface in England than in Scotland if only because the Crown had been the original impetus for church reform. Once Elizabeth became an obstacle to further reforms and her bishops generally complied, Presbyterianism became not simply nostalgia for Geneva but a genuine alternative to episcopacy. The 1570s debate between Thomas Cartwright and John Whitgift was the first English installment of the case for Presbyterianism. It had already played out at Cambridge, where Whitgift, the eventual archbishop of Canterbury (1583), as vice principal of the university expelled Cartwright from his post as professor of theology for lectures that advocated Presbyterianism.

This controversy over church government was not an academic dispute about theology or biblical interpretation. The condition of the episcopacy in England (and in Scotland) was prone to significant abuses. If the Protestant Reformation was a product of discontent about church officers who seemed to protect the powerful and affluent, the extension of that impulse to governing structures was hardly surprising. A major temptation for bishops and their noble patrons was money. Revenues connected to bishops were notoriously available to their own families or served as mechanisms to render tribute to the Crown. According to Gordon Donaldson, at the time of a bishop's appointment in England, he often had "to hand over or lease property to the queen, who sometimes passed it on to her favourites, or even to promise an annual cash payment."[8] Adding to the financial incentives that surrounded episcopacy, benefices sometimes belonged to persons who did not carry out their spiritual responsibilities. In some cases, appointments went to "priests who refused to renounce the Roman allegiance, laymen, youths," and men with little education. At the same time, the Church of England faced a genuine shortage of residential priests. A 1586 survey indicated that out of 2,537 parishes, only 472 preachers were in place.[9] Presbyterianism ideally provided a remedy. Abolishing episcopacy would liberate church revenues for greater distribution throughout parishes and to ministers. Funds administered by deacons could also be administered better to assist the poor.[10] The Presbyterian manner of examining candidates by an assembly of pastors also promised to raise standards for ordination by removing the verdict from a single officer's prerogative. Advocates for Presbyterianism may have been the "hotter" sort of Protestants and prone to the zealous extremes. But their enthusiasm was not blind to ecclesiastical conditions and the obstacles to reform.

The contest between Whitgift and Cartwright followed in the wake of the 1572 *Admonition* to Parliament Protestants upset that the legislature had failed to approve reforms of worship. A second *Admonition* generally attributed to Cartwright was also in the background when Whitgift decided to stand up for the Church of England as a truly Reformed church. His *An Answer to a certen Libel* (1572) addressed five points: the danger of an unlearned ministry, errors in the prayer book, the faults of the bishops, the need for the church's rightful authority (independent from the Crown), and unfounded biblical support for the established church. Presbyterianism was the subtext; the text was the question about which authority had legitimate power to resolve ecclesiastical controversy.

Whitgift's pamphlet was not an elegant argument since its format involved quoting from the *Admonition* before elaborating a refutation. It would have been perfect for the age of blogging, but Whitgift's preface gave away his main point, which was that the Church of England represented the sound third way between the radicalism of Anabaptists and the tyranny of Rome. It may have come as a surprise to Protestants inspired by Geneva to see their understanding of church government lumped with Anabaptists. But Whitgift plowed ahead and likened Cartwright's complaint that "the civil magistrate hath no authority in ecclesiastical matters" and ought not to "meddle" in them to the Anabaptists' ideas. Whitgift even alleged that subtle papists were behind Anabaptists' efforts to "overthrow" the gospel, which in turn appealed to hypocrites and licentious persons.[11] At the other extreme were papists who refused to worship in the Church of England because its priests and bishops were not "canonically called" to their offices. Like Presbyterians, Romanists also condemned England's forms of worship for departing from Rome's. Finally, Roman Catholics resembled Anabaptists in denying any authority of the civil magistrate in the government and affairs of the church. This left the Church of England as the golden mean between the extremes of chaotic liberty and despotic uniformity. Whitgift's implicit ecclesiological point was that the Crown (instead of the pope) as head of the church, with bishops under the Crown's oversight, constituted a properly Reformed church.

Whitgift's *Answer* ran the gamut of historical, biblical, and practical arguments, a reflection of the encyclopedic nature of the original *Admonition*'s complaints. The Cambridge professor attempted to answer everything, even if it meant treating a topic repeatedly and repetitiously throughout a 200-plus-page pamphlet. The debate over godparents at infant baptisms was indicative of the standoff. Objections to the promises godparents made at the sacrament relied on an appeal to scripture (Rom. 7:15, 18) that Whitgift found entirely unpersuasive. These "proofs," he wrote, were too "farre fetched for my understanding" and actually set a standard so rigid as to "condemn all promises made by man."[12] Likewise, the argument often descended into particulars, such as the meaning of words, with Whitgift refusing to let any disagreement go unmentioned. The word "priest" was objectionable to the *Admonition*'s authors, but for Whitgift these were hardly weighty matters. He suspected that the word "presbyter" was derived from "priest." Even when the New Testament authors spoke about the priesthood being abolished, Whitgift countered, those same authors described Christ as a priest forever, a point that barred any argument that the word "priest" was inherently objectionable.[13]

On the matter of church government, again the points ran the gamut from ancient church history and the functions of the apostles to interpretations of Calvin's New Testament commentaries. Whitgift had no trouble finding evidence of episcopacy in the early church. He quoted church fathers, such as Jerome and Cyprian, who not only described the church's hierarchy with bishops firmly at the top but also defended episcopacy as a check on disunity and schism. According to Cyprian, the "chéefe and principal office of an Archebishop [is] to kéepe vnitie in the Church," to address heresies, schisms, and factions, and to oversee all other clergy "whiche be vnder him" to perform their duties.[14] Whitgift also found plenty of evidence that Calvin recognized hierarchies as part of the church. This did not resolve whether some form of aristocratic element in the church was better than parity among church officers, as Presbyterians preferred. But the authority of bishops was not inherently tyrannical. The subjection of deacons to priests, priests to bishops, and bishops to archbishops was no flaw or indication of self-regard by church officers. It was simply a way to preserve order. For Whitgift, when Peter wrote that pastors should feed their flocks, he was not recommending privilege and power. Instead, the apostle condemned "hautinesse, contempt and tyrannie of pastours" toward their congregations. A pastor had "rule and superioritie over his flocke, but it must not be tyrannicall."[15] What is more, a typical pattern in scripture, from Moses to the Jerusalem Council, was rule by a prince within a particular realm. Christ did not appoint one emperor for the world's government or one bishop for the church universal, but he did appoint diverse princes, bishops, and governors, with one prince sufficient "to governe one kingdome, and one Archebyshoppe one Province, as cheefe and principall over the rest."[16]

When it came to the queen's place as head of the church, Whitgift found little with which to disagree in his adversaries. He quoted a pledge of loyalty to the queen, found in the *Admonition*, that at least reflected the realities of English politics if not the authors' actual attitude to monarchy. The *Admonition*'s authors had written:

> Not that wee meane to take awaye the authoritie of the ciuile magistrate and chiefe gouernour, to whome we wishe all blessednesse, & for the increase of whose godlinesse, we dayly pray: but that Christe being restored into his kingdome, to rule in the same by the scepter of his worde, and severe discipline: the prince may be better obeyed, the realme more flourishe in godlynesse, and the Lorde him selfe more syncerely and purely accordynge to his reuealed will serued than heretofore he hath ben, or yet at this present is.[17]

At the same time, Whitgift was prompt to point out that the larger argument against bishops was at odds with this benediction upon the queen. Christ rules his church, he asserted, by the godly magistrate whom he has "placed over his Churche, and to whom he hath committed hys Churche touching externall policie and gouernemente." Whoever was not content with the details of English church government played "the parts of Corah, Dathan, and Abiram," the rebels against Moses in Numbers 16, who met their fate when the earth swallowed them, their families, and all their possessions.[18]

Such a threat could have silenced further criticism of episcopacy, but Cartwright was not so intimidated. Later Presbyterians might have looked to the Old Testament for instruction about the monarchy, but for rule in the church, Cartwright went straight to the apostles and the early church. In fact, as much as the debate between Whitgift and Cartwright may have appeared to boil down to the Reformation's formal principle (sufficiency of scripture), interpreting the New Testament veered into debates about church history. What was the church's status without any recognition by the civil magistrate or, worse, under persecution? How much was this an exception that awaited an emperor's conversion and religious establishment? If Protestants truly wanted to recover the purity of biblical teaching and apostolic practice, was an established church even imaginable? In effect, Protestantism's impulse to go back to the sources—the apostles and church fathers—was also an invitation to consider the radical position of a church before the rise of Christian emperors.

Cartwright immediately answered the charge of Anabaptism and began where the *Admonition* had ended, with an affirmation of loyalty to the Crown. Unlike Anabaptists, who regarded the sword as an institution completely at odds with Christian devotion, Cartwright acknowledged the lawfulness, necessity, and "singular commodity" of the civil magistrate. He pointed to sermons that Dissenters (Presbyterians) preached to commend the government, prayers for them, and the utter dependence of a "flourishing" commonwealth and church upon the authority of secular rulers: "We love them as fathers and mothers, we feare them as our Lords and maisters and we obey them in the Lord and for the Lord."[19] If he dissented from anything commanded, it was for the sake of conscience informed by the word of God. If Whitgift should have been able to see differences between Presbyterianism and Anabaptism on matters of civil government, that was no less true for matters of church government. Whitgift had argued that Presbyterians, like Anabaptists, believed congregations should call their own pastors (instead of the government) and that ecclesiastical authorities should have power of excommunication. This was a hypocritical charge if only because it rendered defenders of episcopacy in similar company, because in the episcopal system bishops ordained priests and also had a major responsibility for disciplining wayward Christians. "Why do you go about to bring us in hatred for those things," Cartwright asked, "whych you do no more alow?"[20] He knew the answer was to "endevor to discredite" those opposed to bishops. Cartwright wanted Whitgift to play fair.

Part of the rules for debate involved using the Bible as the norm for the church. Here Cartwright revealed a basic tension between advocates for Presbyterianism and episcopacy. What did the Bible say about bishops in the ancient church? On the one hand, it did talk about bishops or overseers in the Greek, but these officers had a very different set of functions than English bishops. The list of contrasts was long: the earliest bishops oversaw one congregation, not thousands; they were engaged in the ministry of a particular congregation as opposed to having no congregational responsibilities; the earliest bishops received their call to office from other pastors, elders, and church members rather than being the ones responsible for ordaining all other ministers; they did not have exclusive power of excommunication but shared it with other pastors and elders.[21]

On the other hand, New Testament silence about bishops akin to the sixteenth-century-England variety allowed Cartwright to turn the tables on Whitgift. If the defenders of episcopacy could level the charge of Anabaptist against Presbyterians, Presbyterians could just as readily accuse bishops of sounding papist. After all, if the New Testament was silent about bishops of the kind that England enjoyed, then advocates of episcopacy needed to go beyond scripture. If Whitgift believed that the apostles established archbishops but left no written record, then "how shall we keep out of the church the unwritten tradition of the papists?" On the flip side, if the apostles had actually left a "perfect and written rule for ordering the church" and the embellishment of episcopacy came later, then Whitgift, Cartwright argued, had implicitly cast doubt on the sufficiency of scripture.[22] At that point, the push for greater reform of church government did not look as much like the perfectionism embedded in the epithet "Puritan." Instead, it went to a deeper point about the structural features of Romanist church life that had failed to prevent corruption of doctrine and worship.

The standard objection to Cartwright's primitivist desire for the church government of 100 CE was that the church under Christian magistrates required a different administration than one under persecution. It made sense, from Whitgift's perspective, for the church in different political and social settings to change standards in selecting ministers. In the apostolic church, without a godly magistrate available, the apostles could devise methods that should not apply to a ministry with a Christian monarch in place. The defense of bishops, in other words, depended on distinguishing the apostles' doctrines, perfect in their content, from their government, ceremonies, and discipline, which were "convenient" for their time.[23]

Cartwright countered that the New Testament showed no sign that relying on one person for the selection of ministers was the pattern of the apostles. The selection of a replacement for Judas in Acts 1 and the call of deacons in Acts 6 both reflected reliance on a consensus among the people and their leaders. Whatever the actual history of the early church, Cartwright's weightier point concerned the wisdom (and potential abuse) of committing ordination to "the power of one" who is allegedly "fittest" to make the determination.[24] He was not explicitly questioning the bishop's capacity for judgment (though of course he was implicitly), but simply the notion that one church officer could discern which men should be ordained to the ministry: "Unless you have your bishop so full of sight that he can leave nothing unseen, and that he received the Spirit without measure"—which gives him Christlike powers—then "the assistance of others" (both ministers and laity) in the process should be welcome.[25]

Part of the reason why Cartwright may have been disingenuous when conceding that bishops were fit to judge candidates for the ministry involved another part of his appeal to the early church. Once the empire had become Christian and emperors were involved in selecting bishops, ambition and politics began to corrupt church processes. Cartwright observed that the pagan emperor Galerius Maximinus "chose the choicest magistrates to be priests." This was the norm for emperors once they became Christian. They selected bishops and endowed them with "wealth and outward pomp" as a way of maintaining the status of priests within the empire. This stateliness, pomp, and "lordship" contrasted starkly with the simplicity of the apostles' ministry and their immediate successors. This was no less true of the Church of England. But the public display and status of bishops for over one thousand years was no justification for its persistence. In fact, since the source of episcopacy's outward glory was "so corrupt," "I conclude that the thing itself which hath sprung from such fountains cannot be good."[26]

The debate between Whitgift and Cartwright went to a second round with the former's response, *The Defense . . . against the Reply of T.C.* (1574), and the latter's *Second Reply* (1575). Like many of these pamphlet battles, the contestants repeated and clarified points already made. In this case, the authors returned to questions about bishops in the New Testament, the extent of apostles' authority (and the ministers they ordained), and the selection of ministers. The political stakes of the debate between episcopacy and Presbyterianism came up in two relatively new ways. At one stage in the exchange, Whitgift and Cartwright discussed the degree to which the apostles and ancient pastors performed both spiritual and civil functions. At issue was the work of deacons in caring for the poor and needy and whether the apostles gave up that activity after the diaconate began. A second question was the interpretation of Peter's condemnation of Ananias and Sapphira for concealing the nature of their private property, a denunciation that brought both excommunication and physical death (Acts 5). Whitgift used these examples to argue for the legitimacy of bishops having civil (temporal) authority. Cartwright, conversely, appealed to the extraordinary nature of the early church to argue that only exceptional circumstances extended the church's ministry beyond strictly spiritual matters. At stake was a sixteenth-century version of the modern notion of the separation of church and state. Although the machinery of religious disestablishment took two centuries to develop, it was implicit in the temporal versus spiritual distinction that went back to Christ's assertion that some aspects of life belonged to Caesar, others to God. In the case of the sixteenth-century church, Whitgift blurred the line between spiritual and temporal spheres. In contrast, Cartwright wanted to delineate those realms to avoid potential abuse of power by princes and bishops.

The disagreement about church–state relations became most obvious and pressing over the legitimate head of the church. For Whitgift, Cartwright's contention that Christ alone was sovereign in the church was a bridge too far. He agreed that Christ (not the pope) was the spiritual head of the church. But in the church's external affairs, the Crown was the head, a power that Christ gave to civil authorities over their people "in all causes."[27] This meant that Christ was "only the archbishop and bishop in respect to his spiritual government." All church officers, bishops, priests, deacons, in their spiritual functions, derived their authority from Christ. For the civil dimensions of church life, ecclesiastical authority came from the queen. This explained why "magistrates are called gods." To be sure, Christ ruled the consciences of Christians in a spiritual manner that guided faith and personal holiness. But the corporate church was bigger than a believer's experience. This ecclesiastical institution required an external government supplied by the civil magistrate. The Crown ruled the church's outward or external affairs by virtue of authority delegated from Christ. If someone wanted a chart of church–state authority with clean lines drawn from Christ to princes, bishops, and priests on Whitgift's scheme, the wait would be long. For him, the queen had authority over the external aspects of the church, while bishops possessed both civil (from the Crown) and spiritual (from Christ) authority.

Cartwright's response played up the ambiguity that lurked in Whitgift's scheme. If Christ were truly the only head of the church, as sometimes the latter allowed, then how could the civil authority also be head of the church in its external functions? Cartwright appealed to the apostles, who reserved the title "head of the church" for Christ. If, however, that appellation also extended to the magistrate, then was it possible to say that Christ was superior to the queen? The question was rhetorical since—here Cartwright was daring Whitgift to follow his logic—no one would call any civil magistrate, as the New Testament described Christ, "the first born of every creature, the first begotten of the dead, the Redeemer of his people." Cartwright added that if the church was the body of Christ and if it had two heads, the result was "certainly monstrous." Consequently, attributing headship of the church to the civil magistrate was a "great violence." "He who is not of the body can be no member of the church."[28]

This exchange set the terms for future debates between defenders of Presbyterianism and episcopacy (which have continued to the present).[29] Ideas and pamphlets, however, were distinct from church life in England and its governance. Here, John Field, one of the authors and editors of the original *Admonition* and a lecturer at a London church, pestered the bishops and Parliament to reform church administration. Some of his efforts involved publication and distribution of pro-Presbyterian arguments, even anti-episcopal texts from Beza in Geneva. But actual plans for ecclesiastical governance through assemblies and synods took shape in the late 1580s when "ministers of the brotherhood" in and near Cambridge met to draft a book of discipline (form of government). Field's work also bore fruit in Parliament (through petitions) that prompted some members to call for leniency in requiring priests to conform in matters of dress and liturgy, and to urge limits on bishops' privileges. In 1587, a bill sponsored by Job Throckmorton, a member of Parliament from Warwickshire, proposed replacing bishops with presbyteries and introducing a liturgy from Geneva. The proposal failed because Parliament had no power over such matters; the question belonged properly to the queen. The reassertion of royal prerogative provoked another pamphlet conflict, with Throckmorton's Marprelate tracts expressing additional discontent with the Church of England. The return volley from the government was a manhunt for authors and presses responsible for the pamphlets. For the establishment, Presbyterianism had become synonymous with "sedicious and factions persons in the commonwealth" who sought the overthrow of the government. Authorities even tracked down Cartwright, who during 1590 and 1591 went to prison on suspicion of subverting the government "by force of arms."[30]

The upshot of England's brief consideration of Presbyterianism was the identification of its advocates with an unacceptable political position that directly challenged the Crown's authority. On the flip side, advocates for episcopacy increasingly conceived of their government as a royalist response to disorder and insurrection, a position that identified the bishops' well-being with the fortunes of the monarchy. The religious calculus that emerged was that the appeal of Presbyterianism grew in direct proportion to the Crown's insistence on religious uniformity. If Presbyterianism gained a reputation for radicalism, much of that stigma flowed from expectations that were unique to English Protestantism. And if episcopacy won the opening round, its victory depended much more on currying the approval of the monarchy than following the teachings of king Jesus. For the losers, the parallels between the papacy's response to the Reformation and the bishops rejection of Presbyterianism were clear.

Scottish Presbyterians

If Scotland (more than Geneva) owns the reputation as the home of Presbyterianism, the reason involves the relative ease by which the Church of Scotland instituted a form of government first attempted in Reformed cities on the Continent. Unlike England where episcopacy was an arm of the monarch, who was head of the church, the Scottish Reformation was anything but stable politically. The ruler of Scotland during the 1550s, Mary of Lorraine, regent to Mary Stuart, was committed to ensuring Rome's ministry in the realm. She also sought a political alliance with France by attracting the dauphin of France (and future king, Francis II) to wed her daughter, an act of diplomacy that would have ensured Scotland's dependence on the French.

These were the sorts of royal policies that in 1558 provoked Knox to write *First Blast of the Trumpet Against the Monstrous Regiment of Women.* As intemperate as Knox's book may have been, it resonated with the state of affairs in Scotland. Mary of Lorraine had to worry about Parliament's suspicion of a French monarch, a growing Protestant movement that saw increasing signs of reform at the local level, and the return of a Protestant monarch in England with Elizabeth I's inauguration. Once Mary of Lorraine perished—the same year (1560) that Francis II died from an inner-ear infection—her eighteen-year-old daughter, Mary Stuart, now a widow, became Scotland's sovereign. When Mary Queen of Scots returned to her native land after living fifteen years in France (between the ages of three and eighteen), she knew little about Scottish government or the kingdom's ways. The vicissitudes of the Scottish monarchy meant that circumstances were not advantageous for Protestantism, but they also created religious and political opportunities. Perhaps because of her inexperience but also owing to the strength of Protestant lords in Scotland, Mary Stuart refused to discourage advocates of church reform. Protestants dominated her council, and she abandoned cultivating French ties—all French soldiers withdrew. Instead, Mary devoted much attention to English affairs. As the granddaughter of Margaret Tudor (Henry VIII's sister), Mary likely had designs on the kingdom to the south. Her second husband, Henry Stuart, Lord Darnley, was also a grandchild of Margaret Tudor. The Scottish royal couple had legitimate claims on the English throne.[31]

These unsettled circumstances provided openings for Protestantism similar to ones in cities and territories on the Continent. Within six months after Mary Stuart's initial activities as queen, Scotland's Parliament met to resolve religious debates in the kingdom. Mary's own vices and infamous instances of moral misconduct among Scottish nobles may have explained the appeal of a form of church government that had the advantage of instilling moral discipline among the realm's subjects. Historians of the Scottish Reformation and biographers of John Knox do not hesitate to tie the rise of Presbyterianism in Scotland to the Scottish pastor's positive experience in Geneva. Margo Todd, for instance, asserts that Knox used Calvin's *Ecclesiastical Ordinances* and *Institutes* as the "theoretical foundation" for the Scottish Kirk's system of sessions and assemblies. The pattern of moral rigor that Knox observed in Geneva was one that applied to "both princes and common people."[32] Conceivably this standard included church officers. Todd observes that this was a "stunning" rebuke potentially at least to the sexual double standard of early modern Europe. Beyond sexual relations, the rigor of Presbyterian discipline was also a challenge to different standards of justice for political elites (civil or ecclesiastical) and ordinary citizens.

In December 1560, six months after the Scottish Parliament met, Lords of the Congregation abolished the Mass. Parliament also approved the First Book of Discipline. This was the document that Knox drew up in consultation with five other pastors (all Johns—Willock, Spottiswoode, Winram, Row, and Douglas) and became the blueprint for the Church of Scotland.[33] Unlike the debates that played out in England during the 1570s, this First Book did not need to make a case against bishops since Parliament was in the mood for reform.

The proposed document did make several snide references to bishops as "dogs" or "idle," but the expectation throughout was one of starting church life more or less from scratch, or at least from a biblical foundation (with memories of Geneva in mind). Rather than a systematic description of ecclesiastical authority, church offices, rules for ordination and assemblies, the First Book almost chaotically ranged from instruction about the sacraments to explaining sins that should keep a man from being ordained to the ministry. In fact, in the section "The Policy of the Church," the First Book made recommendations for daily sermons, the observance of the Lord's Supper four times a year, meetings where pastors met to assess each other's preaching (prophesying), penalties for adultery, and instructions on burial services ("neither singing nor reading"). The egalitarian nature of Presbyterian discipline also led Knox and company to frown on the tradition of preaching at funerals for the wealthy but keeping silent during ceremonies for the poor.[34]

The most obvious difference between existing episcopal government and the one proposed by Knox was to use structures that Calvin had developed. Instead of priests, ministers were the ones responsible for preaching and administering the sacraments. And rather than a top-down arrangement in which bishops selected priests, congregations called ministers who then needed to be examined by other ministers: "It appertains to the people, and to every several congregation, to elect their minister." A congregation had forty days. After that a "superintendent with his council may present unto [the congregation] a man whom they judge apt to feed the flock." Examinations of ministers included a man's doctrine, ability to communicate, and public reputation. "Public infamy" disqualified a candidate. Sins that rose to the level of endangering the church's reputation were "not the common sins and offences which any has committed in time of blindness, by fragility" but "such capital crimes as the civil sword ought and may punish with death by the word of God." The First Book also included instruction for ordaining ministers, once properly vetted, in a service with a sermon from an "especial minister" that reminded the candidate of his solemn responsibilities and instructed the congregation on its holy duty to respect its pastor. The authors of the First Book may have engaged in more transparency than needed when they admitted that the lack of "learned and godly men" might show the system to be too demanding. Here the example of the early church provided comfort. In the gentile church, godly men were also "rare," but that did not stop the apostles from selecting pastors from non-Jewish ranks.[35] The First Book rounded out a discussion of the ministry with a lengthy section on how to pay ministers and provide for their children. The section on finances included details about assistance to the poor and salaries for teachers.[36]

Beyond describing the nature and duties of ministers, the First Book provided a series of ecclesiastical mechanisms regulating pastors. One came from within the congregation and followed what may have been the genius of Calvin's *Ordinances*. The ordination of laity to roles of oversight was an important measure for preventing clericalism. The work of elders went in two directions. For the laity, elders were supposed to assist the pastor in judging and discerning "all public affairs," such as giving "admonition to the licentious liver," and monitoring "the manners and conversation of all men within their charge." In the other direction, elders had responsibility to "take heed to the life, manners, diligence, and study of their ministers," which included admonishing and correcting him, even to the point of deposing a pastor "with the consent of the church and superintendent." In fact, the First Book prescribed that "if any minister is apprehended in any notable crime, as whoredom, adultery, murder, man slaughter, perjury, teaching of heresy, or any such as deserve death, or [that] may be a note of perpetual infamy, he ought to be deposed for ever."[37]

Superintendents were an additional form of oversight in pastoral relations. These offices had no precedent in Geneva's system. The First Book called for ten or twelve pastors, one for each province, to "plant and erect churches" and oversee other ministers in the vicinity. Superintendents received their appointment from the General Council of the Realm. They were the most episcopal-like piece of the Scottish Kirk and owed their inspiration partly to the ecclesiastical order created by John à Lasco, in Germany, who went as far as to claim superintendents were of divine origin.[38] Even if superintendents were sacred for Reformers on the Continent, in Scotland after three years the responsibility for selecting superintendents switched from the General Council to an election by provincial ministers. To guard against episcopacy, the First Book warned that superintendents "must not be suffered to live as your idle bishops have done heretofore." They needed to preach and travel. Duties were so demanding that contemporaries might have wondered why anyone would serve as a superintendent. These officers should not remain in "one place above twenty or thirty days in their visitation, till they have passed through their whole bounds." They needed to preach three times a week even while visiting churches in their province. Once they returned to their principal residence, they needed to be "likewise exercised in preaching and in edification" in the local parish. Striking the balance of residence and travel was a challenge: "They must not be suffered to continue [in their home parish] so long, as they may seem to neglect their other churches."[39]

The demanding nature of the superintendent's work did not become an issue simply because the First Book's implementation in the initial stages of reform was incomplete. It never received approval from the Crown or Parliament. Aside from evidence to suggest that most popular support for the Reformation came from the urban populations and lesser nobility, the actual workings of church government limped under the burden of pre-Reformation expectations.[40] Earlier financial arrangements—benefices—for underwriting the church remained in place. If pastors could sign a new Confession of Faith and pass professional muster, they could serve in the Reformed church. Patronage also remained in force—an issue that for centuries disrupted peace in the Church of Scotland. Parliament made some provisions for supporting new pastors along lines idealized by the First Book, but in many cases stipends depended on support from local authorities, a sure path to patrons having more say in ordination than congregation members. For superintendents, authorities appointed eight (instead of ten), three of whom had been bishops in the pre-Reformation church. Meanwhile, enough of the older patterns of church hierarchy and ecclesiastical benefices survived the Scottish Reformation to allow for the appointment of new bishops. Not only was the First Book's system of superintendents a hybrid of episcopacy and Presbyterianism, but the Reformed Church of Scotland included episcopal and Presbyterian sectors.[41]

Unlike Elizabeth's firm resolve with the Church of England, Queen Mary's religious life was hardly helpful to Scottish Presbyterians. After returning to Scotland in 1561, she surprised fellow Roman Catholics by accepting the Reformation's changes but insisted upon her right to have the Mass celebrated at her court. This offended the Reformers almost as much as her 1565 marriage to Lord Darnley (Henry Stuart), who was Roman Catholic and an infamous drunk. After two more years of romantic intrigue (with homicides to add spice), the confederate lords led armed forces against the queen, who abdicated. For the next six years, Scotland was divided between those who backed Mary's claims to the throne and those who favored her son, one-year-old James VI. At the age of six, James became king, with the Earl of Morton as his regent. To say that Scottish civil authorities had more pressing concerns than implementing the First Book of Discipline is an understatement.

The inadequacy of both the First Book of Discipline and the lack of order in the church prompted another attempt at reform with the Second Book of Discipline (1578). Part of the motivation for another constitution was the Earl of Morton, who was committed to reform and admired the English monarchy's ecclesiastical authority. On the plus side for Presbyterians, Morton required subscription to the Scottish confession by all benefice holders. Less favorable was his presentation of two men for episcopal office who many believed to be lacking in character. Opposition from the General Assembly to those appointments led to a convoluted compromise that restored the offices of bishop and archbishop, though subordinate to the General Assembly, after being vetted by learned pastors in each province. The difficulty of this plan became so obvious by 1575 that Morton established a commission to provide a new church constitution. Church leaders also asked for advice from the Reformed churches in Geneva and Zurich that produced mixed signals. Geneva recommended parity of elders and warned about the dangers of episcopacy. Zurich praised the monarchy as a valuable aid to church reform.[42]

If the First Book showed a blend of episcopacy and Presbyterianism, the Second Book revealed the influence of Geneva. That city's polity outlined four offices in the church—pastors, teachers, elders, and deacons. The question of bishops was irrelevant if only because the Second Book used the word "bishop" interchangeably with "pastor." The reason was that different words applied to different functions of clergy—"Pastors, because they feed their Congregation," "Bishops, because they watch above their flock," "Ministers, by reason of their service and office," and sometimes "Presbyters or Seniors, for the gravity" of their spiritual responsibilities.[43] The Second Book left no doubt, however, about the rule of the church through assemblies of pastors and elders. The term "bishops," in the older sense, was a corruption of the church. To associate it ever with a name of "superioritie" or "Lordship" was to misconstrue every pastor's responsibility to "watch" and oversee a congregation.[44] Assemblies at the congregational, provincial, national, and international level had the authority and duty to "execute Ecclesiastical discipline & punishment upon all transgressors, and proud contemners of the good order and policie of the kirke, and so the whole discipline is in their hands."[45] This authority also included vetting officers both by providing the necessary training (the task of doctors) and by examining candidates before licensure and ordination. This process did not exclude the consent of—or election by—the congregation. The Second Book prohibited the "intrusion" of officers upon the laity.[46] It followed Geneva by granting excommunication solely to the church's spiritual authority.[47]

By reserving the most serious penalty of church discipline—excommunication—to the church, the Second Book put Scotland in the camp of rejecting Erastianism. The conception of church power developed by Thomas Erastus, a physician who opposed Calvin's insistence that excommunication was not a civil but an ecclesiastical prerogative, held that churches turn offending parties over to the civil magistrate, who in turn meted out appropriate penalties. The Second Book followed Calvin's view. It stipulated that church discipline was a spiritual power that belongs to the church as a spiritual institution. The church's power of discipline came "immediately from God, and the mediator, Jesus Christ." It was not civil but flowed from "the spiritual king and governour of his kirk," Jesus Christ. To usurp Christ's headship over the church was the conceit of the Antichrist. In addition, the headship of Christ required the church's ministry to be based exclusively on scripture, "the kirk hearing the voyce of Christ the onely spirituall king, and being ruled by his lawes." This left to the civil magistrate power over "external things for external peace and quietness amongst the subjects" in contrast to the church's rule over conscience. This separation of powers, spiritual and temporal, meant no disrespect to kings and princes. Subjects should still refer to these authorities as "Lords," who were legitimately "dominators over their subjects whom they govern civilly." But only Christ was "Lord and master" in the church.[48]

This division of ecclesiastical and civil power was relatively easy to keep straight in theory, but the Second Book sometimes blurred church–state spheres of authority. A Christian magistrate had a duty to "assist and fortify the godly proceedings of the Kirk in all behalfs; and namely to see that the public estate and ministry thereof be maintained & sustained, as it appertains, according to Gods word." Civil magistrates should make "laws and constitutions agreeable to Gods word, for advancement of the kirk, and policy thereof, without usurping any thing that pertains not to the civil sword," such as the ministry of word and sacrament. In cases where the church strayed from the correct path, kings and princes could "restore the true service of the Lord, after the example of some godly Kings of Juda, and diverse godly Emperors, and Kings also in the light of the new Testament."[49] Scottish Presbyterians were claiming for their church government nothing different from what Calvin had argued in print and sought in practice. They were not giving up on the ideal of the godly magistrate and the Christian commonwealth. They even tried to find support in the New Testament, the very place where Cartwright and Whitgift agreed (in a way) that under persecution the church had no bishops. But granting power to the king to discern whether the church measured up to biblical standards opened the gates to state interference. Even the implementation of the Scottish General Assembly in 1567 required the Scottish Parliament's approval.

Not So Hot Protestants

Even with Parliament's approval, the fortunes of Presbyterianism in Scotland still depended on the Crown. Scottish pastors may have thought the odds were in their favor after the General Assembly ratified the Second Book of Discipline. They may have also been optimistic given their king's tutor, George Buchanan, one of the finest humanists of the time (Hugh Trevor-Roper called him the "greatest Latin writer" of sixteenth-century Europe), who in 1570 became one of the young king's teachers and was responsible for James VI's intellectual achievements.[50] Born in 1509, Buchanan adopted a moderate outlook akin to Erasmus's during the initial decades of church reform. By the 1560s, though, he aligned with Protestantism and even held the post of moderator of Scotland's first General Assembly, the only layperson to hold the office during four hundred years of history. Buchanan not only taught James a humanist curriculum. He also tried to instill the basics of Presbyterian church government. The humanist sometimes tried literally to beat the material into the king. One apocryphal story has it that Buchanan, in response to objections of his treatment of the boy king, said, "Madam, I have whipt his arse, you may kiss it if you please."[51] That likely left a sour taste in James's mouth for Presbyterianism.

What also colored the king's outlook was Buchanan's history of the Scottish constitution and defense of popular sovereignty. This case for Presbyterian church government was several steps removed either from appeals to the apostles or Old Testament politics. Still, it reinforced Presbyterian objections to episcopacy and raised questions about the monarch's relationship with the church. Part of James's instruction in Latin came from Buchanan's 1579 book, *De jure regni apud Scotos*, likely written more than a decade earlier to justify the deposition of James's mother. There the humanist propounded a theory of monarchy based on popular sovereignty. Ideally, the people appointed sovereigns to perform a set of specified duties. Bound up with this understanding was the right of the people to depose a monarch who failed to fulfill royal responsibilities. Another text that Buchanan was writing while educating James was *Rerum Scoticarum historia*, published posthumously. This book provided a narrative that read into ancient Scotland an elective monarchy consistent with reason and the laws of nature. Buchanan contended that the Scottish monarchy's degeneracy was the product of abandoning natural law, which led to sexual immorality. In both books, in fact, Buchanan linked tyranny to sexual infidelity. This theme not only reflected the humanist's insistence on subjecting baser instincts to reason, but also made plausible the case against Mary, James's mother. Buchanan's rationale for deposing a monarchy stood in contrast to medieval notions that granted this right exclusively to the papacy. It also reinforced at least indirectly Presbyterians' recognition of the laity's legitimate responsibility in the life of the church.[52]

In the autumn of 1582, when Buchanan died, prospects for Presbyterianism in the Church of Scotland must have looked promising. The General Assembly was able to meet independent of civil authorities and was in the good hands of Andrew Melville, a gifted humanist scholar and university administrator, who had the imprimatur of Geneva's Beza thanks to a term of study in the city. James VI was coming into his own as a young king and had received a classical and theological education from a man firmly committed to church reform and a godly realm. The previous year, the king had signed a confession of faith (the Negative or King's Confession of Faith) that committed him, Parliament, and the church to Protestantism, with an explicit rejection of the Roman Church.[53] These changes, however, were skin-deep. Scotland's political strife, the setting for the Scottish Reformation, persisted, and again may explain the outward and relative success of Presbyterianism. The Ruthven Raid during the summer of 1582 may have been all someone needed to know about the health of church and state in the early days of James's rule.

Kidnaping a king is several steps removed from regicide but also on the spectrum of obsession with royal abuses of power, a psychological state that James and his sons repeatedly provoked in their subjects. The Ruthven Raid, Steven J. Read observes, was business as usual during the first decade of James's reign. The ten-month coup d'état that began at the end of August 1582 was one of six palace coups between 1578 and 1585, only one of which was unsuccessful. For anyone tempted to blame such instability on rancorous Presbyterians, attention to the rivalry among Scottish nobles may add perspective. Church government was at times a rationalization for the standard conflicts that arise from either political ideals or self-aggrandizement. The fifteen raiders, led by William Ruthven, fourth Lord Ruthven, all of them with ranks or titles, rallied roughly 1,000 men to execute the coup and hold James initially at Stirling Castle (for six days) and then at Holyrood Palace. Their chief grievance had less to do with James than his advisors, the Duke of Lennox (Esmé Stewart) and the Earl of Arran (James Stewart). The raiders wanted to correct a political imbalance that occurred after the Earl of Morton's (James Douglas) loss of power as regent. This change promised also to redress financial profligacy by the Crown.[54]

Even so, the raid echoed debates between Presbyterians and Episcopalians. The raiders had sympathies to Presbyterian church government such that the coup appeared to be a victory for the Melville wing of the Kirk. In May 1583, James escaped from his captors during a hunting trip to Linlithgow and Falkland. His flight took him to the castle of the archbishop, Patrick Adamson. The ecclesiastical significance of the raid became all the more apparent the next year (1584) when James, with help from the Earl of Arran, instituted the Black Acts. These were church measures that explicitly rejected presbyteries, confirmed the power of bishops, and asserted the Crown's authority over the church. Adamson, who had visited England during the fall of 1583 and sought assistance unsuccessfully from Whitgift in subduing Presbyterians, supplied James and his advisors with a theory of imperial kingship that granted the Crown's supremacy over the church. His theory may have been congenial both to James and church officers who favored episcopacy, but it was out of step at least with a Scottish national identity that Buchanan had expressed in his *Rerum Scoticarum historia*. Roger A. Mason writes that when the Scottish humanist "dismissed" Constantine as "the bastard son of a Roman general's concubine," he was tapping a widespread hostility "to the idea of empire which was at once both thoroughly patriotic and essentially presbyterian."[55]

Adamson, however, offered a distinctly pro-Constantinan account of the Crown's supremacy in his *A declaratioun of kings maiesties* . . . , a work published in 1585 in defense of the Black Acts. Countering the Presbyterians on the two-kingdoms doctrine was one obvious point for Adamson to make. Conceiving of ecclesiastical power as independent of civil authority, with Christ the sole head of the church, was implicitly a seditious position for Presbyterians to take. The archbishop asserted that "faithful" preachers had a duty to "exhort" their people to obey their king, which was the opposite of Presbyterians' troubling the political order. Adamson supported his own case for the king's supremacy by appealing to Constantine. The history of the primitive church—which went conveniently back to the Christian emperors, not to the apostles—proved that magistrates had power over both civil and ecclesiastical affairs. Indeed, Roman emperors had appointed judges, that is, bishops, to decide ecclesiastical matters. Adamson even appropriated Eusebius's praise of Constantine as "bishop of Bishops," a "vniuersall Bishop within his Realme." Such a rank gave kings responsibility for bishops' faithfulness. Mason observes that Adamson was "thinking along the Constantinian lines already so familiar in England."[56] Melville saw what was happening and thought the king had abandoned Buchanan's tutelage for Adamson's folly.

James may have favored Adamson over Buchanan and Melville, but the politics of the realm and the Kirk left the archbishop as a lone voice in debates about church government. For that reason the king needed to qualify the hardest positions of the Black Acts. Whatever Presbyterians and advocates of episcopacy thought about royal supremacy in the church, James wanted to keep Scottish nobles happy. As beneficial to James's imperial aspirations as defenders of episcopacy were—including the view that Presbyterianism was "the mother of all faction, confusion, sedition, and rebellion"—the king's own negotiations with elites and churchmen paved the way for his effort to domesticate Presbyterianism.[57]

As such, the Golden Acts of 1592 appeared to be a victory for Presbyterians. That policy granted power to presbyteries to form ecclesiastical courts. A sense of victory may have encouraged strident Presbyterians to object to James's wife, Queen Ann (of Denmark), who was Lutheran at the time of their 1590 wedding but by 1596 was suspected of being Roman Catholic. Sermons against the queen and a riot in Edinburgh by ministers opposed to false religion provoked James to imprison the ministers involved. He also threatened to remove his residence from Edinburgh, a gesture that local burghers saw as a direct threat to their livelihood. The city's businessmen turned on the pastors, apologized to James, and paid a sizable fine. That confrontation in 1596 was in the air in 1597 when the General Assembly next met. James called the body and set its agenda. He even had a small pamphlet published that instructed delegates on the questions he wanted discussed. Instead of working through bishops, James decided to execute his sovereignty in the church by presiding over the Presbyterians' highest council.

The Melvillians (pro-Presbyterian party) objected vociferously to James's Erastian involvement in the church. At the same time, their earlier celebration of the king's Golden Acts contradicted their opposition to what D. G. Mullan described as "a new godly Constantine presiding at a Scottish Nicea."[58] James's subsequent appointment of three bishops to Parliament (albeit without power in the Kirk) was a further rebuke to Presbyterians. Compensation for Presbyterians came in the king's double pledge to rid the Highlands of zealous Roman Catholics and to provide the church with improved revenues. These concessions notwithstanding, the General Assembly that met at Perth accepted terms that were going to prevent the sort of reforms laid out in the Second Book of Discipline's publication. Commissioners in 1597 accepted the king's proposal to appoint fourteen commissioners to manage church affairs between meetings of the General Assembly. James may well have thought, David D. Hall suggests, that his voice in selecting these commissioners was a form of the Crown appointing bishops.[59] If so, James had taken to heart Queen Elizabeth's 1590 warning that in both England and Scotland "a sect of perilous consequence" had arisen that "would have no kings but a presbytery."[60]

That counsel was a harbinger not only of James's succession to the English throne but also of the fate of the iconic Scottish Presbyterian Andrew Melville. A scholar of considerable ability such that he upgraded Scotland's universities while working as a pastor and theologian, Melville was also as zealous for church reform and as willing to challenge his social superiors as Knox had been. In the context of James's control of the church in 1597, Melville had a private meeting with the king. When James asserted that special meetings of pastors were "illegal and seditious," Melville replied, even with the king's sleeve in his grasp, that "there are two kings and two Kingdoms, in Scotland." Christ, he added, was the king of his kingdom. In the church, James was "not a king, nor a lord, nor a head, but a member."[61]

Melville had been forced into exile roughly fifteen years earlier owing to his associations with those behind the Ruthven Raid. This time Melville did not suffer for his remarks to James other than losing his rectorship at St. Andrews and being demoted to dean of the theology faculty. But in 1606, three years after James became the dual sovereign of Scotland and England, Melville went to London, summoned by the Crown, for what was supposed to be a consultation about the church. The meeting turned out to be a pretext for sending Melville to prison, where he remained for four years. After special pleading by the Duke of Boullion for Melville's release, he took a theology position in Sedan, France, and taught there for the last eleven years of his life (1611–22). Assertions of

Christ's kingship over the church were no match for the actual supremacy of earthly kings in their realms.

No Bishops, Two Kings

Presbyterian reforms of church government met resistance from English and Scottish monarchs, along with their allies, but the idea of governing the church by councils instead of bishops was no more antimonarchical than Parliament's efforts to restrain a sacral monarch. Initial efforts in the British Isles to import a system of church government implemented in Geneva were designed to reform a type of ecclesiastical oversight that was old, ineffective, and privileged. Calvin's church government was roughly thirty years old when Thomas Cartwright started to write against bishops and Scottish church officials wrote their First Book of Discipline, but the idea that the monarch should be the chief executive of the church was equally young. The English Parliament's Act of Supremacy came only seven years before Calvin's *Ecclesiastical Ordinances*. A city council could be as jealous of its authority as a monarch, as Calvin experienced in 1538 when he ran afoul of the city council. The difference, though, was that a municipal government had much less credibility in claiming the divine right of committee meetings. Presbyterianism, in other words, need not have threatened Protestant monarchs without kings and queens themselves seeking to aggrandize their own power and revenues.

Developments in Scotland between 1581 and 1582 illustrate Presbyterians' qualified respect for monarchy. The Negative Confession of 1581, a source of inspiration and rock of constitutional and confessional solidity for mid-seventeenth-century Presbyterians, was a covenant somewhat forced on the young King James. In this document, he promised to uphold the true (Protestant) and exclude the false (Roman Catholic) religion. The Negative Confession's main purpose was to signal that the king was not sympathetic to Roman Catholicism and so not susceptible to nobles who sought to increase French influence at court. Historians have speculated on the authors of the Negative Confession. Some credit Esmé Stuart, Earl of Lennox, who knew he needed to mollify the king's critics. Others attribute the document to John Craig, moderator of the General Assembly. Initially, signatures on the Negative Confession included James and his courtiers and a few ministers (roughly thirty), but the king soon circulated the document to all the churches for the people also to sign. This confession reinforced Scotland's Protestant identity but did not resolve religious and political misgivings about James and his inner circle. Worst of all for Presbyterians, it did nothing to secure Presbyterian polity within the Kirk. Within a year, the king was hostage to the Ruthven raiders. By 1584, James backed the Black Acts, which appeared to indicate retaliation against his Presbyterian opponents.

For all of the frustration that Presbyterians experienced with James, they refused to abandon monarchy. Instead of "no bishop, no king," their mantra was much closer to "many councils, one king." Republicanism and democracy were not options. David D. Hall explains that the Scots desired not a social transformation but a Reformed church. For that reason, a major legacy of the Scottish Reformation, despite its hiccups, was to establish a system of church courts, closer to the people than bishops were or had been. These ecclesiastical bodies were supposed to assist with personal and social godliness while carrying out ecclesiastical reform. English Presbyterians hoped for such structures, but the Scots instituted and refined them. The two books of discipline function as both models and inspiration for later attempts at Presbyterianism.

To be sure, Presbyterianism was not simply about elders running the church. Its advocates also hoped and prayed for a godly prince on the order of ancient Israel's kings. The Old Testament was in some ways an odd place to turn since it contained stories of so many unfaithful, idolatrous, and wicked kings. But the appeal of a covenant between God, his people, and the people's priests and rulers, as the Negative Confession of 1581 explained, meant that as long as Presbyterians used covenants to call for reform and faithfulness, they also looked for a monarch to aid the church. The downside for Presbyterians was that when the king became an obstacle to reform, the church had a duty to correct the monarch. Hall describes the situation in Scotland as one where the "struggle for true religion . . . assumed the same shape as the struggle for true religion in ancient Israel—encompassing the same covenant, the same obligation to obey divine law, and the same role for truth-speaking prophets."[62] Bible-based reform of church and society was unthinkable without a king.

CHAPTER 2

The Problem with Scottish Kings

James VI/I may have been the best Protestant monarch that any European society could muster, at least by Reformed standards. He was responsible, after all, for commissioning a translation of the Bible that English-speaking Protestants of all stripes, from Baptists to Episcopalians, used for the better part of three centuries. Never mind that the proposal for this translation came from Puritans at the 1604 Hampton Conference, the one that lured Andrew Melville to London and sent him to prison before exile was his path to freedom. England already had a Bishops' Bible (1567, rev. 1572). It was not as popular among Puritans as the Geneva Bible (1560). The politics behind this translation were obvious. The new edition of the Bible meant that James could assert his authority over the church, show he was willing to include critics and promote unity, and also prove his competence as a lay theologian. By displacing the Geneva Bible, James was also ridding his realms of a Bible that contained advice on resistance to wayward monarchs, the inevitable outcome of reflection on the reigns of Old Testament kings.[1]

The King James Bible was published in 1611 during a decade when James had another opportunity to combine his understanding of theology and political power. Even if advocates of Presbyterianism worried about the Crown's and bishops' influence on the church, James I seemed to be sympathetic to the theology of Puritans and Presbyterians when he supported the Synod of Dort (1618–19). He sent bishops as part of an English delegation to that international body of churches. The synod was a response to a decade-long theological controversy in the Dutch Reformed churches over the doctrine of election and the scope of salvation—all of humankind potentially or only those for whom Christ died. The king did appear to side with those at Dort who took the seemingly hard line on the depths of human sinfulness and the consequent need for divine intervention to achieve salvation. Popular understandings of Calvinism associate Dort with the "Five Points of Calvinism"—TULIP—whose first three letters indicate the severity of Dort's verdicts: "Total Depravity," "Unconditional Election," and "Limited Atonement." The bishops he sent also made useful interventions on the side of Reformed orthodoxy, an indication that the Church of England was not always faulty, even in the hands of bishops. To be sure, James I's support for Dort dovetailed with his political interests. He needed strong diplomatic ties with the Netherlands because Spain was an ongoing threat. Siding with the Dutch churches that favored religious uniformity was one way to reassure a political ally.[2]

Another indication that James I was not the worst monarch came from the experience of Nonconformists. Even if the Pilgrims, a group of separatist Puritans, had migrated to the Netherlands thanks to James's religious policies, he still allowed Dissenters to settle in the colonies of North America. Whether or not he deserves credit (or blame) for the Christianization of lands in the New World that sprang from settlements in Plymouth and Massachusetts Bay, James did in effect oversee the transplanting of Puritanism in the New World. The first group of Puritans to gain the Crown's permission to settle in North America were separatists, sometimes called "Brownists" for holding the views of Robert Browne, a priest inspired by Puritans who tried to establish a separate congregation outside the oversight of a bishop. Later known as Pilgrims, those Protestants were supposed to join the colony at Jamestown. They wound up settling for Plymouth as the result of a myriad of obstacles, which included needing to gain the favor of the Virginia Company's governor. The Pilgrims' leaders presented themselves to Sir Edwin Sandys, the company's executive, as part of the mainstream of Reformed churches, adjacent to French Protestants. English officials, for their part, were willing to ignore what they knew then about the Pilgrims thanks to a desperate need for anyone willing to work in the colonies. No matter the amount of dissembling involved in the origins of the Plymouth colony, the Pilgrims regarded themselves as the king's loyal subjects. Even on the other side of the Atlantic, when the settlers arrived at a joint description of their endeavor, their Mayflower Compact—short and to the point—asserted that they were firmly subject to James I, the "Defender of the Faith." That affirmation of the king's sovereignty and faith was fully compatible, in their minds, with their mission to "glorify God" and "advance Christianity."[3]

Presbyterians who had yet to seek passage to British colonies in North America were not confident in the king or his involvement in the church's growth. Soon after James became king of England, he looked for ways to consolidate the churches in both of his realms. In 1606, he called for a meeting of bishops and Presbyterians (including Andrew Melville and his nephew, James Melville) with the Privy Council in London. Discussions revealed no common ground between the two sides of church government. In fact, at one point Andrew Melville became frustrated with Richard Bancroft, archbishop of Canterbury, grabbed the prelate's sleeves, shook him, and declared himself to be the bishop's enemy until death. That outburst sent Melville to house arrest for three years. But to his nephew, James offered the bishopric of Dunkeld. The younger Melville informed the king that episcopacy was inherently "devilish and satanical . . . the mother of all dissolution and atheism."[4] These remarks put the younger Melville, by order of the king, also under house arrest.

As much as Presbyterians objected to bishops, the higher hurdle was the Crown. For the first half of the seventeenth century, that challenge grew even more onerous as the Stuart line passed from James I to his son Charles I. Reckoning with the second Stuart king of England was hard enough. Facing the consequences of civil war and regicide was harder still. Presbyterians possessed many arguments that assisted critics and legislators who opposed royal absolutism. Those church reformers were unwilling to overthrow the sovereign, who was, for better or worse, the Lord's anointed.

No King, No Presbyterian

The history of Presbyterianism in the British Isles and North America would likely look very different without the Stuart monarchy. To be sure, as Reformers such as Thomas Cartwright discovered, the Tudors in the case of Elizabeth I were no bargain. This was especially true since the last of the Tudors was partly the inspiration for the divine right monarchy that James I and his son Charles I asserted. Yet, if the Stuart monarchs had not insisted on royal supremacy in both the civil and ecclesiastical realms, the appeal of Presbyterianism may well have been confined to biblical commentaries and an occasional lecture in church polity at Cambridge or St. Andrews.

In his *True Law of Free Monarchies*, published in 1598 soon after James I had gained control over Presbyterians in the Church of Scotland, the thirty-two-year-old king drew upon his humanist education under George Buchanan to instruct the Scots about the best—because biblical—form of civil government. A monarch was a kind of earthly god because he sat upon God's throne and ultimately gave an account of his or her administration to the sovereign of the universe. This was clearly the pattern of monarchy taught by the Old Testament, he argued, an assertion to which covenant-minded Presbyterians could object only awkwardly. A monarch's subjects owed obedience in all things except any command or law that was contrary to God's law, James added. That qualification gave Presbyterians ground for their arguments about the sufficiency of scripture. Where the rubber of civil polity hit the road of ecclesiology came when James invoked at least implicitly the Negative Confession's (1581) terms. A true monarch had a duty to maintain the true religion and punish those of his subjects who dared to alter or disturb the national church. Although James I did not mention church polity directly in *True Law*, his contemporaries and later historians interpreted the book as a rejection of the Genevan/Presbyterian notion of two kingdoms: the king was head of the civil realm and Christ was the spiritual king of the church.[5]

James I made his preference for episcopacy explicit, however, in a book published the following year, *Basilikon Doron*, another text about the virtues and duties of monarchy, written for his son Henry Frederick, Prince of Wales. He warned his son about Puritans. They were pests in both the church and the commonwealth "whom no deserts can oblige, neither oarthes [*sic*] or promises bind, breathing nothing but sedition and calumnies, aspiring without measure, railing without reason, and making their own imaginations . . . the square of their conscience." James also cautioned against "proude Papall Bishops."[6] Indeed, the Crown's command of the episcopate and its finances was essential to social order and stability. James wrote that along with reestablishing the three estates in Parliament, banishing the "conceited parity" of ministers was essentially to order in the church, "the peace of the commonweal," and a "well-ruled monarchy."[7]

One further indication of James I's understanding of the Crown's churchly duties came early in his rule as king of England in the book *Triplici nodo, triplex cuneus* (1607). This work was a reply to Pope Paul V and Cardinal Bellarmine in which the king defended England's policy of requiring an oath of loyalty from Roman Catholic subjects. On the one hand, the king needed to guard against a history of popes and bishops working up sedition against emperors and kings. On the other hand, the sort of loyalty he demanded did not reach to matters of conscience or to the soul. The issue was simply a matter of civil allegiance to the God-ordained magistrate.[8] James was not deciding between the merits of the Presbyterian or episcopal systems. He was making political claims for the sake of social stability. That left Presbyterians little room to maneuver, especially when the king tried to institute uniformity between the national churches of England and Scotland.

In 1612, James's first-born son, Henry, died. That left James's son Charles as heir to the throne. His reign began in 1625 and relied on his father's advice to his brother in *Basilikon Doron*, minus some of the finesse. For English Protestants in the orbit of the Puritan desire for further reform (which included Presbyterians), Charles I and his archbishop, William Laud, were a significant departure from the religious policies of James and Elizabeth. Charles I did not grow up with Presbyterian tutors, as his father had. He was also sympathetic to Roman Catholicism, given his marriage to Henrietta Maria of France. Although a diplomatic arrangement, the marriage also meant a retinue of Roman Catholic priests followed the queen to the royal family's private chapel. Charles I also preferred external forms of worship as indicators of devotion as opposed to the personal and informal, sometimes called "experiential," Calvinism of most Puritans and Presbyterians. To add insult to injury, his chief religious advisor, Laud, eschewed the Calvinist theology that was generally the consensus among Church of England bishops before him. Charles I did continue his father's policies of religious uniformity. Laud was content to carry out this policy in England by insisting on the use of the prayer book and vestments. He also required kneeling in worship for prayer and the Eucharist. When the king began to impose similar practices on the Church of Scotland, his vulnerability among the Scots, his native people, became apparent. Agnes Mure MacKenzie explains that Charles's awkwardness with his subjects was as true in England as in Scotland:

> To *all* his subjects he was a foreigner, and neither they nor he were aware of it enough to make allowance for the fact. By training he was too English to understand Scotland. By temperament he was far too much of a Scot to understand England; he loved (what an Englishman hates) a clear definition, an action based . . . on reasoned principles—a dangerous habit in a politician, for one can do many things with a mass of people if one will only refrain from explaining. The Tudors, in practice, were immensely more tyrannous than any Stewart: but they did not state any absolutist theory of government, and England accordingly put up with them.[9]

MacKenzie could well have added that Presbyterians generally adore explanations as long as the reasons are correct. No one should have been surprised to see a resurgence of Presbyterianism during Charles's reign.

Even before Charles I's coronation, seventeenth-century Presbyterian convictions among the English echoed Thomas Cartwright's arguments from a previous generation. Again, because English advocates of Presbyterianism never had the chance to formulate clear mechanisms of ecclesiastical rule by council or assembly, as the Scots had, Presbyterians in England were more prone to criticize episcopacy and its excesses than to prove the virtues of an alternative church polity. Unlike the earlier period under Elizabeth, English Presbyterianism during the reign of James I and Charles I was confined primarily to pamphlets. Even then, publishing dissent could be punished for threatening the established order. Samuel Ward, a Puritan minister in Ipswich, for instance, ran afoul of both James I and Charles I, once in 1622 and later in 1635, not so much for advocating church reforms as for disagreeing with the Church of England's operations. Other English ministers of Presbyterian leanings, such as John Forbes and John Paget, went into exile in the Netherlands, a place where many English Dissenters migrated to escape the Stuart government's religious policies.[10] Robert S. Paul asserted in his study of the Westminster Assembly that during the first third of the seventeenth century, ministers with "keen" Presbyterian convictions "had either been suppressed and doomed to a life of penury and obscurity, or else they had been forced to exercise their talents abroad." For the rest, conformity was the only option.[11]

Paul's description of Presbyterianism before the Westminster Assembly implies that advocates of church government by synod and council were more or less inconsequential between the 1590s and the English Civil War, a notion that historian Polly Ha, *English Presbyterianism, 1590–1640*, challenges. Her book clearly recovers the vigor of Presbyterian convictions between 1590 and 1640. It does not, however, reveal patterns of institutional expression that matched what the Scots had accomplished with officially approved books of discipline, the regular meeting of assemblies, and even the actual power that such bodies sometimes exerted over church life. To be sure, in the 1590s James VI had outmaneuvered Presbyterians in the Church of Scotland and defanged their potency. Still, the documents, the acts, and even the vows of the king in the National Confession (1581) were touchstones to which Scottish Presbyterians could return for justification and inspiration. The best English Presbyterians could do was echo the arguments of Thomas Cartwright and John Field and meet informally.

The sound heard most often in the English Presbyterian echo chamber was an objection to the civil functions of the episcopate. Several Presbyterians complained that bishops meted out civil penalties in church courts. Fines or imprisonment for religious or spiritual offenses, they observed, blurred the civil and ecclesiastical realms. Presbyterians countered by arguing that church penalties should be solely spiritual. Related to the error of mixing the ecclesiastical and civil functions of bishops was the problem of church officers holding multiple benefices. This was another way that private (or nonspiritual) interests became factors in church government. Sometimes, arguments in favor of Presbyterianism pointed out that the bishops' prerogatives were at odds with royal supremacy, since the episcopate was supposed to have independence from the Crown in ecclesiastical judgments. If the arguments for the powers of episcopacy invoked medieval canon law, writers in the Presbyterian camp were quick to observe that Reformation acts of the 1530s Parliament overturned those laws.

Sometimes, too, the arguments against bishops questioned their standing among the three estates of England—the Crown, the Lords, and the Commons. The logic here was that spiritual power was no proper qualification for civil authority within Parliament. That jurists who sought to roll back the church courts' jurisdictions sometimes used Presbyterian objections is not an indication that these lawyers were convinced of Presbyterian ecclesiology. Rather they primarily sought to clarify the scope of affairs beyond the church's competency. Common law jurists took a page out of the Presbyterian playbook when they argued that questions of wills, estates, marriages, and even tithes should be adjudicated not in church courts but under civil jurisdiction. The overlap between Presbyterians and legal reforms designed to reduce the authority of church courts foreshadowed the fault lines that drove the Civil War of the 1640s.[12]

Opposition to episcopal church courts was not simply a product of legal or theological ideals, but it also followed the Puritan desire for a godly society, sometimes referred to as a "reformation of manners." For Presbyterians, the episcopal system was too distant and abstract from ordinary citizens and church members. Presbyterianism ideally facilitated a system of holiness that placed spiritual oversight within each congregation as opposed to the remote ecclesiastical care of bishops. This had been a big part of Calvin's Geneva appeal to English Protestants during days of exile. A difference between Geneva and British church life, however, was the possibility in the latter's case of implementing these reforms nationally, from the local level of the session up through presbyteries in regions, and beyond to a nationwide jurisdiction in a General Assembly. French, Dutch, and German Protestants laid out similar forms of church polity, but the surrounding political structures, either hostile or decentralized, could not achieve reforms available to Presbyterians in the British Isles thanks to a Protestant monarch. A godly king working in tandem with a church that was truly reformed offered the possibility of even greater uniformity of morality and doctrine.

Presbyterian support for godly magistrates might have seemed to compromise the barrier between civil and spiritual matters. But, like Calvin, many advocates of Presbyterian polity insisted that temporal punishments—fines, imprisonment, execution—were matters for the state, whereas the church's measures of discipline were spiritual—admonitions, censures, excommunication. If monarchs failed to recognize the superiority of Presbyterianism over episcopacy for creating mechanisms of social control, the reason was likely the exacting morality that church reform required of magistrates. (Imagine Charles I with the piety of Samuel Rutherford.) At the same time, a call for godly magistrates became for jurists and legislators a way to use Presbyterian reforms to check the Crown's supremacy and restrain the bishops' power.[13]

For Scottish Presbyterians, the Stuart monarchy's twin rule of Scotland and England brought the unwelcome development of even greater episcopal influence in the Kirk than under James VI. The original instance of "no bishop, no king" traces back to 1604 when James I was trying to bring uniformity to the churches in his realms. Although he was still opposed to papal supremacy, he was equally "an enemie to the confused Anaarchie or paritie of th Puritanes."[14] In the king's mind, bishops were part of his own claims to supremacy within his kingdoms. During the first decade of the seventeenth century, James ended the practice of annual gatherings of the Scots' General Assembly and paved the way for his nobles to attend ecclesiastical assemblies as voting members (whenever they could meet). In 1609, he appointed three Scottish bishops to the Council of State and created a Court of High Commission for administering the Kirk's affairs (similar to one in England). A year later, he arranged for three Scottish bishops to be consecrated by their counterparts in the Church of England. By 1612, James persuaded the Scottish Parliament to require ministers to take an oath that recognized the king as the "only lawful supreme governor of this realm" in matters both spiritual and temporal.[15]

In the next decade, the king shifted his attention to the Church of Scotland's liturgy. What began with instructions on set times to administer the Lord's Supper proceeded to rules for a uniform order of worship, and culminated in the Articles of Perth (1618). Here the king required new practices in the Kirk, all objectionable to Presbyterians: the observance of feast and saints days, private services of Holy Communion, private administration of baptism to babies about to die, confirmation of church members by bishops, and the requirement to kneel during the reception of bread and wine in the Lord's Supper. If Melvillians thought James VI in 1597 had enervated Presbyterianism, as James I he placed Presbyterian reforms on life support.

Presbyterianism for the Nation

Samuel Rutherford may have been the brains of Scotland's Covenanters, but Alexander Henderson was the architect of the kingdom's odd mix of Hebrew theology and medieval political theory that came together in the National Covenant (1638). Rutherford would become, for nineteenth-century British Protestants, a model of Puritan (experiential Calvinist) piety. As such, his name has been more familiar than Henderson's, whose 1646 death occurred when the prospects for Presbyterianism in England and Scotland looked bright. During their lifetimes, what distinguished Rutherford from Henderson was the former's *Due Right of Presbyteries*, published in 1644. This work became the textbook for serious Presbyterians on church government and proper relations between church and state. Before that book, however, Henderson was much more important to the fortunes of Presbyterianism and the attendant challenges to Charles I's religious policies. During the 1630s, a pivotal decade in Scottish politics, Henderson (born 1583), then ministering in Leuchars, emerged as one of the most prominent Nonconformist ministers. His reputation was partly the outcome of his previous good standing with his archbishop, George Gledstanes of St. Andrews. Henderson had also been a fierce critic of the Five Articles of Perth (1618). Rutherford, in contrast, labored in obscurity in the town of Anwoth in southwest Scotland. He, too, was known for harboring Nonconformist views, which resulted in little more than a summons to appear before the Court of High

Commission. Neither pastor qualified as a member of elite Scottish society, but Henderson's path to Presbyterian leadership was straighter than Rutherford's.[16]

Decisive for Henderson's emergence as the leading voice among Presbyterians in the Church of Scotland was his association with the National Covenant, signed first by leading nobles on February 28, 1638, in Greyfriars Church, Edinburgh. Although the National Covenant represented Presbyterian convictions about church government (anti-episcopal) and proper relations between church and state (the independence of the church from the king as head), the document also asserted Scottish sovereignty against Charles I's perceived neglect of his native people. The king's apparent indifference was evident in the ceremonies he used to sacralize his rule. His 1633 coronation in Scotland at Holyrood was unprecedented and took place within a Communion service that trafficked in popish symbols—crucifix, candles, altar, and vestments for the attending bishops (some of them wore the traditional Scottish black gowns).[17] The king's oath also included a new promise to "defend the Bishops, and the churches under the government," a clear affront to the Presbyterian sector of the Scottish population.[18] Yet, as much as Charles's antics offended the sensibilities of committed Presbyterians, for many more Scots, John Morrill argues, the king was guilty much more of a "naked authoritarianism" that was "indifferent" to Scotland's "laws, customs, and traditions."[19]

In this context, Presbyterianism emerged as the voice of protest against Charles I's mishandling of the northern kingdom. Scottish nobles grew frustrated with the king's absence from Scotland and the coincident decline of national institutions, such as the Scottish court.[20] The king's isolation also annoyed lesser elites who had enjoyed greater access to government offices after reforms begun with the 1560 Scottish Reformation. Other nobles resented Charles's secretiveness. The main instrument for administering Scotland's affairs was Edinburgh's Privy Council. Although it remained in place, the king used it infrequently, which also diminished participation by nobles. Charles I's reliance on English advisors was also annoying, such that even sensible reforms in the courts, such as those he had instituted in 1626, came across as heavy-handed.[21] The Crown's imposition in 1636 and 1637 of a new prayer book, one of English vintage no less, highlighted the king's disregard for the Scots. Riots in the summer of 1637 prompted the organization of resistance that eventually produced the National Covenant. Conceived and written by Henderson and Archibald Johnstone of Wariston, an Edinburgh lawyer, the document received signatures from a broad swath of the Scottish public—from nobles, lairds, ministers, burgher councillors, and the male heads of household from many parishes. Suddenly, the Covenanters—a relatively small strain of Scottish Protestantism—became the vehicle for asserting Scottish national identity.

The Covenanting wing of the Scottish church drew inspiration from the National Covenant of the Church of Scotland of 1581 (also called sometimes the King's Confession or the Negative Confession). Both covenants drew on similar ideals—anti-Catholicism, suspicion of episcopacy, and the benefits of (not to mention biblical warrant for) Presbyterianism. The National Covenant of 1638 drew partly on an idealized understanding of the Scottish Reformation, which was responsible for establishing a church "without mixture of human invention." As the embodiment of "Christ's true religion . . . and a perfect religion," the Scottish Reformed church was part of larger work of "destroying" the Antichrist.[22] Some of this rhetoric reflected the need for ideals capable of gaining popular support. Another factor, however, was the apocalypticism that animated Scotland's most ardent Presbyterians. In the case of Samuel Rutherford, the National Covenant was a sign that Christ's return was near, and the conversion of the Jews imminent. He used the eschatological language of the Bible to describe the situation in Scotland as "fetching a blow upon the Beast, and the scarlet-coloured whore."[23]

Of course, those who signed the National Covenant did not necessarily share the millennialism of Scotland's devout ministers. For nobles and lairds, the National Covenant's appeal was mainly constitutional. Charles had too much power, had neglected Scotland's political institutions, and the kingdom needed to recover its own administrative powers. Soon after the National Covenant's publication, officials at the forefront of the movement demanded several reforms that included civil and ecclesiastical changes, such as eliminating the Court of High Commission, permitting the annual meeting of the General Assembly, granting Parliament freedom to endorse the General Assembly, and granting parishes and presbyteries a say in the call of pastors.[24]

The National Covenant's call for a General Assembly may have seemed innocuous, but James VI's policies five decades earlier forbade a gathering of pastors and elders. In 1636, Scottish bishops reminded the government that holding an assembly usurped the Crown's authority. Although an assembly challenged the king's wishes, the Marquis of Hamilton (James Hamilton), who represented Charles I, tried to outmaneuver Henderson by allowing a General Assembly to meet even while setting the agenda and selecting delegates. Once the Assembly began, Hamilton departed. His absence emboldened Henderson, the moderator, to assert the church's right to meet without the king's approval and its duty to subject its determinations to the true king, Jesus Christ. The General Assembly proceeded to reject acts from previous assemblies (conducted by bishops). Among these rulings were the Articles of Perth (1618), which imposed Anglican forms on the Church of Scotland.[25] To add to the anti-episcopal character of the body, the assembly excommunicated most of the Church of Scotland's bishops. These bold decisions inspired many of the nobles and lairds present as observers to support the National Covenant. The Earl of Argyll remained at the assembly for its entirety, an indication of implicit support. Meanwhile, Lord Erskine, according to reports, was in "tears" and begged to lend his support to the Presbyterians.[26]

The Scots' break with episcopacy and embrace of Presbyterianism may have looked like zeal for a Reformed church, but some pastors mixed pragmatism with biblical fidelity. One of the Presbyterians in the minority at the 1638 General Assembly, for instance, was Robert Baillie, a pastor and University of Glasgow professor. He expressed reservations about the conflict that suggested he spoke for more Scots than just himself. He was willing, for example, to concede that a mix of bishops working in tandem with assemblies and presbyteries was an agreeable model for Reformed churches. Baillie conceded that a bishop had a superiority of "order" but not one of "degree" above fellow presbyters. A bishop's powers of ordination and jurisdiction could still be subject to presbyteries and assemblies. The main question was what was "expedient." This was a far cry from a defense of episcopacy that relied on apostolic succession or legal precedents. But Baillie's position implied approval of the church order that had emerged under James VI/I. The professor agreed with the Covenanters that Charles I had crossed the line of proper church–Crown relations and that the king's religious policies were destructive for the Church of Scotland. For that reason, Baillie supported most of the aims of the National Covenant, even as he preferred order and stability in the church.[27]

Reservations about the National Covenant could not prevent the armed conflict that began the following year. The First Bishops' War attracted military veterans such as Alexander Leslie, who on March 21, 1639, led a charge against the king's forces defending Edinburgh's castle. A veteran of the Thirty Years' War, Leslie had served with distinction in the Swedish army. In 1627, King Gustavus Adolphus knighted him for his courage and leadership in combat against the imperial army. Born in 1582, the illegitimate child of Captain George Leslie (of Blair Castle) and a woman sometimes referred to as the "wench of Rannoch," the younger Leslie made his way into Scottish society through military service. By 1638, he had retired from the Swedish army and was an obvious choice by Scottish authorities to be lord general for the Army of the Covenant.[28]

Leslie's own reasons for siding with the Covenanters were not obvious. Since 1634, while in Hamburg, Leslie met with other Scots and heard complaints about Charles I's disregard for the Scots and their Parliament. His loyalty to the *religio patria*, Alexia Grosjean and Steve Murdoch indicate, may have even preceded that of the Covenanters. At the same time, Leslie's relationships first as a foster child and then through marriage put him in close company with the Campbells, a leading clan among the Covenanters. This tie suggests that his decision to side with Charles I's Scottish opponents had less to do with religion than with nationalism and kinship. Leslie was dismayed, for instance, when other Scottish generals—who had served in Sweden's military—decided to fight for Charles. They had separated "themselves from the rest of this kingdome."[29] According to Grosjean and Murdoch, Leslie "seldom committed" his views on religion to paper.[30] Even Swedish officials saw the advantages of Scotland's National Covenant. They were willing to relinquish Leslie's services in part because they feared Charles I's alliance with Denmark.

Scotland's National Covenant also drew support from segments of England. Covenanter preachers crossed the border into northern England to explain Presbyterian convictions. They persuaded certain English nobles to refuse to fight for Charles I, a decision that led to prison. Some of the Covenanters' success, to be sure, owed to psychological tricks that Leslie had learned as a commander for Sweden. In Newcastle, he sent his barber into the Royalist camp with stories about a Covenanter army of 20,000 soldiers. Leslie also entertained Royalist commanders for dinner so they could see Covenanter preparation for battle. The king's officers were treated to the intimidating sight of 1,000 Highlanders, along with broadswords, bows, and Highland style of dress. These Scots "struck more fear into the English 'than any other terror.'"[31] In sum, an odd assortment of factors—religious, national, military—fueled the Covenanters' opposition to Charles I and his religious policy. The growing antagonism between the king and the Covenanters was not simply English versus Scots or Episcopalians versus Presbyterians.

The conclusion to the First Bishops' War was almost as docile as its start was dramatic (casualties on both sides were in the low hundreds). In May 1639, Charles I gestured to appease the Scots by convening the Scottish Parliament in return for an end to hostilities. But the presence of the Royal army in Scotland gave the Covenanters reasons to continue opposition. They did so by occupying the border town Kelso. The size and strength of the Covenanters' army forced Charles I to reaffirm his father's National Confession (1581), which indicated a determination to protect the rights, religion, and laws of Scotland. The pattern of assembling troops and then negotiating led one writer to describe the First Bishops' War as "non-events with little real fighting." In other words, the war was mainly "an excuse for feuding between local families in the north east and west of Scotland."[32]

The Covenanters' superiority in outmaneuvering the Royalist forces in the First Bishops' War drove the king to negotiate at Berwick. The prominence of church affairs in Scottish discontent explains in part why the National Covenant's authors, Archibald Johnston and Alexander Henderson, made up two-thirds of the Covenanters' team of negotiators (the third was John Leslie, Earl of Rothes) with the king. The Scots were adamant that the General Assembly and the Scottish Parliament be restored to their rightful authority. Charles made concessions on the General Assembly and agreed to the convening of Parliament. The resulting Treaty of Berwick (1639) was too ambiguous to end the hostilities. The king returned to London keen to subdue the Scots.[33]

Unable to secure funding from England's (Short) Parliament, Charles formed a militia to fight in the Second Bishops' War. The Covenanters' generals again outwitted the king's forces by invading northern England and showing sufficient strength to prompt a Royalist retreat. The Treaty of Ripon (1640) ended hostilities, allowed Scottish soldiers to occupy parts of northern England, and promised further negotiations in London.

By this point, Charles I's mishandling of Scottish affairs was affecting control of England. Desperate for funding, in the fall of 1640 the king called another Parliament (Long), which met until 1660. Scottish commissioners arrived a week after Parliament began. Their negotiations with Charles I produced the Treaty of London (1641), whose terms were favorable to the Covenanters. The king pledged financial assistance, clemency for anyone who had signed the National Covenant, and suppression of publications against the Covenanters. At roughly the same time in Scotland, the General Assembly removed pastors who had opposed the National Covenant, in areas where support for episcopacy and Charles remained strong (especially Aberdeen).[34]

The Bishops' Wars (1639–40) were a prelude to the English Civil Wars (1642–51), and the opening to the Wars of the Three Kingdoms (1639–53), which for a time ended episcopacy and even monarchy in England. Hostilities between Crown and Parliament were the chief drivers of the English war, which acquired a distinctly Presbyterian hue when the English Parliament commissioned the Westminster Assembly to recast the main features of the kingdom's church. At the same time, Puritanism, a looser category than Presbyterianism for reforming the English church, was also a prominent presence at the Westminster Assembly. Most scholars split the pastors, and theologians at Westminster into the Presbyterian and Puritan parties mainly because of differences over church polity. Most of the English commissioners safely fit under a Puritan tent that allowed a measure of diversity in theology and church government. Presbyterianism still appealed to those English Protestants who looked to Geneva and other Reformed churches on the Continent as models of reform. The kind of commitment to Presbyterianism that survived among the Scots was weak in England. Robert S. Paul observes that "books advocating Presbyterianism" in England had not been written since the days of Thomas Cartwright, the most important critic of episcopacy in the 1570s.[35]

In the short run, the Civil War improved the prospect for Presbyterianism in England. With the king seeking to gain power over Parliament and rumors circulating of Irish soldiers from the Continent rallying to Charles I's side, the conflict turned sectarian. Parliament saw the king through the lens of his objectionable tendencies toward Roman Catholicism. Charles I did not help by resorting to divine-right conceptions of the monarchy in opposition to Parliament. In 1642, Charles saw war as a better option than negotiating with Parliament for maintaining his authority. By then Parliament had excluded bishops from the House of Lords. Because Parliament's army was ineffective in the early stages of the war, members of the Commons reached out to the Scots. The result was an alliance between Parliament and a Scotland where Covenanters were still ascendant. Part of the Scots' condition in this alliance was for England to ratify the Solemn League and Covenant. With this agreement, Scotland's National Covenant became the norm in effect for England, Wales, and Ireland. This also implied that Presbyterianism, as the Scots had developed it, would become the established religion through the British Isles and Ireland. Alexander Henderson was the author of four of the Solemn League and Covenant's six articles. When presented to the General Assembly, according to one pastor, the new covenant received applause "with heartie affections, expressed in tears of pitie and joy."[36]

Ratification of the Solemn League and Covenant coincided with the opening of the Westminster Assembly. More than one hundred pastors and a smaller group of lay delegates gathered to reform the Church of England's confession of faith, catechisms, form of church government, and liturgy. Debates over the application of the Solemn League and Covenant raised the question of whether England's national church needed to conform to the Church of Scotland. A revision to the Covenant's terms established that the standard for reform was "the word of God." For Henderson, this language only strengthened the case for Presbyterianism since the Bible mandated this form of church government.[37] Despite Henderson's understanding of these debates, the Scots' participation at Westminster was small and only advisory.[38] Among the eleven Scots who served at different times in London were the authors of the National Covenant, both Lord Johnston (Archibald Johnston) and Alexander Henderson. Another was Samuel Rutherford, whose famous book *Due Right of Presbyteries* was published in the early years of the Westminster Assembly. Despite war with Charles I, England appeared to be moving into the Presbyterian column of Europe's post-Reformation national churches. The drama of war also heightened eschatological imaginations at Westminster. For the Covenanters looking on from afar, the Westminster Assembly promised "an international Presbyterian revolution" on the way to "the latter-day glory itself."[39]

Though the Scots were small in number, their Presbyterian rigor, by some reckonings, saved the English from an unfocused Protestantism.[40] Still, the Scottish delegates were only advisors among a body of pastors and theologians who were far from a consensus on church government and ecclesiastical establishment. Historians typically group the delegates into Presbyterian, Independent, Erastian, and Melvillian camps, even as the preferred form of church government (Congregational or Presbyterian) did not correspond to the civil government's responsibility for aspects of spiritual discipline. The inability to agree on these questions of ecclesiastical and civil polity were far removed from actual fighting in the Civil War, which saw Oliver Cromwell's New Model Army prove its superiority to Charles I's armed forces. A defeat of the king by the Independent Cromwell was no guarantee of a victory for Presbyterianism in any of the kingdoms. Samuel Rutherford's famous book *Lex, Rex* (1644) was the closest the Scots came to making a case for Presbyterian politics (civil and ecclesiastical) in the context of both civil war and ecclesiastical debate.

Rutherford was responding directly to John Maxwell's *Sacro-Sancta Regum Majestas* published the same year. Maxwell (1591–1647) was a Scot and served as a bishop in Ireland, and his royalism led to an understanding of the monarch's authority coming from God, hardly a controversial position. But Maxwell's argument took issue directly with the consent theory that traced royal authority to the people. Although Rutherford's response was arguably the fullest expression of Covenanter political theory, it relied on standard notions of natural law, human nature, communities, constitutionalism, and political representation that had circulated throughout medieval and early modern Europe. Even if Rutherford appealed to the people, he was no populist. Parliaments in England and Scotland were the embodiment of the people and as such had powers, ordained by God, independent of the king. For this reason, the king had obligations to the people by virtue of his oaths. The people could also expect the monarch to comply with their beliefs. Rutherford extended this logic to religion. The people had duties to God irrespective of their loyalty to the king: "The people may swear a Covenant for Reformation of Religion, without the King."[41] Political theory aside, Rutherford's aim was to defend the Scottish Reformation's church reform, which was synonymous with Presbyterianism. "What really motivated Rutherford was not his belief in the popular origins of royal authority," according to John Coffey, "but his passionate conviction that the king was obliged to defend true religion and purge the land of idolatry."[42] The armed struggle against Charles was not over "constitutionalist arguments" but concerned the true religion that emerged in the Church of Scotland under James VI. Rutherford added to his defense of Presbyterianism an understanding of Scottish history in which Roman Catholicism had replaced Scotland's original and true Christianity (from the third century). The Reformation was a process of recovering the kingdom's ancient and pure faith.

However plausible Rutherford's arguments, he was no match for the course of events transpiring in the Civil War, Parliament, and the Westminster Assembly. The tipping point at Westminster came in 1646 when coincidently Cromwell's army gained the upper hand against Charles I, and the Westminster Assembly decided on a presbyterial-synodical structure for the Church of England. The consensus on church government, however, was capacious enough to include Erastians and Independents. The result was hardly a replica of Calvin's Geneva. According to some Scottish observers, this was a "lame Erastian presbytery."[43] This was also the year that Henderson, the most prominent of Scottish observers at the Westminster Assembly, died. His millennial hopes could not overcome disappointment with developments in England. Before his death, Henderson even met with Charles to seek an end to the war. During the second meeting, royal forces were spent, and the king appeared willing to accept compromise. True to his Covenanter convictions, Henderson proposed the National Covenant in return for peace. Henderson's position, outlined in several documents, combined law and theology with respect for royal authority. His biggest request was for Charles I to emulate the great Hebrew monarchs, who had abolished idolatry to serve God. The king refused. Instead, Charles I came away distrusting Presbyterianism as a form of church government that relied on popular consent and was consequently antimonarchical. Charles dismissed Presbyterianism by arguing that if episcopacy were unlawful, "I doubt not but God will so enlighten mine Eyes."[44] Henderson returned to Scotland and died a few weeks later.[45]

If Henderson were no match for Charles I, the Scottish divines at the Westminster Assembly had much more to fear than compromises on church government. In Scottish affairs, the war took a surprising turn when the king authorized the Earl of Montrose (James Graham), an erstwhile Covenanter, to lead a Royalist army division against his homeland. The earl's rationale for battling the Covenanters was that the Scots' alliance with England had betrayed the National Covenant. Montrose's military success enabled him, as royal commissioner, to convene the Scottish Parliament. That resurrection of Scottish government was short-lived, however, because Covenanter troops decamped from England to defeat Montrose's dwindling ranks. To make a difficult situation worse, the Civil War coincided with an outbreak of bubonic plague in Scotland. With the realm's social fabric unraveling, leading Covenanters, such as Lord Warriston (Archibald Johnston), became even more attached to the National Covenant. This time, a return to first principles included a reign of terror that punished "enemies of the commonwealthe."[46] The Scottish government executed a handful of nobles, fined, banished, or excommunicated rebels (depending on the degree of rebellion), and fickle ministers lost their pulpits.

The crisis that loomed for both Scotland and England was a political theology (couched in the language of biblical covenants) that functioned as national myth for the Scots and an exotic burden for the English, who were a few steps removed from the Covenanters' outlook and zeal. Rutherford's arguments that the Covenants of 1638 and 1643 had reestablished Christ's headship over the church were small consolation. For the most ardent of Covenanters, the failures of war were indications of the Scottish peoples' unfaithfulness. But for moderates, the inability to reconcile church and civil government at Westminster was the responsibility of Protestant sectarians who had rebelled against the king. Led by James Hamilton, these moderates, or "Engagers," offered Charles I support against Cromwell in exchange for concessions about church government at the Westminster Assembly. A firm conviction behind engagement was the need to suppress the religious chaos rife among Cromwell's army. The Engagement turned out to be as controversial as episcopacy. "Covenanters" who viewed the Engagement as a betrayal, became known as "Protesters." Their opposition was minor compared to the Engager army's defeat in July 1648 at the hands of the New Model Army, a battle at which the king's forces were notably absent.[47]

The crisis in England and Scotland could not have been more dire as a result of the warring factions turning on each other at the Solway–

Tweed line. To the south, the New Model Army took out its frustrations against the English Parliament, transferred power to a Council of State, tried and executed Charles I for treason, and established a form of a republic with Cromwell as lord protector. To the north, another purge of the political class occurred when the Protestors defeated the Engagers. In January 1649, the new Scottish Parliament reaffirmed the Solemn League and Covenant and prescribed punishments for those who had sided with Charles I, running from fines and excommunication to executions for a few. The Scottish Parliament also banned Engagers from politics. But allegiance to the National Covenants prevented Protesters from forming an alliance with Cromwell. The Scots demanded a king who stood in continuity with both the King's Confession of 1581 and the National Covenant of 1638. Consequently, the Scots determined to receive Charles II as their sovereign.[48]

Negotiations with the next in the line of Stuart monarchs began in 1649 when envoys from Scotland consulted with Charles II, who was then in the Netherlands assessing his options. The sticking point was church government. The Scots wanted Presbyterianism to prevail throughout all three kingdoms. They also needed the king to guarantee that General Assemblies met independently from royal control. Charles II wanted to restore the Crown in England with help from supporters in Ireland. Alliances with the Irish ended when Cromwell brutally defeated Royalist forces at Drogheda and Wexford during the late summer of 1649.

Charles II then relocated to Scotland and under duress agreed to the Covenanters' terms. Cromwell's army then invaded Scotland. In a surprising and dispiriting battle at Dunbar, 3,000 Scots died and 10,000 were taken prisoner. In the wake of defeat, Presbyterians divided again into camps either still loyal to the Covenant or moderates who hoped to salvage order by recognizing Charles II as their king. Between 1651 and 1653, rival assemblies of presbyters met, the 1653 General Assembly being the last during the Commonwealth era. During the same period, Cromwell gained control of Scotland. The religious toleration (some thought chaos) that prevailed in England now became the norm for Scotland, with Independents, Quakers, and Baptists making their first appearances.[49]

David D. Hall observes that the ironies of the situation were difficult to count: "What Charles I had failed to accomplish became a reality in

1651, unity among the three kingdoms in how religion should be practiced."[50] He could have included Covenanters on the list of ironies thanks to their willingness to recognize a king whose religious sympathies were far from theirs but who was useful because of his standing as monarch. Even more ironically, Cromwell's religious policies reduced advocates of Presbyterianism and episcopacy to the same status as Protestants—like Baptists and Quakers—whom General Assemblies and bishops would have countenanced as sectarian threats to social order. This was a Presbyterian revolution that might well have been a lesson to future Presbyterians who considered political rebellion a remedy for religious and social grievances.

Covenantally Entangled and Independent

Presbyterians emerged in the late 1630s as a serious option for reforming the Church of Scotland in a substantial way. Thanks to war with the Crown, both in Scotland and England, Presbyterianism even seemed to be the best option for the English, Welsh, and Irish churches. With the 1643 ratification of the Solemn League and Covenant and the convening of the Westminster Assembly to rewrite the norms of the Church of England, Presbyterians in England and Scotland had their best chance for success since sixteenth-century English-speaking exiles in Geneva first became enamored with Calvin's system of church government. The major hitch to this almost dream come true was war, not to mention the varied interests of those sponsoring or conducting the battles. Hostilities among competing groups were almost too many to count—divisions among English and Scottish rulers (king and Parliaments), antagonisms among nations (Scots, English, and Irish), divisions between Royalists and those who wanted constitutional limits on the Crown, sectarian divisions between Protestants and Roman Catholics, radical Protestant (Quakers and Baptist) animus toward establishmentarian Protestants (Presbyterians, Episcopalians, and Independents), not to mention military leaders (Cromwell) who were sufficiently crafty and brutal to prevail without political or religious allies. To think that Presbyterianism might have emerged from this chaotic situation, even if only in Scotland as the national version of Calvin's well-ordered Geneva, was delusional.

The problem for advocates of Presbyterianism was that the national churches in both Scotland and England could not start (more or less) from scratch—something easier to achieve on the scale of Calvin's Geneva or later when Presbyterians migrated to new societies in British North America. The English and Scots inherited church structures that had existed for centuries and were deeply entangled with other civil institutions. Robert S. Paul writes in his useful study of the Westminster Assembly that the divines and their patrons in Parliament faced "the problem of superimposing . . . a church order drawn wholly from the New Testament . . . upon a society that still held substantially medieval views of the relation of church and state." This was a dilemma that Protestants had faced more generally when seeking autonomy from the papacy during the first half of the sixteenth century. But the argument for Presbyterianism only intensified the challenge of general church reform among Western Christians. Adding to the predicament were the relatively novel claims of royal supremacy over a Protestant church. Paul adds that Presbyterianism may have taken deeper root among the Scots than the English thanks to a smaller "attachment. . . to medieval ideas and customs, particularly in relation to the sacraments" in Scotland.[51]

Presbyterians were not merely victims of circumstances beyond their control, however. Their own views about a godly society and the need for a ruler like the Hebrews' King David or King Josiah, the faithful monarch who ensured that true worship prevailed in his holy commonwealth, ran contrary to Presbyterian insistence on the spiritual autonomy and sovereignty of church officers to run their own ecclesiastical affairs. This tension became especially evident during the heady days of the Westminster Assembly when some of Presbyterianism's finest minds made the case for their ideal church government and when it looked like church government by council might prevail in both England and Scotland.

In addition to Samuel Rutherford's *Lex Rex*, the faculty and supporters of London's Sion College, founded in 1630 by royal charter, produced a sustained brief for Presbyterian church government. Even if, Paul observes, Sion College ministers were not as committed to Presbyterian church government as such Scots as Rutherford, its membership produced in 1646 one of the best defenses of Presbyterianism. *Jus divinum regiminis ecclesiastici* was a reply to a query from the House of Commons to the Westminster Assembly. Not only did the book use the language of divine right for Presbyterianism, but it elaborated fairly standard biblical and theological reasons for rule by elders through councils and assemblies.[52] Those rationales included points about Christ (neither the king nor the pope) as head of the church, the New Testament's teaching about elders and councils, the spiritual independence of the church, and the historical origin of bishops only after the conversion of Constantine. The most unusual aspect of *Jus divinum regiminis* was an eighty-page defense of the divine-right nature of elders and their rule in the church. In addition to invoking the Apostle Paul's instruction in the pastoral epistles (1 Timothy, 2 Timothy, and Titus), the authors also appealed to his teaching in Romans 12 on the diversity of gifts God gave to the church. Because "all gifts and endowments in the Church in general, and in every member in particular" were "from God," rule by elders in councils was not pragmatic, but indeed the divine pattern for church government.[53] This norm for rule in the church was not provisional, as if it awaited the arrival of a Christian emperor. Instead, the authors insisted that it was an order for all times and all places because it was the teaching of Christ's apostles under the "power of the Holy Spirit."[54]

As coherent as the case for rule by elders meeting in councils may have been among English and Scottish advocates of Presbyterianism, the Sion College faculty tied themselves up in knots insisting on the church's spiritual independence while reminding Christian magistrates of their duties to maintain a true church. On the one hand, the king had no special office in the church but was merely a lay member subject to the church's officers within ecclesiastical affairs. On the other hand, the civil magistrate had a duty to enforce the Ten Commandments, which included rules about worship and Sabbatarianism. Sion College authors, as did Rutherford, distinguished between the temporal and external (or ceremonial) aspects of church life as opposed to its spiritual or eternal qualities. These spheres allowed advocates of Presbyterianism to locate the magistrate's churchly responsibilities in the outward (external) matters of the church, and the pastors' and elders' duties in questions of conscience or personal belief. According to this two-kingdoms scheme (spiritual and temporal), Christ was lord of both realms and delegated to church officers spiritual authority and to magistrates temporal power. This distinction allowed the Sion College authors to state confidently that "no proper Ecclesiastical power was ever given by Jesus to the Magistrate as a Magistrate."[55]

Rutherford was also equally bold when he wrote that the "Magistrate as the Magistrate is to procure that there be Preachers and Church-officers to dispense Word, Sacraments, and Discipline."[56] By so providing a reformed Christian ministry, the magistrate was ensuring a godly society. Rutherford explained that he had "never denied" the magistrate's authority to guarantee a faithful Christian ministry, but the two-kingdom distinction allowed him to render the king's power as merely temporal and external.[57] He clearly raised the stakes for magistrates and strained the case for ecclesiastical autonomy:

> Magistrates as magistrates are to extend their power for Christ; that is, that not only there be Iustice and Peace amongst men, but also that there be Religion in the land, yea, that the Gospel be preached; so all our Divines make the King to be *custos et vindex utriusque tabulae*; Yea, I think he is a keeper and preserver of the Gospel also, and is to command men to serve Christ, and professe the Gospel, and to punish the blaspheming of Iesus Christ: and this is royall and magistraticall service that the King as King performeth to God, and to Iesus Christ the mediator, *ex conditione operis*, in regard that good which he procureth as King, materially and externally, is consonant to the supernaturall Law of the Gospel, but it is not magistraticall service to Christ.[58]

However coherent and devotionally appealing the case for Presbyterianism may have been, the temporal/spiritual distinction was no match for the real-world politics of seventeenth-century England, Scotland, and the Stuart monarchs. Making church reform dependent on a godly monarch, no matter how much Hebrew kings provided inspiration (which was more the exception than the rule, by the way), involved a host of political actors in ecclesiastical affairs, from the Crown and the monarch's fortunes in Parliament to pious generals' ambitions and the preferences of nobles who funded local pastors. This set of chefs stirring the pot of Christian ministry did not even encompass the sorts of compromises pastors and elders themselves would need to make during their councils, much like the reduced plans for Presbyterian church government in the Westminster Assembly. In other words, the magisterial Reformation, the one experienced by all Protestants (Reformed, Lutheran, and Anglican) except for Anabaptists, depended on civil government. Once political controversy and civil war emerged, the church was an easy target in the political and literal crossfire.

The Scots' National Covenant and the English Parliament's Solemn League and Covenant seemed to promise a better future for Presbyterianism. Those agreements appeared to produce both church reform and a holy commonwealth. And yet, from the angle of British political history, those expressions of godly endeavor were merely chess pieces in the realm of temporal politics. Effective government of the kingdom became much more pressing than public worship or the proper administration of the church. Perhaps the greatest irony of political and military conflicts during Charles I's reign was that ecclesiastical reform wound up a second-order consideration to the rights and prerogatives of temporal authorities, who, in Reformed Protestant theory, derived their powers from the very Christ whom Presbyterians sought to restore as head of the church. Presbyterians claimed to know the true arrangement of divine rights, but their spiritual power was weak compared to the temporal authority of kings, Parliaments, and armies.

CHAPTER 3

Presbyterianism (Finally) Established

After almost two decades of war and political (and religious) recalibration, England and Scotland welcomed the return to monarchy, "running unto the King as Israel to bring back David," writes historian Philip Benedict.[1] The religious question of proper church government and worship that had greatly fueled war and political antagonism during the 1640s was even more unsettled in the 1650s. The Cromwellian church order, "broad, decentralized, and antihierarchical," was unacceptable to both advocates of Presbyterianism and episcopacy.[2] Some proponents of each had gone into exile despite Oliver Cromwell's policies of toleration. After the Restoration, those who favored bishops were content to return to Laudian policies and the old prayer book. Presbyterians remained committed to simple worship and church government through assemblies. Some Presbyterians were hopeful about Charles II, who had—albeit under duress—agreed to the Solemn League and Covenant. In fact, the king's negotiations with the Covenanters in 1650 soured him on Presbyterianism. Edward Hyde, Earl of Clarendon, reinforced the king's coolness toward Presbyterianism. The earl's hope was that God would "preserve us from living in a country where the church is independent from the State" and where "all churchmen may be kings."[3] Despite the return of the monarchy, a new religious order took two years to be implemented.

In England, Charles II's policies were initially concessive to as many groups as possible. A dozen Puritans, among them Richard Baxter and Edmund Calamy, became royal chaplains. When they preached before the king, the prayer book was not necessary. To make the church inclusive, Charles II appointed Baxter and Calamy as bishops. Each man refused the office. Initial plans for the church order involved a hybrid between episcopacy and Presbyterianism. Plans required bishops to preach regularly. They also needed to work in consultation with elected presbyters. The new terms of church government were sufficiently attractive to woo 695 ministers, who had been ejected from the Church of England between 1641 and 1659, back to their parishes.[4] These initial policies never became law, however. Parliament defeated them by a narrow vote.

Under the next Parliament (called Cavalier for its ties to Royalist combatants during the Civil War), which lasted from 1661 to 1679, the king changed course. The Act of Uniformity of 1662 was indicative of Parliament's attitude after the Civil War and the Interregnum. The act required all ministers to assent to "everything" in the Book of Common Prayer and do so publicly in their parishes. Parliament threatened fines for any minister refusing to use the prescribed liturgy for sacraments. The act also required ministers to swear allegiance to the king and abjure the Solemn League and Covenant. One last issue of importance to Presbyterians was ordination. The act granted to bishops the power of conferring the rights and privileges of the ministry. In this climate, the Restoration church reverted back to an Erastian pattern, with the civil government taking an active role in church administration. That period also nurtured divine-right justifications for episcopacy among bishops and royalists. Theologically, the church veered away from Calvinism toward Arminian views. The reputation of William Laud, the controversial (to Puritans and Presbyterians) former archbishop of Canterbury, also improved. The recovery of Laud's stature was responsible for Gilbert Sheldon's (archbishop of Canterbury, 1663–77) publication of Laud's *Diary, History and Prayers*.

The Act of Uniformity obviously jeopardized a range of English Protestant ministers. In the Puritan camp, some objected to the imposition of the prayer book. Others, who had sworn the Solemn League and Covenant, were unwilling to renounce the godly society that alliance with Scottish Presbyterians had promised. Still other pastors, who had been ordained during Cromwell's rule by the Triers, a commission appointed to vet candidates for the ministry, were unwilling to be reordained by a bishop. The result was that on St. Bartholomew's Day, August 24, 1662, more than 1,000 ministers refused to submit to the Act of Uniformity and thereby gave up the stipends that came with their callings.

Dissenting ministers were now on the outside of the Church of England, both figuratively and literally. Some tried to meet with parishioners secretly for worship and edification. If detected, authorities arrested them. Some ministers went to jail, where they conducted worship for other prisoners. Laws in support of conformity banned any gathering for religious purposes larger than five people who were not part of the same household. Legislation also penalized dissenting ministers who came within five miles of any parish where they had served either in the old national church or through conventicles. Charles II himself was uncomfortable with the persecution that followed. In 1672, he issued a Declaration of Indulgence, which created a way for Dissenters to qualify for a license to conduct worship. More than 1,600 ministers applied and received an indulgence. Parliament was jealous of its prerogatives and retaliated in 1673 with the Test Act, which required all public officials (civil, military, and legal) to commune within the Established Church.[5] Caught between Parliament's rock and the king's hard place, Dissenters had no hope for church reform.

In Scotland, frustration with Presbyterianism was a close rival to suspicions about Charles II. To his credit, the king avoided the mistakes of his father, Charles I. He did not require liturgical uniformity, a reversal from his grandfather's Articles of Perth (1618). Neither did Charles II venture into the contested domain of a prayer book—the spark that ignited the Bishops' Wars. As late as 1672, worship even appeared to conform to Presbyterian standards. According to an English Nonconformist studying in the north, worship in Scotland was "in all respects," even when the archbishop preached, "after the same manner managed as in the Presbyterian congregations in England."[6] Church order returned to the awkward mix of bishops and assemblies.

Yet, Scotland's Parliament had grown tired of Presbyterian precision and saw the advantages of episcopacy. The same was true for Charles II, who recognized that, with an episcopal order, the Crown had greater control of the church and its resources. In 1661, Parliament had passed a resolution that called for a frame of ecclesiastical government that was both "agreeable to the word of God" and "most suteable to monarchical government." Episcopacy seemed to promise "public peace and quyet" in the kingdom.[7] Later that same year, Charles II made official what was more or less the way the Kirk functioned—a return to the church order under his grandfather. Sessions, presbyteries, and assemblies carried out the work of church government under the oversight and direction of bishops.

For the most zealous of Presbyterians, the Restoration order was unwelcome, but the new provisions for ordination were especially objectionable. The new order required ministers to be ordained by bishops and gave local lords a prominent voice in the selection of pastors. If the old Presbyterian objections to the inherent corruption of episcopacy were insufficiently alarming, inserting local elites into the mechanism of church government was an affront to claims of ecclesiastical independence and spiritual authority. As many as 270 Scottish ministers (roughly 25 percent) refused to comply. Scottish dissent was greater than in the English church "despite the narrower range of issues."[8] In the vicinity of Glasgow, Presbyterian dissent was the greatest—more than half the pastors. Such resistance was an outgrowth of the second line crossed, the National Covenant. Opposition to the new church order provoked secret assemblies and conventicles where pastors continued to lead worship. Presbyterian zeal also spurred armed confrontations with the government. In the 1660s and the 1680s, in particular, members of the conventicles, still loyal to the terms of the National Covenant, engaged in armed skirmishes with Scottish soldiers. During the 1670s, Charles II's government attempted to accommodate those who led ecclesiastical resistance.

The king's occasional flexibility on religious policy may seem odd in the context of both Tudor and Stuart conceptions of royal supremacy over the church. But his reasons for religious toleration were connected to a desire to open English society to Roman Catholics. That aim explains Parliament's opposition and insistence on religious uniformity (thanks also to the presence of bishops in the House of Lords). Suspicions of Charles II also explain English and Scottish Presbyterian activities during the Restoration. Even as English Presbyterians cooperated with their kingdom's bishops, their Scottish counterparts, still harkening for the promise of a covenanted and godly nation, mixed militant and millennial motivations to complete (finally) the Scottish Reformation. Only another revolution, this one "glorious," could tame the Stuarts, suppress Roman Catholics, and sort out the competing claims of bishops, moderators, and zealous English and Scottish Protestants.

Presbyterian Dissent

If Charles II was no Elizabeth, Richard Baxter was no Thomas Cartwright (the leading voice of sixteenth-century English Presbyterians). Still, Baxter was to English Presbyterianism what Cartwright had been a century earlier. Baxter may well have been a weaker vessel for English Calvinists than John Owen, who defended Reformed orthodoxy against the spread of Arminianism. But the popular and widely read minister from Kidderminster, a small town southwest of Birmingham, dominated discussions of church life during the second half of the seventeenth century. Part of Baxter's prominence owes to a massive literary output (150-plus titles, with several weighing in at around 600 pages in print). Remarkably, this productivity was not the result of a cloistered life. At the age of twenty-five, Baxter became a minister in Kidderminster. During the Civil War, between 1642 and 1647, he left the ministry to serve as a chaplain in Parliament's army. His military service exposed him to—and inoculated him against—religious radicals. Baxter opposed the execution of Charles I and refused to take an oath to the new Commonwealth.

Nevertheless, the Kidderminster pastor reconciled himself to Cromwell (and especially to Cromwell's son Richard), a shift that colored his Presbyterian convictions. Baxter's version was by no means the divine-right Presbyterianism on the order of Cartwright, Melville, or Rutherford. Baxter's ecclesiology was a middling sort, a position somewhere between episcopacy and Congregationalism. This meant, according to Tim Cooper, that for Baxter a Presbyterian "need not have been Presbyterian in any formal sense."[9] His attitude about authority in the church was akin to his outlook on civil government—skeptical about monarchs, lords, and bishops, especially as a means to living a holy life or establishing a godly commonwealth. His *A Holy Commonwealth* (1659) was a brief for a form of theocracy that depended on cooperation between the civil magistrate and local ministers in the cultivation of personal holiness and civic righteousness. The details of actual political forms, whether civil or ecclesiastical, were inexact. The primary goal was sanctity no matter how achieved.

Baxter's flexibility on church polity owed partly to the influence of James Ussher, archbishop of Armagh. The Irish bishop's proposal for reduced episcopal authority informed Baxter's outlook during debates over religious policy in the initial stages of the Restoration. Ussher had died in 1656. His ideas about church government, long in development, became public thanks to the efforts of his biographer, Nicholas Bernard. The idea behind a reduced episcopacy was a hybrid of episcopal authority and local responsibility. Ussher sought to limit the size of each see to the footprint of a single congregation. A bishop's authority extended to his own congregation and included advisory input from presbyters. Within the wider arena of a diocese, a bishop acted in a presidential capacity in relation to other pastors and congregations. Ussher's idea stemmed from an understanding of the early church, which supposedly revealed a pattern of one bishop per congregation, who was also active in all parts of church life, from worship to governance.[10]

What Baxter was thinking (with help from Ussher) was not as important for religious policy in England as it was for civil authorities. Charles II began to clarify the Crown's views even before Parliament restored the monarchy. Negotiations between the king's aids and representatives of Parliament had begun in March 1660 when the chief concerns were for protection of the army—pay for soldiers, pardon for revolutionaries in exchange for declarations of loyalty. But another controverted matter, obviously after Britain's wars of religion, was church policy. The Declaration of Breda, ratified by the king in April and the basis for the May 1, 1660, Restoration, handled religion in remarkable continuity with the more or less laissez-faire policies under Oliver Cromwell. In order to heal wounds and end confusion in the realm, the Declaration of Breda affirmed freedom of conscience in the following terms: "We do declare a Liberty to tender Consciences; and that no Man shall be disquieted or called in Question for Differences of Opinion in Matter of Religion, which do not disturb the Peace of the Kingdom; and that We shall be ready to consent to such an Act of Parliament as, upon mature Deliberation, shall be offered to Us, for the full granting that Indulgence."[11]

Austin Woolrych observes that the masterful stroke in Breda was to put the burden of religious policy in Parliament where "animosities" were still likeliest to surface.[12] If someone were to revoke the religious liberties the king favored, Parliament would have to do the unpleasant work. This was a very different stance from the pattern of royal supremacy over the church that had so agitated Presbyterians and Puritans.

The Declaration of Breda, however, proved too flimsy for a restored national church. How was the revamped Church of England supposed to comprehend Independents, Presbyterians, and Episcopalians? In June 1660, the leading Presbyterians—Baxter, Thomas Manton, and John Wallis—met with the king and Edward Hyde, the first Earl of Clarendon, to negotiate an agreeable religious settlement. According to Baxter's account, the Presbyterian nonnegotiables were an agreement on what was essential to church life, the practice of discipline within the church, and the inclusion of worthy ministers only. Notions about divine-right bishops or presbyters were as far from view as were debates about who was the head of the church, the king or Christ. The king's response was to ask the Presbyterians to flesh out these matters. They complied when London's Presbyterians gathered for a conference at Sion College with a broad range of English Protestants. These ministers produced terms for a restored establishment under three main heads—the return of a modest episcopacy (smaller dioceses to ensure discipline), a commission to revise the prayer book, and a resolve to view contested rituals and ceremonies as matters indifferent.[13]

Over the summer of 1660, negotiations took place with meetings among different groups of ministers and communications with Charles, the culmination of which was the meeting in October at Worcester House, Lord Clarendon's residence. At this consultation, which included Presbyterians, bishops, and the king and his advisors, several sticking points emerged that were ominous for Presbyterians. One was the extent to which ministers could determine affairs in their own parishes. The king objected to granting priests a negative voice against the bishops. Another point of contention was the validity of Presbyterian ordination. The bishops argued for reordaining Presbyterian ministers. When the king proposed toleration for Independents and Anabaptists as long as they were peaceful, Presbyterians and bishops balked at a policy that could eventually embrace Roman Catholics too. Baxter himself opposed toleration for Romanists. Charles II countered that the law contained plenty of restrictions on the Church of Rome.[14] Overall, the Worcester House meeting revealed the incompatibility of the Crown's, bishops', and Presbyterians' positions. Baxter left the meeting dejected. "To the best of my knowledge," he wrote, "the Presbyterian Cause was never spoken for."[15]

Baxter's mood brightened, however, when he read the final version of Charles II's proposal for a restored church, the "The King's Declaration Concerning Ecclesiastical Affairs." In its preamble, Charles jumped right into the fray that had absorbed English Protestants for most of the past century. After professing his "high Affection and Esteem" for the Church of England "as it is established by Law" and its ministry in supporting us "with God's Blessing," the king explained his decision to return to episcopacy. This form of church rule was "the best support of Religion," and "the best means to contain the Minds of Men within the Rules of Government." Charles II was aware—how could he not be after his experience with the Scots nine years earlier?—of those who wanted to "restrain the exercise of that holy Function within the Rules which were observed in the Primitive times." Here the king dipped into arguments that bishops had used against Presbyterians a century earlier to assert that church authority in the primitive church, "those blessed times," was "always subordinate and subject to the Civil." The precise relationship of spiritual and temporal power was not always clear. But just as civil government had evolved over time, so too church government adjusted to different circumstances. For the time being, monarchy and episcopacy were best suited to England. This argument did diverge from divine-right arguments for bishops. Just as other countries had governments that were not monarchical, and even a time when England had tried a "Democratical Government here in the State," so other national churches may legitimately erect churches with "Aristocratical Government," an apparent reference to Presbyterianism. Either way, experimentation was past. "The Hearts of this whole nation," thanks to the "wonderful Blessing of God," rejoiced in monarchy. So too, the Church of England had returned to "that Government . . . Which is established by Law, and with which the Monarchy hath flourished through so many ages." Not to mention, which Charles II did, that episcopacy was "as ancient in this Island" as the Crown itself.[16]

After that agreeable introduction, the king proposed reforms of the episcopate that Puritans had long favored. He declared, for instance, an intention to promote "the Power of Godliness," especially in the observance of the Lord's Day as a time devoted to "the exercises of Religion, both publick and private." He opposed "insufficient, negligent, and scandalous" ministers, but his disapproval was ambiguous about removing such clergy. He also insisted that bishops be "Men of great and exemplar Piety in their Lives," and "of great and known sufficiency of Learning." As such, bishops needed to be examples to the priests under their watch. They also should be "frequent Preachers" in their respective dioceses unless they "be hindered by Sickness, or other bodily Infirmities." To encourage bishops to preach, Charles II proposed suffragan bishops for large dioceses who would share duties in weekly worship.[17]

From here followed a series of instructions sympathetic to Puritans if not also those who favored Presbyterian government. In matters of ordination and church discipline, bishops needed to consult with "Pious Presbyters" within the diocese. The king's declaration in some cases even specified the composition of ecclesiastical committees. On those with six members, the bishop was responsible for appointing three and presbyters decided among themselves who would fill the other slots. Charles also reminded church officers that standards for admission to the Lord's Supper required a credible profession of faith. If church members departed from the pattern of a godly life, bishops needed to ensure that such sinners had displayed repentance before being readmitted to communion. The church needed to use "all possible diligence . . . for the Instruction and Reformation of scandalous Offenders, whom the Minister shall not suffer to partake of the Lord's Table, until they have openly declared themselves to have truly repented and amended their former naughty Lives." Would the king require use of the prayer book? Charles II called it "the best we have seen."[18]

The king knew liturgy was controversial and so outlined procedures for ministers to take exception to forms within the prayer book, called for a committee to review corporate worship, and allowed for other forms that gave ministers flexibility in leading worship. The principle to which the king appealed was freedom of conscience. Charles II explained that "Our present Consideration and Work is, to gratifie the private Consciences of those who are grieved with the use of some Ceremonies, by indulging to, and dispensing with their omitting those Ceremonies; not utterly to abolish any which are Established by Law."[19] This remark likely explains why the King's Declaration's longest sections addressed matters of liturgy, ceremonies, uniformity, and freedom. David Fuller, who studied the relations of church and state in seventeenth-century England, judges that if Charles II's Declaration had become the realm's policy, thanks mainly to its concessions to the Puritans, the statement "would have changed the face of the Church of England forever."[20]

Presbyterians with ties to Baxter were pleased with the King's Declaration even though the proposed restoration of a national church fell well short of what English Reformers had argued for a century earlier. In addition to liturgical reforms, sixteenth-century English Presbyterians, Thomas Cartwright and Walter Travers, had advocated the abolition of episcopacy on the grounds that it was incapable of instilling holiness among clergy and the laity, and that it was too entangled in English legal and civil structures to carry out its spiritual duties adequately. After the Civil War and the Interregnum, Baxter knew that doing away with bishops was a nonstarter. That is why Ussher's idea for a reduced episcopacy was preferable. In addition, the king's own proposals for encouraging bishops with smaller responsibilities to take on the work of spiritual care went a long way to acknowledging Presbyterian objections to episcopacy. At the same time, the Restoration church was so bound up with English legal and administrative structures, along with built-in royal prerogatives, that Presbyterian ideals of ecclesiastical independence and sovereignty were impossible. Yet, the king's pastoral manner as opposed to an exertion of royal prerogative took away some of Presbyterians' vocal criticisms of episcopacy.[21]

Presbyterians were not the only voices among English Protestants with possible objections to episcopacy. At the Savoy Conference of 1661, which included a dozen bishops and Puritan ministers, some Protestants still held out hope for the Solemn League and Covenant's model for a Presbyterian establishment. Others leaned toward independence for congregations. That spectrum left Baxter's reduced episcopacy in the moderate middle. This diversity among Independents, Puritans, and Presbyterians (hardly rigid categories) was partly responsible for the bishops' inflexibility at the Savoy Conference. Puritanism and Presbyterianism connoted political instability to several bishops, who themselves had lost their livings during the war and Interregnum. For this reason, the twelve bishops who attended the Savoy Conference "were in no mood to make concessions," according to C. G. Boling and Jeremy Goring.[22] The Presbyterian cause also suffered from pushy proposals for worship that ignored the bishops' positions on liturgy. Savoy's deliberations continued, per the king's commission, into the summer. The tone of the conference echoed the mood of the nation. That year's elections for Parliament revealed the triumph of a Royalist sensibility in England. A return to episcopacy in the Church of England looked like a safe and preferable outcome after decades of political and ecclesiastical conflict. Support for the Crown may not have determined approval of bishops. But Royalism and Presbyterianism were invariably at odds.[23]

Baxter usually takes the blame for Presbyterians' failure at the Savoy Conference. His defenders counter that Presbyterians' prospects were always grim. Tim Cooper argues that they had virtually no support in the restored Long Parliament or its two subsequent assemblies. "The groundswell toward restoration seemed inexorable" and "carried the bishops along." In turn bishops required Presbyterians "to take every initiative," "stalled and delayed," never put anything in writing, and "never offered a meaningful concession."[24] The bishops' performance was, according to Mark Goldie, a "betrayal of Breda," or a "statutory coup accomplished by the 'prelatical party,'" in the words of Michael Winship.[25] Even James Sharp, the archbishop of St. Andrews present in London to advise Presbyterians, concurred with these verdicts. "The Episcopal Men have the Wind of them," Sharp wrote, "and know how to use it."[26]

The rise of a strident episcopate in England was one of the least likely developments of the seventeenth century's turbulent church history. Jeffrey R. Collins argues that the bishops of the Restoration church embodied the resurgence of Laudian *jure divino* episcopacy. Whereas in the pre-revolution church, Archbishop William Laud's brief for episcopacy included a strong defense of royal supremacy above spiritual authority, during the Restoration bishops went further and severed episcopal rights from deference to the Crown. Fifteen of the twenty-six bishops appointed after 1660 had ties to Laud. In addition, twenty-one of that same body of bishops were sixty-three years old or older, which placed their ecclesiastical formation in the Laudian era. Four of the bishops had gone into exile with the king and twenty-one had lost their livings during the revolution. These upheavals, according to Collins, funneled an already high view of episcopacy into a divine-right argument that rivaled royal supremacy.[27] In this view, bishops became not only "the immediate institution of Christ," but they possessed a unique and superior role in ruling the church.[28] As such, the king became a layman over whom the bishops had spiritual (and higher) authority.

By defending episcopacy this way, the Restoration bishops had ironically adopted a position on the spiritual and temporal spheres and relations between church and state that Presbyterians had set out a century earlier. In both cases, pastors and bishops wanted to limit the Crown's control of the church and preserve the integrity and import of spiritual matters. Bishops were less inclined to speak of Christ as head of the church than Presbyterians. Other than that, the Restoration bishops were conceding the century-old Presbyterian point.

Despite the overlapping regard for spiritual authority, Presbyterians faced penalties in Restoration England. When the Act of Uniformity went into effect (August 1662), all ministers needed to "assent and consent" to everything contained in the Book of Common Prayer. They were also required to renounce publicly the Solemn League and Covenant. At the same time, anyone who hoped to work within the Church of England—including schoolmasters and tutors—needed to be ordained by a bishop. In what became known as the Great Ejection, 2,000 ministers refused the terms of uniformity. That decision had consequences for ministry even outside the Church of England. Parliament followed up in 1664 with the Conventicle Act. This law threatened imprisonment for anyone over sixteen who attended a private worship service that did not follow the Book of Common Prayer. Charles II wanted leniency for Dissenters, and the next year proposed that non-Anglicans be allowed to pay for permission to worship. Parliament remained resolute. The body passed the Five Mile Act, which forbade any ejected minister from living within five miles of the town or village of his previous charge.[29]

Not all Dissenters gave up on the church, nor did all bishops abandon efforts to include Presbyterians in the Church of England. Yet, meetings in 1667 among Baxter, Thomas Manton, and William Bates, led by Bishop John Wilkins, could not forestall further penalties against dissent. The Conventicle Act of 1670 was designed to suppress worship among Dissenters that allegedly used sensitive consciences as a cover for sedition and even revolution. The act even allowed for accusations based on hearsay.[30] Charles II rallied with another Declaration of Indulgence

(1672) designed to ease the penalties against dissent and Roman Catholics. This proposal reflected England's war with the Dutch and efforts to secure an alliance with the French. Parliament revoked the Declaration of Indulgence as unconstitutional. English Presbyterians were left without a national church that embodied true reform. The only remedy available apparently was a political party that could soften Parliament's resolve.

Scottish Resilience

If divine-right episcopacy cut into hopes for Presbyterianism in England, the appeal of bishops in Scotland was more the product of political fatigue than theological argument. At the beginning of the Restoration in Scotland, Presbyterians understood the National Covenant was a political liability. Archibald Johnston of Wariston, the Covenanter leader, in 1660 recorded in his diary that "the bulk of the nation was turned . . . against . . . presbyterial government." He estimated that as many Scots had turned "against the covenant" as had supported it seventeen years earlier. A Presbyterian minister, William Row, confirmed Johnston's observation. "Too many in Scotland . . . had an evil eye to the covenant and presbyterial government" Row wrote.[31] Unlike England where the shadow cast by Cromwell's government made the Church of England attractive, in Scotland Presbyterianism became an easy target for civil authorities and church ministers who wanted a return to moderation in the kingdom and its church. If the form of government that John Calvin had instituted in Geneva was going to become the national norm, Presbyterians needed to overcome themselves (as their worst enemy) and their ecclesiastical rivals, the bishops. Meanwhile, what royal supremacy meant for the Church of Scotland was hardly clear. For advocates of Presbyterianism, such as Robert Wodrow, author of *The History of the Suffering Church of Scotland* (1829), the Restoration period was "one of the blackest periods" in the history of the Kirk.[32]

Despite these conditions, Presbyterians repeated antagonisms from the previous two decades. The Resolutioners, the party that advocated cooperation with Charles II in the early 1650s as the best way to save the National Covenant, had been willing to work with the king to complete the Scottish Reformation. Their opponents, the Protesters, refused to trust Charles II with the fortunes of Presbyterianism. After the Interregnum, in the early stages of the Restoration, these two parties had not changed their views of the same monarch. For the Resolutioners, Charles represented a "settled" government and relief from anarchy. For Protesters, the king was a "matter of terror" to prospects for a godly realm and faithful Kirk.[33]

In the summer of 1660, the king expressed respect for Scottish Presbyterians and a willingness to accommodate them in the restored church. A letter from Charles II to the Presbytery of Edinburgh in August pledged resolve to preserve and protect the Church of Scotland's government as settled by law. Charles II also indicated his intention to recognize the acts of the 1651 General Assembly led by Resolutioners and the last to meet before the Restoration. The letter's intentions, not to mention the timing of its delivery, led some to speculate that the king was appeasing Presbyterians to make room for episcopacy in his final plans for the church. Either way, the letter indicated that the Resolutioners held an early lead in the competition for the Kirk's governance. The king's ecclesiastical diplomacy received confirmation when Scotland's Committee of Estates ordered the arrest of eleven Protesters (ten ministers and one elder). Their fault was drafting a letter that called upon Charles II to remedy the "vast toleration" that had damaged Scotland under Cromwell. The Protesters' missive also warned that Scotland's prelatical party was thwarting the work of church reform. For good measure, the offending Protesters had implored the king to uphold the Solemn League and Covenant and restore "true" religion throughout the three kingdoms.[34]

This arrest was indicative of the Committee of Estates' intention to maintain adversarial pressure on Scots loyal to the Covenants. A proclamation that made illegal all conventicles and seditious meetings provided the grounds for further action against Protesters, as did a ban on any slanders against the king. To add insult to injury, the committee banned two books, one of which was Samuel Rutherford's *Lex Rex*, the other was James Guthrie's *The Causes of God's Wrath*, whose author was another Covenanter and prominent figure in the Protester Assemblies of the early 1650s. Anyone who owned these books needed to turn them in to the solicitor or face an unspecified punishment. According to one Scottish official, the king was not inclined to meddle in the Covenanters' lives. But if they caused political trouble, Charles II was disposed to send them to Barbados.[35]

The timeline available to the Resolutioners for securing control of the Church of Scotland was short, however. Whatever the political maneuvering between London and Edinburgh and however calm the mood of Scotland, the future for Presbyterians was more dire than in England. To the south, Presbyterians had not been the ecclesiastical establishment, as was the case in Scotland. For that reason, the determination in early 1661 by members of the Scottish Parliament to restore episcopacy was as unexpected as it was stunning. The Rescissory Act, passed on March 28, had the potential of setting a dangerous precedent. In one stroke Parliament wiped away the acts of previous Parliaments enacted between 1640 and 1648. Its effects actually extended to undoing legislating dating back to 1633. The Rescissory Act of 1661 gutted the achievements of the Covenanters and appeared to remove entirely the National Covenant from Scottish legal history. The act also granted authority to the king to institute a church polity faithful to God's word and agreeable to monarchy.[36] This law paved the way for a return to episcopacy in the Church of Scotland once the king could find worthy bishops.

If the Rescissory Act cut off Presbyterian appeals to Scottish precedents, a groundswell of support for episcopacy filled the ecclesiastical and legal void. Members of the Scots Council that visited Charles II in the summer of 1661 viewed Presbyterianism as politically unstable. For some, Presbyterianism was synonymous with a kind of "insolence." According to the Earl of Lauderdale, who had been a member of the Westminster Assembly and imprisoned during Cromwell's reign, episcopacy had the advantage of predictability. He also advised that the king wait for the General Assembly to meet before making a final decision. At the same meeting, Charles II heard a different perspective. Some said that the reason the Rescissory Act passed with almost no opposition was its apparent reassurance that Presbyterianism would remain Scotland's form of church polity. For these advisors, Presbyterianism's status as the established church even preceded the acts by the Scottish Parliament that led up to the National Covenant.[37]

Despite mixed messages, Charles II approved a royal letter in August that announced the restoration of bishops. Once again, Presbyterianism's opposition to royal supremacy was a major consideration. The king may well have recalled his grandfather James I's opinion that Presbyterianism's system of parity was the "mother of confusion." In contrast, episcopacy promised to keep ordinary clergy in line and achieve peace.[38] The meeting had the effect of placing Charles II on the side of Erastianism's view of the church as subordinate to the state in enforcing punishment for spiritual offenses. As such, the Presbyterian ideal of the king as head of the civil realm and Christ as spiritual head of the church was inherently disorderly: "Erastianism in its extreme form was to be the order of the day."[39] Lord Clarendon (Edward Hyde) likely spoke for the king when he said, "God preserve me from living in a country, where the church is independent from the state, and may subsist by their own acts; for there all churchmen may be kings."[40] The king's formal declaration in August, repeated in September 1661, was a short step from these sentiments. No synods should meet until the king determined the final policy. Any minister who preached or wrote in dissent would be imprisoned.

Over the course of the 1660s, not only did Presbyterianism vanish within the Church of Scotland but royal supremacy in the church became the norm. Four synods had continued to meet during the spring of 1661—Dumfries, Galloway, Fife, and Glasgow and Ayr—but did so cautiously to avoid the Presbyterian stereotype of rebellion. The Synod of Dumfries even followed the king's directive—after crafting a resolution against episcopacy, ministers went home. The Synod of Galloway also complied with the new rules after drafting a complaint against bishops.[41] The example of the Presbyterian minister James Guthrie, convicted in June 1661 of sedition and executed, was one factor in Presbyterian compliance. Such caution also enabled the reinstitution of the bishops in the Kirk.

In 1662, after bishops had returned to the Scottish Parliament, the Privy Council passed acts that banned at least the worst parts of Presbyterianism. In one of these laws, signing the National Covenant became a treasonable offense. Another resolution required that ministers could only remain in the Kirk with the backing of a "lawful patron" and approval (collation) from the bishop. By October 1662, all parishes whose ministers did not meet these requirements were "vacant."[42] The expectation was that Presbyterian ministers leave their parishes, move to another location, and forgo the stipend for clergy. Economic realities may explain why 528 (out of 802 total) ministers abandoned Presbyterianism and accepted the terms of prelacy. Even pastors who refused to accept episcopacy avoided any hint of rebellion. In Galloway, a heavily Presbyterian region, sixteen ministers accused of noncompliance reassured authorities of their loyalty. Although the new church government was unacceptable, they promised to obey the king's directives and to stop preaching.[43]

For the three decades after the Restoration, Presbyterians in Scotland when active needed to conform or work around the givens of the established church. The Assertory Act of 1669 underscored the king's "supreme authority" over the "external government and policy of the church."[44] The king's power extended not only to the government of the church, but also the business conducted at ecclesiastical meetings. Meanwhile, bishops were responsible for all levels of church government. Episcopal domination extended from national meetings down to the existing sessions of parishes through formal and informal mechanisms. In the west and southwest, where Presbyterian convictions ran strong, more ministers left their charges than in the east and the north. But with variations of time and place came different reactions to an episcopal Church of Scotland.

In the initial period after the Restoration, Presbyterian dissent was mild. In the Presbyterian heartland of the southwest and west of Scotland, unauthorized meetings for worship (conventicles) were few in number. Church courts recorded charges against dissenting ministers for conducting services outside the established churches. But evidence indicates that Presbyterian sentiments were "moderate to weak" if holding illegal worship was a sign.[45] In the north of Scotland, Presbyterians also went along in the main. Not only were conventicles infrequent. Dissenting pastors themselves attended the Kirk's services. The Pentland Rising of 1666 was one indication of conflict between the Covenanters and civil and ecclesiastical authorities. Still, estimates of the rebels put their numbers between 200 and 900. According to some, it was mainly an outbreak from "a rabble of private country clowns," not worthy of being called a rebellion.[46] The reason for Dissenters' compliance was twofold: the palpable unpopularity of the National Covenants and a Scottish disposition against schism. One layman, for instance, who attended services at the local parish admitted that episcopacy was "against his will," but because God had allowed it and the king had established it, he decided to submit to the new order.[47] Another Presbyterian, this time a pastor, combined in equal measure opposition to prelacy and to "separation from the kirk."[48]

Such compliance highlights the unusual uptick of Presbyterian convictions in the 1670s. The event that triggered the change was an assassination attempt in Edinburgh on the archbishop of St. Andrews, James Sharp. The perpetrator, James Mitchell, was a Covenanter who had been involved in the Pentland Rising and condemned for treason. He objected to what he perceived as Sharp's opposition to clemency for participants in the rising. Mitchell's case (a protracted series of trials and eventual execution a decade later) was not as consequential for Presbyterianism as the authorities' response to the attempt on Sharp's life. Officials opened a search for Dissenters throughout Edinburgh, which in turn prompted ministers to flee the city. Some of these pastors from Galloway and Nithsdale had earlier led conventicles but moved to Edinburgh when soldiers in 1666 cracked down on Dissenter worship. Once these ministers fled the city after the attempt on Sharp's life, their isolation provided settings for holding large field conventicles.

As risky as that conduct may have seemed, it also coincided with the Scottish government's offer in 1669 of indulgences to Nonconformist ministers. This policy provided for forty-three Dissenters to minister in established parishes and receive clerical stipends. The reasons for this offer were a shortage of ministers and a desire to contain dissent within the confines of the established church.[49] The government's new policy seemed to indicate tolerance for Presbyterianism, which in turn encouraged Presbyterian pastors to be less secret about their endeavors than they had been in the 1660s.

Although the indulged ministers faced restrictions—often not followed—the policy of openness continued with a second indulgence three years later (1672). This change almost doubled the number of Presbyterians laboring in the Restoration Church of Scotland. Another policy in 1674 indemnified preachers who led conventicles from having to pay any fines or penalties. The new measures likely owed to political rivalries between the Duke of Hamilton and the Duke of Lauderdale, the latter of whom sought to secure greater support from Presbyterians and their sympathizers. The new conditions fanned into flame gatherings that for some qualified as a Presbyterian awakening. Such vigor was evident in the ordination of younger Presbyterian pastors, a practice that clearly violated the policies and theology of episcopacy, but that also took advantage of the new ecclesiastical latitude. Another indication of Presbyterian zeal was the proliferation of conventicles in almost complete disregard of the established church's authority.[50]

These worship services, prevalent in several regions, grew from small gatherings inside homes to meetings in fields with large crowds. Sometimes these conventicles met for days at a time, where several ministers, one after the other, preached, administered the Lord's Supper (not at first but later in the 1670s), and even practiced church discipline. The conventicles were not merely expressions of Presbyterian devotion. According to one estimate, thousands sometimes met, even in terrible weather, to hear preachers condemn "the king, the ministers of the state, the officers of the army, . . . and the episcopal clergy, all broadside to hell."[51] This was not true for all pastors. Some called for holiness and personal reformation through spiritual means. Others were explicitly political. One such pastor, John Semple, had a reputation for preaching against the "bishops and their underlings" from practically "any portion of Scripture."[52]

Such resurgence among Presbyterians, in both the parish and the field, nurtured the recovery of older ecclesiastical themes. Instead of complying with prelacy and going to hear the curates preach, in the 1670s devoted Presbyterians began to avoid worship in the Kirk intentionally. Opposition to Erastianism also resurfaced in an oxymoronic way. Although the indulgences had permitted Presbyterians greater access to gather for worship, the policy became a reason to complain about civil interference with the rights and prerogatives of the church. This grievance became so pronounced that some Presbyterians refused to accept clerical appointments, and insisted that attending services conducted by indulged pastors was a mark of infidelity. A growing sense of militancy throughout the 1670s encouraged those gathering in conventicles to carry weapons in case government officials tried to restrict these assemblies.

In March 1675 the inevitable happened. Violence erupted in the shire of Kinross when soldiers opened fire on a conventicle. Not until the spring of 1678 did such violence result in the death of a soldier. From then on, fighting escalated. The assassination of James Sharp, archbishop of St. Andrews, in June by a group of nine still holding out for the National Covenant, heightened the tension. (According to accounts, one of the assassins mentioned the deaths at the Pentland Rising as justification

Figure 3.1. Depiction of a conventicle in progress, from H. E. Marshall's *Scotland's Story*, published in 1906.

for murdering the bishop.) The largest outbreak of violence occurred a year later with the Bothwell Bridge Rebellion. There the conventiclers rallied a force of 8,000 rebels. They eventually marched on Glasgow and seized the city. Royal forces put down the insurrection a few days later. Estimates of the rebels' deaths vary from single digits to as many as 700. Another estimate puts the number of rebel prisoners at 1,200. The Bothwell incident culminated the second period of Presbyterian life during the Restoration.[53]

Despite the 1679 rebellion, the government responded in a way that suggested its own fault in managing conventicles.[54] As a result, that same year, the king's government issued a third indulgence that offered indemnity to rebels and allowed for services in private homes on the condition that ministers maintain the "public peace."[55] These terms had an ironic effect on prospects for Presbyterianism. Its proponents lost the aura of conviction and courage they had enjoyed throughout the 1670s. In turn, the new arrangement instigated the most contentious of covenanting Presbyterians, the Cameronians. According to some estimates, this group had no more than one hundred followers. Their ministerial leaders were initially three men, Richard Cameron, Donald Cargill, and Thomas Douglas. In 1681, the first two were dead and the last was in exile in England. Initial efforts to recruit ministers failed, but by the end of the 1680s the group claimed three pastors and one probationer (all ordained outside Scotland, in Holland, Ireland, and England).[56]

The political profile of the Cameronians was hard to miss, but other radical groups, according to Mark Linden Mirabello's research, such as the Gibbites and the Russellites, also resisted the established order for religious reasons. Not only were they opposed to the Crown, but they were unafraid to resort to violence. Their opposition to the monarchy led one of their ministers to excommunicate Charles II. The Cameronians also believed that even saying "God save the king" was sinful.[57] They conducted a number of violent raids and received support from the likes of Alexander Shields, who defended armed conflict and invoked the example of Old Testament saints rising up against idolaters and false prophets. In some cases the use of force bordered on the trivial. One woman went to church and "beat" the minister after the sermon. She even admitted that her reason for going to church was to assault the pastor. In other instances, Cameronians killed pastors and soldiers. Often the victims were persons who had either informed on or had threatened them.[58]

Despite the problems that Cameronians and the covenanting tradition caused for the government, by the 1680s most Presbyterians in Scotland had embraced moderation. Few could stomach the politics and wars that attached to Presbyterians during the first half of the seventeenth century. If any aspect of civil government separated Presbyterians from Episcopalians, the issue was the Crown. After James VII/II succeeded his brother to the throne in 1685 (after Charles II's death), England and Scotland faced the prospect of a Roman Catholic king. James II had converted almost two decades earlier. His reign undermined the entire question of royal supremacy. How could a Roman Catholic be the head of a communion that repudiated the pope? The birth of James II's first son in 1688 also raised the possibility of a Roman Catholic dynasty for both England and Scotland. The king's religious policy, meanwhile, revolved around securing greater religious freedoms. This impulse had some appeal to Protestant Dissenters, but it gave more room to Roman Catholics. The Crown's policy allowed all subjects to "serve God after their own way," whether in private homes, chapels, or buildings designated for worship. Those who held out for the National Covenants, of course, opposed the king's proposal. The Cameronians, in their Manichaean manner, called the king's proclamations a "preservative brewed in hell" served in papists' "cup of the whore's fornications."[59] Moderates generally supported the Crown's overture, and several Presbyterian ministers sent thanks to James II, a sign perhaps of dwindling commitment to a national church.[60]

Even if Scottish sentiments for Presbyterianism lagged by the 1680s—historians have observed significant levels of indifference to church polity among the public—James II's days were numbered.[61] A Roman Catholic on the English throne threatened too much of the previous 150 years of domestic policy and foreign relations. James II's requirement that bishops in England read the indulgences in their churches, and his government's subsequent arrest and trial of prelates who refused (including the archbishop of Canterbury, William Sancroft), alarmed Protestants. In England, seven nobles sent an invitation to William of Orange to come to fight James. Rather than combat the Dutch prince, James tried to escape to France. William's forces intervened and placed the last Stuart under protective guard in the Netherlands, before allowing James II to reside in a palace (and with a pension) provided by Louis XIV. The English Parliament interpreted James's flight as an abdication and installed William and his wife, Mary (James's daughter), as king and queen of

England in 1689. Scottish support for William III and Mary was strong, and the beginning of their reign was peaceful generally among the Scots.

With a new king came another religious settlement. Since Episcopalians in Scotland had thrown their support behind James II in public proclamation of loyalty, William III saw episcopacy as an indication of loyalty to the Stuarts (Jacobitism). It did not help that, after the Convention of Estates proclaimed the new king and queen, bishops called attention to their refusal to pray for William and Mary by name.[62] Presbyterians took a decidedly different tack as early as 1689. Some observers saw Presbyterian support for William and Mary as merely convenient. Gilbert Burnett, a philosopher and bishop of Salisbury, quipped that Presbyterian boasts of loyalty were little more than "No Presbytery, No King William."[63] In the end, William III's decision to return the Church of Scotland to its Presbyterian form of government was a political calculation based on the Crown's best option for a manageable and peaceful Scotland. Peace was not foremost for the Cameronians, who were now numerous in the kingdom's southwest. In the form of "rabbling" or local mobs, these zealous Protestants ousted the episcopal clergy. The bulk of Presbyterians, many of whom who knew not Rutherford or Henderson, sought to protect episcopal clergy turned out of the Kirk.[64]

The Scottish religious settlement of William and Mary satisfied most Presbyterians, but questions remained about the divine pattern of church government revealed in scripture. In the Claim of Right that bestowed the crowns on William and Mary, the Scottish Parliament conceded "that Prelacy and the superiority of any office in the Church above presbyters is and hath been a great and insupportable grievance and trouble to this Nation." The statement added that prelacy was "contrary to the Inclinationes of the generality of the people" ever since the Reformation and, so, "ought to be abolished."[65] But such resolve could not hide Presbyterian divisions. Moderates, who had received indulgences from the Crown, were accustomed to working alongside bishops. This was, of course, a sensible position given the political realities and the need for ministers, but it was also a departure from old Presbyterian convictions. For ministers still committed to the National Covenants, Parliament's Claim of Right was weak. A serious challenge going forward for Scottish Presbyterians was how to reconcile both parts of relatively recent church history, namely, the ideals of the National Covenant and the policies of the

Restoration Church. Adding to the dilemma of strict and moderate Presbyterianism was the king's own political need to harmonize two national churches under a coherent religious policy. (Two peaceful realms were important for being able to counter France's expansionist aims.) The Glorious Revolution, in other words, gave the victory to Presbyterians over Episcopalians, but it was hardly the reformed church for which earlier generations of Presbyterians had hoped.

Still, some of the vigor (and divisiveness) of old Presbyterianism was evident at the first meeting (1690) of the General Assembly in forty years. One item for debate was whether to seat ministers with ties to the Cameronians. A gathering committed to peaceful and orderly ways also showed generosity to the stricter sort of Presbyterian by receiving Alexander Shields, Thomas Lining, and William Boyd into the national church. This determination was not free from controversy since these pastors had ministered to laypeople who were opposed to the terms of William III's religious policy for the Kirk. For others, the ones committed to the ideals and legal arrangements of Scotland's covenantal tradition, the situation led to forming a separate ecclesiastical body, the Reformed Presbytery. The populist character of this group prevented them from calling their first pastor, John M'Millan, until 1706. In 1712, the Reformed Presbyterians renewed Scotland's Covenants as part of their response to the Scottish Episcopalians Act of 1711 (a law that prevented restrictions on episcopal worship and marriages).[66]

Another point of contention was the fast for which the General Assembly called during its first session. The reason for a national day of fasting and prayer was to call the nation to repentance for sins from Scotland's recent past. This was delicate territory for Presbyterians with different understandings of Scottish church history since at least 1649. Should the sins include those enumerated by the National Covenants? Or should the General Assembly avoid a list that could jeopardize the Kirk's relative calm and newfound prerogatives? An early sign of the Kirk's emerging moderate character was the Assembly's rejection of lists of infidelity that both the Protesters and Resolutioners had created. The Assembly also provided counsel on how ministers should handle divisions without stirring up older conflicts. The decisions of the Assembly went to William III by a letter. Even that missive produced debate since some still conceived of an independent church without a need for the king's approval. The letter went forward even as Presbyterianism in Scotland in the wake of the Glorious Revolution came with concessions that its advocates a century earlier would have opposed.[67]

The terms of William III's religious policy made it likely that older Presbyterian arguments for church reform would not fade away. Although the new religious settlement restored Presbyterianism and set terms for the General Assembly to reconvene, the Kirk faced restrictions from William III that renewed historic Presbyterian complaints about royal supremacy, Erastianism, and the church's spiritual independence. The authority of the Crown became especially pressing during the 1690s when the king encouraged the Assembly to receive episcopal priests into the Kirk. In the south, the Assembly's commission in 1691 deprived five priests of their parishes, an act that William opposed and rebuked directly. Commissioners complied with the king's wishes. But the affair raised the old specter of the Crown's habit of meddling in the church. This was not an unreasonable worry after William issued five separate proclamations that had adjourned regular meetings of the General Assembly.[68]

These initial skirmishes over the rights of the Crown and the prerogatives of the church led to further debates about authority to convene the General Assembly. In the late 1690s, disputes provoked Presbyterians and some civil leaders to insist on the rights of the Kirk over against the king. The idea of "intrinsic right," a reassertion of Christ's headship over the church and its officers' freedom to determine doctrine, polity, and worship, reemerged as a theme among Presbyterian writers. In contrast, the Crown invoked parts of Charles II's religious settlement to justify incorporating Episcopalians within the Kirk. Similar assertions of rights surrounded whether the church or king was responsible for calling fast days. Because Presbyterians regarded such times as parts of regular worship, they wanted the Assembly to appoint days of national piety. The Crown asserted its own authority, even though in England William III did call for national days of fasting in consultation with his bishops. Presbyterians saw the difference between Scotland and England as an indication of Presbyterianism's inferior status. These rivalries continued after William's reign once Anne became queen and Scotland and England united (1707). Alasdair Raffe has argued that the 1690 restoration of Presbyterianism in Scotland may have seemed a victory for the old arguments against episcopacy, but the terms of that settlement were decidedly favorable to the monarch.[69]

The Presbyterian Achievement

If the Glorious Revolution had achieved a middle way between divine-right monarchy and boisterous parliamentarians, it also paved the way for Presbyterians and Episcopalians to coexist. In Scotland, the setting where Presbyterianism was intimately connected to national identity, the model of church rule by councils finally prevailed. The arrangement may not have been what John Knox or Andrew Melville had envisioned, but John Calvin's novel form of church government that had enticed English and Scottish Protestant exiles became the pattern for the Kirk. Throughout their troubled existence with the Stuart monarchs, Presbyterians shed high and holy expectations for the Crown as an enforcer of God's national covenant. In turn, the demise of the Stuarts also made possible a compromise for the Kirk that involved something less than either royal supremacy or divine-right Presbyterianism. Among Presbyterians who had not abandoned the lessons of the National Covenant, the Cameronians and Covenanters (Reformed Presbyterians), the Glorious Revolution's religious settlement for Scotland was unacceptable.

In England, the Presbyterian understanding of the church was a shell of what it had been 125 years earlier. The Heads of Agreement that Presbyterians and Independents in 1691 ratified to form associations regulating church life among Dissenters contained faint echoes of the full-throated argument for rule by assemblies that Thomas Cartwright had used against Elizabethan bishops. English Presbyterians affirmed that the ministry was an office instituted by Christ and that anyone called to it ought "to be endued with competent Learning, and Ministerial Gifts," and "without scandal" in order to carry out their work. From there the authority for calling pastors devolved to members of "a particular Church," ordinarily in consultation with the pastors of "Neighboring Congregations." This was basically a Congregational polity with a hint of associational connections to like-minded churches. Even so, the *Heads* were explicit that all particular churches were equal in status, and that no officer from any congregation had authority over another church within the association. Arguably the most telling part of the *Heads* was their bare mention of the office of elder. On the one hand, the deacons were "of Divine Appointment" and their task was to distribute church funds "by the direction of the pastor." On the other hand, some who assented to the *Heads* were "of the opinion" that an office of ruling elders existed and others thought "otherwise." This difference did not rise to the level of creating a "breach among us."[70]

Also lost in the aspirations of England's Presbyterians was any hope for a godly civil magistrate to protect the church and defend the true religion. The authors of the *Heads* acknowledged an obligation "to pray for God's Protection, Guidance, and Blessing upon the Rulers set over us," and to support them "according to our station and abilities." If for some reason the Crown or Parliament paid the dissenting churches any attention, "we shall most readily" give an account of "our Affairs, and the state of our Congregations."[71]

These terms were too weak to protect the meager unity they promised. Between 1695 and 1700, Presbyterians and Independents brought different expectations for ordination and church authority to the appointment of new ministers. These contrasting views were evident when Edmund Calamy, the son of the notable English Presbyterian of the same name (called Edmund Calamy the Elder), sought ordination. The service in 1694 was the first to occur in London since 1662. Calamy insisted that his call not be confined to any particular congregation but that it should embrace the church universal (i.e., catholic). That position reflected the Presbyterian conception of ordination but was at odds with Independents, who calibrated a minister's authority according to his congregation's borders. As it turned out, only Presbyterian pastors showed up to ordain Calamy.[72]

Such a whimper of Presbyterian resolve illustrated the roller coaster of expectations and disappointments that these Reformed Protestants in England and Scotland experienced throughout the seventeenth century. They began with frustration over James I's policies and then outrage over his son Charles I's government. For a brief period, Presbyterians found their footing with a National Covenant in Scotland, and alliance between the Scottish and English Parliaments against Charles I, and the convening of a church council that seemed to promise a Presbyterian Church for England, Scotland, and Wales. War, the Interregnum, and Restoration of the Crown deflated Presbyterian hopes. From the Restoration to the Glorious Revolution, Presbyterians divided into three camps. Its right wing remained committed to the ideal of church reform and godly commonwealth. A left wing preserved elements of Reformed teaching and worship in dissenting institutional arrangements. For the third group, the ones to catch the ring of the established church (Scotland), the government's blessing required moderation and compromise of some Presbyterian convictions. Compared to the original Presbyterian exiles who wanted to take what they had seen in Geneva and implement such churches in England and Scotland, the outcome of a century's worth of political intrigue and ecclesiastical debate had to be a disappointment. But for any Protestant who had wanted a specific plan for a reformed church—in doctrine, worship, and government—seventeenth-century Presbyterians left a lasting mark by extending the ideals of Calvin's Reformation. If Presbyterians sounded different from their Reformed Protestant siblings in Europe, that variance owed to what Timothy Larsen and Mark A. Noll identified as "distinctive" about British Christianity, namely, the idiosyncratic relationship between Crown and church.[73] Contrary to the shibboleth used to describe Presbyterianism, "no bishop, no king," the better quip arguably is "no crown, no Presbyterians."

CHAPTER 4

No King, No Creed

Francis Makemie is sometimes called the father of American Presbyterianism, and he earned that status thanks to two episodes during the last two years of a life that ran from 1658 to 1708. The first, in 1706, was his organizing the Presbytery of Philadelphia, a grassroots effort of six other pastors that created structures for ordination and church discipline. It lacked oversight from any Old World ecclesiastical body and owed its New World existence to both the exigencies of colonial existence and the religious freedom that Pennsylvania—a colony founded by Quakers—afforded to Protestants from all over Europe.

The second episode that framed Makemie's reputation was his defiance of British colonial policies in New York. On the way to Boston during the summer of 1707 to recruit pastors for Presbyterian congregations in Pennsylvania, Maryland, and Virginia, Makemie stopped in New York. He and his companion, John Hampton, received a cordial welcome from the colony's governor, Edward Hyde, Lord Cornbury. Makemie's meal with the governor never suggested that Presbyterians were unwelcome in New York. Makemie had no awareness of restrictions on worship and accepted an invitation to preach in a home of local well-wishers. Because Makemie lacked a license, his preaching was against the law, as

Lord Cornbury interpreted it. Local authorities had him arrested and imprisoned. Both Makemie and Hampton were in jail for forty-six days. When the case went to trial, Makemie mentioned that Quakers and "Papists" had worshiped without penalty. He also appealed to England's laws of toleration. An intriguing angle on this claim was whether the Church of England's prerogatives applied to the colonies as much as to England itself. These arguments were sufficient for the jury to find Makemie not guilty. That did not clear him for court costs. In *A Narrative of a New and Unusual American Imprisonment of Two Presbyterian Ministers And Prosecution of Mr. Francis Makemie* (1707), the pastor (who also conducted trade in the Caribbean) itemized his legal fees. Between jailers, justices of the peace, sheriffs, and travel, Makemie was forced to pay more than 81 pounds (the equivalent of almost $25,000 in 2023).[1] This instance of British tyranny's threat to religious liberty became seventy years later an easy narrative by which to prove American Presbyterianism's stake in American independence.[2]

Two hundred years later (1906), leaders of the Presbyterian Church U.S.A., the communion that sprang from the presbytery that Makemie had organized, gathered in Accomack County, Virginia, to unveil a statue that memorialized the colonial pastor. Henry Van Dyke, professor of literature at Princeton University, composed a poem for the occasion, "Presbyter to Christ in America." The Dutch American feted the colonial Ulsterman in American cadences:

To thee, plain hero of a rugged race
We bring a meed of praise too long delayed.
Thy fearless word and faithful work have made
The path of God's republic easier to trace
In this New World: thou has proclaimed the grace
And power of Christ in many a woodland glade,
Teaching the truth that leaves men unafraid
Of tyrants' frowns, or chains, or death's dark face.
Oh, who can tell how much we owe to thee,
Makemie, and to labors such as thine,
For all that makes America the shrine
Of faith untrammeled and of conscience free?
Stand here, gray stone, and consecrate the sod
Where sleeps this brave Scotch-Irish man of God.[3]

Commemorating a Presbyterian pastor who paved the way for America's political ideals may have made sense to Van Dyke's audience. Two centuries earlier, however, the liberties Makemie earned were puny compared to the glories promised by the likes of Knox, Melville, and Cartwright. Born in 1658 in Ramelton, a town in Ireland that boasts the oldest Presbyterian church on the island, Makemie's roots go back to obscure Ulster Protestants who settled earlier in the seventeenth century. His family's Presbyterian convictions were no match for either Oliver Cromwell's government or the Restoration. As an outsider to the Church of Ireland, Makemie could not attend Trinity College in Dublin, but he enrolled instead in 1676 at the University of Glasgow. Ordained in 1681 by the Presbytery of Laggan in west Ulster, Makemie left for North America two years later with a commission to plant churches among Presbyterian settlers. When he left Ireland, prospects for Presbyterianism either in Scotland or Ireland were not encouraging. Nothing in Makemie's subsequent career, however, suggests an attachment to the cause of Presbyterianism either in Scotland or Ireland.

In fact, the young pastor's movements within England's North American colonies indicate a strategy of fitting in more than advocating reformation. In the middle of the 1690s, Makemie engaged in a public controversy with the Quaker George Keith, who had objected to Makemie's use of the Westminster Shorter Catechism to train youths. Rather than defending catechesis per se, Makemie argued instead for the primacy of scripture over against the Quakers' notion of an inner light as the source of religious truth. The Presbyterian pastor also aligned himself with the Reformed churches of Geneva, France, Scotland, and England. A few years later during a business trip to Barbados, Makemie lost the polemical edge that had been a trademark of Presbyterianism. He did so in a pamphlet written in 1697 (published in 1699) to defend Reformed Protestants from claims by Anglicans that Presbyterians were a fringe group of Protestants. Makemie argued that Presbyterians were in fact the "truest and soundest part" of the Church of England. At the same time, he constructed an "ecumenical bridge" between the two British Protestant rivals. Makemie objected to using "Presbyterian" or "Puritan" as epithets. One important reason was that Presbyterians agreed with the Church of England "in all points of Faith, and Divine Ordinances, or parts of Worship." The only differences were in "Ceremonies,

Government and Discipline."[4] Did the colonial setting take some of the edge off Presbyterian zeal?

Whatever the demands of his environment, Makemie's attempt to find a common cause with other British Protestants was indicative of Presbyterians in the English-speaking world after the Glorious Revolution. Scotland excepted, where Presbyterianism became the established church, in England, Ireland, and North America those committed to church government by assemblies conducted their ministry as Dissenters. In fact, almost 125 years of British history taught Presbyterians that the original cause of a godly government and church reform working together to implement the holy commonwealth needed serious readjustment. Without a sovereign to protect the church and add the civil component of ecclesial reform, Presbyterians were on their own for reforming the church. Even the triumph of Presbyterianism in the Kirk resulted in a moderate version of church reform that was decidedly cooler than the aspirations of "hot" Protestants during the last third of the sixteenth century. By the eighteenth century, Presbyterians were recalibrating ecclesiastical ideals to gain a foothold in the emerging structures of liberal society. How central Presbyterianism was to other sectors of national life was the question that church officers and members on both sides of the Atlantic needed to answer. Ironically, with the loss of politics as the focus of debate—whether over the Crown or the bishops—Presbyterians even had trouble instituting their own forms of governance within the church.

The Abnormalities of Normal Scotland

After 150 years of church reform inspired by John Calvin's Geneva, Scotland was the only established Protestant church with a Presbyterian form of church government. (Swiss, Dutch, German, and French Protestants relied on governing bodies through councils of pastors and elders, as opposed to bishops or congregations. But most of these were regional and did not rise to the level of a national church.) The Kirk's apparent success had also come at the expense of national political trauma. Lessons learned from zealous overreach (National Covenants) or fickle sovereigns produced a Presbyterianism after the Glorious Revolution that sought moderation on the fine points of Reformed Protestantism while also being fiercely jealous of the Kirk's prerogatives. Holding onto the religious establishment involved resisting episcopalians on the one side but also refraining on the other from the militancy that the National Covenants had required.

One of Protestantism's achievements, for almost 125 years after the initial establishment of Christian communions separate from Rome, was the development of a body of doctrine. Assertions about salvation and worship forced Protestant pastors and theologians to define terms of Protestant faith that contrasted with Roman Catholic teaching. Both sides engaged in corporate acts of definition by convening synods of bishops and pastors to draft confessions of faith and policies. What Roman Catholics did at the Council of Trent, Protestants undertook locally. The high point for Reformed Protestant orthodoxy came in the seventeenth century when first the Synod of Dort (1619) adopted the Belgic Confession (1561) and the Heidelberg Catechism (1563), along with the Canons of Dort itself, as the doctrinal standards for Dutch and (some) German Reformed churches. Roughly twenty-five years later, the Westminster Assembly produced for the English-speaking Reformed churches what Dort had performed for many communions on the Continent. The first and only church in the seventeenth century to adopt the Westminster Confession was the Church of Scotland. In the chaotic days of civil war and political upheaval, the Kirk's General Assembly in 1647 approved the Westminster Confession. Two years later the Scottish Parliament ratified the Assembly's determination. These decisions did not require ministers to subscribe to the Westminster Confession as their own profession of faith or as a test for ordination, but pastors were required to affirm the National Covenant of 1638.

Not until 1690 did subscribing Westminster Assembly's confession become the norm for the Church of Scotland. If the Kirk had any confessional requirement between 1649 and 1660, it was the original Scots Confession (1560), which became official in 1681 with the Test Act. But with Parliament's 1690 act in favor of the Westminster Assembly, ministers needed to approve the Westminster Confession for the sake of "soundness and unity of doctrine." Three years later, Parliament took the lead in the Act for Settling the Peace and Quiet of the Church by requiring ministers to declare the confession to be the same as their own profession of faith and promise to adhere to its doctrine "constantly." A year later, the General Assembly repeated Parliament's rule by requiring ministers "sincerely" to adopt and "declare" the confession as their own statement of belief.[5]

The 1707 Union of Scotland and England may have prompted Presbyterians to worry about ongoing rivalry with Scottish Episcopalians. But the language of the Union was supposed to be reassuring: "The true Protestant religion, as presently professed within this kingdom," according to the Act for Securing the Protestant Religion and Presbyterian Church Government, "should be effectually and unalterably secured."[6] This included a provision that gave Queen Anne's approval to the 1690 terms of subscription. To be safe, the 1711 General Assembly established a form for licensure of probationers and ordination that seemed to be airtight:

> I do sincerely own and believe the whole doctrine contained in the Confession of Faith approved by the General Assemblies of this National Church, and ratified by law . . . to be the truths of God; and I do own the same as the Confession of my faith: As likewise, I do own the purity of worship presently authorised and practiced in this Church, and also the Presbyterian government and discipline now so happily established therein; which doctrine, worship and Church government, I am persuaded, are founded upon the Word of God, and agreeable thereto: . . . And I promise, that I shall follow no divisive course from the present establishment in this Church: Renouncing all doctrines, tenets, and opinions whatsoever, contrary to or inconsistent with the said doctrine, worship, discipline, or government of this Church.[7]

This level of doctrinal rigor ran ironically against theological trends in Scotland, as it did those in England (considered in this chapter's next section), where enlightened Christianity seemed a better way to enlarge the church's influence than a state church. Despite the emergence of reasonable Protestantism, competition between Presbyterians and Episcopalians remained. The precarious position of Presbyterianism itself was an important factor in the Kirk's requirements for subscription. Robert Wodrow, the eighteenth-century Presbyterian pastor who also chronicled the plight of the Covenanters during the Restoration, admitted in his correspondence that "Subscription to our Confession of Faith," and in particular its requirement by Parliament both in 1690 and at the time of Scotland's union with England in 1707, kept the church from the "flames" of a diminished standing with the government.[8] Parliament's determination to grant legal toleration to Scottish Episcopalians (1712) threatened the Kirk's status. In response, in 1712 the General Assembly repeated its requirements for subscription. According to James Cooper, a late nineteenth-century church historian and minister in the Kirk, the Assembly's requirement for adherence to the Westminster Confession was "not so much the preservation of *the Faith*, as the *protection of the party into whose hands the Revolution had placed the ecclesiastical power in Scotland*."[9] In effect, subscription became an alternative to divine-right Presbyterianism; it functioned as a way to protect the Kirk's prerogatives, even as older Presbyterian ideals of national covenants had lost their plausibility.

The pragmatic nature of subscription was all the more plausible in the way the Kirk chose to enforce doctrinal conformity after a minister's initial ordination vow. Two examples from opposite sides of the church suggest how subscription was the letter but not always the spirit of the law. Ebenezer Erskine (1680–1754), a doctrinal conservative who in the 1730s took up the cause of fighting theological latitude in the Kirk even to the point of seceding from the Kirk, may not have actually subscribed the Westminster Confession of Faith in 1703 when ordained. Twenty years later, when the parish in Kirkaldy voted to call Erskine as pastor, members of the presbytery asked if he had subscribed when he started his ministry. Their reason for asking was to draw attention to an apparent inconsistency between Erskine's own biography and his desire for theological conformity throughout the Kirk. Also, ironic in this incident was that Erskine's opponents, who favored less theological rigor, used doubts about Erskine's initial subscription to block his call to Kirkaldy. Because the candidate could not prove to the presbytery's satisfaction that he had subscribed, Erskine's opponents prevailed. Subscribing the Westminster Confession was no guarantee of a minister's soundness, nor did it preserve a faithful church if subscription itself could preserve an ecclesiastical agenda hostile to the teaching of the creed.

The other example comes from the heresy trials of John Simson (1668–1740), a professor of theology at the University of Glasgow. The son of a Presbyterian pastor, Simson studied at Edinburgh and Leiden. In 1705, he received a call to a parish in the Galloway region. Three years later, as a professor of theology, his reservations about the Westminster Confession became apparent to his peers. Simson's theological innovations were not isolated. For at least a century, Reformed pastors and theologians adjusted orthodox theology to social trends that demanded religious toleration or to intellectual developments that rendered Calvinism a challenge to good taste and sense. In 1717 and 1727, Simson faced charges for heretical teaching. The specific departures involved the professor's unease with Reformed theology's apparently severe insistence that people were inherently sinful and that only believers performed truly good works. Reformed theology's notions about human nature and sanctification were not useful for encouraging virtue among citizens and magistrates. Simson escaped the first round of charges. But in 1729, after two years of investigation and in response to mounting pressure from conservatives, the General Assembly removed the professor from his teaching post. Simson continued to receive his academic stipend for another eleven years until his death.[10] Whether rigorous enforcement of subscription would have prevented the controversy over Simson is impossible to say. Even so, presbytery records from Paisley indicate that during ordination exams Simson expressed scruples about the wording of the Westminster Confession. Those reservations did not prevent him from subscribing or the presbytery from approving the candidate. Subscription had become more of a bureaucratic policy than a theological norm for the Church of Scotland.[11]

One (perhaps all too) obvious interpretation of these developments is that they were a reaction to the turbulence of the seventeenth-century church. Ryan K. Frace has argued that even as the Kirk was holding off episcopacy for the third and last time, Presbyterianism blossomed into a moderate and tolerant version of Protestantism. This was not true across the kingdom, and in local settings Presbyterian conservatives were able to prevent episcopal worship (sometimes even violently).[12] But moderates in the General Assembly, a fairly sizable minority, repositioned the Kirk as both Presbyterian and charitable. The incorporation in 1693 of seventy episcopal priests into the Kirk after they had sworn allegiance to William III exemplified this breadth of spirit. By 1703, as many as 200 (out of 936 parishes) Episcopalians were ministering within the Church of Scotland.[13] The reasons for this shift among Presbyterians were primarily social. The moderates wanted to encourage commercial prosperity and political stability after generations of upheaval. They conceded that religious uniformity was not possible. In turn moderates wanted the Kirk to lead in building social cohesion.

What accompanied the Kirk's shift was the absence (at least among moderates) of the old divine-right arguments for Presbyterian church government. The English Presbyterian Edmund Calamy recalled after visiting Edinburgh during the 1709 General Assembly that "*not one* in all the company was for [the old understanding] of church government, though they free submitted to it."[14] Another feature of this new Presbyterian outlook—albeit typical in circles where the Enlightenment had appeal—was to identify toleration as a Christian virtue. One minister, in fact, claimed that religious diversity "promoted charity, and the more active and habitual exercise of . . . candor, meekness, and forebearance."[15]

Even so, the moderate position was the numerical minority among the Kirk's pastors. Most ministers still held on to some version of Presbyterianism as the true form of church government revealed in scripture (and a smaller number still affirming the National Covenants). By one estimate, roughly 25 percent of the General Assembly's 110 ministers were moderate. Part of the minority's influence in the Kirk through its assemblies owed to a close working relationship with William III's advisor and commissioner William Carstares. Another piece of moderate strategy was to control the committees of the Assembly itself. This became evident in the way debates and ratification of the 1707 Union transpired. The prospect of being ruled by one London Parliament, with bishops composing part of the House of Lords, was sure to inflame committed Presbyterians. Jeffrey Stephen argues that conservatives opposed Union. Some in their number merely counseled, "Pray!" for Union to be defeated. Others appealed to the National Covenants. In 1707, Thomas Boston, the minister who became famous during the Marrow Controversy ten years later, warned his congregation that Union was "a nail sent from Scotland to fix the Dragon of the English Hierarchy in its place in our country."[16] Such opposition and related appeals to Scottish covenants and nationalism, however, could not prompt the Kirk to oppose the Union "officially." Instead, the Assembly's stated position followed the logic of self-interest. As long as the terms of Union granted security for a Presbyterian Kirk, the General Assembly would remain neutral.[17]

One irony of the political calculation that Presbyterian leaders made in the two decades after the Glorious Revolution was that a union of England and Scotland should have drawn opposition from anyone still loyal to the National Covenants. Yet, even that remnant in the Kirk had come around to the House of Hanover, the next line of British monarchs who started with George I, an elector of Hanover who was also a great grandson of James I. The Hanover dynasty was under no obligation to Scotland's covenants, which were the burden of the Stuart monarchs. Presbyterians who still carried a torch for the National Covenants also came to terms with the Glorious Revolution and Union. Their political calculation was fairly straightforward. Although abandoning a royal family that had vowed to uphold the Scottish covenants was sinful, worse was the rule of a Roman Catholic prince. Christopher A. Whatley asserts that those who wanted a return to the ideals of the National Covenant "were willing to declare their unflinching support for the Revolution, the Union and the Hanoverian succession." The reason: Protestant succession was "preferable to a return to royal absolutism."[18]

The one group for whom the covenanting tradition still mattered were the Cameronians, who continued to be a nuisance to both the civil government and the Kirk's leaders. Although numerically insignificant, these Presbyterians embodied a piece of Scottish nationalism that featured the kingdom's Presbyterian past. Alasdair Raffe well explains that the governing principle for the most committed Presbyterians was that the Scottish monarchy needed to "profess the same religion as their people." Mere Protestantism was insufficient. Scottish monarchs, accordingly, still needed to swear the covenants, as Charles II had in 1651.[19] For these Presbyterians, George I's claim to the throne was illegitimate. His vows contained no reference to Presbyterianism but merely a pledge to support the Church of England. Cameronian objections, ironically, played into the hands of moderates in the Kirk. They could elevate their own brand of Presbyterianism over against the radicalism of the Cameronians. Appeals to Scotland's Presbyterian past that were too strong could be a treasonous indication of Jacobitism. Despite gains that came with loyalty to the Hanoverians, Presbyterianism in Scotland, both official and nostalgic, started the eighteenth century in a weak position.

The bind in which Scottish history put Presbyterians was especially evident during the enforcement of the Abjuration Oath of 1702. This legislation required anyone holding public office in Scotland—including the military and the Kirk—to renounce both the Stuart dynasty and the temporal power of the papacy. Some ministers in the Dumfries Presbytery refused, a gesture interpreted as an expression of Jacobitism. From another perspective, however, local custom (since 1690) exempted clergy from swearing allegiance to the Crown. With the Hanoverian succession, pastors and presbyteries faced different pressures stemming from England's troubled relations with France during the War of the Spanish Succession and James II's French residence. George I had good reasons for cutting off any hint of Jacobitism. At the same time, Scottish pastors and congregations were more concerned about local churches than about England's foreign policy. The Dumfries Presbytery calmed the situation, but three ministers continued to refuse to show loyalty. Even so, many laity opposed the oath and would not sit under ministers who had taken it. In 1715, the General Assembly intervened. It ruled that Dumfries needed to prosecute the disloyal ministers. Instead of resolving the controversy, the offending pastors chose to renounce the Kirk's authority. The presbytery retaliated by excommunicating the recalcitrants.[20]

This incident in Dumfries not only revealed the ongoing appeal of Scotland's covenants, but also the weakness of Presbyterian church government. On the one hand, the Dumfries dissenters rehearsed Covenanter arguments that used the church's constitution and its commitment to a covenanted nation as the measure of political legitimacy. These arguments also implicated the 1707 Union. If the United Kingdom itself was sinful, as some alleged, then the General Assembly had also sinned by not condemning the Union. The most obvious objection to the oath was its tyrannical nature. Even with a Presbyterian Church of Scotland and the union of England and Scotland, the Scots remained locked in debates from the mid-seventeenth century. Although their arguments—first used with Charles I—no longer made sense in Hanoverian Britain, conservative Scots doubled down on the old categories of church and kingdom.[21] Rejecting the authority of presbytery and General Assembly was a different order of Presbyterian radicalism. Could Presbyterianism actually provide stability for the Church of Scotland?[22]

Discord in Dumfries foreshadowed the largest eighteenth-century secession in Scotland among Presbyterians. In 1733, the Erskine brothers (Ebenezer and Ralph) spearheaded a new communion that maintained the doctrinal standards of the seventeenth century while also providing an ecclesiastical placeholder for those still hoping for a return to the National Covenants. The incidents that led to this departure were the theological controversies surrounding the Glasgow professor John Simson (described earlier). Opponents of the theologian rallied around a popular seventeenth-century Puritan text, *The Marrow of Modern Divinity*, republished by conservatives in 1718 and subsequently condemned for doctrinal errors by the General Assembly. The editors' protest of the Assembly's action in 1722 provoked a formal admonition from Kirk's highest court. Adding fuel to the fire was the Assembly's acquiescence in Parliament's decision to reimpose lay patronage in the Kirk. A medieval custom that allowed the founder of a parish (and later his family) to select ministers for his congregation, patronage directly contravened Presbyterian mechanisms (congregational, presbyterial, and even divine) for calling a pastor. Although the post-1689 Scottish Parliament had abolished lay patronage in concert with Presbyterian wishes, the government also left room for heritors (large land holders) to act in conjunction with the session (elders) in appointing pastors. Presbyterians had long feared that patronage would become a tool to advance family, business, and political interests, which it usually did. For the General Assembly to go along with the reimposition of lay patronage (supporters saw it as preserving "public order") was from the perspective of the "Marrow men" further evidence of a compromised Kirk.[23]

In 1732, these contentious developments reached their breaking point when Ebenezer Erskine, moderator of the Synod of Perth and Stirling, preached a sermon to his peers on the dangers of patronage. Erskine's life, like that of so many Presbyterian ministers, was deeply entangled in the politics of Restoration and the Glorious Revolution. His father, Henry (1624–96), had been ejected from the Church of Scotland in 1662 in compliance with the Act of Uniformity. Denied his living, he went to London to plead with Charles II, a mission that failed and left Henry preaching to conventicles for much of the Restoration era. His ministry resulted in fines, imprisonment, and banishment. These were conditions under which the son, Ebenezer, born in 1680, and his brother, Ralph, born five years later, first witnessed their father and his ministry. The Glorious Revolution, however, provided Ebenezer with opportunities unavailable to his father. In 1703,Ebenezer received a degree from the University of Edinburgh and was installed as pastor at Portmoak, Kinross-shire, a parish slightly north of Edinburgh. He remained there until 1731 when he took a call to Stirling. Erskine embraced the *Marrow of Modern Divinity* and received a rebuke from the General Assembly for doing so. That did not prevent him from becoming the moderator of his new synod, the vantage from which he preached the sermon that instigated a formal secession from the Kirk and the creation of a new presbytery.[24] His sermon, "The Stone Rejected by the Builders," was a lengthy exposition of Psalm 68:22 ("the stone which the builders rejected, the same is made the head stone of the corner"). It echoed original arguments about Christ as head of the church, rejected patronage in the appointment of ministers, and jabbed his peers—still sensitive about the Marrow Controversy—about preaching law and gospel accurately. His biggest provocation was to link patronage to the Church of Scotland's defection from original Presbyterian convictions.[25]

Reactions followed swiftly. Erskine's synod censured him formally and set up procedures for an official reprimand. Erskine appealed to the General Assembly, which upheld the synod's judgment and added their own rebuke and admonishment. Erskine issued a formal protest. Three other ministers supported his statement. When Erskine and his allies refused to remove the protest, the General Assembly deposed him and his supporters. Stewart J. Brown argues the decision was a "crude demonstration of power" that was intended to "silence opposition to patronage."[26] Instead of backing down or gathering parishioners in conventicles, Erskine and his colleagues seceded and formed a new body, the Associate Presbytery. Initially, the new Presbyterian church attracted two additional pastors, one of whom was Erskine's brother, Ralph. Within a decade, the Associate Presbytery had eight pastors ministering to thirty congregations. They also established a school for training ministers in Perth, which met in the manse of a pastor. Although the General Assembly tried to bring the Associate Presbyterians back into the Kirk, Erskine and his colleagues made that impossible once in 1744 some congregations began to ritualize the renewal of Scotland's covenants.

By having church members stand and swear allegiance to the 1638 and 1643 National Covenants, the Associate Presbytery presented itself as the true national church of Scotland.[27] But this covenantal allegiance also included, unlike Reformed Presbyterians four decades earlier, a promise of allegiance to Scotland's governing authorities. This position became a liability when three Scottish cities added a religion clause to the Burgess Oath, a vow required of all citizens, to maintain "the true religion presently professed in this realm." Some Associate Presbyterians regarded this as requiring fidelity to the corrupt Church of Scotland. Others, including the Erskines, saw no reason to refuse the oath just because it involved a general affirmation of Protestantism. Differences over the Burgess Oath led to a split between the "Burgher" and "Anti-Burgher" synods. Antagonisms ran so deep that Anti-Burghers excommunicated the Erskine brothers, who now were no better than "heathens."[28]

One last Scottish effort to escape the compromises inherent in Presbyterianism's entanglement with the civil government came with the Relief Church. This Presbyterian body had roots in the eighteenth-century awakenings made famous by George Whitefield and Jonathan Edwards. Patronage was again the point of contention. In the parish of Inverkeithing, church members and elders refused to ordain the patron's candidate for pastor. The Presbytery of Dunfermline sided with the congregation. But the General Assembly overruled the presbytery and, according to Stewart J. Brown, "under pressure from Scotland's governing elite" deposed one pastor from the presbytery to show the body's authority and prevent further dissent.[29] The pastor deposed was Thomas Gillespie, who trained at a Dissenting English academy and was an advocate of revivals. Gillespie's ouster prompted Jonathan Edwards to marvel that "a church which has itself suffered so much by persecution should be guilty of so much persecution."[30] Gillespie decided against joining the Seceders because of their support for the National Covenants. After Gillespie ministered alone for a decade, other pastors joined him in 1761 to form the Relief Church (i.e., relief from the oppression of Christian privileges owing to patronage). By 1774, the year of Gillespie's death, the Relief Church had nineteen congregations and two presbyteries. This raised the number of dissenting Presbyterian churches in Scotland to four, five total with the Church of Scotland. Were Presbyterians themselves proving Episcopalians right, that rule by bishops was the surest polity for church unity?

No Established Church, No Creed

If Scotland could not contain Presbyterian convictions in one church, in England rule by councils became embroiled in dissent. English Presbyterians were equally sensitive to the abuses of establishment and led

Presbyterians into positions on church government and freedom of conscience that were almost the opposite of what their predecessors had conceived, whether in Scotland, England, or Geneva. Presbyterians throughout the English-speaking world had an opportunity to test the advantages of independence from supreme monarchs or divine-right bishops. In England, Ireland, and North America, Presbyterian pastors had room to match theories about church authority to the creeds that assemblies and synods had written and approved. In practically every case, Presbyterian church government could not yield unity or doctrinal uniformity. In fact, the very argument Presbyterians had used against the heavy-handed impositions of either bishops or the Crown now backfired on church authority itself. What emerged with a vengeance was the idea that church power was itself tyrannical, a threat to freedom of conscience and biblical authority.

These discrepancies became apparent first in England, because of the creaky structures that Presbyterians and Independents had constructed to oversee congregational life among Dissenters. The state of church life within the Exeter Assembly is revealing of the haphazard church polity that functioned as a watered-down Presbyterianism among those outside the Church of England. Alexander Gordon's reflections capture the reasons for putting quotation marks around "Presbyterian." Exeter had three congregations with Presbyterian leanings. One was Huguenot. The French experience of Presbyterianism was to group all congregations within a city under one body of elders and pastors (session). The effect was to give authority to this urban session over each local congregation.[31]

Much more indicative of Dissenter church life, though, were the mechanisms of authority and finance that prevailed over Exeter's other two Presbyterian congregations. These churches had two pastors each who preached either in the morning or evening (all four shared responsibilities for the Huguenot congregation). The Committee of Thirteen oversaw finances in Exeter, a self-elected body that collected stipends from church members to compensate the four pastors. This committee also had some discretion in selecting and appointing ministers. Below this body were proprietors for each congregation. These officers had responsibility for maintaining the buildings where worship services transpired; whether the proprietors owned or were trustees for private owners is debatable and highlights the legal obstacles that Dissenters faced.[32]

Such uncertainty did not mean Dissenters lacked resources or suffered overtly outside the established church. Leaders of the Sacheverell riots in 1710 directed their ire at the many Dissenters (100,000 in London out of 500,000 in the rest of England) who seemed to prosper despite being excluded from political office and universities. Dissenter meeting houses showed off these Protestants' economic status. Tory Party leaders complained that Dissenters' chapels were full and surrounded by coaches, "fine equipages" even, during services. The construction of new and handsome chapels was more evidence of Dissenters' prosperity.[33]

Whatever their social standing, Dissenters' administration of church life was far removed from the high expectations set by Calvin, Cartwright, and Knox. The challenge of eighteenth-century Presbyterian practice became evident when ministers embraced doctrines that departed from Reformed orthodoxy and the broader Christian tradition. The Salters' Hall controversy of 1719 revealed the level of theological diversity that had grown among the heirs of Puritans and Presbyterians.

The controversy's origins stemmed from the 1690s when Presbyterians began to follow Richard Baxter's neonomian views of justification and sanctification (adding some version of obedience to faith). Independents coalesced around John Owen's opposition to neonomianism (keeping works and faith strictly distinct). The debate centered on the Protestant claim of "faith alone." English Presbyterians, perhaps because the Reformed confessions did not support their views, took a dimmer view of creeds and confessions. One minister, John Humfrey, wrote in 1695 that Martin Luther, John Calvin, and the Westminster divines were entitled to their formulas, but "they are but men and I will not Captivate my Understanding to any of them."[34] A related and important factor in opposition to creeds was the government's efforts to achieve religious uniformity. The Act of Toleration (1688) required Dissenting pastors to subscribe a large part of the Church of England's Thirty-Nine Articles in order to minister lawfully in Nonconformist settings. Scholars have typically tied the Salters' Hall controversy to the appeal among Dissenters of John Locke's views on religious toleration. The political context may explain why English Presbyterians were reluctant to insist on their own version of subscription.

Controversy started in 1717 at a meeting of Dissenters in London. One pastor, James Peirce, with clear ties to Arians in England and the Netherlands, preached sermons that seemed to question Christ's deity.

He had also changed worship services at his congregation to remove singing the doxology. Despite his use of orthodox-sounding language in meetings with the local ruling body in Exeter, the Committee of Thirteen, Peirce remained under suspicion. Exeter's leaders eventually appealed to Dissenters in London, which prompted the February 19, 1719, gathering at Salters' Hall. One pastor proposed the body draw up a declaration that affirmed the doctrine of the Trinity and that the statement be signed. The measure lost by a close vote, 57–53. One of the clerks quipped, "The Bible carried it by four." A week later, a similar proposal came to the ministers in London. It also lost.[35] The controversy revealed two parties among English Dissenters—subscribers and nonsubscribers. Of the seventy-three who opposed requiring doctrinal affirmation, forty-nine were Presbyterian (sixteen Baptist, eight Independent). Among the seventy-eight subscribers, twenty-nine were Presbyterian (thirty-four Independent, fifteen Baptist). Despite the theological achievement of the Westminster Assembly only seventy years earlier, a clear majority of Presbyterians preferred the Bible alone to creeds. Nonsubscribers contended that the "the Protestant Principle" used the Bible as "the only and perfect Rule of Faith." Churches should condemn no man "because he consents not to [Human] Forms of Phrases."[36] In his estimate of the "demise" of English Presbyterianism, James C. Spalding concludes that by the eighteenth century these Protestants "believed in the sole authority of the Bible to the exclusion of all human formulas."[37]

Votes in London did little to calm the situation in Exeter, where the Committee of Thirteen waited four weeks for a reply. On March 5, 1717, they asked the four ministers to meet and respond to the affirmation that "the Son of God was one God with the Father." Peirce at first asked for time to consider, but then responded that he could not subscribe to any creed. Although the Committee of Thirteen had no power to exclude a minister from one of the meetinghouses, the trustees responsible for finances and maintenance did. Those who maintained the James Meeting House, where Peirce and Hallett preached, voted to expel the two offending pastors and locked them out of the building. The next week, the trustees from all three chapels in Exeter met and voted to exclude Peirce and Hallett from all chapels in Exeter. Peirce's only choice was to preach the next Sunday in a private home, where 300 attended. The entire episode left the cooperative arrangement among Dissenters divided along the lines of subscription. In the absence of a presbytery or General Assembly, English Presbyterians relied on ad hoc agencies, such as Exeter's Committee of Thirteen.[38]

The fortunes of Presbyterianism in England were not simply dependent on the creativity of ecclesial organizations outside the establishment. Dissenters in England still confronted the influences of the Crown, its government, and episcopal influence on church life. Here subscription could often reveal more about politics than religious conviction. The place of Dissenters in England was almost as precarious as it was fluid after the ascension of William and Mary. The original terms of the "Act for Exempting their Majestyes Protestant Subjects Dissenting from the Church of England . . ." (1689) were largely agreeable to Presbyterians (and other Dissenters) in matters of worship. They needed to subscribe only those parts of the Thirty-Nine Articles silent about church government. They also had freedom to worship in their own meeting houses so long as the structures were registered and services were open to the public (no locked doors). Anyone who failed to affirm the Trinity, along with Roman Catholics and Quakers, did not qualify for exemption.[39]

Access to other parts of English society was not as flexible as the gathering for worship. The Corporation Act (1661) required Dissenters to take Communion in the Church of England once a year if they were to hold public office in a town or city. The Test Act (1673) required Communion in the Church of England three months after receiving an appointment in the military. Further provisions placed restrictions on teaching and education. Although Presbyterians and Congregationalists had held positions as tutors at English universities before the Restoration, after Charles II's inauguration, the Act for the Confirming and Restoring of Ministers (1660) excluded Dissenters from universities. Two years later, the Act of Uniformity required all licensed tutors and grammar school teachers to subscribe the Thirty-Nine Articles. Any Dissenter teaching without a license risked prosecution.[40] The Toleration Act (1689) did little to change these restrictions. William III's government may have tried fewer teachers or imposed fewer fines, but the laws remained in place. Under Queen Anne, laxity provoked High Church leaders and Tories to grouse that Dissenting academies were indoctrinating students with "seditious and antimonarchical principles." According to Samuel Wesley, the father of John and Charles Wesley, Dissenters advanced "KING-KILLING

DOCTRINES."[41] To immunize the English people, the Schism Act (1714) required any schoolmaster, private tutor, or instructor who taught reading or literature to take vows to conform to Anglican worship. Several Dissenting academies closed.

Dissenting Protestantism was not merely important for religious life but became an influence on a growing social divide in the period running up to the Salters' Hall debates. Rivalry between Tories and Whigs mirrored ecclesiastical differences, with High Church advocates finding a political outlet with the Tories, and Low Church Anglicans and Dissenters generally identifying as Whigs. One notable case that illustrated the alignment of partisan politics and the Protestant churches was that of Henry Sacheverell, a popular priest in Oxford who relocated to Southwark. On November 5, 1709, he used a worship service to preach against Whigs and Dissenters. These groups, he argued, threatened the established church by rendering only qualified support for the monarchy. This was a charge frequently raised in connection with the succession from James II to William III during the Glorious Revolution. Although Sacheverell advocated abstract loyalty to the monarchy, Whigs interpreted his sermon as disloyal to Queen Anne. The priest's trial for high crimes and misdemeanors in 1710 led to his conviction and a light sentence. Sacheverell could not preach for three years. His trial sparked riots that showed unexpected popular support for the Tories and High Church principles. Rioters destroyed several Dissenter meeting houses in London. Others hurled epithets at Whig members of Parliament, such as "Presbyterian Bitches."[42] In 1710, Tories picked up seats in Parliament thanks to these sentiments.

By 1715, however, the tide had turned, and Whigs, now in control, repealed many of the laws that regulated Dissenters, such as the Occasional Conformity Act. They also attempted to overturn the Test and Corporation Acts, and countenanced legislation to allow Roman Catholics to hold office as long as church members renounced the pope's temporal power. This was the context for Benjamin Hoadly's, bishop of Bangor, controversial sermon on March 31, 1717, on the nature of Christ's kingdom. In terms that echoed older Presbyterian ideas about the church as a spiritual kingdom with Christ as its true head, Hoadly argued that Christ ruled in the church not by any human authority, either in the church or the state. Christ alone was lord of the conscience. The implication was again a Presbyterian point of contention, namely, the state had no basis for authority within the church. The ensuing Bangorian controversy was by no means a repeat of the High versus Low Church character of Tory and Whig politics. Instead, it divided each party and also Anglicans and Dissenters. Christopher Dudley argues that the conflict changed the alignment of religion in English politics. High and Low Church outlooks after 1722 no longer predicted political partisanship.[43]

It was no coincidence that the majority of English Presbyterians replaced toleration with subscription during this same period. To be sure, Enlightenment ideas and efforts to reconcile Christianity with reason fed trends that moved Presbyterians away from older doctrinal strictness. But the rejection of subscription itself, coupled with a similar disdain for human authority, including church government, fit the mood of English politics at the time. In the Exeter Assembly case, the split between subscribers and nonsubscribers left the Committee of Thirteen and congregations' trustees in the lurch for both ministerial candidates and funds. Initially, the Exeter Assembly found ministers to replace the nonsubscribers who either left or were banned. Over time, the taint of heterodoxy haunted Presbyterian congregations. Wealthy merchants, the backbone of church members who paid subscriptions, in turn left Presbyterianism for the Church of England.[44] Even the ministers who favored subscription grew weary from its demands. By 1753 in Exeter, a majority of pastors, many from a generation that had no experience with the Salters' Hall debates, voted to abandon a requirement for ministers to affirm "the Deity of the Son & the Holy Spirit."[45] In Devonshire and Cornwall, this was the "end of Presbyterianism," according to Allan Brockett. From 1753 on, church members, not the Exeter Assembly, bore the responsibility for "deciding whether any particular minister was sound in the faith" as church members understood orthodoxy.[46]

The fifty-year struggle and collapse of English Presbyterianism was undoubtedly part of trends that saw enlightened Christianity prevail over Reformed orthodoxy. But the political context also mattered. The rationale for and practice of toleration made more sense to Dissenters than did historic appeals to the kingship of Christ and the Bible's blueprint for church government. Earlier generations of Presbyterians may have overplayed their hands when drawing up plans to reform the national church with hopes for reinforcement from a godly monarch. Eighteenth-century

Presbyterians seem to have been incapable of summoning the convictions or resolve of Thomas Cartwright or Andrew Melville. At the same time, prospects for Presbyterianism after the Glorious Revolution owed less to ministers catching up to modern notions about freedom of conscience than they did to the heirs of Presbyterianism recognizing the impossibility of national identity conforming to religious conviction.

Between the Majority and Religious Establishment

Presbyterianism in Ireland was in many ways an extension of its English and Scottish churches, but it developed along two tracks, one in the south with Dublin as the center, the other in the north around Belfast. Presbyterians in the south traced their presence back to the sixteenth century when English Protestantism, heavily Puritan in identity, established an outpost in Ireland. The Anglicans who brought Protestantism to Ireland after the Reformation, led by the archbishop of Armagh and later Dublin, Adam Loftus, were the kind who sought greater reform of the church along the lines set by Geneva and so modified the nature of episcopacy. Thomas Cartwright was Loftus's chaplain, and when Queen Elizabeth in 1592 founded Trinity College, its first five provosts qualified as Puritan. Further evidence of the Puritan character of Anglicanism in Ireland was James Ussher, archbishop of Armagh from 1625 to 1656, whose Articles of Faith formed the background for the Westminster Assembly's own confession of faith and whose view of a reduced episcopacy mollified some Presbyterians. Although the Presbytery of Dublin functioned as a Dissenting body, often similar to the advisory character of English Presbyterians, the Irish presbytery received a share of the *regium donum*, a grant from Charles II and later from William III (see chapter 6 herein). Like the English, Presbyterians around Dublin were less strict about discipline and doctrine, but uncomfortable with the direction of the Church of England after John Whitgift's, archbishop of Canterbury, turn against Puritanism. Dublin Presbyterians cooperated with like-minded Protestants in the north and sent commissioners to the Synod of Ulster.[47]

Presbyterianism in the north had roots in the Scottish church. The Synod of Ulster's origins stemmed from the Irish Rising of 1641. Presbyterian chaplains accompanied the Scottish soldiers sent to put down the insurrection. The Scots who stayed formed the basis for Presbyterian congregations. At first, Presbyterianism was only strong enough for one presbytery. By 1659, Presbyterians constituted five presbyteries. Throughout the Restoration and the Glorious Revolution they remained sufficiently large to hold their first General Synod (1690). Throughout its early history, Irish Presbyterianism in the north corresponded to developments within Scottish Protestantism. As such, Presbyterians supported the idea of an established church, even though they functioned as Dissenters. Dissent in Ireland was decidedly different than in England and Scotland since Irish Protestants, Presbyterians, Quakers, and Baptists faced few of the legal restrictions included in the Conventicles Act of 1670 or the Test Act of 1673. One factor that afforded all Protestants greater freedom was their minority status within an overly Roman Catholic Irish population. As only a quarter of the population, all Protestants possessed a bond absent in Scotland and England. The twist, of course, was the defeat of Jacobites by William III's armies in 1690 at the battles of Boyne and Aughrim. These victories allowed the Church of Ireland to dominate Ireland's Parliament and neutralize Irish Catholic elites. Presbyterians were caught between their status as Dissenters from the established (Anglican) church and their standing as a religious minority among Ireland's Roman Catholic population.[48]

"Thankfulness" is not the word typically used to characterize Presbyterian attitudes to the Church of Ireland, since both groups vied for ministerial supremacy in an environment vastly different from either England or Scotland. After 1690, 90 percent of Presbyterians lived in Ulster and looked like the functional equivalent of the established church by conducting such ecclesiastical functions as marriage, burial, and church discipline. Once Presbyterianism became Scotland's official church, Irish defenders of episcopacy resented the prominence of a communion that shaded politically into resistance and rebellion. To counter Presbyterian strength, the Irish government passed legislation. In 1704, the Popery Act received an additional clause that required all military and civil officials in Ireland to receive Holy Communion once a year in the Church of Ireland. Ten years later, provisions of England's Schism Act also extended to Ireland, where anyone wanting to establish an academy needed to gain approval from the local bishop. These laws sparked serious political opposition in which Presbyterians, who had rallied to William III's side in 1690, thought they deserved better treatment from England's Parliament. Attempts to change the law during the 1710s finally produced the Toleration Act, which softened some of the restrictions against Presbyterians but did little to alter resentment of their episcopal superiors.[49]

Maintaining the Protestant interest in Ireland while distinguishing Episcopalians from Presbyterians led advocates for bishops to dredge up ugly moments of seventeenth-century history. Ian McBride writes that either for rhetorical purposes or based on actual observations of Scottish migration to Ulster during the 1690s, "Anglicans feared that episcopacy would be swept away by a Presbyterian revolution on the Scottish model."[50] George Walker's account of the siege of London-Derry, published in 1689, for instance, alleged the presence of extremist Presbyterians. This was perhaps a way to counter Presbyterians' demographic majority in Ulster. Bishops, such as Tobias Pullen of Dromore, argued against the Toleration Act for Ireland because it would increase the number of Scottish immigrants, whose ministers, he alleged, wanted to eliminate episcopacy.[51] Responses by Presbyterians reflected differences between the north and south. In 1695, Joseph Boyse, a Presbyterian pastor in Dublin, defended his communion by appealing to constitutional rights of those under British rule and raising objections to the abuse of sacramental tests for civil purposes. Boyse was reluctant, however, to underscore differences between Presbyterians and Anglicans over polity and liturgy. In contrast, in 1696, John McBride, a minister from Belfast, responded to Episcopalian defensiveness with a full-blown defense of freedom of worship, but for only Presbyterians.[52]

A sticking point that these salvos underscored was the Presbyterian claim of spiritual independence. The autonomy of the church from the state was potentially or inherently, depending on one's perspective, a threat to an order in which the church coordinated with and supported the Christian monarch. Presbyterians who insisted church courts (assemblies, synods, and presbyteries) could convene without sanction from civil authorities proved to be particularly alarming to Irish Anglicans.[53] In the context of Queen Anne's reign, with echoes of debates over the Glorious Revolution fading, Irish Anglicans tried to link Presbyterian polity to Whig political theory.

A book by William Tisdale, a priest and friend of Jonathan Swift, who shared the writer's disdain for Presbyterianism, provoked a fulsome defense of the Presbyterian cause. Tisdale's complaint, elaborated in *Conduct of Dissenters* (1712), tracked the dark side of Presbyterianism's involvement with rebellion.[54] Two Belfast ministers rose to the challenge of defending Presbyterianism from Tisdale's attack. James Kirkpatrick and John McBride addressed the political point by underscoring how widespread opposition to Charles I was. Defending Parliament's rights against the Crown along with Scotland's ancient constitution was hardly a fault of Presbyterianism. The authors argued that the National Covenants themselves were not republican but monarchical in character.[55] Kirkpatrick and McBride also used the occasion to affirm basic Presbyterian ecclesiology, namely, that church and state were distinct jurisdictions, one spiritual, one temporal, with Christ as king of the church. Christ's kingship meant that the British monarch needed to refrain from intervening in matters of doctrine or worship. But although this ecclesiology limited the state, it also restricted the church's sphere to spiritual affairs. This arrangement still left the civil magistrate with power to suppress blasphemy and infidelity, a point upon which both Anglicans (on paper) and Covenanters agreed.[56]

Even if Presbyterianism found capable defenders, such as Kirkpatrick and McBride, Irish Presbyterians followed the English siblings by abandoning subscription to the Westminster Confession. John Abernethy, the leading opponent of subscription, preached a sermon in 1719 that brought the matter to a head. Influenced by Bishop Benjamin Hoadly, famous for the Bangorian controversy that took a sweeping view of church authority as merely spiritual and prized freedom of conscience, Abernathy used his sermon to defend reason and private judgment. To resort to any sort of imposition of doctrines was not service to God but, according to Abernethy, an "affront [to God], and to debase ourselves beneath the dignity of our nature by neglecting to improve our Reason which is our greatest excellency."[57] Whatever the merits of Presbyterian ties to the Westminster Assembly, in the context of the Hanoverian monarchy, Abernathy's argument created distance between Presbyterians and Anglicans. Instead of details about church government or liturgy providing the grounds for differentiation, in the 1710s English-speaking Presbyterians increasingly embraced the rights of private judgment. Ecclesiastical establishments and their attendant demands for religious uniformity were the tools of bishops. Presbyterians, according to Whiggish logic, were on the side of liberty combating tyranny.

These circumstances moved Irish Presbyterians into virtually the same debates about subscription that their English peers were having in Exeter and London. Since 1698, subscribing the Westminster Confession was necessary for anyone licensed to preach by the Synod of Ulster. In 1705, the trial of Presbyterian pastor Thomas Emlyn for denying the divinity of Christ produced the stipulation that all candidates for minister subscribe the Westminster Confession before ordination. This was the context for Abernethy's sermon on religious freedom.[58] The synod tried to calm the situation and maintain unity. The Pacific Act of 1720 allowed pastors to question the phrasing of statements in the Westminster Confession and propose their own wording. This ruling failed to satisfy the growing antisubscription sentiment. One Belfast minister, Samuel Haliday, refused altogether to subscribe to any doctrinal statement. These divisions came to be known as Old (subscribers) versus New (nonsubscribers) Lights. To avoid division, Presbyterians formed a separate presbytery for the New Lights—the Presbytery of Antrim. By 1725, even this accommodation became untenable, and the new presbytery severed ties with the Synod of Ulster.[59]

However effective subscription may have been, the politics of ecclesiastical establishments was a major factor in driving Irish Presbyterians from the seeming crown jewel of their great-grandparents' theological achievement—the Westminster Confession of Faith. In fewer than eighty years, the doctrinal standards that Puritan and Presbyterian pastors had created for churches in the four kingdoms, and that emerged from Parliament's own resistance (armed and legislative) to divine-right monarchy, became emblems of tyranny. These changes reflect the dynamics of church life at the start of the Hanoverian dynasty. The place of Dissenters in a confessional state (whether Ireland, England, or Scotland) replaced the older Presbyterian logic of a kingdom in covenant with God in pursuit of the holy commonwealth. Whether Presbyterians who embraced Enlightenment schemes of virtue and politics did so because the National Covenants now appeared repugnant is unclear. It was apparent that the most secure route to preserving the rights of minorities from oppressive rulers was an appeal to natural law, the consent of the governed, a mixed constitution, and rights to resistance.[60] In this setting, Abernethy's nonsubscribing position was an application to individual conscience of the old Presbyterian argument that the church was a distinct polity with its own rulers, independent from the king. Ian McBride states that "during the reigns of William and Anne . . . Presbyterian leaders first found it necessary to assert claims for religious liberty against political repression, and found the materials in a Whiggish discourse that would have surprised their more orthodox predecessors."[61]

Politics aside, Irish Presbyterianism—even after the debates over subscription—still had a Scottish accent. Some of this influence was the function of Scottish settlers in Ireland and some owed to education. Irish Presbyterians depended on Scottish universities for theological training thanks to legal restrictions on Dissenters. Glasgow was the chief training ground for Irish pastors. The older Presbyterian groups, divided between New Light (nonsubscribers) and Old Light (subscribers) used their own institutions (presbytery or synod) to maintain coherence. New Lights, though, had a limited appeal, not much beyond "the better-off sections of Presbyterian society" around Belfast.[62] Old Lights fared no better with the Synod of Ulster but evolved into a moderate position akin to the Church of Scotland. Meanwhile, for Presbyterians still inclined to take their cues from the past, the Seceder and Covenanter branches of Scottish Dissent established a presence in Ireland throughout the eighteenth century. In 1733, the Associate Presbyterians formed their own presbytery and showed enough strength to muster a synod twelve years later. Their links to Scotland were clearly evident when the Scottish oath that split the Scottish Seceders into Burgher and Anti-Burgher wings also divided the Irish Seceders (even though that political provision had no parallel in Ireland). The Covenanters, or Reformed Presbyterians, also kept alive the Scottish National Covenants and after 1750 brought to Ireland those convictions. By the end of the century, the Covenanters had one presbytery in Ireland with six ministers and twelve congregations. Although both of these dissenting bodies kept alive the ideal of a covenanted nation, only the Covenanters made the National Covenants a basis for communion. The Seceders tried to hold onto the theology that drove the covenants without insisting on the political implications.[63]

Like Presbyterians elsewhere in the English-speaking world, the Irish were adjusting to the new terms of religious establishment within the British Empire. The old energies that drove National Covenants and rebellion dwindled but remained appealing to smaller groups desirous of conserving the past. No one had yet figured out a way to maintain the luster of Presbyterian orthodoxy (Westminster Confession) while shedding political demands that had been necessary to the very existence of the English Parliament convening the Westminster Assembly. Sometimes the Scottish roots of Irish Presbyterianism showed. But in general, their leaders needed to navigate conditions foreign to other Presbyterians, namely, an Anglican establishment governing an overwhelmingly Roman Catholic society.

New World Variations on the Old World

Presbyterians in North America did not face the same political constraints that their peers did in the United Kingdom and Ireland. The British government's oversight of the colonies came in different forms, but church life was not a high priority. Without a bishop in the colonies, Protestants outside the Church of England experienced few of the obstacles that Dissenters in England, Scotland, and Ireland did (except for life on the frontier). The religious establishments that did exist in the American colonies—Puritanism in New England and Anglicanism in New York and the south—could be restrictive. They sometimes included barriers to the free movement of ministers and imposed taxes in support of established churches. These circumstances left Dissenters having to pay twice, once for the approved minister and a second time for the pastor of their choice. Baptists, in particular, felt the sting of these policies in Massachusetts and Virginia. For Presbyterians, Virginia's Anglican establishment pushed them to side with disestablishment altogether. But for most Presbyterians, who bulked in the middle colonies of Maryland, Delaware, and Pennsylvania, colonial life afforded freedom to establish churches, conduct services, and create structures for ecclesiastical governance. Such liberty made it remarkable that questions about church power and liberty of conscience took root among New World Presbyterians in ways that echoed the Old World.

In 1721, only four years after its formation, the Synod of Philadelphia received an overture that called for doctrinal rigor among its members. The author was George Gillespie, a pastor in Delaware, originally ordained in 1712 in Scotland (Presbytery of Glasgow) and one year later called and established as the pastor in White Clay Creek (now in Delaware). What motivated Gillespie was the recent confession of fornication by fellow minister Robert Cross. Gillespie had petitioned the synod to suspend Cross from preaching for four Sundays. Gillespie's overture received opposition from Jonathan Dickinson, a Massachusetts native, trained at Yale, and pastor in Elizabeth Town (northern New Jersey). Dickinson echoed arguments that nonsubscribers in England and Ireland were making at roughly the same time. For these pastors, scripture and biblical authority were sufficient guides for church government. Dickinson also appealed to Bishop Hoadly's 1717 sermon that took issue with ecclesiastical authorities coercing belief or conduct among ministers.[64] He found this particular section of the bishop of Bangor's sermon to be instructive: "And in this Sense therefore, his (Christ's) Kingdom is not of this World, that he has in those Points left behind him no Visible Humane Authority, no Vicegerent that can be said properly to supply his place, no Interpreters upon whom his Subjects are absolutely to depend, no Judges over the Consciences and Religion of his People."[65]

Dickinson's reservations about church power prepared for a similar debate about subscription. In 1727, John Thomson brought a proposal to the Synod of Philadelphia that called for the church to adopt the Westminster Confession and catechisms as the doctrinal standards for Presbyterian ministry. An Irish Presbyterian who had graduated from Glasgow in 1711, then licensed by the Presbytery of Armagh a year later, Thomson settled in North America in 1715. Two years later he took a call to the congregation in Lewes (later Delaware). Thomson was eager to keep erroneous teaching out of the colonial church, and subscription became a means to achieve that end. He proposed that unless a prospective minister registered his differences with the Westminster Standards, his ministerial peers could expect him to conform to the Westminster Confession and Catechisms. Departures from that norm could lead to censure.[66] The motion took two years to come before the synod thanks to infrequency of meetings. But reactions to Thomson differed in ways that correlated with ethnicity. Irish and Scottish pastors supported subscription, and the English (or those from New England) had reservations about using church power to enforce doctrinal uniformity. Differences also corresponded to perceptions of church life back in Britain. Subscriptionists hoped to avoid the errors of English and Irish Presbyterians, while their opponents wanted to preserve the liberties enjoyed by colonial churches.

At its 1729 meeting, the Synod of Philadelphia adopted the Westminster Standards as the body's doctrinal norm. The so-called Adopting Act has provoked a host of interpretations, partly because it came in two stages, from different sessions of the same day. In the morning, the synod allowed ministers to take exceptions to doctrines that were not "essential and necessary"—whether this applied to general Christian verities or Westminster's version of Calvinism has been an ongoing source of debate. The afternoon session specifically mentioned objections to the confession's teaching on the civil magistrate. Chapter 23, in particular, conceived of a state church, with a magistrate having power to work with the church in securing church reform and a holy commonwealth, a position that made sense of the alliance England forged with Scotland in the Solemn League and Covenant (1643). Although the Adopting Act appeared initially to be less than what subscriptionists wanted, subsequent controversies in the 1730s revealed much greater support for subscription than perhaps 1720s debates indicated.

The 1736 trial of pastor Samuel Hemphill revolved around charges of plagiarism and departure from the Westminster Confession. Adding notoriety to the controversy (and to their memory) was Benjamin Franklin's writing on behalf of Hemphill (usually under a pseudonym).[67] The trial's resolution depended on an agreement that promised order and uniformity of practice. Hemphill needed to step down, and the church continued to use subscription to control for the quality of her pastors. "All the ministers in this Synod, or that hereafter shall be admitted into this Synod, do declare their agreement in and approbation of the Confession of Faith, with the Larger and Shorter Catechisms of the Assembly of Divines at Westminster, as being in all the essential and necessary articles, good forms of sound words, and systems of Christian doctrine," ruled the commission responsible for trying Hemphill.[68]

Charles Scott Sealy has helpfully connected the debates among Philadelphia Presbyterians to the 1710s Irish controversy over subscription. He observes, in particular, the number of parallels between Philadelphia's Adopting Act and Ulster's Pacific Act. In 1720, the Synod of Ulster approved a resolution that required anyone licensed for preaching to "subscribe" the Westminster Confession and "promise to adhere to the doctrine, worship, discipline, and governm[en]t of this church." The Pacific Act, also like Philadelphia's Adopting Act, granted room for ministers to express reservations about particular phrases in the Westminster Confession and for the Ulster Synod to determine if the candidate was still "sound in the faith."[69] In effect, Presbyterians outside Scotland were trying to hold onto the authority of the church, with ordination as the only way to do it.

Still, the yawning gap between seventeenth-century proponents of Presbyterian church government and their eighteenth-century progeny is remarkable. Only a couple generations before Belfast and Philadelphia, Presbyterians worked out a compromise for using the high water mark of Presbyterian reflection, the Westminster Standards, as the norm for preaching and teaching in England and Scotland, with hopes for a godly monarch working in tandem with churches truly reformed. By the time of the Hanoverian monarchy, Presbyterianism had become a shell of its former self. Its advocates had at one time thought the path of true and complete church reform could only come with a covenant that bound the king, legislature, pastors, and people together in establishing a godly commonwealth. By 1730, the best Presbyterians could do was to ask prospective pastors to affirm the Westminster Standards. When they did ask, they did so politely.

The loss of church authority among Presbyterians continued to haunt the colonial church in North America. Only a few years after the Hemphill trial, awakenings prompted another challenge to the authority of synods, presbyteries, and pastors.[70] Here the difficulty had nothing to do with the civil magistrate requiring religious conformity but came from the opposite direction of spirit-filled preachers. In 1726, Gilbert Tennent, son of Church of Ireland priest William Tennent, had migrated to North America. His father established a school modeled on dissenting academies in England and Ireland. Gilbert promoted awakenings that had swelled in public notoriety thanks to the arrival of George Whitefield, the most extraordinary evangelist, according to the revivals' apologists, since the Apostle Paul. Gilbert Tennent preached a sermon in 1741 to expose the alleged malicious designs of the revivals' opponents. "The Danger of An Unconverted Ministry" branded Tennent's foes as unbelievers since they had not experienced the new birth of the Holy Spirit. That was arguably an effective argument if the issue had simply been one of belief versus unbelief. But Tennent's opponents, many of whom supported subscription, faulted the awakened pastors for transgressing Presbyterian rules. Sometimes revivalists such as Tennant visited towns, uninvited by the local pastor and session, and proceeded to preach to residents. In response to Tennent's inflammatory sermon, the Synod of Philadelphia excluded from its fellowship the Presbytery of New Brunswick, a judicatory established in 1738 to accommodate the revivalist party. Eventually, the colonial church split (1745) between the Old Side (antirevival) Synod of Philadelphia and the New Side (pro-revival) Synod of New York. That division lasted until 1758.

The inability of colonial Presbyterians to police their ranks reflected the powerlessness of Presbyterian church government without backup from the civil magistrate. In theory, the spiritual power of presbytery or synod should have mattered to Protestants, who had insisted for almost two centuries that the church's spiritual power was real if only because the apostles did not need help from the civil authorities; as the sole head of the church, Christ's authority was sufficient. But if Presbyterians could challenge civil magistrates meddling in church life, it did not take long to apply the same lesson to church government. Presbyterians themselves failed to comply with the rule of their own institutions.

The crisis of Presbyterian church authority was not restricted to North America but pervaded the English-speaking world. Whether Presbyterians were part of the political establishment (Scotland) or constituted a dissenting church (Ireland, England, British colonies), eighteenth-century Presbyterians were reluctant to enforce basic standards for ordination and administration. Those who favored uniformity and discipline found themselves increasingly in a weak position that required compromise. The result was a Presbyterianism dialed down several notches from the hotter forms that had challenged monarchs, inspired war, and aspired to the international cooperation of Reformed churches. Eighteenth-century Presbyterianism was not modernist in the twentieth-century sense of self-conscious adaptation to modern society and ideas. Even so, after the Glorious Revolution, Presbyterianism turned away decidedly from zeal for an integration of church and society. British politics taught Presbyterians to recalibrate their hopes for reform in the church. For Presbyterians outside the Church of Scotland, any appeal to a godly magistrate or National Covenants was a luxury. The best the most conservative Presbyterian could muster was a church with sufficient authority to enforce spiritual norms on consenting officers and members.

PART 2

Presbyterian Modern, 1700–1875

CHAPTER 5

Liberal Presbyterian Rebellions

By the late eighteenth century, Presbyterians in Britain's thirteen American colonies and in Ireland had learned to run reformed churches without the added demands of a godly monarch or a covenanted nation. To be sure, the heroic achievements and inspired visions of John Knox, Samuel Rutherford, or the architects of Scotland's National Covenant, Archibald Johnston and Alexander Henderson, continued to enchant sectors of the Presbyterian world. But even for those who carried a torch for Scotland's Presbyterian Reformation, the reality of ministering and worshiping in denominations, as opposed to a church that was truly reformed, was a reminder that the descendants of the Kirk had come to terms with modern administrations of church and state. By the middle of the eighteenth century, some Presbyterians were coming around to the advantages of voluntary as opposed to state churches, policies that tolerated religious dissent and that restricted church authority to ecclesiastical spheres rather than the wider society. Presbyterians in America and especially in Ireland, as Protestants outside the religious establishment and as minorities in their societies' populations, had recalibrated their forms of church government and theological expectations to settings where they hoped for liberty to administer their own affairs and build sustainable communions without obstacles from government or other churches.

Such ecclesiastical adjustments in modernizing societies make Presbyterian support for the American Revolution and the Irish Rising of 1798 surprising and even confounding. Being Presbyterian in North America and Ireland was significantly different from the social vision that had inspired English and Scottish church reformers before the Glorious Revolution. If American and Irish Presbyterians could accommodate the place of churches in eighteenth-century societies, why did they become involved in political rebellions against British rule? Could the American Revolution and Irish Rising have possibly been the outworking of Presbyterian zeal for a reformed church within a godly, covenanted society? Or were those uprisings a reflection of the specific political grievances that Presbyterians in America and Ireland shared with their neighbors?

The trajectory of Presbyterian adjustments to British government and church life between 1650 and 1750, explored in the previous three chapters, highlights how unusual late eighteenth-century political rebellions were as expressions of Presbyterian zeal for a reformed church and godly society. As much as contemporaries and later historians may have regarded 1776 and 1798 as further instances of Presbyterian ecclesiastical and political ideals, the American and Irish rebellions were several steps removed from the political agitation that emerged in Scotland in the 1630s, fueled England's Civil War of the 1640s and execution of a king, and resulted in a temporary experiment with republicanism during the Interregnum. In fact, Presbyterian support (by no means unanimous) for the American Revolution and the Irish Rising revealed a shift among these Reformed Protestants from a Christendom model to a liberal understanding of the churches' place in modern society. Instead of demanding national return to the true faith, Presbyterian support for the 1776 and 1798 rebellions demonstrated an acceptance of religious freedom, a voluntary church, and a generically Protestant understanding of good government.

The Presbyterian Revolution in America

John Witherspoon was an "enigmatic figure."[1] A Presbyterian pastor and president of the College of New Jersey, an institution that contributed to the intellectual formation of James Madison and so to the American Founding, Witherspoon was hardly mysterious about either the North American colonies' rights within the British Empire or the American cause of liberty. The only clergyman to sign the Declaration of Independence, his life gives immediate plausibility to the idea that the War for Independence was a "Presbyterian rebellion." In addition, Witherspoon's sermon "The Dominion of Providence over the Passions of Men," preached on a fast day six weeks before the original July Fourth and widely circulated through the colonies at the call of the Continental Congress, was a standard treatment of the relationship between Presbyterian piety and civil liberty.

As significant as these circumstances may be, Witherspoon's enigma, Mark A. Noll explains, had much to do with the way he transformed instruction at the College of New Jersey. Rather than following in the philosophical footsteps of Jonathan Edwards's revival-friendly idealism, Witherspoon purged the school of the Northampton minister's academic preferences and instituted instruction based on the philosophical realism of his homeland, Scottish Common Sense. Noll also observes that this left the college with a dilemma for harmonizing faith and learning, a challenge with important implications for training Presbyterian ministers in what became the United States. The political lessons remained clear, and Witherspoon's influence on Madison remains a standard entry point for assessing religious influences on the American Founding.[2]

Some of the mystery surrounding Witherspoon stems from the actual toll that the Revolutionary War took on his literary estate. The Battle of Princeton (January 3, 1777) was no Battle of the Boyne or Battle of Culloden, but it was a pivotal episode in George Washington's campaign against the British army. Along with the Colonials' victories at Trenton (December 26) and Assunpink Creek (January 2), Washington's success forced the British to abandon most of New Jersey. Witherspoon experienced that victory differently. Earlier in December, he and his wife escaped before the British troops captured Princeton. Those soldiers ransacked the Witherspoon home, including the college president's library and personal papers. British troops also took over Nassau Hall, the building that housed most of the college's operations. Soldiers either stole or destroyed the college's scientific apparatus, which included a planetarium considered to be one of the best in the world.[3] One of the final confrontations during the Battle of Princeton involved the British running for cover behind Nassau Hall's large stone walls. The exchange of gunfire that led to the British surrender wreaked additional havoc on the college's signature building. The damage did not render Nassau Hall unusable. Six years later when American troops threatened Congress for back pay, Witherspoon made Nassau Hall available to the Continental Congress (of which he was a member). These events surrounding a Presbyterian minister and a college founded by Presbyterians justify George III's quip that "Whigs and Presbyterians" led the American Revolution.[4] Considering the leadership of Virginia's and Massachusetts's elites in the Americans' quest for independence, the better place to look for Presbyterians in the American Revolution was in the ranks of the Patriots' advisors and publicists.[5]

When Witherspoon arrived in America almost two decades earlier (August 1768) with his wife and five children, he came with high hopes for his work at the College of New Jersey. Students showed their support by lighting tallow dips, one in each window of Nassau Hall. This gesture culminated a series of festivities that had started in Philadelphia, where city officials welcomed the Scotsman by presenting him with a special edition of his popular book *Ecclesiastical Characteristics*. From there he journeyed north through Trenton to Princeton. Along the way, officials and residents lined the roads to greet the man colonial Presbyterians had hired to preside over the institution that was not an official church college but was the center of Presbyterian intellectual life. Two years earlier, college officials had offered the presidency to Witherspoon with a generous package of 200 pounds sterling, and a residence complete with a garden and firewood. As attractive as that compensation may have been, Elizabeth, his wife, was not impressed. The recent history of the college's first five presidents all dying in office was one concern. She worried that if the pattern persisted, she would be left alone in a strange land. Elizabeth was also reluctant to leave Scotland, where she had buried five children. While studying in Edinburgh, Benjamin Rush, a College of New Jersey alumnus and influential figure in Philadelphia politics, colonial medicine, and Presbyterian churches, had visited Witherspoon in Paisley to repeat the college's offer. Rush succeeded.[6]

Witherspoon's arrival in North America culminated a thirty-year period in which the fledgling Presbyterian communion achieved a measure of coherence. Unlike the Puritans or Anglicans, colonial Presbyterians had no colony of their own and were not part of an established church (not even a missionary effort of the Kirk). This explains why Maryland and Pennsylvania, two colonies that had at different intervals instituted religious freedom, were the favorite places for pastors and congregations to settle. By the early eighteenth century, this area between New York and Philadelphia became a beachhead for Scottish and Ulster immigrants, who either stayed in New Jersey or relocated to New York and Pennsylvania.[7] After a split within the colonial church over revivals (see chapter 4 herein), American Presbyterians recovered by doing what their form of government did best—establish a system of councils from the local (presbyteries) to regional levels (synods). Another important institution for Presbyterians was the College of New Jersey (so that Americans did not have to train in Scotland). When Witherspoon arrived, he was in a prominent position to lead the American church to the next level of institutional maturity. His Scottish background only enhanced his standing among the colonists.[8]

Witherspoon beefed up the Scottish side of colonial Presbyterianism, but the Church of Scotland from which he came was an uncertain guide to establishing a new communion. Born in 1723 and educated at Edinburgh University between 1739 and 1743, Witherspoon was too young to have taken part in the division of 1733 that saw conservative Presbyterians form a Secession church (Associate Presbytery). Witherspoon's background prepared him to be a reformer within the established church. In his Paisley parish, a stronghold for conservatives in the Kirk, Witherspoon assumed leadership within the so-called Popular Party. Opposed to the Moderates then in the majority, these conservatives rallied around two causes: one was the protection of congregations' power to call their pastor (as opposed to appointment by wealthy elites or lairds); the other was a defense of Calvinistic doctrine (over against morality as the hallmark of Christianity). Witherspoon's *Ecclesiastical Characteristics* was a popular satire of the Moderates. Its premise was that good taste, polite manners, and proper learning mattered more to church leaders than doctrine and worship. The Popular Party shared concerns with the Seceders but not to the point of exiting the Kirk. Witherspoon's support for revivalistic piety, willingness to engage in controversy, and ability to work within existing institutions were important to his appeal to colonial Presbyterians.

The political dimension of Witherspoon's Presbyterianism also stood him in good stead in North America, but he still had to navigate competing Scottish ecclesiastical networks. Some Scots brought to the colonies convictions forged in the seventeenth century's tumultuous covenanting politics. Others, by way of Ulster, were less strict about Scotland's rights but still demanding about doctrine and church government. For Witherspoon himself, as neither a Covenanter nor a Seceder, political philosophy ran in grooves cut by Scottish philosophers more than Presbyterian reformers. His outlook led to his support for American independence, but his revolutionary convictions were substantially different from ardent Scots, such as the Covenanters or Seceders. For instance, Hugh Simm, one of Witherspoon's fellow Scottish immigrants, also relocated from Paisley to New Jersey. Unlike Witherspoon, who fit in almost immediately within the Americanized Scottish community, Simm grew nostalgic for his Scottish roots and could not find kindred spirits. Partly from this frustration, Simm moved to New York City and later to Albany, where he joined a Seceder congregation. Thanks to the National Covenants' dependence on the Crown, Simm and fellow Seceders rejected the Patriots' cause against King George III and Parliament. Simm became a Tory and eventually returned to the United Kingdom.[9]

Such differences between Witherspoon and Simm indicate that Scottish politics did not map neatly in the colonial setting of North America. The long struggle for Presbyterianism as the national church in Scotland produced arguments that could be royalist, republican, or some variety in between. As it turned out, Witherspoon's own support for American independence likely owed more to ideas he shared with Ben Franklin and Thomas Jefferson than any theological tradition that ran from John Knox to Thomas Chalmers.

The same challenge of running the American situation through the grid of Scottish expectations applies to Witherspoon's views on education, which had a significant influence on his understanding of American independence. Historians who have followed Witherspoon's migration to America often stumbled over the Presbyterian's views on the Scottish Enlightenment. Although he opposed Scottish moral philosophy's influence on the Church of Scotland's theology (strong among Moderates), his use of Scottish philosophers at the College of New Jersey indicates inconsistency. Noll puts the predicament well when he observes the intellectual changes that Witherspoon introduced at the college and their consequences for political theory. Before coming to America, Witherspoon had affirmed that social welfare depended on a virtuous people. This was a common theme in much eighteenth-century theorizing. What made Witherspoon's outlook different was the insistence that such virtue depended on a supernatural infusion of grace. To propose that men and women were able by their own natural efforts to achieve moral goodness was, he argued in a 1758 sermon, a "beautiful but unsubstantial idol, raised by human pride."[10]

When Witherspoon came to Princeton, he changed his tune. Not only did he rid the curriculum of the philosophical idealism that Jonathan Edwards in 1758 had instituted while president. Witherspoon also began to speak of society in ways similar to the Kirk's Moderates. In one of his lectures on moral philosophy, he argued that reason was capable of discovering the demands of virtue and duty. In fact, human inquiry could discover the will of God through "enlightened" reason and experience. From here it was a short step to standard Whig political convictions, such as society based on "voluntary compact," humans originating in a state of nature "equal and consequently free," and participation in society for "the protection of liberty, as far as it is a blessing."[11] Historians may debate whether Witherspoon was a Lockean (liberal individualism) or a classical republican (communal virtue), but his influence made room for Christian supporters of American independence to present their interests as communal, objective, God-given, or free from the taint of secularism.[12]

As much as Witherspoon's philosophical loyalties may explain his politics, his intellectual history misses an aspect of Scottish experience that was even more basic than moral philosophy. That was the ecclesiastical settlement of England's 1707 Union with Scotland. Unlike older Presbyterian politics informed by the National Covenants, eighteenth-century colonial Presbyterians looked to the 1707 Union for protection. Gideon Mailer notes that in 1746, Witherspoon had opposed a Covenanter faction that wanted to restore a descendant of the Stuart line to the throne in hopes of recovering the National Covenant. Mailer locates Witherspoon within a group of Presbyterian preachers who remained loyal to the Hanoverian monarchy over against the tyrannical abuses of Parliament in London.[13] These Presbyterians did not adopt the rhetoric of some

New England radicals who conceived of the patriotic cause as an extension of the Solemn League and Covenant. Instead, Witherspoon appealed to British norms derived from the 1707 Union.[14] Politically, the Union between England and Scotland also served as a model for confederation. For Patriots such as Witherspoon, this meant the North American colonies should enjoy a status within the British government similar to Scotland's position within the United Kingdom.

Standard accounts of Witherspoon's support for American independence feature his famous 1776 sermon, "The Dominion of Providence over the Passions of Men." Even here, his calculations were as political as they were religious. He delivered the sermon six weeks before he signed the Declaration of Independence and likened the controversy between Britain and America as mainly one of a legislative body, "independent of us" and interested in "opposing us," making laws for the colonies without the colonists' input.[15] When he did invoke religion in the sermon, Witherspoon used standard-issue civil religion that looked to Christianity as a bulwark of social stability.

In other writings produced around the same time, however, Witherspoon reflected on the colonies' situation within the British Empire and defended the protection of local prerogatives within a united kingdom. In his posthumously published essay "On Conducting the American Controversy," Witherspoon was at pains to disassociate the American cause from radicals such as John Wilkes, who, in addition to ridiculing King George, lacked the good sense to avoid mocking the Scots. Wilkes, according to Witherspoon, was guilty of "gross, and indecent, and groundless abuse of the king and his family," so much so that Wilkes became "odious to the nation."[16] The issue facing Patriots was a British prejudice that elevated Parliament and the Crown over any sympathy with the colonists' lack of representation. London's power to tax might have seemed "agreeable" to the form of the British constitution, but its daily practice was "inconsistent with [its] spirit." This left Americans in the awkward situation of being "dutiful and respectful" of the king as "any in his dominions," yet without any meaningful voice in the British government.[17]

When in May 1776 (the same month he preached his famous sermon) Witherspoon wrote *Address to the Natives of Scotland Residing in America*, he was again keen to blame the Scots' lukewarm support for

American independence on Wilkes's radicalism. The idea that the cause of American liberty was the same as "Wilkism" had spooked many Scots into support for the king. But now Witherspoon was confident that the merits of American independence were distinct from any inherent opposition to the king or the British constitution. The American colonies had prospered demographically and economically in ways that were evident to all Europeans. The reason for this prosperity was not the attributes of a specific people (the colonies were diverse) or the advantages of land and climate. The main reason was independence.

Contrary to British writers who claimed that the colonies had advanced because of their close ties to Great Britain, Witherspoon argued the opposite. The colonists had benefited from "British liberty," which they transplanted from the homeland and wrote into their "several constitutions." Political independence would only formalize what the colonies had enjoyed. It would also benefit Great Britain. Witherspoon invoked Montesquieu and asked rhetorically, "If the trade of America has hitherto been of so great benefit to England, how much more valuable may it be when these countries shall still be more highly improved?" He even speculated that American independence could make up for the revolution of 1649 and the execution of Charles I. If Parliament could have settled on a "regular form of government" as soon as it had achieved "superiority," British liberties would never have "been shaken."[18] But delay cost those opposed to the Crown's tyranny: they broke into "parties," became "bewildered in their views," and submitted tamely to "that very tyranny" (Oliver Cromwell) against which they had fought. America's declarations of independence were giving "union and force" to defenses of liberty in ways that in the 1640s eluded Presbyterians. Witherspoon said nothing about the Scottish Reformation's National Covenants or the politics they inspired.

Witherspoon found an ally in Francis Alison. The vice provost at the Philadelphia Academy (later University of Pennsylvania) and pastor at nearby First Presbyterian Church, Alison in 1735 had like Witherspoon come to North America by way of Scotland. Upon his arrival, he pastored and started an academy in New London, Chester County, and emerged as a leader in the antirevival Old Side Presbyterian Synod (the result of a split among colonial Presbyterians that ran from 1741 to 1758). Like Witherspoon also, Alison followed the Scottish philosophical categories he had learned at University of Glasgow. Although Alison was initially suspicious of Witherspoon thanks to the College of New Jersey's pro-revival and New Side reputation, neither of these Presbyterians brought church divisions into their perspective on the British government. Alison and Witherspoon were both situated within the political settlements achieved by the Glorious Revolution and the Union of England and Scotland.

When it came to the colonies' relationship to Parliament's policies after the Seven Years' War, no matter what his moral philosophy may have required, Alison was especially keen to defend American liberties. Although Witherspoon was not present to feel the effects of the Stamp Act (1765) or Townsend Acts (1766/67), Alison was, and he participated in assemblies of Presbyterian clergy responsible for giving advice to colonists on proper political responses. As tensions rose and colonists became frustrated over Parliament's apparent disregard for British subjects in North America, Presbyterian pastors sent mixed messages. Sometimes they called for restraint, humility, fasting, and prayer. Other times they contemplated legitimate forms of resistance to political tyranny. Through it all, Alison and his colleagues were quick to assert their loyalty to the king. In a 1775 letter to Scottish Highlanders resettled in North Carolina that Alison coauthored with James Sproat, George Duffield, and Robert Davidson (all in Philadelphia congregations), colonial Presbyterians revealed themselves to be friends of "the house of Hanover." At this late date, they did not see a contradiction between support for American liberties and a "sacred obligation" to remain loyal to the Crown.[19] The letter even warned southern Presbyterians that if such loyalty failed to support American liberties, the North Carolinians would lose fellowship with Presbyterians in the north.

This 1775 missive also repeated an earlier affirmation from the Synod of New York that opposition to Parliament did not signify "disaffection to the King" or a desire of separation from "the parent State." Alison and others explained the nature of the conflict, namely, whether Parliament had the legitimate authority to "dispose of our money without our consent." If colonists had to pay taxes without representation in London, "where is our English liberty?" That logic was easily translated into the patriotic shibboleth "no taxation without representation."[20] But it came with an understanding of British politics that many Americans would soon forget.

These Presbyterians' historical narrative followed the high points of British politics that moved from the Magna Carta and the Glorious Revolution to the Union of England and Scotland. For Scottish Presbyterians who still maintained their kingdom's duty to uphold the National Covenant, the coronation of William and Mary was inglorious. Parliament's peaceful victory over James II provided no obvious advantage to Presbyterians within the Church of Scotland. Not until the Union of 1707 did Presbyterianism (minus its Covenanting aspirations) become the national church's approved polity. Even with all that history, colonial Presbyterians such as Alison regarded their status as British subjects through the lens of the United Kingdom's blessings.

Alison and fellow pastors went on to explain that Parliament was "limited by the fundamental laws of the Constitution, and by the Great Charter of England." As such, failure to support the colonists' cause was to oppose the "British constitution." It was akin to fighting on the opposite side of Presbyterians at the Battle of Newtonbutler, one phase of the Williamite War in Ireland between the armies of William and Mary and James II's forces. The letter's specific reference to the Williamites' victories at Londonderry and Enniskillen, familiar to Protestants who regarded the Glorious Revolution as insurance against Stuart tyranny and infidelity, meant that Presbyterians had turned a page from their seventeenth-century policies. In fact, according to the Presbyterian pastors, when "our forefathers" fought in that war to "set aside that bigoted Prince, and the Stewart family, and set the Brunswick family on the throne," they were not rebels. They were, like American patriots eighty years later, loyalists, "firmly devoted to the present reigning family, as the assertors of the British privileges and English liberty."[21] This letter was part of a strategy to gain support for the American cause from Presbyterians who opposed the radicalism of John Wilkes.[22] These patriots were pairing their British provincial rights "alongside more commonly conceived English liberties." By making this connection, Alison was employing a logic distinct from the older Presbyterian tactic of insisting the king uphold his vow to promote the true faith.

Presbyterian loyalty to the British constitution did not surface often in debates about the religious influences on the American Founding. Even so, Witherspoon's and Alison's assessments of the 1707 Union's significance for church life put these pastors on the side of the "royalist revolution," as Eric Nelson calls it. Unlike the formation of the

Commonwealth (1649) or the Glorious Revolution (1688), he writes, the American Revolution was "for a great many of its protagonists—a revolution against a legislature, not against a king." It was even a "rebellion in favor of royal power" because the colonists wanted to deny that Parliament possessed any jurisdiction over British North America.[23] As much as this pro-royalist position may have ceded ground to assertions of royal supremacy, Witherspoon, Alison, and their colleagues understood that their communion's place within a united kingdom after the settlements of the Glorious Revolution was better than the adversarial conditions that had prevailed throughout the seventeenth century. Resistance to tyranny was, of course, a popular trope employed to support independence and popular consent, but it did not address the church's place within the political establishment. When it came to protecting the Presbyterian church's prerogatives in British North America, the provisions of the British constitution looked more appealing to colonial pastors than the religious policies of either the Tudors or Stuarts.

No Bishops

A further indication of the importance of British religious policies to colonial Presbyterianism was a bond forged between the American Presbyterian Church and the Congregationalist churches of New England. Well before the Quebec Act (1774) inflamed Protestants already suspicious of episcopacy to think that Britain's incorporation of the French colony reflected indifference to Roman Catholicism and presaged the advent of an American bishop to regulate colonial church life, Alison was on the lookout for any trace of episcopacy in colonial society. Between 1764 and 1768, he corresponded with the New England Congregationalist pastor (and eventual president of Yale College) Ezra Stiles about the dangers of an American bishop. Alison himself created the anti-episcopal newspapers, *Centinel* and *The Remonstrant*, to expose the political power that bishops possessed beyond their spiritual duties. He encouraged Stiles to start similar publications in New England. This coordination led to the formation of a General Convention of Presbyterians and Congregationalists to promote good societies and fashion a "firm union against Episcopal encroachments."[24] Within a year of his arrival at Princeton,

Witherspoon became a regular participant in this General Convention, until 1775 when it ceased to meet.

The threat to civil and religious liberty from the Anglican establishment reinforced colonists' general fears of tyranny and their accompanying consecration of liberty. If membership in the Church of England were necessary for civil appointments and military service, the colonists could face the same sorts of constraints that Protestant Dissenters endured in England and Ireland. If, also, bishops had the power to establish civil courts, as Alison alleged, again the colonists' way of life could change dramatically.

Nevertheless, worries about episcopacy were not distinct from the colonists' objections to Parliament's schemes for generating revenue from North America. Ever since 1701, when the Church of England's Society for the Propagation of the Gospel started to send missionaries to the colonies, American pastors, notably Jonathan Mayhew, argued that London was plotting to create a diocese in North America that would turn colonial Congregationalists and Presbyterians into Dissenters. Fears of an American bishop reached a crescendo in the 1760s with the imposition of the Stamp Act in 1765. Here the issue of taxation without representation mingled with opposition to episcopacy. Aside from theoretical questions of citizenship and representative government, the Stamp Act's procedures were particularly objectionable. Boston's patriots John Adams and Samuel Adams opposed powers given to the Vice-Admiralty Court's judges to hear cases without a jury. The act's provisions also required the payment of duties on documents used in ecclesiastical courts (warnings, summons, admonitions). When Lord Grenville, lord of the treasury and chancellor of the exchequer, heard that no such courts existed in North America, he replied that "at some future period it was very possible they might be."[25] The link between taxes and bishops escalated the colonists' opposition to the Anglican Church. Anglican priests and missionaries became synonymous with the English government and its tyrannical policies.[26]

New England Congregationalists had reasons for opposing a bishop that were distinct from those of Presbyterians. With the loss in 1684 of Massachusetts Bay's original proprietary charter, the colony became a potential location for Anglican missionaries. For Presbyterians, in contrast, the 1707 Union of England and Scotland was the significant milestone.

That settlement united the two nations under a single government but two separate national churches. Even though the Scottish Episcopalians Act of 1711 was a setback for Presbyterians, the reformed character of the Church of Scotland remained. Such security was not available in British North America, where a similar religious settlement had yet to be tried or implemented. Witherspoon's conception of the American colonies as a satellite within the British Empire drew specifically on Scotland's place in the United Kingdom.

For the Ulsterman Alison, British policies touched a different political nerve. Although Alison had emerged as one of the most distinguished educators and pastors in the colonies, Yale's Ezra Stiles called him the "greatest classical scholar in America," Alison's background contrasted significantly with Witherspoon's.[27] By 1768, when *Centinel* first appeared in Pennsylvania newspapers, Alison had lived in the colonies since 1735 when he had migrated from Ireland. The son of a weaver in County Donegal, his ancestors were Scottish planters who had settled during the reign of James I. His intellectual capacities were impressive enough for his family to send him to Edinburgh and further study in divinity at Glasgow. This was good preparation for ministering in the Presbyterian Church of Ireland, but Alison's time at Edinburgh also exposed him to the natural and moral philosophy of the Scottish Enlightenment. When he returned to Ireland, he found few opportunities for either ministry or teaching. He left his native land "as a poor man to the wilds of America" in hopes of imparting the new learning.[28] In America, he ministered at a church in New London, in Chester County (Pennsylvania), and also offered classes for local boys. That instruction eventually blossomed into an academy that leaned toward the antirevival side of the colonial Presbyterian church. The academy at New London lacked resources, however, and Alison relocated to Philadelphia to take an appointment at the school established by Benjamin Franklin.

Alison's lack of opportunities in his homeland was partly a function of Presbyterianism's minority rank in Ireland. For the first fourteen years of his life in Ireland (until 1719), penal laws prevented Presbyterians from observing important parts of their church's ministry. The government did not recognize marriages performed by a Presbyterian pastor. Participation in sacraments officiated by any clergy other than the Church of Ireland's priests prevented the observers from serving in government, the military, or attending university. Members of Ireland's Protestant Ascendancy (Anglican) had a monopoly on Parliament and duly protected the economic interests of the Anglo-Irish landholders. Although the Toleration Act of 1719 removed certain penalties attached to Protestant Dissenters, and though Protestants did not experience the degree and persistence of legal opposition that Roman Catholics did, Presbyterians remained second-class Protestants behind the episcopacy-based Church of Ireland.[29]

Alison likely had more reasons than Witherspoon to resent Anglicanism, but among Irish and Scottish settlers in British North America, he found the politics of the empire to be more aggravating than debates about church polity. Colonial Presbyterians saw imperial policies in North America through the prism of eighteenth-century adjustments to national churches after the Glorious Revolution. Contrary to James I's adage "no bishop, no king," by the second half of the eighteenth century, with the older challenge of an absolute monarchy subdued, Presbyterians regarded monarchy differently. In the context of American independence, the Crown looked to Presbyterians more congenial than Parliament thanks to the latter's plans for economic and political uniformity in the empire. The best hope for American Presbyterians was not a return to National Covenant but national independence.

Presbyterian Rebels Who Stayed Behind

Henry Joy McCracken (1767–98) was no Francis Alison or John Witherspoon. He was a Presbyterian in Belfast of Scottish descent. The son of Presbyterians (with some Huguenot blood), he worked in the city's textile business, as his father did, first in linen and then managing a facility that produced cotton. He was sufficiently devout to form the first Sunday school in Belfast.[30] Unlike Alison and Witherspoon, McCracken was not a minister. In fact, he devoted himself at the age of twenty-four to politics. He was among the founders of the United Irishmen, one of several expressions of reformist politics in Ireland. The failure of liberal reforms during the 1780s, which pushed for greater legislative independence for the Irish Parliament, combined with inspiration from the French Revolution and the circulation of Tom Paine's *Common Sense*, added a radical tinge to political reform in Ireland at the end of the eighteenth century. In 1791, as a prominent figure in the United Irishmen, McCracken hoped the republican organization might do for Ireland what revolution had accomplished in the United States and France.

Although initially appealing to some Irish Presbyterians, the United Irishmen also enlisted Anglicans and Roman Catholics who wanted Ireland's own Parliament to have greater power in Irish society. They also sought to have penalties against dissenting religious groups revoked. McCracken's Presbyterian colleagues in the United Irishmen included Henry Munro (1758–98) and William Drennan (1754–1820), but the list of Presbyterians in and around the Irish Rising is long. Munro's biography was similar to McCracken's. Born near Belfast in Lisburn, Munro worked in the linen trade and joined the United Irishmen four years after its initial organization. Drennan grew up in Belfast and practiced medicine after training at Edinburgh. He started in the north of Ireland before moving in 1789 to Dublin, where in addition to his practice Drennan composed poetry, including lyrics for some of the United Irishmen's most beloved songs. Munro grew up in a Presbyterian family. Drennan was the son of a Presbyterian minister. Being Presbyterian was not essential to joining the organization. It was an ecumenical effort that played on the second-class status that Roman Catholics, Presbyterians, and other dissenting Protestants experienced under British rule. But in the north, the region where the influence of seventeenth-century Scottish settlements was strongest, the United Irishmen's composition was largely Presbyterian. This explains the prominence of McCracken and Munro. The latter was, in fact, a direct descendant of Robert Monro, a highly acclaimed Scottish general who commanded troops during the Thirty Years' War under Gustavus Adolphus and then led a division of Scottish Covenanters during the Irish Confederate Wars of the 1640s.[31]

The French gave much-needed help to the Americans during their quest for independence, but by the 1790s France had different reasons for deciding whether or not to help the Irish. As early as 1793, the United Irishmen had cultivated support from the French. By then France's dominant political ideology was radically egalitarian and antimonarchist. Irish associations with the French, consequently, implied revolution rather than mere political reform. For this reason, Dublin Castle, the seat of government in Ireland, was suspicious of the United Irishmen from the beginning. Wariness turned into opposition once Theobald Wolfe Tone, a leader of the group, reached out to the French. In May 1794, the Irish government suppressed the United Irishmen. As a secret society, the Irishmen's plans escalated to outright overthrow of the government. An armed revolt, coordinated with help from France, in December 1796 failed when adverse weather conditions prevented 14,000 French soldiers from landing at Ireland's southern coast. At the time, the Irish government's efforts to infiltrate and disrupt the Irishmen were largely successful.[32]

The United Irishmen remained intent on overthrowing the government, partly in reaction to reports of brutality by Unionist forces—approximately seventy persons, suspected of belonging to the Irishmen, had been executed (half were prisoners) in or near County Wexford. Leaders planned to attack the government on May 23 and 24, 1798, first in Dublin and then in other parts of the country. The uprising in Dublin, sometimes called "The Hurry," was unsuccessful because of confused plans and execution, as the name suggested. But in Oulart, County Wexford, the Irishmen fought successfully against government militia. Encouraged by news of the battle in Wexford, Irishmen in Ulster wanted to move forward with rebellion. At a meeting of the Ulster Provincial Council in late May, members selected McCracken as their leader and made plans for an attack. A little more than a week later, McCracken led the Irishmen in the Battle of Antrim. His "spirit-stirring words" before battle and his organization of 500 men into three divisions—musketeers at the front, pikemen in the middle, and an artillery unit at the back—suggested McCracken was well suited for the uprising.[33] The initial conflict on June 7 allowed the Irishmen to commandeer the town. This success lasted only two hours, however. Superior Union forces surrounded McCracken's units, and the Irishmen disbanded. According to James Hope, a survivor in the battle, "every effort to rally on the part of McCracken was ineffectual." "Panic" set in and "the rout followed."[34] A similar fate attended Henry Munro a few days later. On June 11, he led Irishmen into battle in Ballynahinich in County Down. The rebels again had no success. According to estimates, three died and thirty were injured. Munro and his soldiers retreated. Three days later, three Orangemen found Munro under a heap of trash in a field of potatoes.[35]

The defeat of the Irishmen came with enormous consequences. For instance, if the War for American Independence had turned out differently, Witherspoon and Alison could have been tried and found guilty of treason. But McCracken and Munro did not write tracts or preach sermons. They took up arms. Worse, they lost. On June 16, 1798, after his defeat at Ballynahinich and discovery by Orangemen, Munro was tried, sentenced to death, and executed—all on the same day. Between his sentence and execution, Munro received the Lord's Supper from an Anglican priest. After the execution, Munro's body was decapitated. Authorities mounted his head on a spike in the market, where it remained for several months until Lord Bredalbane, a commander of Scottish troops stationed in Lisburn, ordered its removal. McCracken was on the loose for a month or so before informants told government authorities of his location.[36] In prison for a day, his trial took place on July 17, and he was convicted of treason. Later on the same day, a guard informed him that orders had come for his immediate execution. He met with his sister and asked for counsel from Presbyterian pastors. McCracken agreed with his sister that his death by hanging was as much a part of God's will as if he had died of natural causes.[37]

Although much more dramatic and less well known than the Presbyterian-tinged American Revolution, McCracken's and Munro's participation in the 1798 rebellion may suggest another data point of affinity between Presbyterianism and political rebellion. Still, drawing direct lines between these Protestants and the Irish Rising is a mistake, because a constellation of factors—resentment of English overlords, economic and legal obstacles, and a variety of Presbyterian traditions—did not cohere around either Irish or British politics.

Bishops in Charge (Mainly)

If Presbyterians in North America looked to Scotland for an analogy to their status within the British Empire—for example, the Union of 1707—lessons learned in Ireland should have given them pause. In the minds of Irish Protestants, mainly in the Church of Ireland (episcopal), their kingdom enjoyed all the benefits of a separate and coequal partner within the Hanoverian monarchy.[38] In addition, the British constitution with its model of a constitutional monarchy was a further indication of the benefits Ireland enjoyed within the United Kingdom. This meant that the Irish kingdom was not a British colony the way Virginia and New England were. Ireland was ideally a "complete kingdom within itself."[39] Ireland's equality to England or Scotland had its challenges. The Declaratory

Act of 1720 gave Westminster, the English Parliament, authority to interfere in Irish affairs. Ireland's Parliament enjoyed a measure of autonomy and often appealed to its ancient privileges. Those rights turned out to be largely medieval and provided rhetorical points for Irish polemicists to claim a status on a par with England's. Throughout most of the seventeenth century, Ireland's Parliament met infrequently, but after 1690 it met once every two years. The Irish Parliament was also a chief political mechanism for the "Protestant Ascendancy," a badge historians attribute to the kingdom's elite. The defeat of Roman Catholic power in Ireland during the Glorious Revolution brought with it Protestant hegemony that took root in the Irish House of Commons. This was the Parliament that passed a series of acts that destroyed Roman Catholic access to power, whether by confiscating land or by penal laws that restricted public office and the franchise to members of the Church of Ireland. The penal code was similar to England's laws that regulated Roman Catholicism.[40]

These laws point to the role that the Church of Ireland played in the Protestant Ascendancy within Irish government. They also illustrate the way that a Christendom model (with church and state as "two expressions of the same national community") appealed to Protestants as much as it did to Roman Catholics. The problem for Ireland was that the national church included only a small percentage of the population—about one-eighth of all Irish. The highest concentrations of the national church were in Dublin and plantation settlements in the north. Otherwise, Anglicans in Ireland were sparse. This was not the case in Parliament, land ownership, or the courts. Edmund Burke himself conceded that Anglicanism was "not the religion of the people of Ireland." In fact, he added, "no church, in no Country in the world, is so circumstanced."[41] After 1719, when the Toleration Act removed some penalties against Protestant dissenters (chiefly Presbyterians), the Church of Ireland lost some of its hold on the Protestant Ascendancy. Landed elites and the monarchy viewed the church as the weakest part of Ireland's establishment. Ireland's national church, rather than integrating national identity as Anglicanism did in England, represented increasingly an alien and privileged presence. At the same time, Anglicanism was present in most public institutions and gatherings. Clergy presided at national or royal anniversaries, priests dominated intellectual life, and the Church of Ireland controlled the mechanisms of welfare and education.

The Rising of 1798 emerged from a general opposition among Irish people against the Protestant Ascendancy, but Presbyterians themselves were not sufficiently unified to qualify as the most important influence on the Rising. They were divided into four groups: (1) the oldest, aggregated within the Synod of Ulster, drew upon Presbyterians who after the Glorious Revolution began to distinguish themselves from Anglicans; (2) refusing subscription to the Westminster Confession was a major factor in creating a second Irish Presbyterian body, the Presbytery of Antrim (1725); (3) Scots coming to Ireland, who carried with them loyalties from seventeenth-century Scottish church politics, accounted for a third group, but these wound up as separate communions—either Seceder or Reformed Presbyterian (Covenanter); (4) one last group of Irish Presbyterians was the Southern Association, a loose affiliation that claimed congregations outside Ulster, primarily located around Dublin. Estimates of Presbyterian membership across all the communions ran close to 600,000. This gave Presbyterianism roughly 15 percent of Ireland's 4 million people.[42]

Whatever differences may have existed among these Presbyterian groups politically, most Irish people—Anglican, Presbyterian, and at least elite Roman Catholics—supported political reform in the 1770s. One factor was a capacity to manage Ireland's economy in ways that were more congenial at least to Irish landowners and businessmen. One way to achieve this was through Irish representation in London at Britain's Parliament. Ireland's support for Britain during its war with the American colonies—by raising volunteer militias to protect the country from the French—was a signal that gave Parliament room to reinstate an Irish Parliament in Dublin. The British constitution demanded that those within the Union secure necessary rights for their political and economic well-being. In 1783, the British Parliament passed the Renunciation Act, which gave the Irish Parliament power to legislate its local affairs. For reformers and patriots, this milestone appeared to give Ireland all the benefits secured in the Glorious Revolution of 1688.[43]

That success was short-lived. The incorporation of Quebec into the British Empire with the Quebec Act of 1774, for instance, raised questions about Roman Catholics' place in an independent Ireland. Meanwhile, Ireland's legislative independence could not break the Protestant Ascendancy's control of Irish affairs. Once the French Revolution started,

France became an inspiration to Irish radicals who sought complete independence from Britain. At their founding in 1791, the United Irishmen ran in channels of liberal reform by supporting an Irish Parliament. The appeal of the American and French Revolutions, however, coupled with a Roman Catholic population and paramilitary groups with plans for armed insurrection prompted the Irishmen's radicalism. Underground revolutionary forces numbered as many as 280,000, and the Irish government determined to crush it. Armed skirmishes began in 1796 and ended in 1798 when French ships stalled in high winds at Bantry Bay and left Irishmen leaders, such as McCracken and Munro, to suffer defeat and face execution for their participation in the Rebellion of 1798.[44]

Presbyterian support for reform and ultimately rebellion (where it radicalized) tapped religious sources as much as wider currents in British politics. One argument generally unavailable to Irish Presbyterian patriots was an appeal to Britain's ancient constitution. For Presbyterians, that theoretical path led awkwardly to bishops and ecclesiastical hierarchy. In contrast, republican opposition to arbitrary central government, fears of corruption, and promotion of religious toleration were more congenial to Presbyterian purposes. It also helped that these ideas were available at Scottish universities where Irish pastors invariably trained. One further link was the work of a native Irishman, from Armagh to be precise, Frances Hutcheson, whose instruction in moral philosophy at the University of Glasgow provided some of the intellectual foundation for republicanism.[45] Although defenders of the monarchy and Anglicanism invariably saw Presbyterianism as socially subversive and doctrinally intolerant, the basic contours of Presbyterian church government did encourage hostility to hierarchy in church and society. Between affirmations of the congregation's rights in calling a pastor and assertions of Christ's headship over the church, Presbyterians were instinctively predisposed to point out the abuses and errors of bishops and monarchs.

Because of Presbyterianism's association with civil war and regicide (fair or not), Irish Presbyterians always needed to be circumspect when challenging the Protestant Ascendancy. At least, this was the case for the Ulster Synod, which ministered in respectable middle-class commercial society.[46] For the Covenanters and Seceders, support for rebellion, where it existed, appealed to precedents in Scottish church history. The Covenanters were disproportionately more involved with rebellion than any other Presbyterian body (at least among pastors). A high regard for popular sovereignty as a kind of divine-right populism was one factor. God had, according to this view, instituted government, and its source of legitimacy came from popular consent. Echoes of the English Civil War's millennialism encouraged Irish Covenanters to interpret the French Revolution as the final stage of the age-old battle against the Antichrist (the Roman Church). The abolition of the ancien régime and the corrupting influence of religious establishment would finally usher in the rule of Christ. Irish Covenanters still affirmed the Solemn League and Covenant and saw no contradiction between the seventeenth-century ideal of a Presbyterian religious establishment and their hopes for disentangling church and state.[47]

For Seceders, a path to rebellion was arguably even more convoluted than that of the Covenanters. A later exit from the Church of Scotland in 1732 did not allow Seceders to claim the merits of Scotland's National Covenants. Some Seceders supported rebellion. But the reasons often invoked the ideals and millennial associations of the French Revolution as much as the Scottish Reformation's pursuit of Christ's lordship over church and society. For other Seceders, the politics of rebellion prompted a turn away from reforming society to cultivating personal devotion.[48] Ian McBride observes that what was true for Irish Presbyterians was no less the case for Seceders (and for Covenanters): radicalism was the product of a kaleidoscope of influences: "theological inheritance, social factors, and political circumstances." Above all, "exclusion from the institutions of state" bred antagonism to the Anglican Ascendancy and the British government that upheld it.[49]

Belief and Rebellion

Between the time when Henry Joy McCracken received his death sentence and his execution, he asked to see Sinclare Kelburn, his pastor at the Third Presbyterian Congregation on Rosemary Street in Belfast, where the McCracken family were members. Kelburn was unwell, and so the convict's sister recommended William Steele Dickson, a Presbyterian pastor from Portaferry, who was in Belfast (roughly thirty miles away) in the aftermath of the rebellion. McCracken's ties to these two pastors, both New Light Presbyterians, could well suggest an affinity between this strain of Protestantism and the rebellion. That implication leans heavily on New Light Presbyterianism's opposition to creedal subscription. And yet that deviation from Presbyterian convention was hardly radical. New Light Presbyterians appealed to middle-class and respectable parts of Ulster society, where finding a moderate form of Protestantism was more congenial than following the demands of either Scotland's National Covenant or Irish republicanism.

New Lights remained respectable throughout the eighteenth century and were still part of the Synod of Ulster. Kelburn and Dickson may have had their critics, but they hardly labored on the fringes of Irish Presbyterianism. The moderation of New Light Presbyterianism may account for its ties to the United Irishmen, even if radicalism seems to go hand in hand with rebellion. Kelburn, for instance, delivered a series of sermons during the years of political tumult, published as *The Divinity of Our Lord Jesus Christ Asserted and Proved* (1795) by a Philadelphia printer. An American Presbyterian pastor, John B. Smith, welcomed Kelburn's sermons as a refutation of Joseph Priestly's unorthodox Christology. Another example of New Light moderation comes from Dickson's collection of sermons, published in 1817 in Belfast, that prioritized morality over doctrine. The title of one sermon, "The Goodness, Truth, and Mercy of God, the Foundations of Public and Private Thanksgiving," captured the Anglo-American Protestant equation of theism with public order and stable government. Even if Dickson were straying from the Westminster Confession's doctrine, he maintained the Westminster Assembly's practice of singing psalms in worship. He may have included some hymns, but was closer to old Presbyterian worship habits than many of his orthodox peers in the United States. His 1792 book, *Psalmody*, argued that Irish Presbyterians, who had only twelve tunes available in their Psalter, needed to emulate the Covenanters, who had 140 melodies for congregational song.[50] New Light ministers may have favored innovation in theology and worship, but their modifications in religious life were hardly radical.

If New Light Presbyterians differed from Covenanters and Seceders, their stance resembled more the Church of Scotland than any radical form of Protestantism. Andrew R. Holmes argues, in fact, that New Light Presbyterians were "the embodiment of Enlightenment sensibilities," like those dominant in the Church of Scotland.[51] Their primary traits were a good rhetorical style in the pulpit, stressing morality over doctrine, and the value of natural theology (truths revealed apart from scripture). According to Holmes, New Light preaching "exalted reason over revelation, the benevolence of God the Father overshadowing the person and work of Christ, the duty of submission to the divine will replacing the need for faith and repentance."[52] This was precisely the sort of polite religion that the Popular Party in the Church of Scotland, of which John Witherspoon had been a member, opposed. For conservatives, moderate Presbyterianism rounded off the edges that had characterized Reformed Protestantism's quest to reform church and society. Common sense and good taste in religion may have fit well with a rejection of the tired hierarchies of Ireland's Anglican establishment. But it provided few arguments for armed rebellion.

In other words, New Light Presbyterians' profile was some distance from the quip by A. T. Q. Stewart, a historian of Presbyterian political radicalism, that a Presbyterian is "happiest when he is being a radical."[53] That line may have described the Covenanters in opposition to the Stuart monarchs, but it did not capture United Irishmen such as McCracken. His sister's description of his last hours included religious ideals straight from the warm and reasonable piety of New Light pastors. Mary Ann McCracken described her brother's motivation in remarkably pious terms. The form of religion necessary for social "regeneration" was no less than "to do to others as we would wish others to do to us; to do no evil that good may come of it; . . . to be guided by the parable of the good Samaritan, to consider all who are within reach of our kindness as our neighbours, however they may differ from us in our religious belief."[54] In a letter to his sister, McCracken himself had used similarly simple terms, but with less direct piety: "These are the times that try men's souls. You will no doubt hear a great number of stories respecting the situation of this country: its present unfortunate state is entirely owing to treachery. The rich always betray the poor."[55]

This was not the language of Presbyterian politics, whether moderate, Covenanter, or Seceder, no matter its New Testament resonance. It was, however, Ian McBride argues, much more the outworking of Jacobin ideas that became popular during the 1790s thanks to the millennial hopes inspired by the French Revolution and the rights-based language of writers such as Thomas Paine. That was a time that encouraged ordinary people to think for themselves, even if they were also echoing ideas that cast the world in the simple dichotomies of rich and poor, elites and commoners, hierarchy and equality. The Presbyterian aspects of the 1798 Irish Rising were distinct from the procedures and petitions of American Presbyterians and the covenant theology of 1640s London. In fact, compared to either the American or English revolutions, the Irish version was an aftershock to rebellions more noticeably Presbyterian.

From Ireland to the United States

It is tempting to link Presbyterian participation in the American Revolution and the Irish Rising to the old Reformed Protestant ideals of a John Knox or Samuel Rutherford, but the late eighteenth-century upheavals in Ireland and North America appealed not to a common theology but to distinctly political discontents influenced by piety. American Presbyterians belonged to a prosperous society that benefited from Britain's benign neglect of its North American holdings. They had also experienced church life under voluntarism in the middle colonies, and saw no need for an ecclesiastical establishment to operate a communion in a diversely Christian society. In Ireland, the situation was significantly different. Economically, Presbyterians in the north were better off than the Irish in agricultural settings where laws and soil made farming difficult. As Protestant dissenters, Irish Presbyterians were also outside looking in at the institutions—legal, civil, educational—that the Protestant Ascendancy controlled. Unlike American Presbyterians who did not share a common Scottish ancestry, Irish Presbyterians evoked memories and ideals of Scottish church history that were nearer in time, geography, politics, and church life for Ireland than for America's thirteen colonies (turned states). For these reasons, not only were the Irish Rising and the American Revolution several steps removed from mid-seventeenth-century political upheavals in England and Scotland, but they were also markedly different from each other, despite common aspirations of republicanism and political independence.

An illustration of this difference comes from the case of Thomas Ledlie Birch, a radical Presbyterian pastor from Saintfield, County Down.

The son of a middle-class home, Birch graduated in 1775 from Glasgow University, where he belonged to debating clubs and aligned with American Patriots. He later penned a letter (1784) to George Washington on behalf of the Masonic Lodge to which Birch belonged. In it, he congratulated the American general on winning his war against the British. The Saintfield pastor belonged to the Presbytery of Belfast and attended the Synod of Ulster. Contemporaries regarded him as orthodox, if only because he supported subscription to the Westminster Confession and opposed Arianism of the New Lights.

Determining whether theology drove politics or vice versa was often a challenge in Birch's career, however. When during America's War for Independence, Ireland needed militia to replace British soldiers sent to North America, Birch became a captain of the Saintfield branch of Volunteers. In 1792, he formed a local society of the United Irishmen. The millenarian aspect of his radical politics came out in full force in a 1793 sermon preached before the Synod of Ulster. Here he interpreted the French Revolution as an era of light and truth that was finally overcoming the unholy Constantinian alliance of church and state. Losing members from his congregation did not deter Birch from his embrace of radical politics and Roman Catholic relief. He preached against monarchy, landlords, episcopacy, and English rule. Despite being arrested for high treason in 1797—acquitted in part because a witness for the prosecution was assassinated—Birch continued to agitate against British rule. In April 1798, local members of the United Irishmen elected him captain. On the eve of the uprising in June, he preached a sermon that exhorted his company to "drive the bloodhounds of King George the German king beyond the seas. This is Ireland, we are Irish, and we shall be free."[56] For his words and efforts, authorities arrested and brought Birch to trial in late June. Thanks to the efforts of his brother, George, a loyalist and friend of Lord Castlereagh, Birch's life was spared on the condition that he go into exile.

In September 1798, Birch sailed to New York and soon migrated to the town of Washington in western Pennsylvania where other exiles from Saintfield had settled. He adapted his millenarian beliefs to his new country and began referring to the United States as the fulfillment of biblical prophecy. He hoped that the town of Washington would become the foundation for building a Christian republic that would in turn inaugurate the kingdom of God.

Although some Presbyterians on the frontier shared Birch's politics and doctrine and were inclined to vote for Thomas Jefferson's Democratic-Republican Party, the official outlets of the American Presbyterian church, closer to Witherspoon and Alison, aligned with the Federalist Party. That division was partly responsible for the Presbytery of Ohio's rejection of Birch's 1801 petition to become a member. The matter did not stop there or then. For two more years, Birch appealed to both the Presbytery of Ohio and the General Assembly. In 1803, the higher judicatory upheld the rulings of Ohio. Part of the difficulty Birch faced, aside from his own mercurial temperament, was his opposition to the revivals that were then spreading among Presbyterians from Kentucky to western Pennsylvania and Ohio. The chief opponent to Birch was John McMillan, a prominent figure in the presbytery and a strong advocate of the awakenings. Birch struck McMillan not only as a political firebrand but also a morally dubious character—witnesses reported instances of the Irishman's drunkenness.[57] After a decade, American Presbyterians finally resolved Birch's predicament. They upheld the Presbytery of Baltimore's 1810 approval of the pastor as a member even while allowing him to minister outside the boundaries of the Maryland presbytery. To obtain this resolution, Birch needed to acknowledge and apologize for his errors in ways similar to his previous renunciation of treason in Ireland. Birch lived until 1828, but after 1815 had ceased to be a controversial American Presbyterian.

Birch's rough ride in the American church reflected a mismatch between Presbyterian rebellions in Ireland and the United States. Even if the revivals on the American frontier leaned toward egalitarian social arrangements, its leaders, such as McMillan, were politically conservative. David Wilson argues that Birch's combination of "religious conservatism with political radicalism" made him one of the "aliens" that the Alien and Sedition Acts (1798) were designed to silence. In contrast, Birch's nemesis, McMillan, "was firmly aligned with the Federalists" and a strong supporter of officials responsible for 1798 laws to restrict immigrants and their influence. McMillan used Birch's involvement in the Irish Rising to discredit the immigrant pastor and condemned his congregation as "followers of Tom Paine."[58] Although Birch always conceived of the Irish and American rebellions as part of a common millenarian struggle of political and spiritual liberty against the tyranny of royal supremacy and priestcraft, his experience in America revealed the degree to which Irish and American Presbyterians were politically out of sync. Wilson puts it well when he writes that Birch's "political radicalism and his theological conservatism were deeply rooted in the northern Irish Presbyterian culture," as were his combination of millenarian and "secular hopes" for revolutionary change. By the time of the 1798 Rising and Birch's exile to America, Presbyterians in the United States were content to work within the nation's major political parties and expand the church's influence in church planting and higher education. The Presbyterianism of the Irish Rising, consequently, "combined and clashed" with the politics of American Presbyterians in their support of political independence.[59]

If Birch's beliefs and politics did not align with American Presbyterians, who had opposed British tyranny on the way to supporting a federal republic, neither did late eighteenth-century Irish or American Presbyterians value the politics of the Scottish National Covenants. On the other side of the Glorious Revolution and the Union of England and Scotland, the politics of Presbyterians depended more on local circumstances than on the ideal of church reforms supported by a godly government and backed by a devout people.

CHAPTER 6

Presbyterianism after Establishment

Instead of the American War for Independence emerging from Presbyterians' cussed quest for a Reformed church and society, the political struggle in the British Empire actually drew a mixed reaction from John Calvin's and John Knox's followers. In Scotland, especially, the leadership of the established church was divided by nonreligious factors that ranged from economics to the new science of politics associated with the Scottish Enlightenment. According to Dalphy I. Fagerstrom, the "sharpest division" in Scottish society over the American Revolution was in the Kirk.[1] The split broke down according to the Moderate and Evangelical Parties. The latter failed to form a consensus. John Erskine, a minister most widely known as an American sympathizer, wrote the pamphlet *Shall I Go to War with My American Brethren?*, published first in 1769 and republished seven years later in time for the Declaration of Independence. This was not a full-throated defense of republicanism. In fact, Erskine objected to some of the excesses of colonial arguments. But the Edinburgh minister recognized the legitimacy of the colonists' defense of their British rights, fear of an American bishop, and London's tolerance of Roman Catholics in Quebec. Fast-day sermons from Evangelical pastors told worshipers that the political crisis was a sign of divine judgment for Britain's religious and moral declension.[2]

In contrast, Moderates in the Kirk eschewed associations with republicanism and even insinuated that Evangelicals were little more than Wilkites (disciples of the radical and indiscreet journalist and member of Parliament John Wilkes)—that is, "enemies to government" and "fomenters of the rebellion in America."[3] In pamphlet literature, critics of Evangelicals observed that ministers failed to pray for the king and asked instead for God's blessing on American success. Among other charges was the complaint that some Evangelical pastors heeded American calls for during the War of Independence.

At the General Assembly of 1776, surface support for the British government obscured the subtext of mixed reactions to the American war. The official results showed that commissioners unanimously approved a statement of loyalty to the Crown from the lord high commissioner. Subsequent reports indicated that some commissioners felt their support was coerced, especially if a negative vote was interpreted as sympathy for the American rebellion. In addition, several ministers, with reservations about Scotland's place in the United Kingdom and the Kirk's status within the British political establishment, pinned their own hopes for reform on the possibilities opened by the American cause. At the General Assembly of 1782, ministers had second thoughts about endorsing yet another formal statement of loyalty. These pastors also expressed a desire for the government to include the voices of the Scottish people in "constitutional arrangements."[4]

Scottish responses to North America were part of larger questions about church–state relations. The issue of patronage, a constant in Scottish church history, had arisen again and may have been a factor in shaping perceptions within the Kirk of the American struggle for independence. Fagerstrom observes that during the late 1770s, church officials feared that Evangelicals "would seize the opportunity to express radical and republican sentiments." The reason was that American independence was more appealing to "the Presbyterians of Scotland than any other Rebellion."[5] Whether or not these worries were plausible, Scottish officials did keep London apprised of the situation. Overall, Scottish debates about America corresponded to objections to patronage in the Kirk. Evangelicals, the party most critical of the place of elites and government in selecting parish pastors, were the most inclined to see the American colonies' political ideals in a favorable light. Fagerstrom highlights in particular a change of rhetoric among Evangelicals during this period. In contrast to what had been an appeal to the divine right of the people in the choice of their pastor, pamphlet literature during the 1780s against patronage began to employ the language of natural rights.

One of the Kirk's Evangelical pastors who sympathized with the Americans was Charles Nisbet, a minister in Montrose (part of the presbytery of Edinburgh) who eventually migrated to Carlisle, Pennsylvania, to preside over a fledgling academic institution, Dickinson College. During the initial battles of the American war, Nisbet had preached a sermon, while still in Scotland, about the destruction of the Babylonian Empire that offended some but also made him attractive to college officials in Pennsylvania. Nisbet warned about the instability of empires built on violence and the shedding of innocent blood. His background was mixed. Nisbet was the son of a poor Scottish schoolmaster and a university graduate (Edinburgh). His politics in Scotland were also a mix of opposition to the wealthy Scottish merchants for exploiting the poor and comfortable interaction with lords and ladies from the nation's upper echelons. Those social skills were similar to ones he would need in America since, in its initial republican phase, the United States was more aristocratic than the democratic society that emerged in the 1820s. Nisbet himself feared democracy and worried that egalitarianism would lead to anarchy.[6] Once settled in Carlisle, he continued to fret that the new nation was not producing the sort of public men who could form and maintain good government.

One issue that did not appear to concern Nisbet before he moved to America was the lack of an ecclesiastical establishment. The congregation in Pennsylvania that he joined and where he sometimes preached had experienced the antagonisms of the First Great Awakening that split Presbyterians into Old Side and New Side camps. But neither of those branches of the colonial church expressed any particular affinity for a state church. In addition, by the time of Nisbet's move, American Presbyterians were in the initial stages of revising the Westminster Confession to make it compatible with freedom of religion and ecclesiastical disestablishment. Nisbet's America was moving toward an official embrace of voluntaryism, which placed all religious groups on a par and required them to find their own means of support and mechanisms of oversight—all independent of the civil authority.

Nisbet had reservations, however, about a voluntary church. As he observed the new nation's political dynamics, he worried about more than the mere dangers of populism or America's capacity to cultivate political elites who could put aside self-interest in pursuit of the common good. He fretted about what would become of a nation without an established church. Although Nisbet generally supported the new Constitution of 1787, he faulted the Constitutional Convention for not providing public support of religion. On the one hand, Nisbet was not confident that the people on their own would support Protestant ministers. On the other, he argued that civil laws were insufficient to nurture a stable society without the help of religion: "Regard of Man" depended on "fear of God," he wrote to a friend.[7]

Nisbet's dilemma was emblematic of a concern among Presbyterians about church life without the civil magistrate's support and defense. How much help did the church need from the civil magistrate, if only to show that religion was important to the life of the nation? On the flip side, how much more dignified or noble could civil government be without the blessing of an established church? As much as Presbyterians had always insisted on the spiritual independence of the church, they had also supported religious establishment. Whether on the grounds of National Covenants or the general ethos of Christendom, Presbyterians were reluctant to abandon the benefits that came from political authorities endorsing the Christian faith. At the same time, they were hardly reluctant to complain when public authorities meddled in the church's affairs. Patronage was the ever-present reminder that the church lacked the spiritual independence Presbyterians idealized. The Presbyterian hope for autonomy over ecclesiastical affairs, consequently, was never far from a recognition that voluntarism was a remedy to the church's entanglement with civil authorities. Yet, as Nisbet himself was aware, venturing into the unknown world of complete ecclesiastical independence, and the undesirable reality of having no more social standing than even Baptists or Methodists, was a bridge that few Presbyterians at the end of the eighteenth century were prepared to cross. Sixty years later, as Presbyterians in Scotland, England, and the United States reassessed relations to their respective national governments, many came to see that disestablishment and voluntarism were the best paths to church reform.

From "Hot" to Moderate

If Presbyterians initially had a reputation for political rabble-rousing, by the end of the eighteenth century descendants of Calvin, Knox, and Melville had become respectable and bland. The Church of Scotland on the eve of the nineteenth century was characteristically balanced about its place in the kingdom's established order. This was partly the fruit of the Moderate Party's dominance within the General Assembly, even as Evangelicals (i.e., those devoted generally to the theology of the Westminster Assembly) hoped for greater zeal within the church and more holiness in Scottish society. Reactions to the French Revolution and the church's role in academic appointments took the temperature of the Scottish church at the turn of the nineteenth century.

"Everything rung, and was connected with the Revolution in France," Henry Cockburn, later the solicitor general for Scotland between 1830 and 1834, recalled about his youth. "Everything . . . literally everything was soaked in this one event."[8] Scottish Presbyterians may have purged revolution from their system 150 years earlier than their Irish and American cousins, but France's reproach to the old European order still stirred some Scots to question their own version of throne and altar (or pulpit) politics. According to Emma Vincent, the number of newspapers in Scotland between 1782 and 1790 increased by 400 percent (from eight to twenty-seven).Thomas Paine's *The Rights of Man* circulated as widely as Scots planted trees of liberty. In 1792, political riots broke out in Lanark, Aberdeen, Perth, Dundee, and Peebles. An Edinburgh demonstration planned to coincide with the king's birthday as a show of loyalty turned into another riot to protest the British government. About these developments, Church of Scotland minister Thomas Somerville later wrote, "The safety of all surrounding nations was at stake. The very existence of civil society was in danger."[9]

Gone were the days when Presbyterians sought to bring the church and society into conformity with God's word. Instead, the Church of Scotland firmly supported the political establishment and many of its ministers preached against the French Revolution in terms that reflected their approval of the status quo. In a study of Scottish preaching during the 1790s, Vincent identifies three main themes. The first was divine sovereignty and providence. God's control of all things was an indication of the superiority of the British constitution over against republican competitors, whether in America or France.[10] The implication here for subjects of the king, as ministers explained, was to carry out duties rather than assert rights. It went without saying, though many said it, that mobs and riots were at odds with the subjection to governing authorities taught in scripture. The error of protest was part of the second theme of Scottish preaching, namely, the evil consequences that befell national sins. Social and economic upheaval did not justify political change but instead reflected divine judgment upon a disobedient people.[11] This left a call for national repentance as the sermons' third dominant theme. Such appeals made hasty references to Old Testament prophets who admonished Israelites to walk in the ways of their covenant with Yahweh. The consensus among Church of Scotland ministers gave the 1794 General Assembly room to send a letter to George III that assured him "that the sound principles of loyalty, and of attachment to the Constitution in Church and State, are fixed in the hearts of the great body of Your Majesty's subjects in Scotland." They were also ideals that the Kirk promised through "our most zealous care" to "cherish" and "promote."[12]

The Kirk's stature in Scottish society had taken at least a century to cohere. After seeing wings of Presbyterianism still committed to the politics and theology of the National Covenants form separate communions (the Covenanters and the Associate Presbytery), and after weathering the challenges of ministers and laity awakened by the likes of George Whitefield, the Church of Scotland was largely content in its assigned station. The nature of church government was aptly orderly and reassuring as summarized in the so-called Moderate Manifesto of 1752. In questions about how to resolve the protests of ministers, congregations, or presbyteries against rulings of the General Assembly, Moderates recommended not the righteous zeal of biblical prophets but the path of balance, order, and decorum. These Presbyterians insisted that the church was a society in which members needed to heed the "judgment of the society." It followed that a united society provided many more benefits than a "disunited" one. For that reason, "regulations for public order" needed to come not from the "fancy" of private individuals but the "judgment of the majority" expressed within the legislative component of the society. This did not mean that everyone in the church thought the same way. It did mean, however, that as long as someone, especially ministers, continued to enjoy emoluments and status by virtue of religious establishment, they needed to follow society's norms. To do otherwise was to be guilty of "disorderliness" and "dishonesty."[13]

This Moderate Manifesto was the embodiment of the Moderate Party's theology, which, according to Stewart J. Brown, originated from an effort to adapt the Kirk's ministry to Scotland's elites. On the one hand, this outlook generally aligned with the direction of the Scottish Enlightenment. Moderates were often friends with thinkers such as David Hume and Lord Kames, and pastors "shielded" philosophers "from censure by the Church courts."[14] Such receptiveness to new ideas included approval of toleration, freedom of inquiry, moderation, virtue, polite manners, and optimism about the future (or belief in progress). On the other hand, this embrace of moderation brought skepticism about superstition and religious enthusiasm. Without identifying the National Covenants or the Westminster Confession as examples of religious extremism, the Moderates overwhelmingly lost touch with the theology and politics that had inspired ardent Presbyterians between 1570 and 1660.

The contrast between the Church of Scotland in 1650 and its successor in 1760 is remarkable. The earlier iteration of the Kirk had envisioned a covenanted society in which the Crown, church, and people sought further reformation in ecclesiastical and civil institutions for the sake of God's glory and the people's edification. The Kirk of the Moderates also contended for an integrated society with church and state cooperating to cultivate a Christian nation. But the Enlightened version replaced scripture's covenants and Reformed Protestant convictions about godliness with the virtues and reasonableness of the new sciences of politics, economics, and morality. Brown states that Scottish Moderates emphasized "Christian moral culture" by appealing to an "innate" moral sense that checked bodily passions, and a godly society that was the outworking of divine benevolence in both the natural order and human interactions.[15]

The Moderate Manifesto of 1752 made sense of Presbyterianism for an enlightened Scotland. The old idea of Christ as the head of the church, in contrast to the Crown, resurfaced. But for Moderates this conviction applied to all Protestants. The "characters which we bear," as officers of the Church of Scotland, made it unnecessary to acknowledge that Jesus Christ is "the only King and Head of His Church."[16] For added emphasis, the headship of Christ, the Manifesto explained, meant that the church was no mere voluntary society but a body formed by the "laws of Christ." Moderates wanted to uphold the rights of liberty of conscience but not to the point of allowing officers to appeal to the laws of Christ over against the external administration of the church. Liberty of conscience employed to overturn the oversight even of fallible men was the equivalent of the "most extravagant maxims of Independency" and an assault on "that happy ecclesiastical constitution which we glory in being members of."[17] The need for uniformity and good order also required the church to have common standards for doctrine, worship, and government. For that reason, the Manifesto stipulated that every minister and elder in the church should "acknowledge and subscribe our *Confession of Faith*." Anyone who "departed from or denied the *form of sound words* therein contained" became liable to the censure of the church.[18] For those wondering how the Confession of Faith harmonized with Enlightenment philosophy, the obvious answer came by maintaining a stable social order.

George Hill, one of the most influential figures in the Moderate Party, enunciated aptly the adjustments that Scottish Presbyterians made to life in the emerging world of reason, tolerance, and social order. The son of a minister in St. Andrews, Hill's life never strayed far from the Kirk's presence in that university town. He studied at St. Andrews, preached at one of the city's parishes, taught Greek at the United College of the university and then divinity at St. Mary's College at the University of St. Andrews. He was one of the founders of the Royal Society of Edinburgh and served as the moderator of the General Assembly in 1789. His book on Presbyterian polity, not often mentioned among his most important works, was another window into how far removed the moderate understanding of the Kirk was from sixteenth- and seventeenth-century proposals. Hill republished the material on church polity as a separate title, *A View of the Constitution of the Church of Scotland* (1817), originally the second in a three-volume set of lectures on theology (1803). In it, he explained, the Kirk's place within the Scottish establishment.

Arguably, the most telling part of Hill's book came in a chapter on Presbyterianism's basic principles. Although many previous defenders of Presbyterianism said little about the importance of elders (lay officers invested with the power of oversight), because the goal was to replace bishops with councils or assemblies, Hill used Enlightenment confidence in human abilities to recommend a church government dominated by elders. He conceded that if Kirk sessions included "mean unlearned men," then they would inevitably bring an "unwise, illiberal, and violent spirit into the church's government." But under instruction from a learned pastor, elders promised a form of church polity "better calculated to conciliate the respect and good will of the people, to restrain their vices, and to minister to their improvement."[19] Hill painted this picture before invoking Presbyterians' favorite biblical passage—the Council of Jerusalem in Acts 15. This was convenient on Hill's part because the elders who gathered in first-century Palestine were not products of a polite society, as was the case at St. Andrews or in Edinburgh.

Such anachronistic juggling persisted when Hill distanced the Kirk from the divine-right Presbyterianism of seventeenth-century Scotland. He did, of course, acknowledge the bravery and suffering that his Scottish forebears exhibited. At the same time, "the progress of science and good government" had "exploded the horrid practice of persecution for conscience's sake."[20] That same intellectual advance allowed Presbyterians to use "more liberal" justifications for their form of church government. That opening let Hill invoke, of all people, Richard Hooker, the great sixteenth-century Anglican theological slayer of Presbyterians. Hill read Hooker to argue that the New Testament did not require one particular form of church polity. A careful reading showed that the apostles set up churches with varying polities depending on local circumstances.[21] The same principle applied to Scotland. Presbyterianism was the best form of government for the nation because it was "agreeable" to the Scottish people, who typically held "liberal sentiments."[22] Hill was willing to trace Presbyterian polity to scripture. Still, what made Presbyterianism thrive in Scotland was a group of ministers who were accountable to each other in "our general conduct, and our attainments in literature." These were the means by which to "maintain the honor of that dignified station" possessed by the Church of Scotland.[23]

Attempts to bridge older Presbyterian convictions with contemporary notions of good taste were partly responsible for the ridicule that the Moderates' received from their Evangelical opponents. In 1753 before he left for North America, John Witherspoon penned a satire of Moderates. Then a Church of Scotland minister in Beith, Witherspoon's *Ecclesiastical Characteristics* was published a year after the Moderates gained control of the General Assembly. He characterized the majority of pastors by their "Athenian Creed":

> I believe in the beauty and comely proportions of Dame Nature, and in Almighty Fate, her only parent and guardian . . .
> I believe that the Universe is a huge machine, wound up from everlasting, and consisting of an infinite number of links and chains . . .
> I believe that there is no ill in the Universe . . . that those things vulgarly called *sins* are only *errors* in judgment, and foils to set off the beauty of Nature . . .
> In fine, I believe in the divinity of Lord Shaftesbury, the saintship of Marcus Antoninus, the perspicuity of Aristotle, and the perpetual duration of Mr Hutcheson's works . . . Amen.[24]

Witherspoon may have deflated the aspirations among Presbyterians for enlightened respectability, but by the time of his death in 1794, almost four decades later, the Moderate Party was still dominant in the Church of Scotland.

Yet, debates surrounding the French Revolution's aftermath created spaces for discontent among the Moderates' opponents, the Popular Party. To observers, the Kirk may have looked like it was "saddled with the Westminster Confession," according to Andrew L. Drummond and James Bulloch, and unable to move into new fields of thought and ministry. But the challenge to historic hierarchies in Europe spawned by the French Revolution, whether Protestant or Roman Catholic, was also a threat to Scotland's political and religious establishment. The Kirk's ties to the government relied on Henry Dundas, the most formidable Scottish politician between 1775 and 1810 and lieutenant for Scotland to British prime minister, William Pitt. Dundas's so-called despotism could damage the Kirk's reputation because his administration relied heavily on patronage. David J. Brown observes that Dundas's system allowed MPs, if loyal, to nominate most posts in his constituency, including church appointments.[25] In fact, according to Drummond and Bulloch, after 1782, a congregation's participation in signing the call of a minister had become merely "a formality."[26] A patron nominated a minister for a congregation and the presbytery inducted the nominee, while church members' participation in the call, the middle piece in the sequence, dwindled to an inconsequential step in bureaucratic process. This arrangement provided the Kirk with security. But in the wider political context of securing rights to citizens and subjects, the Church of Scotland looked increasingly aristocratic and remote from the lives of ordinary people.

This perception spread in an unlikely way during the early days of foreign missions. Linking the French Revolution to the rise of Protestant agencies for the support of evangelism overseas among indigenous peoples seems strange on the surface. To be sure, earlier examples of missions, especially in the English-speaking world, came from the peculiar circumstances of European colonists settling near native populations. Before the 1790s, however, missionary efforts were local and happenstance. What changed at the end of the eighteenth century was the formation of missionary societies, some the result of denominations, others interdenominational, under lay leadership. In the case of Robert Haldane, the hopes for an age of spiritual and social progress, prompted by France's promise of a new age, were incentives to Protestant hopes for extending Christianity around the world. A graduate of the University of Edinburgh, who converted in his early twenties in 1795, Haldane's hopes for a mission to Bengal ran up against the ecclesiastical and political status quo within the Kirk. Presbyterians opposition to Haldane stemmed from fears of French radicalism. Haldane tried but failed to assure Scottish authorities that his mission, set up with lay ministers such as himself, reinforced Presbyterian church order.[27]

Haldane may not have been his own best advocate since he and his brother relied on training lay pastors (one estimate was as many as 200),[28] encouraging the formation of Congregational churches in Scotland, and questioning the Kirk's ministers' orthodoxy. Once the General Assembly turned the Haldanes down, the brothers looked to nondenominational missionary societies in England and the Netherlands. The General Assembly did not merely reject the proposal but also warned against an autonomous Christian ministry:

> There have arisen among us a set of men whose proceedings threaten no small disorder to the country. They assume the name of missionaries, as if they had some special commission from heaven: they are going through the land as universal itinerant teachers, and as superintendents of the ministers of religion; they are introducing themselves into parishes, without any call, and erecting in places Sunday

> Schools without any countenance from the Presbytery of the bounds or the minister of the parish; they are committing in these schools the religious instruction of youth to ignorant persons, altogether unfit for such an important charge; and they are studying to alienate the affections of the people from their pastor, and engaging them to join their new sect, as if they alone were possessed of some secret and novel method of bringing men to heaven.[29]

The Church of Scotland's investment in the existing political order stood in marked contrast to the sometime radical provocations that earlier generations of Presbyterians used when confronting bishops and unfaithful monarchs.

If Scotland's religious establishment rejected the Haldanes' populism, the Kirk's alliance with Scottish universities was further evidence of Presbyterianism's membership within the establishment. Ties between the church and universities had always been close. The medieval church was largely responsible for creating Europe's academic institutions, and Protestants did little to challenge relations between church and academy. By the late eighteenth century, the church's involvement in the life of Scottish universities was still pronounced. Most professors were clergy, and many of the students, though small in numbers, were training to be ministers.

Aside from the religious skepticism that sometimes accompanied the Enlightenment in its many variants, the rise of academic specialization strained the bonds between church and academy. The controversy over the appointment of John Leslie as professor of mathematics at the University of Edinburgh revealed tensions between academic inquiry and settled religious convictions. The incident also created an opening for the Popular Party to challenge the Moderate Party's dominance in the General Assembly. On the one hand, Moderates and the Populars both advocated the independence of the church to protect it from interference by the Crown. The leader of the Moderates, George Hill, for instance, echoed the themes of earlier Presbyterian theory in his lectures. The church, he deduced, existed before it became part of the political establishment and, as such, its ecclesiastical authority conceivably existed without an alliance with civil authorities. As such, the church did not depend on the state for its own spiritual authority: "When the Church receives the countenance and protection of the Civil Power, she does not, by this alliance, lose those rights and powers which are implied in Church government as such." Hill also insisted on the parity of ministers and repeated the older Presbyterian arguments against episcopacy and the older understanding that church power was spiritual (not temporal).The church's domain, he wrote, was "concerned only with the consciences of men, and gives no claim to any authority over their persons or their properties."[30]

On the other hand, Scottish universities, as the Leslie case showed, were subject to a mixture of authorities—civil, ecclesiastical, and intellectual. On the specific component of church influence, Presbyterian involvement in academic appointments was an irritant to Scots who wanted to free universities from the Kirk's dominance. Although university professorships were technically not under church control, the learning and prestige that pastors possessed in an age before academic professionalization gave church officers leverage in regulating and staffing Scottish universities. The Leslie case proved to be a contest less about curriculum and ideas than a proxy battle between the Kirk's two factions. At the same time, the ecclesiastical dispute created an impression that the church was an obstacle to an institution—the university—upon which the modernization of Scotland depended. The economic, political, and intellectual demands of a liberalizing society were exposing the Church of Scotland to be an anachronistic institution.

The Moderates' choice for the Edinburgh post, Thomas McKnight, was a minister from South Leith. Although odd by modern university norms, this was still the norm as part of the presbytery and General Assembly's outsize role in Scotland's intellectual life. Ecclesiastical politics surfaced when Moderates in the Edinburgh presbytery supported McKnight and also insisted that he retain his clerical post. That demand was a bridge too far for academic reformers, who opposed the Kirk's domination of the university. It also created an opening for the Populars. The rival to McKnight was Leslie, a layman whose qualifications rested on his proficiency as a natural scientist. He had published articles and a well-received book. Rumors also circulated that Leslie was a skeptic thanks to his praise for David Hume. If the academic appointment rested solely on theology, the Popular Party should have opposed Leslie and Moderates should have recognized Leslie as someone in tune with Scottish intellectual life. But the controversy went in the opposite direction. Doctrinal conservatives supported Leslie and Moderates opposed him.[31]

In March 1805, the Moderates in the Presbytery of Edinburgh prevailed narrowly in blocking Leslie's appointment. Two months later when the matter came before the General Assembly, the Popular Party prevailed by a twelve-vote majority (96 to 84). Drummond and Bulloch observe that "here was a landmark in the history of the Assembly, for the Moderates, who for so long had controlled it." The appointment of Leslie, in turn, marked the secularization of intellectual life in Scotland: "The old categories of 'general' and 'special' revelation, dependent on Nature and Scripture respectively, had been shaken." With this weakening of Reformed theology's old categories came the understanding that "Christian faith must be vindicated on other grounds," Drummond and Bulloch add.[32] The irony was that the Popular Party, "by arraying themselves on the side of irreligion," wound up abetting university reformers who, according to J. B. Morrell, were intent on overturning "a hypocritical and erastian clerical . . . domination" of Scottish universities.[33]

Such discontent within the Church of Scotland—more than a century removed from the Glorious Revolution—was indicative more generally of discontinuity between Reformation ideals (and zeal) and the realities of ecclesiastical establishment. For Moderates, the old model of a covenanted nation was a threat to the stability and order that the Church of Scotland needed. The Popular Party still affirmed the old theological ideals of the Westminster Assembly even if they had moved on from covenanted nationalism. At the same time, the Popular Party desired a strong church government that avoided the compromise that came with currying favor from civil authorities. In both cases, the Kirk appeared to be drifting along with trends in Scottish society for the sake of maintaining its status as the established church.

Voluntarism Comes for the Scottish Establishment

If the "hotter" zeal of Presbyterian reform was cooling within the Kirk, the wider public was also wondering about the value of ecclesiastical establishments altogether. Between 1829 and 1843, a Voluntary campaign among Scottish Dissenters made the Kirk's polarization between Moderates and the Popular Party look irrelevant. The Voluntarist position, not far removed from what had evolved in the United States, took the

Figure 6.1. *The Skating Minister* (1790s), by Henry Raeburn.

church out of the civil magistrate's administration and located ecclesiastical life within the realm of voluntary association. Voluntarism's appeal grew among the middle classes and in urban areas, environments where traditional Scottish hierarchies were increasingly out of place. Scottish proponents of voluntarism looked for support and established networks with Dissenters in England and Ireland who were also conducting church ministry outside traditional establishment expectations. In the words of Stewart J. Brown, the voluntarists desired "a more individualistic and egalitarian society," one dominated by voluntary associations, "in which neither the State nor the Established Church would exercise power over individual conscience" and "all religious denominations would be equal in law."[34]

The Voluntary movement lasted from 1829 to 1840, a consequential time for both civil and ecclesiastical politics in Scotland. It began with the premise, anti-Catholic in effect, that religious establishments might bring the wrong kind of Christianity into power. The Catholic Emancipation Act of 1829, which allowed Roman Catholics to vote and serve at certain levels in civil and military offices in Britain, raised the prospect of a non-Protestant majority, like in Ireland, utilizing a numerical majority to use state funds for Roman Catholic institutions. One way to avoid this outcome was to disestablish the church altogether.[35] Advocates of voluntarism set up local chapters and published periodicals to appeal to a growing middle class with increasing access to education and desirous of representative government. The desire was to challenge a government and church beholden to Scottish elites. One specific policy that gained traction in Edinburgh was a campaign against the annuity tax. The payment of 6 percent on rentals of houses and shops was part of a fiscal mechanism to pay the stipends of city pastors. What made the tax especially objectionable was the arbitrary manner in which authorities collected it. Some wealthy families gained exemption. Some who lived outside the city but worshiped at one of Edinburgh's parishes also avoided the tax. Opposition to the tax tended to be popular among the Dissenters, whose churches saw no benefit from the policy. As much as the Voluntary movement was a modernizing trend in Scotland, it did come at the expense of the old parish ideal. Instead of an implicitly covenanted nation of clergy, landed elites, teachers, and magistrates working together within a moral consensus, the Voluntary movement encouraged projection and protection of personal interests. At the same time, voluntary associations also functioned as outlets for like-minded citizens. This was an attitude learned partly from creating Dissenting churches, 650 of which had been started in Scotland since 1733, all on the basis of voluntary contributions and membership.[36]

Resonance between voluntarism in religion and democratic politics had immediate repercussions for the Church of Scotland. The recurring contest over patronage—the role of lairds in the appointment of ministers—became a large target of those Scots who resented the prerogatives that social elites enjoyed in Scottish institutions. Thomas Chalmers, who had emerged as a leader among the Evangelical Party, a wing of the older Popular Party in the Kirk, was an odd combination of populism and establishmentarianism. For instance, he opposed the system of patronage because it undermined the rights of laity in the call of pastors. At the same time, he defended the social ideal of a nation organically connected with the Kirk providing religious and educational guidance for a godly commonwealth. As much as the piety surrounding revivals ran in the direction of interdenominational cooperation in antislavery associations, foreign missions, and societies for the distribution of Bibles, Chalmers, who himself had experienced an evangelical conversion, still threw his support behind an established church. In 1834, the General Assembly, with Evangelicals as the majority, passed the Veto Act, a policy that gave husbands and fathers in parishes the right to veto a patron's candidate for minister. At the same time, the Kirk ratified plans to extend the Church of Scotland throughout the country by creating new parishes and schools.[37] The hope was to reach Scotland's unchurched population and answer the complaint that the Kirk solely rested on its ties to the civil authorities. The popularity of these decisions, even among the landed classes who contributed significant sums to the budget for extension, put pressure on Parliament in London to honor its own commitment to the ecclesiastical establishment in Scotland. At the same time, the Popular Party's plans ran directly contrary to the Voluntary Campaign. Chalmers still echoed the old Presbyterian ideal of church and state working harmoniously for a Christian Scotland, even as the Voluntaryists wanted to separate the church from the state's oversight.[38]

The Popular Party was soon to learn the wisdom of voluntarism and the limits of establishment, however painful the moral of the story. The British government, in consultation with the General Assembly, determined to improve the spiritual conditions of Scotland. In 1835, London's Whig government (led by William Lamb, Lord Melbourne) appointed a Royal Commission to survey the unchurched population in Scotland and determine what resources were needed. The commission was an immediate though indirect threat to the Kirk since the assessment took into account the capacity of both the established church and Dissenters. Even more alarming was the commission's scrutiny of mechanisms for funding clergy. This inquiry had the potential to expose the landed classes' power of the purse and the byzantine nature of medieval tithing systems that the sixteenth-century Reformation had not displaced. The Royal Commission took three years to issue a report. The results were disappointing to the Kirk and especially to Chalmers's Evangelical Party, which favored church extension. The study refused funding for new churches in part because Dissenters had already started churches in locations where the Kirk was absent. The report did recommend new rural parishes but chose to fund them with existing church endowments.[39]

The challenge of cooperating with the state became even more apparent when the British government decided to overturn the Kirk's earlier objections to patronage. In the same year that the General Assembly reaffirmed the church's spiritual independence from external interference (read patrons) and the rights of church members in calling a pastor, the Earl of Kinnoull nominated Robert Young for the parish in Auchterarder. In a lopsided vote, more than three-quarters of the congregation refused the nominee. The case went to presbytery, synod, and General Assembly. In each instance, church courts sided with the laity. Kinnoull then appealed to the civil courts, and four years later the British Court of Session upheld the patron's rights. This was a clear affront to the Presbyterian conviction that Christ was the sole head of the church. According to the General Assembly, the church's courts "possess an exclusive jurisdiction founded on the Word of God, which . . . flows immediately from God and the mediator Jesus Christ, and is spiritual, not having a temporal head on earth, but only Christ, the only King and Governor of his Kirk."[40] But the Court of Session rejected this assertion of the church's spiritual independence. British authorities countered that although the church oversaw a candidate's qualifications, civil authorities administered mechanisms of appointment and related financial matters. According to this logic, the Veto Act was contrary to the Patronage Act of 1711, which specified the role of patrons in nominating candidates for ministry. By not specifying the reasons for rejecting the ministerial candidate, the Kirk had violated that 1711 law. This judgment was one more indication of religious establishment's risks.

The state's failure to uphold the Kirk, combined with growing support for voluntarism, reignited the conflict between the Moderate and Popular Parties in the Kirk. Although Moderates in the General Assembly supported a policy that granted congregations the right to object to nominees for the ministry while also providing for presbyteries to overturn the laity's choice if deemed fractious, the Evangelical Party championed the cause of ecclesiastical sovereignty within the Kirk.[41] A series of statements from 1841 and 1842 outlined a position that was increasingly untenable—a Knoxian conception of church and state in a modernizing United Kingdom. In 1841, a "Solemn Engagement in Defence of the Liberties of the Church and People of Scotland" outlined standard points of Presbyterian polity: the kingship of Christ over the church, the spiritual jurisdiction of the ecclesial realm, and the independence of the church from the civil magistrate in all explicitly religious matters. The older Presbyterian model of national godliness resurfaced in an updated matter with the addition of "People" to the affirmation's title. Of course, the old National Covenants had always included the Scottish folk in the bonds of the holy commonweal that also included the king, Parliament, and church. Still, the rights of the laity had not been prominent in older disputes between bishops and councils. Now, in a society that was becoming more democratic and in a church increasingly sensitive to patrons intruding in parish ministry, "the people" tapped a new found Presbyterian regard for all Scots. The "Solemn Engagement" asserted that God had "invested ordinary members of His Church with important spiritual privileges." As such, the consent of the congregation was an "indispensable condition" in the formation of the bond between pastor and members. Without that consent, settling a minister was an "act of oppression."[42]

The authors of the "Solemn Engagement" believed they stood on solid ground prepared by the legal precedents of the Revolution Settlement and the Treaty of Union. But they were prepared to do more than appeal to law and tradition. The duty of the Kirk's ministers was to remove "the yoke" of civil interference. That responsibility constituted the basis for another covenant, this time among ministers and well-wishers, to combat the church's subjection to civil government in the form of patronage.[43] By 1841, the protest against patronage mainly amounted to a call to unite against the existing hardship.

By 1842, however, objections extended beyond patronage to religious establishment and mere protests turned into a threat. The recent high-handedness by the civil courts led to the conclusion that the Kirk must act to protect its authority. In a series of resolutions passed in 1842, the Evangelical Party voiced a willingness to go without "the endowments or emoluments secured to them by the civil law."[44] This appeared to be the only way to alert "Her Majesty's government" of the dire circumstances that afflicted the Christian ministry in Scotland. The old "civil advantages" that came with establishment had become oppressive. Those aids restricted the church's "spiritual freedom and jurisdiction."[45]

Forgoing the state's support and coordination was just one step removed from the determination in 1843 to leave the Church of Scotland altogether. On May 23, 1843, the "ecclesiastical revolution" of Scotland took place at the Church of St. Andrew in Edinburgh: 121 pastors and 73 elders withdrew from the established church by leaving the General Assembly; the ministers gave up their manses and stipends.[46] The "Protest and Act of Separation" that explained this revolt made fewer references to patronage and the rights of laity and relied more on Presbyterian arguments that had become part of Scottish law. A list of eight grievances underscored the Evangelical Party's opposition to the civil court's involvement in the church's spiritual and independent authority. Only in the final objection did the Protest and Act of Separation come to the matter of patronage. For the Protesters, conditions were so bad that no pastor could be "admitted into the Church Courts of the Establishment" without the "sanction of the civil courts."[47] These abuses violated the terms of the church's original constitution in the Claim of Right of 1689, upheld again in the Treaty of Union of 1712. Although the Protesters remained formally committed to "the right and duty of the Civil Magistrate to maintain and support the establishment of religion in accordance with God's word," they could not abide the Church of Scotland. The only way, ironically, for the Protesters to retain an authentic established church was to form a communion outside the establishment.

The Free Church of Scotland eventually attracted more than 450 ministers, compared to the 121 pastors who left the General Assembly on the day of the Disruption, May 18. (The rest of the Kirk's delegates remained silent on the Protest and Act of Separation, a gesture that implied assent to the civil government's allocation of temporal and spiritual powers in Scotland.) Five days later, the Free Church convened its own assembly and elected Thomas Chalmers moderator. Independence from the state's stipends, manses, and church buildings meant the Free Church started from scratch. For Scottish church historian James Bryce's interpretation of the Disruption, the split finally achieved for the Church of Scotland what the Scottish Reformers had intended. In 1843, the true Church of Scotland was free from "spiritual tyranny and thraldom" by clearly separating the government and discipline of the church from "the State and its tribunals." Presbyterians had finally rid themselves of the "remnant of Papal usurpation and tyranny, which the Reformation and Revolution had failed to extirpate." The Free Church's separation had placed the Kirk safely beyond all "idle and unprofitable 'disputations.'"[48]

What Bryce saw in 1850 as the triumph of original Presbyterianism was actually a victory for voluntarism. In 1838, when Whigs refused to fund church extension, the British government "had determined that the social influence and authority of the establishment should be allowed to decline," according to Stewart J. Brown. Instead of a church that provided religious services for the entire population, Scotland was becoming "increasingly pluralistic and voluntary in its religion" with "the needs of the towns and cities . . . met through voluntary means."[49] Although the Free Church continued to affirm the establishment principle, it functioned practically as a voluntary communion. If Brown is correct that with the Disruption and spread of voluntarism an "individualistic and liberal Scotland had emerged," it also bears noticing that during the same process the Presbyterians who defended the Scottish Reformation embraced a social world their early modern heroes could not have imagined.

The Other Presbyterian Voluntarists

The realities of voluntarism in England took an unexpected turn when two unlikely developments occurred: one was the rise of Unitarianism, the other was the extension of the Kirk into England. English Dissenters paved the way for Unitarianism among those who claimed English Presbyterian lineage. A commitment to independence of thought and organizational autonomy both combined to give English ministers and laity a Unitarian identity. Some Unitarian proponents were aggressive about their convictions, but others, especially among those who attended Unitarian chapels, would "have been appalled had anyone called [their meeting] 'Unitarian.'"[50] Meanwhile, not everyone who traced their ecclesiastical lineage to sixteenth-century Presbyterians worshiped as a Unitarian. According to information on church life from 1835 records, Unitarians attracted 37,000 attendants to their chapels, led by roughly 175 ministers. In contrast, English Presbyterians counted roughly 80,000 members and 81 ministers. The latter statistic comes from a convention of ministers and elders who attended the English Presbyterian Synod.[51]

Presbyterianism in England persisted chiefly in the north throughout the eighteenth century, but in the 1830s its congregations began to form ties with the Scots. Like Baptists and Independents, English Presbyterians established congregational unions that Protestant dissenters forged outside the Church of England. In 1813, Unitarianism itself became a recognized communion through an act of Parliament. Despite a breadth of doctrine, English Presbyterians continued to teach and practice parts of Reformed Protestantism even without coherent ecclesiastical structures. Some English Presbyterian conservatism also owed to the migration of Scots who labored in shipbuilding and textile industries located in the north of England. That geography explains in part why English Presbyterianism was strongest in Manchester, Liverpool, and the towns of Northumberland and Tyneside, while London retained a small Presbyterian presence. Throughout much of the eighteenth century, pastors supplied the bulk of officers in local presbyteries. But from the 1780s into the nineteenth century, English Presbyterians began to rely more on elders. By the 1830s, Hugh Ralph, a Presbyterian pastor in Liverpool, and Alex Munro, Ralph's counterpart in Manchester, petitioned the Church of Scotland for a formal ecclesiastical connection. The Kirk's General Assembly recommended that the English churches form a synod according to the constitution and laws of the Church of Scotland. That advice led the English Presbyterian Synod in 1835 to adopt the Westminster Standards and the discipline, government, and worship of the Church of Scotland. The English Presbyterians added to their name, "in Connection with the Church of Scotland." The earlier passage of the Sacramental Test Act (1828), which repealed the Test and Corporation Act's restrictions on Dissenters and Roman Catholics in British society, facilitated this chapter in English Presbyterian history.[52]

English Presbyterians had been dependent on voluntary contributions to finance their activities and training, but ridding their number of Unitarians improved their resources. Since the formation of a General Body of Protestants outside the establishment in 1727 (Baptists, Presbyterians, and Independents), Unitarians had been influential participants in the legal and economic levers available to dissent. This included access to the Lady Hewley Trust, an endowment set up in 1710 by the widow of John Hewley, Lord Mayor of York, to fund Presbyterian pastors. Over time, Unitarians gained access to the Hewley Trust by serving as trustees of the estate. Unitarian presence was not inherently deceitful or corrupt but a reflection of the fluidity of English Protestantism outside the Church of England. After 1830, however, Trinitarian Dissenters pressured Unitarians to forfeit their place among the orthodox. They initiated a suit in 1830 in the Chancery, not decided until 1842, to remove Unitarians permanently from the Lady Hewley Trust. After 1842, the seven trustees included three Presbyterians, two Baptists, and two Independents. Midway through these legal proceedings, at the same time as the formation of the English Presbyterian Synod (1836), Presbyterians also succeeded in pressuring Unitarians to abandon the institutional connections they had cultivated since the 1720s.[53]

The rise to prominence of Scots among the English churches was a quality that most nineteenth-century accounts of English Presbyterianism acknowledged without the slightest hint of national pride. When the English Presbyterian Church in 1876 formed a communion with requisite church polity among English and Scottish congregations within England, the synod sponsored a collection of essays to commemorate the event. Peter Lorimer, for instance, a Presbyterian pastor in London of Scottish descent, wrote an essay on English Presbyterianism that featured the English side of Presbyterianism. John Knox may have been the North Star of sixteenth-century Presbyterianism by virtue of his ties to churches in England, Scotland, Geneva, and even Frankfurt, but, according to Lorimer, England had its own worthies in Thomas Cartwright and Walter Travers. Still, Lorimer conceded that English Presbyterians had been no match for royal supremacy or bishops' intrigues. As such, eighteenth-century English Presbyterianism was an example of "perpetual decline and ever increasing disaster."[54]

Twenty years later, Alexander Hutton Drysdale, who had served as moderator of the English Synod, again tried to give English Presbyterians a sense of identity. Still, he needed to acknowledge that Knox's ministry in England (1549–53) was the origin of Presbyterianism in the realm. Drysdale went on to highlight Cartwright's subsequent and local rumblings against episcopacy at Wandsworth, Jersey, and Guernsey. But in the seventeenth century, Presbyterianism became either a political position to combat Charles I or it occupied a small place in English church life. Only with the migration of Scottish Presbyterian pastors to English congregations in the late eighteenth and early nineteenth centuries did Presbyterian fortunes in England improve.[55] English Presbyterianism's humble past was also evident in its leaders' rejection of any claim to establishment status. Independence from the state did not mean that the English had rejected Presbyterian assertions about Christ's headship over the church or that pastors and elders were anything less than ministers executing laws of the supreme legislator. In 1844 the English synod entertained and approved overtures from several presbyteries that affirmed ecclesiastical independence. This involved submission to Christ, "its only King and Head," with the appointment of officers "to make and execute such regulations and orders" only that accorded with "His Holy Word." As such, the church was a "spiritual" kingdom, invested with all "requisite powers and spiritual jurisdiction to administer its own ecclesiastical economy." Submission to Christ was the guarantee of the church's independence. The church possessed "exclusive jurisdiction and supreme authority, subject only to Christ, in all its own spiritual affairs."[56]

Such an assertion of church power, historically a source of friction with English civil authorities invested in an established church, also came with standard regard for the powers of synods and assemblies. Part of why the English Presbyterians' assertion of real, spiritual authority, the kind ordained by Christ himself, remained unthreatening in the nineteenth century was that it did not include a demand for recognition as the national church. The English Presbyterian Church possessed its "own inherent powers of self-government and jurisdiction." Although Knox and Cartwright had conceived of their church as maintaining "inviolate all the rights, powers, and privileges wherewith Christ [had] invested it," English Presbyterians in their voluntary capacity downgraded what had been political prescriptions to pious proclamations.[57]

The ongoing vigor of Presbyterian claims to real, though spiritual, authority also came across as mild if not inspirational thanks to the Whiggish narrative that undergirded their logic. Long gone were the claims of a Christian nation that united all ranks of society, from the king to the ordinary church member, in a reformed church and godly commonweal. Instead, Presbyterianism had become an example of representative and constitutional government. For the author of "The Polity of the Presbyterian Church" (which may have been the Presbyterian pastor Alexander Hutton Drysdale), the representation of church members through elders assembling in sessions, presbyteries, and synods was obviously an extension of the original general assembly at the Council of Jerusalem, even if the Bible did not provide the "minutia" of Presbyterian government. Even more notable was the way this form of government functioned for the ordinary Christian. In a well-regulated Presbyterian church, any member could appeal any grievance to its "united eldership." If the elders' judgment was unsatisfactory, said church member could appeal from his session to his presbytery and on up the chain of church courts. The appellant could have confidence in Presbyterian formal structures to be treated with "affection and fidelity" by elders, who would do their "utmost to decide his case according to the mind of Christ."[58] This form of church government was notably the same administration characteristic of nations moving from "the yoke of oppression" to "sound views of national liberty." Presbyterians could, in fact, take pride that the advance of liberal politics was an "approximation" of the "great principles—particularly the principle of elective representation—which Christ has laid down for the government of His Church."[59]

Liberal affinities between civil and ecclesiastical procedure was the closest English Presbyterians came to religious establishment. Representative government may have been desirable in church and society, but in contrast to the establishment principle of a national church, English Presbyterians remained firmly voluntarist. Although English Presbyterians had strong associations with the Church of Scotland, in 1843 when forced to take a side in the Scottish Disruption, the English sided with the Free Church. To make this disposition clear, English Presbyterians removed references to Scotland from their official name and abbreviated it to the Presbyterian Church of England.[60]

This determination made sense of the theological ties—largely Calvinistic—that English Presbyterians saw in the Scottish church's Evangelical Party. But it was odd to the extent that the Free Church's insistence that leaving the Church of Scotland was in no way a rejection of the establishment principle. The Free Church was still committed to this ideal, even as it received no stipends from the British government but depended on voluntary contributions. English Presbyterians, in contrast, explicitly upheld the "voluntary principle." In 1849, the English Presbyterian Synod clarified that the communion had always been a "voluntary association" of congregations.[61] This was the preferred way for nineteenth-century Presbyterians to assert both their independence and "spiritual authority."[62] It was also the best way to protect the church from such intrusion of civil authorities in the work of the church that had afflicted the Church of Scotland.[63] A voluntary church was truly an independent one.

Voluntarism was a political path for Presbyterians to signal support for democratizing and liberalizing politics, especially since ecclesiastical independence echoed calls for removing the state's regulation of private conviction. By insisting that ecclesiastical power came directly from—and was an extension of—Christ's kingly rule, a power that the state had no legitimate right in which to meddle, advocates of Presbyterian polity were making the church entirely dependent on financial gifts not from political subjects but Christians who followed personal convictions. Arriving at that understanding among Presbyterians took the better part of three centuries, so powerful was the legacy of Constantianism and the model of Old Testament Israel's covenanted people, priests, elders, and monarchs. Even the Free Church of Scotland's ongoing defense of the establishment principle suggests that heirs of Calvin, Knox, and Cartwright deserve only minimal credit for ushering in the modern shibboleth of religious freedom. As damning as such faint praise may be, Presbyterianism in the British Isles still deserves mention at least for ushering in modern norms of religious freedom and pluralism. What was true, though, was that an affirmation of Christ's supremacy in the church laid the groundwork for an independent and a voluntary administration of the church.

Voluntary Presbyterianism and Denominationalism

Presbyterians in the colonies that became the United States never had to worry about an ecclesiastical establishment. The creation of a presbytery in Philadelphia (1706), a synod in the same city (1717), and eventually a General Assembly (that met in the nation's original capital in 1789), all happened without aid from colonial governments. Those colonies that lacked religious establishments, Pennsylvania (including Delaware) and New Jersey, provided Presbyterians the most room to maneuver. But even when it came to gaining approval from what was in effect "the mother church," the Kirk, American Presbyterians assumed independence and acted accordingly. Unlike German and Dutch Reformed communions that depended on approval and regulation from European authorities (e.g., the Classis of Amsterdam), American Presbyterians implemented ecclesiastical and doctrinal traditions from Britain entirely on their own.

Such independence from British civil and Scottish ecclesiastical oversight did not mean American Presbyterians were indifferent to their denominational siblings in Scotland, Ireland, and England. In fact, the faculty at Princeton Seminary, the first Presbyterian institution for training pastors, founded in 1812 under the auspices of the PCUSA General Assembly, used the pages of the *Biblical Repertory and Princeton Review* to monitor theological and ecclesial developments, including the 1843 Disruption. Those assessments by Princetonians revealed not simply the different social and political contexts of transatlantic Presbyterianism. They also indicated the speed with which the various Presbyterian communions were reckoning with the failure of ecclesiastical establishment and the benefits of a voluntary church.

Commentary on Kirk politics in the years leading up to the Disruption allowed American Presbyterians to compare themselves to the original Presbyterians of the Scottish Reformation. The first to comment was Archibald Alexander, the senior member of Princeton's faculty. Before him were the four strands of Scottish Presbyterianism—the national church, the Covenanters, the Seceders, and the Relief Church. In the context of the American dispute between New and Old School Presbyterians (which involved controversies over revivals and cooperation with Congregationalists to plant churches on the frontier), Alexander and his colleagues at the seminary may well have been looking to Scotland for perspective on American Presbyterianism. Alexander's first two articles from 1835 looked almost exclusively at the example of the 1732 Secession, but he could not assume his readers knew much about their Scottish Presbyterian cousins. Alexander provided statistics on the contemporary religious scene in Scotland, a description of the powers and composition of the General Assembly, a history of ecclesiastical establishment before and after union with England, and information on clerical salaries. Although Alexander repeated that he was simply reporting on the Scottish scene, the statistics he included showed that the Kirk was not growing in comparison to other Scottish Protestants. "While the established church has neglected to furnish the people with the means of religious instruction," Alexander wrote, "the object has been accomplished by the Seceders, and other dissenters."[64]

Nevertheless, Alexander was also critical of the Seceders. As much as he regarded the Reformation as a recovery of the people's rights in calling ministers—a clear disapproval of patronage—Alexander also favored order over anarchy, respect for authority over suspicion of hierarchy. This perspective led him to judge Ebenezer Erskine and his peers as "unreasonable" when deciding to reject the judgments of presbytery and General Assembly.[65] Then at the 1747 Synod of the Seceders, when the Anti-Burgher faction deposed Erskine from the communion he was instrumental in founding, Alexander judged the action "most extraordinary." He wrote that it was "remarkable" for the founder to be deposed by "that very ecclesiastical body which he had been the chief instrument of forming."[66] For readers inclined to look for a subtext, Alexander gave hints of disapproving of both the orneriness and disorderliness of the first great secession in Scottish Presbyterian history. He could not help but wonder if such cussedness stemmed from the Seceders' origins in the Marrow Controversy. Although Alexander's American readers may well have expected a professor at a seminary that held closely to the Westminster Confession to side with the doctrinally orthodox "Marrow Men," he detected problems similar to those in the 1748 contretemps. He wrote: "There seems to be too much evidence of a captious temper, a wish to find some appearance of heresy in a church from which they had seceded; and we are constrained to say, too much leaning towards antinomianism, or rather too friendly a feeling towards forms of expression which are capable of an antinomian sense. If they had nothing worse, in regard to doctrine, to object to the established church, the ground of their secession is reduced to very narrow limits."[67]

If Princeton's faculty were inclined to regard the Seceders as disruptive, observers may well have thought the same scholars would take a similar line on a potential split in the Kirk of the 1830s. Alexander had a chance to establish an interpretive strategy when he wrote an article about the debates over the Veto Act of 1834 (where the Popular Party prevailed in the General Assembly to restore the rights of congregations and presbyteries against patrons in the call of pastors). Alexander opined that "orthodox Presbyterians" in the United States should take a "lively interest" in Scottish developments, not only because Scotland was the birthplace of Presbyterianism, but also because Americans themselves were needing to rely on civil courts to sort out ecclesiastical squabbles that resulted in 1838 in two separate communions.[68] This time he wrote with the aim of presenting "a fair view of the nature of the case."[69] This left commentary to Alexander's biological son, Joseph Addison Alexander, and his spiritual son, Charles Hodge, both of whom taught at Princeton Seminary. Between them, Alexander and Hodge wrote three articles total, one of which was coauthored. Along the way they rendered opinions that transcended Scotland's party lines—such as that the Secession may have been responsible for giving control of the Kirk to Moderates,[70] and that Thomas Chalmers's popularity was excessive or incompatible with "good taste and Christian moderation."[71]

Americans had no trouble taking the side of Scots who opposed patronage, but they also saw ecclesiastical establishment as an obstacle to the Kirk's spiritual independence. Charles Hodge understood how patronage compromised Christ's lordship over the church: "Christ has established a church and has given it a government distinct from that of the state, and its officers, in the administration of that government, must follow his directions and not the directions of men." In Hodge's estimate, Christ's rule over the church was the Free Church's cause.[72] The junior Alexander echoed Hodge by linking the Free Church to "the genuine original natural Scotch Church of the Reformation."[73]

Where the Americans departed from the Free Church was over the establishment principle. The Princetonians had little trouble appreciating the Free Church's claim to be the ongoing national church of Scotland. The logic of this position involved an assumption that the state was obligated to provide for the religious instruction of the people through "some branch of the Christian church." The church was not a creature of the state but an independent organization with spiritual powers derived from Christ, and the church could not relinquish any of its spiritual power without also forsaking the lordship of Christ. This was, from the Americans' perspective, a "grand" vision of the church. "There is something really sublime in the determination to assume the rank of a National Church," Hodge and Alexander admitted, perhaps sensing the limitations of their own denomination's claim on the United States.[74] But one significant challenge was the Free Church's insistence that the civil government not only provide for religious instruction but also support the clergy." We do not think this the best plan," Hodge and Alexander wrote. "In this country, the very phrase 'church and state' is enough to frighten us from our propriety."[75]

The Americans' last reservation about the Disruption echoed the elder Alexander's observation about the zealotry and sectarianism of the Seceders. Did an established church, the Americans implicitly wondered, inherently nurture factions and breed incivility? Alexander the younger and Hodge questioned in particular the Free Church's "tone" toward other churches. On the one hand, the Free Church stood on the high ground of Christian ecumenicity in its relations with other Protestant communions. On the other hand, in the case of the Church of Scotland, the Free Church appeared to regard the Kirk as an alien body, not part of the "church of Jesus Christ."[76] The Princetonians reminded readers that both the Free Church and the Kirk professed the same confession of faith. The only difference was "the important doctrine of the lordship of Christ over his church." Even here, the Princetonians conceded that the Church of Scotland affirmed this doctrine. But even if the Kirk's affirmation was flawed, its error did not rise to the level of infidelity or unbelief. For proof, the Americans observed that both communions regarded the Church of England as a true church, even though the English body was hardly capable of affirming the lordship of Christ on Scottish Presbyterian terms. "The Church of England is bound hand and foot by the state," they wrote. "It is Erastian in principle and Erastian in practice." But "a doctrine which leads to the conclusion that the church of England is not and never has been a church of Christ . . . is refuted by the reductio ad absurdum."[77]

Clearly the Americans were an ocean removed and three centuries away from the original Presbyterian Reformation debates on the relationship between Reformed churches and the civil magistrate. For them, a denominational system within a society that made churches voluntary associations was not only the norm but also a practical solution to religious establishment. However propitious the Glorious Revolution had been for finally making the Church of Scotland Presbyterian, the American Revolution appeared to Presbyterians in the United States even more glorious. The new nation made possible a truly reformed and orthodox church without the obstacles of civil magistrates, local patrons, or General Assemblies needing the approval of civil government. Presbyterianism in the United States lacked much of the glory that British Presbyterians associated with Knox, the Bishops' Wars, or the National Covenant. But it set the trend for Presbyterians in the Anglophone world whenever they recognized the benefits of voluntarism.

Tepidly Bold Presbyterianism

Even if American Presbyterianism lacked the prestige that religious establishments added to church life, its thinkers showed no deficit when explaining the government God had instituted for Christians. Divine-right Presbyterianism might have sounded risible to the likes of Mark Twain, but American Presbyterians, especially those in Princeton's network, repeated arguments about church polity that would have made Cartwright, Knox, and Rutherford proud. In the United States, a self-conscious Presbyterianism emerged that continued to insist on sixteenth-century church polity and seventeenth-century Reformed theology as the guiding lights for church life. To be so intentionally traditional on church government and doctrine while also praising a republican and liberal political order was one of the chief anomalies of Presbyterian adaptations to nineteenth-century American politics.

Two figures who made notable contributions in this line of thought were Samuel Miller and Stuart Robinson. The former was the second professor at Princeton Seminary, whose duties included teaching church history and ecclesiastical polity. Miller had an auspicious start to his writing career when, caught up in the spirit of the Enlightenment, he wrote *A Brief Retrospect of the Eighteenth Century; Part the First in Three Volumes; Containing a Sketch of the Revolutions and Improvements in Science, Arts, and Literature during That Period* (1803, 1805). Not only was the title an oxymoron but Miller needed three volumes to document all of the positive developments of the previous century. Completed after studying at the University of Pennsylvania and while a Presbyterian pastor in New York, the book has regularly attracted the attention of intellectual historians eager to trace the genealogy of ideas in the new nation. In those excavations, Miller generally receives favorable assessments, just as he did in his own lifetime when he received an honorary doctorate from his alma mater. Historians have not, however, followed the rest of Miller's literary output, especially his protracted defense of Presbyterian church government. The first *Letters concerning the Constitution and Order to the Christian Ministry* (1807) was the product of Miller's defense of Presbyterianism while ministering in what had previously been an Anglican establishment (New York). The second *Letters concerning the Constitution and Order to the Christian Ministry* (1840), published after almost two decades of classroom instruction, also reflected the vigorous restatement of Presbyterianism inspired by the Old School Presbyterian experience.

In the former work, Miller wrote specifically against Presbyterians' old nemesis, Episcopalians. A claim of bishops' superiority to presbyters had caught Miller's eye and prompted him to clarify differences between Presbyterians and Episcopalians. He first explained that "bishop" was actually a legitimate word for church office that Presbyterians themselves also applied to elders. Where Presbyterians differed was the matter of a bishop's "character and power."[78] Although a Presbyterian pastor and an Episcopalian priest each had the right and duty to perform the work of word and sacrament, the latter had no power of ordination but relied on his bishop. Presbyterians in contrast believed the power of ordination belonged to a company of officers. In fact, Miller claimed, as Presbyterian proponents had long before him, that the New Testament recognized no such office or function as a metropolitan or diocesan bishop. Instead, all ministers share a parity of office that denied to any single pastor an authority greater than his peers.[79] Miller admitted that Episcopalians were not of one mind about the importance of episcopacy. Some held that it was merely optional; some that it was preferable. But the one group that alarmed Miller was made up of Episcopalians who regarded bishops as essential to Christianity, as if faith in Christ apart from being baptized and confirmed by a bishop was inadequate for salvation. Such a view automatically excommunicated "nine-tenths of the whole Protestant world."[80]

The choice of "letters" to describe Miller's 1807 book may have attracted initial readers, but in a 360-page book with only nine entries, *Letters* was likely a slog for the faint of heart. Miller's survey of biblical, patristic, Reformation, and Anglican history in those nine letters rarely introduced new material to older Presbyterian arguments. Still, he made no reference to Thomas Cartwright, John Knox, Andrew Melville, or Samuel Rutherford. Miller did credit John Jewel (1522–71), Joseph Hall (1574–1656), John Davenant (1572–1641), and James Usher (1581–1656) as bishops who exhibited "*real religion*."[81] They were also notable for not combating Presbyterians. Meanwhile, to counter arguments for apostolic succession, Miller invoked William Chillingworth (1602–44), Isaac Barrow (1613–80), and Benjamin Hoadly (1676–1761) to demonstrate that sensible bishops understood proving direct ties to the apostles was as "futile as it is unnecessary."[82]

That point forced Miller to put his own cards on the table. How was it that Presbyterian ministers justified their own ordination and authority? Here Miller came up with a Presbyterian version of apostolic succession that involved two steps. First, the original Presbyterians of England and Scotland had been ordained by bishops. That rite validated their ministry and in turn all Presbyterian pastors whom they and their successors ordained. Second, Miller turned the tables on advocates of episcopacy and asserted that his previous biblical and historical investigations had shown that bishops emerged only in the postapostolic period. For Miller, this chronology indicated that councils preceded bishops. In other words, "it is only so far as *any* succession flows through the line of *Presbyters*, that it is either regular or valid." Because Protestant bishops were essentially "*Presbyters*, and assisted in all other ordinations by *other Presbyters*," their ordinations were "valid."[83] Miller's later book, *The Primitive and Apostolic Order of the Church of Christ Vindicated* (1840), was essentially a reworking of the 1807 *Letters*, this time as a critique of the Oxford Movement and claims of episcopal supremacy based on apostolic succession.

Stuart Robinson's brief for Presbyterianism was similar to Miller's and useful for distinguishing his denomination from the variety of Protestant communions that were competing for souls and resources. Born in Strabane, Tyrone County, Ireland, in 1814, the grandson of a Presbyterian Church of Ireland pastor, Robinson's parents migrated to Virginia when he was a young boy. He overcame several obstacles—his father's business failure, his mother's death, a disabled arm (thanks to a nurse who failed to catch him after a throw in the air as a baby)—to become a pastor at several churches in the U.S. South and a professor at Danville Seminary (Kentucky). Robinson's specific reason for extending what had been an inaugural lecture at the seminary in 1857 into a book was "the Church question" raised by the Oxford Movement. Miller's 1840 book provided answers closer to the beginning of the ecclesiological inquiry, while the Mercersburg Theology of John Williamson Nevin and Philip Schaf (among the German Reformed) answered in a manner that conceded the validity of apostolic succession. Robinson divided the Protestant world of the United States between the "anti-evangelical Churchism" of the high church advocates, and the "anti-ecclesiastical evangelicalism" of those who promoted revivalism and parachurch organizations.[84] He presented Presbyterianism, found in the Church of Scotland's *Second Book of Discipline* and the Westminster Assembly's "Form of Government," as a third and best way.

As predictable as Robinson's invocation of those iconic documents may have appeared—the book included both sources as appendices—his case for church government by councils was one of the most original produced at a time when textbooks on church polity were abundant. Instead of turning to the ancient church, as so many Presbyterian advocates had before him, Robinson went even further back, namely, to God's eternal decree. That audacious turn situated Presbyterianism in God's covenant of redemption, the work of Christ to save the elect as the body of Christ, the manifestation of the family of God in the institutional church, and the governance of those believers through officers ruling in coordinated settings at congregational, presbyterial, and synodical levels. The pattern of church government, for Robinson, derived not merely from the New Testament but also from Old Testament structures of elders (heads of tribes) and the coordinated rule or prophets, priests, and kings.[85]

Robinson also included a set of columns, almost like a chart, that ran for several pages and listed the chief differences among Presbyterians, Congregationalists, and advocates of episcopacy. Here again Robinson refined and extended arguments against bishops that earlier Presbyterians had not always made explicit. For instance, on the nature of church power, Presbyterianism reflected God's design to redeem an elect group, and form them into a spiritual commonwealth, with "laws, officers, and ordinances." In contrast, prelacy started with the apostles and "their successors in office," from the top down, akin to a monarchy. Unlike episcopal hierarchy, Presbyterian government originated from "an organic body composed of rulers and ruled."[86] This difference persisted in Presbyterians' and Episcopalians' relationship to the civil government. For Presbyterians, the church's power was strictly spiritual and independent of the magistrate, the conviction that over and over had troubled English and Scottish authorities going back to the seventeenth century. In contrast, prelacy implied a hierarchy with an order "superior to the civil government," or one that should at least have "concurrent jurisdiction" with the magistrate. It went without saying, though Robinson said it anyway, that the chief offices for the two sides were elders (teaching and ruling) and bishops. This, in turn, led to the different settings in which church administration took place. For prelacy, bishops acted on their own, sometimes consulting with advisory councils of bishops. For Presbyterians, the chief outlet was a tribunal or council. Presbyterians relied on representative bodies with "well-defined and limited powers from the lowest to the highest court."[87]

As much as Robinson acknowledged a debt to the Scots, he argued that the prospects for Presbyterianism were much better in the United States than in Scotland. He was not comfortable with this observation. Scottish Presbyterians were a "noble race," too great in the "grandeur of their character" for subsequent generations of British Protestants to recognize thanks to the latter's "dilettantism."[88] The Scots' great achievement was to "recognize those great constituent truths" that underlay both the spiritual and the civil commonwealths. But the perils of Scottish society forced the Kirk to adopt a peace treaty with the civil government that compromised the spiritual character and independence of the church. Scottish Presbyterianism, accordingly, descended into the "Church of the Martyrs," then the "Church of the Moderates," and finally Babylon itself. In the United States, Presbyterians could freely rally the "elect of God under the banner of Christ's Crown and Covenant."[89] Robinson knew American Presbyterianism still needed reform, but he was nonetheless optimistic. Providence "seemed" to indicate that American Presbyterians had a "high and glorious mission" to institute ideals of the Scottish Reformers.[90]

However convincing Robinson and Miller may have been to their peers outside the United States, their arguments were among the most sustained assertions of Presbyterian church government in the nineteenth century. The reason may be that disestablishment and voluntarism finally allowed Presbyterians to voice, full throttle, the spiritual independence of the church. A voluntary church may have been a plausible outcome to Presbyterian assertions of the church's spiritual authority. What prevented that position from blossoming, at least in the practice of ecclesiastical independence, was Presbyterians' dependence (like other magisterial Protestants) on a supporting monarch, prince, or city council. Only a Christian civil magistrate could underwrite a church in a Christendom setting. In places and times such as nineteenth-century England and the United States, however, spiritual independence was a reality as much as it was a doctrine. Once past the fears of upheaval from the late eighteenth-century republican revolutions, voluntarism and a spiritually independent church looked like the best option for Presbyterians.

CHAPTER 7

Divine-Right Stipends

Few historians of Christianity confuse Nova Scotia with Geneva in the annals of Protestant history. Even so, the eighteenth-century peninsula in the most eastern part of what became the Dominion of Canada had all the ingredients that made the city of John Calvin's ministry famous. This was no less true even if Nova Scotia entered Presbyterian history almost two centuries after the French pastor's death. Despite its remote location, Nova Scotia became the object of Protestant interest when in 1713 Louis XIV ceded the territory to Queen Anne in the Treaty of Utrecht. That agreement was a significant moment for Dutch Protestantism since it put an end to war with Spain (and its French ally). From this point, Nova Scotia's narrative was one part Ireland and another part Geneva.

The peninsula's resemblance to Ireland stemmed from the British government's intention to settle a loyal population that could supplant the majority of Acadian inhabitants, who were French-speaking Roman Catholics. "Plantation" may not be the word to describe British rule, but the similarities between the way Protestantism spread to both Ireland and Nova Scotia are hard to avoid. Recruitment appeals for North America—which included land grants—were sent to British Protestants and to Reformed believers in Switzerland, the Netherlands, and Germany.

Failure to attract enough settlers, hostility between the French (and Native Americans) and Protestants, and the larger international hostility between Britain and France, prompted the British government between 1755 and 1764 to deport large numbers of Acadians to colonies in the south; most went to Massachusetts, but others were spread between Pennsylvania and Georgia. Roughly 2,600 remained by 1763 at the end of the French and Indian War.[1]

Nova Scotia's need for pastors gave an opening to Presbyterians, who eventually became the largest rival to the Church of England throughout Canadian society. Initially, the religious settlement looked like a repeat of England's ecclesiastical establishment. A 1758 act made provision for religious worship and required conformity to the Church of England's norms. The next year brought a guarantee of religious freedom for "persons of all persuasions, except Papists." The legislation also exempted Dissenters from taxes "levied" for the support of the established church. That provision became attractive to Protestants in Ulster and New England who were looking for a new home. In the calculations of nineteenth-century church historian William Gregg, ships landing in the early 1760s brought 200 settlers from Boston, 180 from Plymouth, 100 from New London and Rhode Island, and 200 from Northern Ireland.[2]

The large number of Presbyterians among these settlers prompted the people of Halifax to ask the Presbytery of New Brunswick (New Jersey) for a pastor. In reply, the presbytery sent James Lyon, a recent graduate of the College of New Jersey. New Brunswick had ordained Lyon in 1764 before he moved to Canada, on the condition that he labor for at least ten months in the new church. The nineteenth-century American theologian Charles Hodge referred to this incident in his history of colonial Presbyterianism. He quoted a letter from the Presbytery of New Brunswick to Lyon to calm fears about lax subscription among American Presbyterians who were still recovering from controversies over the awakenings led by George Whitefield. The letter insisted that the Westminster Confession was received in New Jersey "without equivocation, and in the true and proper sense of the words." In addition, discipline was "faithfully and regularly exercised."[3]

Pastor Lyon lasted only a few years in Halifax before taking a call to a Presbyterian congregation in Maine, a short tenure that indicated the challenge of planting European-style congregations on the frontier.

Between 1765 and 1795, Presbyterian inhabitants of Nova Scotia sent requests to Scotland for pastors with mixed success. The communions most responsive were the Seceders (Associate Reformed Presbyterians, ARP). In fact, James Murdoch was the pastor with the longest tenure in Nova Scotia and came from the ARP's Anti-Burgher synod. After roughly a year in Halifax, Murdoch moved to Horton on the Bay of Minas and preached to scattered Scottish and Irish settlers as an itinerant. The general state of church life was typical of Protestantism in North American British colonies—scattered, haphazard, and underfunded. A 1769 financial petition to England rendered a bleak estimate. The people were in "such low circumstances" that they could not "get a bare subsistence for their families." The past year had seen the crop of corn fall so low that "many suffered for want of bread."[4] This left the residents unable to "perform contracts with their ministers, which, under other circumstances, they would be willing and desirous to do." Without pastors, the people would likely abandon the province. For that reason, "all well-wishers to religion," and "advocates of liberty of conscience and the right of private judgment" needed to provide charitable assistance for the support of clergy.[5]

That petition for support of Presbyterians and Congregationalists did not mention Church of England priests and school teachers also working in Nova Scotia. According to Gregg, at least six Anglicans were already working in the province. What is more, they received "liberal grants of land and money" from the imperial government and the Society for the Propagation of the Gospel.[6] Such political favoritism was responsible for the unlikely persistence of debates almost two centuries old between Presbyterians and their episcopal adversaries. Although revolutions—Glorious and American—tamed the wildest political features of Presbyterian zeal, a Presbyterian sense of superiority died hard. The ideals of a covenanted nation may have vanished except among those who still adhered to the National Covenant (1638). But vestiges of religious establishment lived on through the curious mechanisms the British Crown and its governments used to fund deserving Presbyterian pastors outside the established churches. Arriving at the point where such financial support was either not needed or unwanted was the final transition to a voluntary church. Being willing to abandon an established church that was also the Christian lifeblood of the nation was a long way to go for Presbyterians thanks to their historic attachment to a godly magistrate. Internal divisions among Presbyterian communions added to the challenge.

The Crown's Generosity

Isaac Watts has for almost three centuries competed with Charles Wesley for the most hymns by one writer in any average Anglo-American Protestant hymnal, but Presbyterians generally favored the former thanks to his status as an English Nonconformist pastor. Before becoming a private tutor for the Hartopp family, Watts was the minister for a Congregationalist church in London. He was pastor most notably during the time of the Salters' Hall debates, and his own attempts to bring peace to Congregationalist and Presbyterian disputes about the deity of Christ led him away from the Savoy Declaration's doctrinal norms. After his death, Unitarians claimed Watts as one of their own. Whatever the merits of that case, Watts was part of a generation of dissenting Protestants who resisted the state's imposition of orthodoxy through creedal subscription (see chapter 6 herein).

Watts's doctrinal positions notwithstanding, Presbyterians had little trouble selecting from among his 750 hymns for their hymnals when awakenings tempted them to turn away from exclusive use of the Hebrew Psalter for congregational song. Some of the favorites that have remained in Presbyterian hymnals (until the rise of praise bands) include "Alas, and Did My Savior Bleed," "Give to Our God Immortal Praise," "Jesus Shall Reign Where'er the Sun," "Joy to the World! The Lord Is Come!," "Our God, Our Help in Ages Past," and "When I Survey the Wondrous Cross."[7] Watts's verse was not confined to public worship but extended to honoring the civil magistrate. For the coronation of George II and Queen Caroline, Watts wrote these words:

> Rise, happy Morn, fair Sun arise,
> Shed radiant Gold around the Skies,
> And rich in Beams and Blessings shine
> Profuse on GEORGE and CAROLINE.

Despite the challenges of ministering and worshiping outside the Anglican establishment, Watts was not the only dissenting minister to offer effusive praise for the new monarch. James Clegg, another dissenter, echoed Watts by declaring that the coronation of George II was "the most magnificent and the joy the most universal that had been known." The Presbyterian pastor at Exeter, John Enty, was similarly ebullient. The new king showed himself to be a "zealous Protestant" and a "*Nursing Father*" to the faithful. The same was true for his wife, who, in Enty's words, was a queen of "such justly admired Accomplishments, to be its *Nursing Mother*."[8]

Such fulsome praise from dissenters may sound odd without considering the treatment that English Protestants received from the Crown in the form of the *regium donum*. This gift to Protestant Dissenters, ostensibly for support of pastor's widows (eventually extended to impoverished pastors also) was a significant part of English and Irish Presbyterian life during the eighteenth and nineteenth centuries. Historians offer different explanations for the Crown's grant to Dissenters—whether it was a way of minimizing opposition to the religious establishment or a reward that Whigs used to maintain power. Either way, it was a curious feature of church politics at a time when voluntarism and freedom of religion were becoming the norm. Denominationalism was the flip side of this trend. By accepting that different denominations were parts of one Protestant currency, English-speaking churches hastened an ecumenism that dissolved distinct attachments to the bishops, presbyteries, awakenings, or specific means for achieving personal holiness.

Before the voluntary principle for sustaining church life became government policy, however, the *regium donum* was a mechanism for softening the civil penalties that Dissenters experienced thanks to the Test and Corporation Act of 1673. Although not draconian, these laws specified that anyone occupying a civil, military, or religious office needed to swear an oath to the Crown's supremacy. The legislation also required subscribing a declaration against transubstantiation. Within three months of taking these vows, officials needed to take Communion in the Church of England. The 1673 legislation obviously restricted Roman Catholic participation in British public life, but also hampered Presbyterians who either objected to royal supremacy or the prayer book (or both). A gift from the Crown seemed on the surface to contradict the purpose of religious uniformity. The grant system began in 1722, when George I, on the advice of Prime Minister Robert Walpole, set up treasury payments of 500 pounds for the relief of dissenting ministers' widows. Soon the grant expanded to poor pastors. The English body used by government to administer these funds was a group of ministers who served as trustees to a trust established by Dr. Daniel Williams, a Congregationalist pastor and theologian. Williams had left an estate and library for training dissenting ministers. Of the ten trustees in the 1720s, eight were Presbyterian.

This royal grant had precedent in Irish Protestantism. Charles II had established a *regium donum* for Irish Presbyterians at the level of 600 pounds. But an inadequacy of revenues allowed the treasury to make only the 1676 payment. At roughly the same time, the king also made provision for allocating fifty pounds a year to roughly ten English Presbyterian ministers, headed by Richard Baxter. At the time of the Glorious Revolution, William III revived the grant to Ulster Presbyterians. Queen Anne eventually extended the grants to ministers in the south of Ireland. Throughout the period running up to George I's policy, Presbyterians (and other Dissenters) were ambivalent about the funds since they gave the appearance of buying off objections to the Test Act. And because pastors administered the *regium donum* in secret, critics could always allege that the trustees were guilty of favoritism.[9]

In 1736, Samuel Chandler, a Presbyterian minister, brought a motion to a meeting of Dissenters at Salters' Hall to refuse the grants because Dissenters should not receive "money from persons in power." Chandler also objected to the secrecy of the trustees' activities. The proposal failed, but the concerns behind Chandler's motion lingered. Despite a generally equitable and charitable distribution of funds to widows and destitute ministers, the grants' trustees—the majority of whom were Presbyterian—continued to face criticism. (Baptists and Independents were not excluded and had their own procedures for distribution.) The governing body was the subject of a minor pamphlet battle in the 1770s that alleged the administrators were the "king's men," more interested in cooperation with the government than in repealing the Test Act. At issue in part were changes in doctrinal requirements for receiving the funds. The trustees wanted to use the Thirty-Nine Articles as criteria for ministers (and their families) to receive funding. They feared growing dissent from the doctrine of the Trinity. For critics of the trustees, however, this doctrinal requirement appeared to place the fund's administrators on the side of the "rank tories," who had voted recently to uphold the Test Act.[10] None of the critics suggested trustees had used the funds for personal gain. Moreover, each of the administrators remained respected figures among Protestant Dissenters.

After several decades of calm, the *regium donum* returned to public scrutiny in the 1790s in ways that made the program unsustainable. One of the grant's administrators, Thomas Martin, a Baptist, made an offhand remark, as the French Revolution was playing out and England and France were still at war, about Dissenters supporting French soldiers if they landed on English soil. Patriots took exception, and rumors circulated about the possible destruction of Dissenters' homes and meeting houses. In response, the trustees reorganized their membership to include equal numbers of Presbyterians, Baptists, and Independents. At the same time, Dissenters themselves recognized that the *regium donum* was a small part of their revenues. According to K. R. M. Short, "thousands of pounds were raised and allocated each year" by wealthy London congregations, annual sermons, and other forms of solicitation, to "ease the conditions of the less fortunate nonconformists."[11] Such breadth of support was likely responsible for one dissenting pastor, who argued in the *Morning Chronicle* (1792) that Nonconformists should give up the "Queen's Bounty" in return for the freedom to conduct marriage ceremonies.[12] By 1828, at the time of the Test Act's repeal, such quid pro quo arrangements became obviously unnecessary. Free from penalties, Presbyterians and other English Dissenters no longer needed financial incentives to go along with the established religious order. Even so, six years after the Test Act's repeal, Thomas Rees, a Presbyterian, continued to defend the grant as completely above reproach.[13]

After the repeal of the Test Act, however, debates about the *regium donum* spawned wider appreciation for voluntarism. For critics of dissent, Noncomformist pastors' need for charity was a sign of the weakness of Protestants outside the Church of England. In fact, maintaining the *regium donum* became a technique by which to stigmatize Protestant Dissent as incapable of self-sufficiency.[14] Dissenters such as the Presbyterian Rees, meanwhile, did not seem to understand the contradiction between recommending the royal grants even after removing legal restrictions on Noncomformists. Here older arguments that Christianity flourished most when freed from civil obligations made little sense of any continued reliance on the *regium donum*.[15] Presbyterians suffered more in these debates than Baptists and Congregationalists because of their associations with the Church of Scotland and their history of arguing for a religious (read Presbyterian) establishment. When opposition to the *regium donum* intensified in 1841 with the formation of the British Anti-State Church Association, Baptists and Congregationalists were noticeably active compared to Presbyterian indifference. Moreover, Presbyterians' associations with Unitarianism gave Baptists and Congregationalists more reasons to distance themselves from the royal grants. Even so, Presbyterians dominated the administration of the *regium donum*, but they benefited least from actual allocation. In 1847, for instance, the trustees' report showed that of the 1,070 recipients, 166 were Presbyterian, 443 Independents, and 461 Baptists.[16]

When the *regium donum* finally ended in 1851, it did so with little fanfare or controversy. In 1849, a vote in Parliament went against the grants

Figure 7.1. *Battle of the Boyne, Ireland, between Kings James II and William III, 12 July 1690*, oil on canvas by Jan van Huchtenburgh.

by a majority of five votes for every three in support. Two years later, the chancellor informed the House of Lords that "the grant would not be proposed for the coming year."[17] Through it all, the grants gave English Presbyterians a weak tie to religious establishment, even though hopes for a Presbyterian Church of England had vanished almost two centuries earlier. In return for receiving the *regium donum*, Presbyterians gave up on reforming the national church. As good English subjects, Presbyterian objections to the tyranny of prelacy or royal supremacy went silent.

The Crown's Irish Problem

The history of the *regium donum* for English Nonconformists was bound up with a similar arrangement for Irish Dissenters. In fact, the end of the English grants in 1851 coincided with debates about the value and legitimacy of the Irish *regium donum*. In both cases, critics of the funds regarded the payments as a way to calm opposition both to the Church of England and the Church of Ireland. "The mendicant multitude—English and Irish, orthodox and heterodox, Papal and Protestant, Socianian and Calvinist—all are huddled together in one motley group, like so much quarry rubbish collected on the beach," one Congregationalist pastor wrote, "to constitute a sort of breakwater to beat back the surge of popular opinion which threatens to sweep away the foundations of Ecclesiastic Establishments."[18]

That framing of the objection may well have expressed resentment over the preferential treatment that Presbyterians in Ireland received through the payment system. At the same time, the *regium donum* had for Irish Presbyterians a measure of plausibility that their ecclesiastical siblings in other parts of the English-speaking world lacked.

From one angle, the history of the Presbyterian Church in Ireland mirrors debates over subscription and polity that played out in Scotland and North America, but with an important difference. The support Irish pastors and congregations received from the Crown was one factor. Another was the assistance Presbyterians supplied to William III during the Glorious Revolution that made the *regium donum* a reward for their loyalty to the Crown. Yet an additional layer to the unique character of Irish Presbyterianism was their minority and dissenting status in a place where the religious establishment was episcopal and the country's population was mostly Roman Catholic. Altogether, these considerations made the *regium donum* not simply a matter of financial support for indigent pastors, widows, and congregations. It was also a marker of ecclesiastical and political respectability.

On the one hand, thanks to the Test Act of 1673, Presbyterian ministers in Ireland labored under significant restrictions. The marriages they performed were technically invalid. Ministers could not teach in schools. To perform a burial service they needed to use the rites of the Church of Ireland. Laws forbade the meeting of church assemblies (presbytery or synod). They could not preach. And civil authorities imposed fines of 100 pounds for celebrating the Lord's Supper. For Presbyterians who were not ministers, the Test Act prohibited them from holding public office. One way that government encouraged compliance was to threaten the cessation of the *regium donum* for a period after said offense.[19]

On the other hand, the grants became harder to administer as Presbyterians in Ireland diversified. After a lapse during the first two decades of the eighteenth century, thanks to legislative uncertainties, personal preferences of the British monarchy, and desire to protect the religious establishment, the system returned with George I. Initially the grants went to the Synod of Ulster and then generally to dissenting ministers in the south. But as Irish Presbyterians experienced divisions over subscription and grew to include Scottish transplants, such as the Seceders (the Associate Presbytery), the *regium donum* went to the largest and most respectable, namely, the Synod of Ulster, the Presbytery of Antrim (nonsubscribing), and the Secession Synod. (In the nineteenth century, the grants even included Unitarians among the provisions for Nonconformists.) Defenders of the Church of Ireland repeatedly objected that the grants undermined the established church. Irish demographics, however, required the enlistment of all Protestants under the umbrella of the British government's policies.[20]

If the civil authorities lumped together Irish Protestants for political ends, the system also surprisingly consolidated Presbyterians. This was particularly true of relations between the Synod of Ulster and the Seceders owing to the appeal and rationale of the *regium donum*. When the latter began to organize congregations in Ireland in the 1740s, they were generally distrustful of the existing Irish Presbyterians (Synod of Ulster).

On the one hand, the subscription controversy of the 1720s among the Irish indicated a doctrinal laxity that ran contrary to Seceder rigor. On the other, the *regium donum* was a scheme that could either easily be abused or compromise the church's independence. Relations between the two sets of Presbyterians were testy for most of the eighteenth century, even while the Seceders tended to suffer less from penalties against Dissenters than the Synod of Ulster, which looked askance at the Seceders because of their novelty and small numbers.

By 1784, however, when Seceders began to receive the *regium donum*, antagonisms between the two groups started slowly to subside. In fact, when the Seceders became part of the grant system, their thirty-eight pastors were divided into the Burgher and Anti-Burgher branches (see chapter 4 herein), even though the oaths responsible for the split were part of Scotland's politics and irrelevant within Ireland. But the classification system for dispersing the grants, initiated in response to the 1798 Rising, raised questions about political loyalty as a condition for eligibility for the grants. The British government, especially after the 1801 Act of Union, had incentives to use the grants to ensure allegiance from Presbyterians of all stripes.[21] These new political realities reduced antagonisms between the Synod of Ulster and the Seceders. Suspicions remained, and sometimes Seceders were especially attuned to preferential treatment for the Ulster Synod, whose history and size made its congregations eligible for larger subsidies. But in 1809, the Seceders began to receive funds in proportions similar to the Synod of Ulster.[22]

Such equal treatment in financial matters may have eased Seceder suspicion of the Synod of Ulster, but concerns about doctrinal laxity persisted. Seceders had legitimate reason for alarm in the 1820s when another subscription controversy erupted in the Synod of Ulster. The debate arose with the appointment of an apparently Arian-leaning professor, William Bruce, at the Belfast Academical Institution, a school established in 1815 to bring higher education in reach of Presbyterians wanting to enter the ministry. Debates again pitted those who insisted on subscription to the Westminster Standards against those opposed for the sake of liberty of conscience. In 1835, the Synod of Ulster voted by a fairly large majority to require anyone seeking ordination to subscribe the Westminster Standards. The controversy lingered because of ecclesiastical and civil politics. Within the church, the matter of subscription raised questions about enforcement. Because the nature of church power within the Ulster Synod was largely congregational, requiring subscription through church courts was mainly wishful thinking. Also at play were changes that came with Catholic Emancipation (1828) and differences among Presbyterians over the proper response: religious freedom for all or restricting political participation to Protestants.[23]

The Synod of Ulster's resolve to require subscription was not alone responsible for reassuring Seceders. Also persuasive was the response in 1839 from four ministers in the synod to an assertion of episcopal superiority by Archibald Boyd, a Church of Ireland curate in the cathedral at Londonderry. He was also a distinguished preacher, and in 1838 delivered a series of sermons on episcopacy and Anglican liturgy to cultivate a high church position in the Irish church. His *Sermons on the Church*, four in all, relied on older arguments for bishops drawn from readings of the pastoral epistles that corrected Presbyterian interpretations of words such as "elder" and "overseer." Whatever the Apostle Paul may have written about elders, Boyd could not help noting that the letters went directly to one person, either Timothy or Titus, who functioned as bishops in the ancient church. Despite slander directed at the Church of Ireland, and the bishops' sometime bashfulness, Boyd implored confidence: "Our church is scriptural in her constitution and can claim kindred with the oldest and purest communities in the peculiarities of her government."[24]

Given their minority position in Irish society at large, Presbyterians were generally deferential to the Church of Ireland, but Boyd's attack produced a vigorous defense of Presbyterian government. *Presbyterianism Defended* (1839) was the work of four Irish Presbyterians. W. D. Killen drew the assignment on apostolic succession, William McClure on episcopacy, James Denham on the church's spiritual independence, and Alexander Porter Goudy on worship. The tone was less dramatic—not as zealous and self-righteous—than older briefs for Presbyterianism before the Glorious Revolution. Killen, for instance, warned that Presbyterians not adopt a superior attitude since God honored faithful Independents and some in the national church. A Presbyterian church without love was "a temple from which the glory has departed." At the same time, Killen told his audience to expect that the "purest piety" will emerge where Christians worship according to the "purest forms."[25] So too, McClure answered the charge that Presbyterians were being divisive by maintaining their separate and peculiar worship. On the one hand, Presbyterianism best functioned as a hedge against the "pernicious doctrines" that were circulating in the Church of England.[26] On the other hand, no one would plausibly entertain charges against Luther, Knox, Melville, and Rutherford for disrupting the peace and unity of the church in their day.

When Denham turned to the church's spiritual authority, he also contended that Presbyterianism was particularity propitious for contributing to the general good of the church. To insist on this government was not selfish, but biblical. Even more, it was the only church government to bring "*all* the people and *all* the ministers, the *humblest* member and the *highest* ruler under a free government, and yet an effective control."[27] Perhaps the feistiest of the chapters was the one Goudy contributed. Although he recognized the Church of Ireland and the Church of England were home to genuine believers, the author was alarmed that any bishop or priest would claim that "prelatic supremacy" was "essential to Christian unity." "We cannot be expected to stand tamely by and see everything we hold dear as Presbyterians flouted at and scorned," he insisted, not only by "ignorant or infidel declaimers" but also by "the educated and learned of the land."[28]

Yet, the most startling part of the book was the introduction from Henry Wallace, moderator of the Synod of Ulster. He framed the four discourses by admitting Presbyterians had lost their former zeal. Wallace lamented that defenses of Presbyterianism had become rare and the reading public had not seen for some time the credentials of the Presbyterian Church's "Divine commission." Even among Irish Presbyterians, pastors had avoided the distinguishing characteristics of their church polity for fear of stirring up needless controversy. But that changed with the assertions of episcopacy and apostolic succession, first in the Church of Ireland and then with the Oxford Movement. Claims from High Church Anglicans of "exclusive apostolicity" reserved for bishops smacked of "haughty superciliousness" and "intolerant severity" in ways reminiscent of Rome.[29] In fact, Wallace thought recent developments in the Irish and English established churches proved Presbyterians were right to worry that prelacy bred Romanism. Of course, the claim from advocates of episcopacy that Presbyterianism was an invalid ministry because its ministers were not ordained by successors of apostles was nonsense, he added.

The commission that Presbyterians held was from "the Messiah, the Head of the church." For good measure, Wallace added that Presbyterianism was better adapted than Anglicanism for "promulgating truth" and "suppressing error."[30]

For historical support, Wallace looked to Scotland, the incubator of Ulster Presbyterianism, in ways that may have surprised fellow members in his synod. Although opposition to bishops did not require the same "stern practical necessity" as in the early days of "our Scottish forefathers," Presbyterians could claim victories by limiting "royal prerogative" and diminishing the influence of prelates in national assemblies.[31] Still, the real historical inspiration for Irish Presbyterians were the Covenanters. By no means remembered fondly thanks to "fashionable ignorance and prejudice," the "tales of [the Covenanters'] sufferings . . . hallowed the converse of Presbyterian firesides."[32]

In the days of Catholic emancipation and expanded suffrage, Wallace's was an unusual appeal to the dark days of religious war. But the memory of those devout Presbyterians in popular paintings by George Harvey—*The Covenanters' Communion* (before 1840) and *The Covenanters' Preaching* (1830)—Wallace wrote, should not be limited merely to piety. In fact, the recent celebrations in Edinburgh, Glasgow, and Derry of Scotland's "deliverance from prelacy" had revived "sympathy with the spirit" and admiration not just for the zeal but also "the deeds" of the Covenanters.[33] Wallace sensed that among Irish Presbyterians the "old spirit," expressed under the banner "CHRIST'S CROWN AND COVENANT," was growing. Moreover, it was time for Presbyterians no longer to be ashamed of "our convictions of the unscriptural character of prelacy."[34] Granted, the Covenanters' "stern" stand was no longer necessary. Thanks to Presbyterian victories already secured, the Irish church was free to follow "the less perilous duty of argumentative warfare." For that reason, the recent assertions of divine-right episcopacy required a forceful response, namely, that Presbyterians were legitimate, scriptural, and deserved credit for the advance of British liberties.[35]

This revival of Presbyterian-versus-episcopal polemics may have been surprising in the Irish context, but it was important for consolidating the Presbyterian Church of Ireland, even as ministers were losing financial support from the Crown. The exchange between Irish Presbyterians and Anglicans went on for several more years. Archibald Boyd countered in the same year that Wallace and others were writing. His reply came as *Episcopacy, Ordination, Lay-Eldership, and Liturgies* (1839). Presbyterians responded with *The Plea of Presbytery* (1840). According to Andrew R. Holmes, this skirmish instilled among Presbyterians a "different spirit." No longer deferential to the religious establishment, now Presbyterians were eager to "debate as equals."[36] The Synod of Ulster in 1840 passed a resolution of thanks for the ministers who had advocated and defended the claims of Presbyterianism. That these assertions took place at the same time that the Synod of Ulster and the Secession Synod were planning a union was not a coincidence. Irish Presbyterians' recovery of ecclesiastical militancy was important in persuading Irish Seceders that the two parties held the same convictions and followed the same practices. The formal ratification of the union took place on July 10, 1840, in Belfast and paved the way for Irish Presbyterians to hold their first "General Assembly of the Presbyterian Church of Ireland." The Ulster Synod contributed 292 congregations to the union compared to 141 from the Secession Synod. Combined, the Presbyterian Church in Ireland had roughly 650,000 members. (In the religious census of 1834, the Church of Ireland had about 850,000 members.)

As welcome as the consolidation of Irish Presbyterians may have been, it put the Presbyterian Church in an awkward position. On the one hand, they still suffered under laws that rendered them Nonconformists and so unable to perform marriages that the civil courts recognized. A case came before the courts in the 1840s that questioned this code and led to the Marriage Act of 1844, which removed some barriers to Presbyterian weddings.[37] This was another instance in which Presbyterians complained forcefully about Anglican persecution of fellow Protestants and blamed Puseyism, a word used synonymously with the Oxford Movement's High Church ideals, for influencing the Church of Ireland. On the other hand, Presbyterians still benefited from the *regium donum* and so enjoyed a quasi-establishmentarian status. While voluntarism was emerging as the standard way of sustaining churches in liberal societies, vestiges of the codependent relationship between church and state persisted even in Ireland.

Awkwardness increased especially in the 1860s during debates over disestablishment of the Church of Ireland. Members of the General Assembly divided between continuing the *regium donum*, which the Irish

Church Act would have ended, and looking for alternative mechanisms of financial support. Arguably, the most sustained attack on the royal grants came from an anonymous pamphlet, published in 1865, under the title *The Irish* Regium Donum: *Its History, Character, and Effects.* Although the pamphlet added little to the history of the grants, the discussion of their effects was stunning if only for exposing Irish Presbyterian hypocrisy. The author noted a policy from 1850 that required Presbyterian pastors to use the sign of the cross when administering a baptism, a clear indication that the royal grants regulated and controlled pastors. The *regium donum* was nothing less than "a State collar for the necks of recipients."[38] If fear of state control of the church was one reason for discontinuing the grants, another was the civil government's indifference to religious truth through its support for groups as diverse as Unitarians and Roman Catholics.[39] One more damning aspect was that although competition between the Ulster Synod and the Seceder churches for the grants had led to the 1840 union, that outcome owed more to financial than spiritual motives.[40] Worst of all was the glaring evidence, with an accountant's rigor, of Irish Presbyterians' stinginess. For support, the author quoted an official report that concluded "no class of Christians have been in the habit of paying so little to their ministers as the laity of several Presbyterian Synods endowed by Parliamentary grant."[41]

The pamphlet's anonymous author (who used the name, "A Voluntary") concluded with even stronger words about voluntarism. The *regium donum* had taught Presbyterians the wrong lesson, namely, one of not living on the merits of their ministry but instead trusting "princes and governments to do the duty for them." From here, the argument shifted to church history and what Presbyterians did best—or at least thought they did. They looked to the ancient church not merely for examples but models and norms for ministry. There, readers could see that the voluntary principle was "our Divine Master's own ordinance for the maintenance and extension of his Church." Christ had taught his disciples to "look for support from those whom they taught." A *donum* from Nero would have been unthinkable and "refused had it been offered." "Ten thousand times . . . would we eke out, as Paul did, by the labour of our hands, the scanty subsistence that a weak or young Church may be able to give, than accept wealth and comfort from any other source than our supreme Head and King."[42]

That appeal to the ancient church, of course, dredged up perennial disagreements between Presbyterians and Anglicans about the character of the pre-Constantinian church and the degree to which it was the norm for all subsequent churches. The author claimed that during the first three centuries of the church, its "palmiest and most successful," no other principle other than voluntarism "was in operation." The most recent example of placing the church on a voluntary setting came from the Free Church of Scotland. The author conceded that Free Church advocates still maintained the establishment principle, but this left the communion as the "poorest State Church in Christendom." More accurate was the reality that "no sooner did [the Free Church] appeal to the Christian voluntary liberality of her people, than she had laid in heaps at her feet twenty times over as much as she had in vain sued the Government to give her." This was a call not only for the elimination of the *regium donum* in Ireland but the removal of state churches in England and Scotland altogether. "Episcopalian, Popish, and Presbyterian endowments" always prevented voluntarism "from thriving."[43] All of these considerations led to a final plea: "Relieve Ireland of her Church Establishment, which has for ages been an incubus on her improvement, and a mockery to the world."[44]

The advantages of voluntarism soon became apparent, even as the loss of the *regium donum* opened a whole new set of challenges for Irish Presbyterians and the British government. Thanks to the growing opposition to an established church and the financial arrangement that sustained the Church of Ireland, the Liberal Party under the leadership of William Gladstone supported disestablishment. The son of Scots with evangelical convictions (the mother Episcopal, the father Presbyterian), Gladstone became a High Church Anglican later in life, even as his politics switched from Conservative to Liberal. He also changed his views about the Irish religious establishment. His book *The State in Its Relation with the Church* (1838) advocated a confessional state under the tutelage and ministry of Anglicanism—both in England and Ireland. By the 1860s, as the leader of the Liberal Party (prime minister in 1868), Gladstone switched course. The change, he explained in an 1869 speech, owed to the Church of Ireland's place within the Protestant Ascendancy. This form of establishment was "odious and dangerous" and restricted evangelism among the ordinary Irish people.[45] Disestablishment had the advantage of placing the Church of Ireland on an even footing with other Irish communions and making Protestantism more attractive.

Irish disestablishment became the centerpiece of Gladstone's Liberal government thanks to the rise of Fenianism (a radical republican group driven by Irish nationalism) among the concerns of the electorate in the 1868 elections. Disestablishment was one part of the Liberal Party's effort to try to pacify radical violence. Gladstone's strategy was to isolate the Fenians from the Irish people, who would prefer liberal reforms over an independent Irish republic. Presbyterians may have dabbled in republicanism in the 1790s, but Fenianism changed that outlook. Even so, with disestablishment would come the loss of the *regium donum*. Debates for almost an entire year revealed problems with Gladstone's plan. The Tories, led by Benjamin Disraeli, proposed a "concurrent" establishment that would have funded Presbyterians and Roman Catholics along with the Church of Ireland. Queen Victoria herself objected to the Crown losing its status as head of the Irish church. No matter the reservations, Gladstone was able to prevail, and on July 26, 1869, the Irish Church Act passed into law.[46] Although it disestablished the Church of Ireland, it did not freeze assets. Several provisions for short-term funding, payments to clergy, and financing for schools were part of the legislation that went into effect two years later. (To this day, the Church of Ireland declares that disestablishment was the "greatest gift" to Irish Anglicans.)[47]

The outcome did not please Presbyterians because it meant life with the blessing of the *regium donum*. Thomas Hamilton described in *History of the Irish Presbyterian Church* (1886) how many feared that disestablishment would "inflict the severest blow" on Presbyterians that they "had ever sustained."[48] But the arrangement came with a golden parachute. Ministers who had been receiving the grants could opt between either receiving it for the remainder of their lives or receive one final "lump sum." Either way, these funds would have been for the pastors' private use. Since many ministers depended on the stipends, Hamilton explained, no one would have begrudged a decision based on the personal needs of each pastor, congregation, and dependent families.

Many worried how the church could sustain itself financially in the future. But two meetings took place that seemed to prove the author of *The Irish* Regium Donum correct about a voluntary church. In 1869 in Belfast, a large Lay Conference took place in which all local congregations sent representatives. This body established a Sustentation Fund to which those attending pledged annual support at the level of 30,000 pounds (total) each year. The next year, the pastors who met at the General Assembly contributed their revenues in a freewill offering to an endowment fund for the Presbyterian Church. The total received was more than 585,000 pounds, which generated an annual interest of roughly 25,000 pounds. According to Hamilton's tallies, the total income in 1886 from both of these funds was close to 50,000 pounds, 11,000 more than Irish Presbyterians had received from the *regium donum*.[49] Voluntarism did appear to be more lucrative than state generosity.

Despite good relations between Irish Presbyterians and the Free Church of Scotland, the latter communion's loyalty to the establishment principle prompted its members to criticize voluntarism. Even if the Free Church needed to find private sources of funding, leading voices in the communion still affirmed establishmentarianism. James Begg, moderator of the Free Church in the mid-1860s, explained that in a voluntary system, the state abdicated its duty to promote the true religion. Disestablishment meant, at least implicitly, that the government had no obligation to support truth but merely looked on as a neutral bystander. This was "monstrous" because it set Protestants and Roman Catholics on an equal footing—he insisted—in a "Protestant kingdom."[50] For Begg, the folly of this policy followed directly from Ireland's demographics. Disestablishment would lead to Presbyterianism's "weak congregations" being "swamped," "Protestants persecuted," Presbyterian children "trained up in popery," and Protestants unable to maintain "the cause of truth."[51]

From a different perspective, one less attached to the lessons of the Reformation than from the realities of liberal society, came Robert Elder's argument for abandoning the civil magistrate's patronage. Elder was pastor of the Free Church in West Rothesay, Scotland, and moderator of the General Assembly for 1871, and his pamphlet *The Irish Church Question: Considered with Special Reference to Free Church Principles* (1868) clarified the issue between voluntarism and establishmentarianism. The pastor professed his wholehearted support for the Irish Presbyterian Church. The church deserved respect for its "purity, soundness, zeal, and usefulness" and for "faithful witness to Christ in that dark land where Providence has planted her."[52] At the same time, Elder counseled that perpetuating the *regium donum* would inflict "deeper injury on the cause of truth." Elder knew that this put him on the side of disestablishment and conceded that his position was at odds with Scottish Presbyterian history. He knew that the Free Church was not of one mind.

Elder was compensating for reactions from some Free Church leaders who looked at the Irish situation as a defeat for the establishment principle. This view, Elder contended, contradicted the very terms that brought the Free Church into existence. "We judged it *unspeakably better* to have *no Establishment at all*, than one in which" the rights and liberties of Christ's church "should be trampled on."[53] In a word, the Scottish establishment was basically "Erastian," that is, the "subjection of the Church to the control of the State."[54] The Crown's rule over the Scottish church may not have been as direct as it was over the Church of England and Church of Ireland, but the dynamic was basically the same. Royal supremacy was at the root of ecclesiastical establishments in the United Kingdom.[55] The loss of the *regium donum* was a positive step because it ended the state's control of the church. Elder would not call himself a "voluntary" in "the ordinary sense."[56] But just as the 1843 Disruption in Scotland had proved that older establishmentarian ideals were no longer tenable, so too did the Irish Church Act indicate that Presbyterians needed to adjust to modern social circumstances.

Old World in the New

If Presbyterians in Ireland and Scotland were catching up to the demands of liberal society, their cousins in Canada were still playing by the old rules of church–state expectations. Presbyterianism came to the territories that eventually became Quebec and Ontario by sheer demographics. Presbyterian churches grew up around Scottish settlers, who like other colonists came to the New World for a host of reasons, largely inflected through economic motives. Congregations grew and institutions caught up. No committees from Scotland's churches planned for church extension. Not until the early nineteenth century did the idea of foreign missions even emerge among Protestants in the West. Its roots were in the evangelical awakenings and its mechanisms were agencies outside church structures.

The spontaneous origins of Canadian Presbyterianism could not obscure the predominance of Scottish influence on church life. The earliest structures of Presbyterianism emerged in Nova Scotia.[57] The first two presbyteries of exclusively Scottish origin were located in Truro (1786) and Pictou (1795). (Previous to this a haphazard group of Reformed ministers, French, English, and Scottish, had organized for purposes of ordination and cooperation.) The first two presbyteries were created by Seceders from Scotland. When in 1747 the Seceder Scottish communion split into Burgher and Anti-Burgher camps, Canada's first two presbyteries did so too: Pictou's Presbytery was Anti-Burgher, Truro was Burgher. Although these differences prevented cooperation, over time leaders recognized that Scotland's church politics did not transfer easily to the New World. After almost three decades of relative independence, in 1817 the two presbyteries agreed to form an overseeing body, the Synod of Nova Scotia. This higher administrative unit united not only Burghers and Anti-Burghers but also ministers ordained in the Church of Scotland.[58]

In the west (what became Upper and Lower Canada), the pattern of Presbyterian activity was similar to Nova Scotia. In the 1790s, settlers petitioned the Church of Scotland to send pastors. At the time, the national body was not in a position to help (only in 1825 did Scots work through the nondenominational Glasgow Colonial Society to provide ministers for Canada). In the short term, Presbyterians and Dutch Reformed churches from the United States sent pastors to Upper Canada. But for a sustained presence, the Seceders again proved to be the most flexible and willing communion to work in Canada. In 1817, they formed the Presbytery of the Canadas and held their first meeting in Montreal. At the time, these Presbyterians had sixteen ministers, compared to twenty-four Anglican and thirty-eight Methodist. The total population of the Canadas was just short of 500,000. Of those who identified as Protestant, the Anglicans accounted for 58,000, Presbyterians 47,000, and Methodists 37,000. In his *Short History of the Presbyterian Church* (1892), William Gregg observes almost in passing that two of the Presbyterian ministers were chaplains to the British army and accordingly received 50 pounds each in compensation.[59] Two others received 100 pounds from government resources. Anglican priests received almost double that sum from funds generated from the Society for the Propagation of the Gospel (Anglican). Methodist pastors depended on church members.

Presbyterians who came from Seceder backgrounds were Dissenters compared to Anglicans, but the arrival of Church of Scotland ministers added a level of complexity not seen since James I. The vehicle by which Church of Scotland ministers came to Canada was the Glasgow Colonial Society, an evangelical missionary organization. Although this may have been a welcome development for Canadian Presbyterianism, it set off a dispute on two fronts. Old rivalries between the Church of Scotland and the Seceders were now present in colonial North America. Even more controversial was a second conflict between Presbyterians and Anglicans. With the presence of Presbyterians, who possessed establishment status within the United Kingdom, Canadian officials now needed to decide how to fund Britain's two state churches. Was it simply a question of funding both Anglican priests and Presbyterian pastors equally or in proportion to their members? If Canada's government supported establishment ministers financially, were all other groups in Lower Canada (including Presbyterians such as Seceders and Covenanters) reduced to dissenting churches?

This dilemma became especially vexing when the policy of government grants (Clergy Reserves) defrayed costs of Canadian church life. Although Anglicans controlled many of the levers of colonial administration, in 1826 the Canadian government approved grants to the Church of Scotland of Upper Canada. Seceders, who struggled to attract ministers from Britain and Ireland and who needed financial assistance, thought they, too, should be eligible for such funding. In 1830, the United Presbytery (Seceders) of Upper Canada appealed to the provincial government. The government responded by requesting Presbyterians form a union so that grants could go to a single administrative unit. In 1831, this policy prompted Church of Scotland ministers to form a body whose purpose was, albeit not conveyed by its name, efficiency: the Synod of the Presbyterian Church of Canada in Connection with the Church of Scotland. Seceders from the United Presbytery did likewise the same year by transitioning into the United Synod of Upper Canada.[60]

Even so, Seceders did not qualify for government grants until 1832 when they appealed directly to King William IV. Their petition noted that the government was already funding Roman Catholic priests. They also argued that if Church of Scotland ministers were eligible, Seceders should be also since the United Synod held to the same theology and church government as the Scottish religious establishment. What is more, the Seceders warned the king about diminished loyalty to the Crown in their ranks if the government refused to fund their pastors. The petition succeeded. In 1833, Upper Canada's lieutenant governor informed Seceder leaders that the king's government had awarded their communion 700 pounds (annually).[61]

The connection between eligibility for government grants and the colonial administration's need for bureaucratic efficiency dissolved the antagonisms that had animated Seceders and the Church of Scotland in the homeland. Such a merger made no sense in the Old World, but under a colonial British government, historic antagonisms were hard to maintain. Tensions surfaced in negotiations for the union of synods. For instance, Church of Scotland leaders required Seceders to present certificates of good standing for inclusion. Even so, union prevailed. Seceders contributed roughly sixteen pastors to the United Synod; the Church of Scotland had sixty. The letter sent by the moderator of the United Synod back to church officials in Scotland (the Church of Scotland's Colonial Committee) explained that the civil magistrate's oversight was key to the union. The first step was to grant the Seceders' a share of government support. The second was the Canadian provincial government's desire to work with "one church" rather than two Presbyterian groups.[62] The report to Scotland offered no adverse commentary on the Seceders but praised the union itself for exhibiting "an almost perfect unanimity."[63]

As encouraging as the report from Canada to Scotland was, Presbyterian claims upon the Clergy Reserves for colonial churches revived the historic rivalry between Anglicans and Presbyterians. John Strachan (the first) bishop of Toronto, objected to Presbyterians receiving government grants. The son of an Aberdeen family—his father an Episcopalian and his mother a member of the Relief Church (Presbyterian)[64]—Strachan had to endure charges that he grew up Presbyterian and became Anglican thanks to the "lure of two hundred pounds a year."[65] At St. Andrews, he had read divinity as a university student. Later in life he confessed his "abhorrence of Calvinism, as presented in the Scottish Confession of Faith."[66] Upon his arrival in Upper Canada in 1799, he was a school teacher in Kingston. There he received more instruction in Anglicanism and was ordained a curate at Cornwall three years later. As he moved in North American Episcopal circles, he befriended John Henry Hobart, the bishop of New York. Strachan wrote a biographical pamphlet about Hobart in 1830 after the bishop's death. He cast it in the form of a letter to Thomas Chalmers. Strachan moved smoothly in Upper Canada's Tory circles and received further encouragement for his religious convictions from the Oxford Movement that, in his view, regarded the Church of England rightfully as the one, holy, catholic church. Strachan maintained that position to the point of condemning John Henry Newman for taking his High Church views all the way to Rome. In an 1841 charge to an ordinand, Strachan referred to the Church of England as "a city on a hill," a model "of the Primitive Church, so beautiful and perfect."[67]

His Anglicanism left little room for Presbyterians. In 1827, Strachan's *Observations on the Provision Made for the Maintenance of a Protestant Clergy* set out the Anglican position as "the church" and "an integral part of the state." Three years later he preached on the unity of church and state in a way comparable to Chalmers's defense of establishmentarianism. The cooperation of ecclesial and civil authorities was "the brightest ornament of the British constitution." Conversely, those who argued for the separation of church and state violated the "appointment of Heaven," "the constitution of human nature," and so were guilty of "wickedness" and "infidelity." This was precisely the form that Christianity assumed when "it was freely recognized in the world," an assertion that echoed older and ongoing debates about church polity before Constantine.[68] With this position came Strachan's opposition to voluntarism. A church free from the government turned clergy into salesmen who only appealed to their congregation's tastes. His High Church views also ignored the value of the other Protestant communions. Methodists were simply outlets for fanaticism and republicanism. Meanwhile, Presbyterians, though established in Scotland, were guilty of "unmerited and vulgar abuse of the Church of England."[69] In other words, for Strachan, non-Anglican Protestants were schismatics.[70]

Such a defense of the old ecclesiastical and civil order on the Canadian frontier was impressive even if political realities in a new society required compromise. As bishop of Toronto, and with easy access to the colony's civil authorities, Strachan could overestimate the Anglican population of Upper Canada in ways that ensured his communion received the majority of the Clergy Reserves. The disparity between the bishop's reports and actual church membership generated complaints from other Protestants and created headaches for the colony's government. The specific issue was how to disperse funds for clergy. Once Presbyterians invoked their establishment status within British society, Canadian officials needed to find a way that satisfied heirs of both national churches.[71]

Distribution of the Clergy Reserves, thanks in part to Strachan's ties to the colony's government, favored Anglicans, but not to the point that suppressed complaints from Presbyterians. By 1836, the lieutenant governor (Colborne) had endowed forty-four Anglican rectories. Presbyterians countered by sending a representative to London to petition the Crown. William Morris was the appointed messenger, and his trip to England included side journeys to Scotland, where he met Kirk leaders. There the advice was disheartening. For instance, Chalmers recommended that Canadian Presbyterians accede to the Church of England in most financial and legal matters. Back in Canada, Presbyterians continued to pressure the government through church meetings, contacts with officials, and communications in the press. The moderator of the United Synod, Alexander Gale, summed up ecclesial and national sentiments: "Is there really a just cause why Scotchmen should not enjoy equal privileges—why they should be held inferior in Canada to Englishmen?" He added that, after all, "Canada is a British, not an English Colony."[72] The question for most Presbyterians was not about ecclesiastical establishment but an equitable sharing of the trust's funds. At the time, Anglicans accounted for twice as many church members as Presbyterians but received five times the income. Some Presbyterians even advocated a system used in New South Wales where the government had agreed to match the voluntary contributions of all denominations.[73] The union of 1840 improved the ratio of Presbyterians to Anglicans by increasing the total to seventy ministers.

Canada's colonial status meant debates about the Clergy Reserves needed input from English officials, including bishops in the House of Lords and the archbishop of Canterbury, as the Constitutional Act of 1791 required. With episcopal counsel, the English government established new terms for church funding. Any income from reserves sold before 1840 would be shared between Anglicans and Presbyterians at the rate of two to one. All income from sales after 1840 would be shared among all the colony's churches. Anglicans and Presbyterians would receive equal sums, while three-eighths of any surplus income went to Methodists and Roman Catholic priests. Canadian historian John S. Moir did the math and concluded that the Church of England with 20 percent of the colony's residents received 42 percent of the Clergy Reserves. Meanwhile, Presbyterians, who had roughly the same number of church members, received 21 percent. The rest of the Christian population (60 percent) received the remainder of the funds—38 percent.[74] Aside from these disparities, the new rules allowed communions, such as Methodists and the United Relief Church that had relied on voluntary contributions, to become part of the government's funding.

Presbyterian challenges to church funding in colonial Canada did not stop with these new terms. The 1843 Disruption of the Church of Scotland sent ripples to the New World.[75] Although the issue of patronage that drove the Disruption (see chapter 6 herein) was not a factor in Canada, ties among Scottish churches created conditions for a New World version of rupture. At the 1843 Synod of Canada meeting, ministers who followed the struggle in Scotland passed a declaration (28 to 11) that expressed their "deepest concern" for the "present condition and prospects" of the Kirk. What made this declaration divisive was specific language that indicated sympathy with "those of her rulers and members who leaving the establishment at the bidding of conscience have thereby sacrificed temporal interests and personal feelings." Free Church resolve must "command respect and admiration of the Christian Church."[76] Visits from Kirk representatives to Canada during the preceding year were partly responsible for sides taken among the Canadians. Opposition to the declaration stemmed from a desire for the Synod of Canada to retain good relations with the Church of Scotland. Opponents argued that Canadians should continue to receive ministers from all Presbyterian communions that adhered to the same doctrinal standard. Some who supported the declaration were convinced that the Church of Scotland had compromised its spiritual independence and trampled on the "crown rights" of Christ.[77]

The next year, the Synod of Canada entertained a motion to remove "in connection with the Church of Scotland" from the North American church's name even if it meant the loss of funding from the Clergy Reserves. A substitute motion called for the synod to maintain good relations with the Kirk. The synod was closely divided, but a majority (56 out of 96) supported the proposal. In response, twenty ministers and nineteen elders left the United Synod to form the Synod of the Presbyterian Church of Canada, popularly known as the Free Church. Canadian church history was mirroring Scottish Presbyterian history. Because of its commitment to the establishment principle, the Free Church of Scotland technically refused support from a government that did not acknowledge Christ's rule over his church.

This logic presented Free Church Canadians with a potential dilemma of whether to receive funding from the Clergy Reserves. Five congregations resolved the quandary when in 1848 the provincial government opened the reserves to all denominations. They applied for government assistance. But when the synod met later in 1848, a majority of officers voted to reject state funding. The synod also forbade congregations from applying for Clergy Reserves. The reason was that government funds diminished "the usefulness of ministers and liberality of the people in contributing to the support of the Gospel." This policy also protected the church from "the evil influence which an irreligious government might exert" through an unhealthy financial dependence. With that resolve, Free Church Canadians followed their Scottish siblings by becoming functionally voluntarist but still officially establishmentarian.[78]

The Synod of Canada with ties to the Church of Scotland did not object to government assistance but soon confronted the difficulties that Free Church Canadians imagined. The demands of religious pluralism and its political cousin, religious freedom, made government support for churches, even if interdenominational, awkward. For that reason, Canada's government looked for ways to secularize support for clergy. A common turn in the nineteenth century was to channel support for churches into funds for schooling. Still, Canada's officials did not cut off clergy immediately. As in the case of Irish Presbyterians, Canada's pastors already receiving funds would continue to do so for life. This concession paved the way to a voluntarist system. The plan required a permanent endowment to sustain roughly two-thirds of the Clergy Reserves' budget. Despite objections from Christian communions not eligible, the system of reserves persisted into the twentieth century. In 1900, a cash payment of the remaining funds (almost 89,000 pounds) went to the last twelve qualified clergymen and to sixty-two widows and orphans.[79] "Thus ended the Church of Scotland's search for co-establishment in Canada," writes John S. Moir.[80] It was also the last gasp of Presbyterianism's establishment principle that had for three centuries informed various communions with hopes for a Christian society.

Yet Another Presbyterian Rebellion?

As unlikely as Presbyterian rebellions were in an age of voluntarism and disestablishment, between 1837 and 1838 political violence erupted in

Lower and Upper Canada that paralleled the 1798 Rising in Ireland (see chapter 5 herein).The initial struggle in Lower Canada depended on Louis Joseph Papineau, who led protests against the provincial government by gathering popular assemblies and boycotting British goods. His creation of the Conseil des Patriotes in 1837 was the straw that broke the back of political order and forced him and his collaborator Edmund Bailey O'Callaghan into exile in New York. In Upper Canada, the rebellion's leader was William Lyon Mackenzie, a Scottish colonist who came to British North America in 1820 and worked as a journalist before entering politics. Frustrations with the legislature provoked Mackenzie to abandon political reform and take up arms. His militia of roughly 200 was no match for Canadian soldiers and volunteers, which numbered close to 1,000. On December 7, 1837, Mackenzie went down to defeat at the Battle of Montgomery's Tavern. In all, four (three rebels) died and ten were wounded (five rebels).

The way William Morley Kilbourn tells it, the rebellion in Upper Canada could very well have been another instance of Presbyterian revolution, but historians have not agreed. Mackenzie's mother was a devout Presbyterian in Dundee, and his father died when the boy was an infant. According to Kilbourn, Mackenzie's knowledge of the Shorter Catechism and the Bible were important influences on the "fireband's" politics. Despite a period of wandering away from religion as a young man, and siring an illegitimate child, he "remained a faithful Presbyterian in his later days."[81] In fact, Kilbourn insists that Mackenzie held as tenaciously to Calvinist doctrine as he did to "rationalist liberalism" and never recognized conflict between the two.

Instead of Presbyterian doctrine, liberal expectations were more likely behind this insurrection. According to Allen Greer, the Canadian civil wars were part of a wider constellation of rebellions in the British Empire that included the Irish Rebellion of 1798. Like the situation in Ireland, Upper and Lower Canada included English and non-English speakers, Protestants and Roman Catholics that clashed among themselves and with "the existing order."[82]

The 1839 report, prepared by Lord Durham to investigate the rebellions, revealed that the Clergy Reserves were at the bottom of Canada's unrest. In the case of Lower Canada, where law excluded Roman Catholic priests from government assistance, the influence of religious commitment was noticeable. To encourage the dispersion of Roman Catholics in the colony, Durham argued, "a wise Government would have taken care to aid, in every possible way, the diffusion of their means of religious instruction."[83] In Upper Canada, Durham reported, the "Reformers" used the reserves to show the government's "disposition to act in direct defiance to the known sentiments of a vast majority of its constituents."[84] In fact, the pacification of Canada depended on a prompt and fair resolution of these inequities, since "it was . . . one of the most important questions referred . . . for investigation."[85] Not only had the Church of England received a disproportionate share of the funds, but even Church of Scotland pastors had sought to exclude Protestants from other denominations and so increased hostilities. When the imperial government had a chance to address the situation, officials "never interfered once" but left the "unhappy system of 'clergy reserves'" in place.[86]

Durham underscored a basic tension in the colonial government's support for clergy. The nature of a colonial society required clergy to function more like missionaries than settled pastors or priests. Their congregants or parishioners lived in a frontier society without the infrastructure, social and ecclesiastical, that sustained churches in England or Scotland. Yet support for clergy in the Canadas assumed an Old World model of ministry—the parish with parochial ministers. In an unsettled society, combined with the need for colonists to spread out, cultivate land, and generate economic growth, Clergy Reserves were more an obstacle than an aid: "The great objection to reserves for the clergy is, that for those whom the land is set apart never have attempted, and never could successfully attempt, to cultivate or settle the property."[87] By setting aside land for pastors and priests to use to generate wealth, the policy withheld valuable assets from settlers who could well have been much more productive than clergy. As such, "much land is withheld from the settlers, and kept in a state of waste," to the "serious injury" of the entire region.[88] Worse, the provincial government had acted with "reckless profusion" and in direct contradiction to the secretary of state's directives.

Lord Durham did not recommend voluntarism, but that was the direction in which Canadian church–state relations were headed. Despite Old World expectations for religious establishment (not only among Presbyterians), the conditions of a new society in need of settlers from different Christian backgrounds meant that New World church life needed to accommodate such diversity by divesting ecclesiastical institutions of government support. Yet, this was not simply a dilemma posed in colonial societies, since England's dissenters also exposed the challenge of state support for nonestablished religious bodies. The Canadian Civil Wars of 1837–38 did not show signs of classic Presbyterian resistance to tyranny, even if discontent with Clergy Reserves was a factor. These wars were of a piece with Presbyterian hostility to religious establishments that excluded them. Since 1560, when English and Scottish Protestants sought to take the Reformation all the way to revisions of church government and relations with the Crown, Presbyterians had objected repeatedly to established churches that did not conform to biblical teaching about worship, church polity, and national morality.

The nineteenth-century shift to voluntary support for churches erased the feature of British church life that had animated most Presbyterians for three centuries. Voluntarism left Presbyterianism as merely one denomination in a wider sea of Protestantism. Presbyterians' calling card to the wider world was no longer a godly nation and a true church. It became instead a system of doctrine and a form of church administration apparently based on scripture. Depending on the circumstances, Presbyterians came to voluntarism reluctantly, especially when civil government devised ways to support even Dissenters. Without hope for a covenanted nation, an established church, or even special favors from the Crown, Presbyterians faced a future that their most inspiring and passionate exponents had not considered.

CHAPTER 8

Presbyterian Politics after Establishment

Presbyterianism emerged in the sixteenth century as a wing of Protestant attempts to reform the church in the West. Whatever the precedents were for John Calvin's *Ecclesiastical Ordinances* (1541), his design of a polity that relied upon elders and pastors meeting in councils to oversee ecclesiastical matters became the model form of church government for Reformed Protestantism in England and Scotland. Because of the interconnectedness of civil and ecclesiastical authorities in those kingdoms (and Europe more generally, of course), the introduction of Presbyterian polity over against episcopacy was sure to affect church–state relations. Put simply, church reform inevitably led to adjustments in the political order. That consequence drove British politics between (roughly) 1560 and 1712. Monarchs intervened in church affairs, Parliaments checked the overreach of monarchs, pastors and bishops appealed for the favor of state officials, not to mention the momentous events of civil war, regicide, an experiment with republicanism, the introduction of constitutional monarchy, and finally the establishment of Presbyterianism in the Church of Scotland. The dispute between Presbyterianism and episcopacy was by no means the sole or major influence on Elizabethan and Stuart politics. At the same time, fights over church polity invited civil authorities to intervene.

These political and ecclesiastical developments continued to reverberate in the British Isles and British North America during much of the so-called long eighteenth century. Once civil authorities found ways to accommodate Christian diversity, Presbyterianism lost a crucial piece of its initial motivation. For Reformed Protestants, the problem with Europe's Christian society before the Reformation was not cooperation between church and state. It was rather an erroneous understanding of the faith and a system of political and ecclesiastical administration prone to corruption and hypocrisy. The Protestant solution was to reform the church's teachings, worship, and ministry. The further outworking of the Reformation in England and Scotland provoked Presbyterians to question episcopal control of the church along with the Crown's cozy relationship with the bishops. A covenanted society promised to coordinate civil government, the church, and the people into a godly whole, with a reformed church only a part, though a large one, of the nation's Christian expression. For Presbyterians, reform of the church obviously meant doing away with bishops and implementing ecclesiastical oversight through assemblies. Reform of church and society also involved the independence of the church. Presbyterians did not object to monarchy. How could they since so much of their inspiration for a godly society came from Old Testament Israel under the rule of godly (sometimes not so godly) kings? Their objection to monarchy, instead, proceeded from ecclesiastical prerogatives that kings and queens enjoyed, whether through specific customs and laws, or from the accumulated expectations of medieval society. For Presbyterians, the kingship of Christ over his church was the basis for challenging any monarch's control of church life.

This Presbyterian zeal for a reformed church and a covenanted nation lost most of its energy once British law turned to the protection of the rights of religious groups outside the established church. Since Presbyterians outside Scotland (and even Seceder groups inside Scotland) led the brief for freedom of speech and worship, they were partly responsible for the predicament in which they found themselves in the early nineteenth century. What form should a godly society take now that the church, reduced to a denomination among other communions, could no longer be the religious spine of a Christian nation? The obvious answer was political participation. Presbyterians could vote (or lobby for greater suffrage) for representatives or hold public office in the political parties available in various local contexts. But since the Anglophone world consisted of a republic and a monarchy overseeing an empire, could Presbyterians agree, even informally, about a common set of political convictions? Only in the late nineteenth century, during the era of Protestant ecumenism, did Presbyterians on both sides of the Atlantic begin to coordinate activities and chart common social ideals. But even before those days of transatlantic progressivism, Presbyterians intuited principles about politics and economics that echoed, however faintly, their older aspirations for a godly nation. Remarkably enough, those intuitions produced similar responses as the English-speaking world transitioned to a liberal, commercial, and modern set of societies.

Whiggish Presbyterian Politics

American Presbyterians had a head start on their ecclesiastical siblings thanks to a national government that on paper eliminated deferential social relations and freed citizens from many of the theories and debates—ancient, medieval, and modern—that had justified monarchy. But in Scotland, the home of Presbyterianism's success in the Reformation's contests for gaining the favor of civil magistrates on a national scale, the norms and ideals of religious establishment persisted. That reality and set of expectations colored the way that Presbyterians calculated support for either liberal or conservative policies. An established church also cultivated respect for tradition and older social arrangements that hindered liberalism. As such, even if Presbyterians—by virtue of ideas about vocation, property, work ethic, personal responsibility, and economic productivity—were generally inclined to embrace and defend the political economy that grew up with liberal politics and free markets, Scots also needed to make room for an established church. In Scotland, those deliberations were the most extensive. But in other settings where the Scots had influence, such as Ireland and Canada, expectations for an established church also colored Presbyterian politics. Where hopes for religious establishment were virtually nonexistent, such as the United

States and England, Presbyterians adapted to modern Whiggish and liberal political arrangements more readily than those in Canada, Ireland, and Scotland.

Early indications of the difference that a constitutional republic made for Presbyterianism came when in 1789 the Presbyterian Church in the United States of America revised the Westminster Confession and Catechisms' clauses on the civil magistrate. The original version's conception of the ruler posited a kind of Constantine with responsibility to keep the church faithful. Those 1640s commissioners to the Westminster Assembly described the magistrate's duty as taking "order, that unity and peace be preserved in the Church, that the truth of God be kept pure and entire; that all blasphemies and heresies be suppressed; all corruptions and abuses in worship and discipline prevented or reformed; and all the ordinances of God duly settled, administered, and observed." Those same divines may very well have had Constantine in mind when they added that the magistrate had power "to call synods, to be present at them, and to provide that whatsoever is transacted in them be according to the mind of God" (Westminster Confession, 23.3).

The Westminster Assembly's conception was clearly a tall order with Charles I on the throne, but now with George Washington as president of the federal government, who was an Anglican of sufficiently soft conviction to also join the Masons, Presbyterians recognized the time-bound character of the Westminster Confession's chapter on civil government. For that reason, they revised it to be compatible with the principles of disestablishment, free exercise, and voluntarism, both explicit and implied in the U.S. Constitution. For the American church, civil magistrates now functioned as "nursing fathers" who were responsible "to protect the church of our common Lord, without giving the preference to any denomination of Christians above the rest." In case anyone thought this statement merely recognized the plurality of Protestant denominations in the new nation, the revision also asserted that magistrates were bound to "protect the person and good name of all their people" such that no one should suffer any "indignity, violence, abuse, or injury" on the basis of "religion or infidelity." It almost went without saying that civil government also should protect "all religious and ecclesiastical assemblies" from "molestation or disturbance" (Revised Westminster Confession, 23.3).

This conception of the state's obligations to the church was overtly American (Presbyterians in Scotland, Ireland, and Canada still use the original version) and did not settle how Presbyterians as citizens should conduct themselves in the new republic beyond general admonitions to obey the law and honor officials. On the explicit responsibilities for temporal affairs, Presbyterians were generally on their own. The question of suffrage, however, was obviously large. If a church member had no voting rights, a basic method of political participation in a liberal society, then Presbyterian influence on political affairs would necessarily be slight. Related to suffrage was the organization of political parties. Presbyterians in the transatlantic world did not take the step that Dutch Reformed did in late nineteenth-century Netherlands of forming a political party based on religious convictions and networks. Meanwhile, aside from the activity of church members in elections and political organizations, the churches themselves could and did issue statements on national affairs. All of these layers constituted a fuzzy conception of Presbyterian political involvement that was basically Whig or Liberal. This outlook leaned heavily on personal responsibility and self-sufficiency for ordinary people, even while looking favorably on government efforts to improve economic conditions and uphold moral norms.

Why Presbyterians in different settings—from colonial society in Canada and republican federalism in the United States to ecclesiastical establishment in Scotland—would arrive at a similar political disposition is arguably a mystery. Nonetheless, the Whiggish outlook of Presbyterians (and other Anglo-American Protestants) is a given that few historians question. Harvard University historian David Hempton has aptly summarized the consensus: British Nonconformists for most of the nineteenth-century were generally opposed to remnants of the religious establishment and championed democratic reforms and individual responsibility: "This progressive liberalism was underpinned by a vigorous emphasis on temperance, sabbatarianism, philanthropy and sexual purity."[1] The American historian Daniel Walker Howe points to a similar set of convictions among Anglo-American Protestants. Whigs in the United States were committed to improvement through "careful, purposeful planning." They also stressed morality and "duties" rather than "rights." "The community, like its members, was expected to set an example of virtue and to enforce it when possible." Whigs also believed in the "organic unity of society" in ways that downplayed social conflict and promoted harmony and consensus.[2] Oxford University historian Richard Carwardine agrees that Anglo-American Protestants belonged to a Whiggish political culture on both sides of the Atlantic. Their instincts combined a willingness to support "an interventionist state to advance a Christian society, through temperance and Sabbatarian legislation, for example," and an "optimistic faith" in technology, "economic progress and social development." Often postmillennial beliefs that associated social improvement with the inauguration of Christ's millennial rule fueled this outlook, which found political outlets in the Whig and Republican Parties (United States) and the Liberals (United Kingdom).[3]

The United States

Charles Hodge (1797–1878), professor of systematic theology at Princeton Seminary, is arguably a representative figure among American Presbyterians, where signs of republican influence on political theology are easy to find. A third-generation Scots-Irish American, Hodge grew up in Philadelphia, a Presbyterian stronghold, but then moved to Princeton, New Jersey, when his father died from smallpox. His mother ran a boardinghouse in the college town. The largest male presence in his life (at least religiously) was Archibald Alexander, the first professor of theology at the local seminary. After completing the undergraduate course at the College of New Jersey, Hodge enrolled at the seminary and qualified for ordination. He was twenty-five when the seminary hired him to teach Hebrew and Old Testament. After Alexander's death in 1851, Hodge took over courses in systematic theology. Although he lived in a small town midway between Philadelphia and New York City, Hodge brought to his political outlook an urbanity that betrayed his place of residence. He had ties to Philadelphia society through marriage to Sarah Bache, a great-granddaughter of Benjamin Franklin. His brother, Hugh, was an accomplished professor of medicine at Philadelphia's College (later the University of Pennsylvania). Meanwhile, Hodge's education took him to rabbis in Philadelphia and to Protestants in New England (to learn Hebrew) and eventually to Paris, Halle, and Berlin for two years of exposure to European theological scholarship.[4]

Hodge was a serious academic, absorbed in theology, biblical scholarship, and church politics. He was also something of a polymath who rarely let his thoughts about government and society go unpublished. From the platform of the seminary's theological journal, *Biblical Repertory and Princeton Review*, Hodge held forth on everything from the most recent General Assembly to major political controversies. Richard Carwardine says that Hodge's progression from Federalist to Whig to Republican showed little angst or hesitation. What informed the Presbyterian's navigation of the nation's politics was an outlook that prized "social order" and the "economic activity and meritocratic opportunities of responsible, self-discipline, self-improving, and publicly educated citizens."[5] As much as Hodge leavened his opinions and arguments with references to scripture and natural law, the broadly powerful science of political economy (not to mention sanctified self-interest) was never far from view.

In the first chapter of America's two-party system, Hodge's background among Scots-Irish Philadelphia merchants was partly responsible for his loyalty to the Federalist Party. The sort of trade at the city's docks and warehouses that Hodge's father, Andrew, had cultivated found greater returns with Federalists responsible for business policy rather than with the Jeffersonian Democratic-Republicans' preferences for farmers. Rivalry between Federalists and Republicans was even part of Charles Hodge's college experience. An 1807 student revolt reflected a division between the college's administration, still committed to the Federalist politics of the American Revolutionary generation, and a student body increasingly from the South, where Jefferson's agrarian and honor-based conceptions of public life prevailed.[6]

During the 1820s, debates that propelled the Democrats-versus-Whigs era of electoral politics, Hodge saw the Whigs as the better vehicle for preserving economic expansion and public order. He was no fan of the populism that Andrew Jackson's political machinery introduced into what had been a fairly genteel system of selecting presidents. The Jacksonian habit of voting for candidates of only one party meant that government officials sacrificed "private opinion, conscience & everything else."[7] Carwardine traces Hodge's opposition to Jacksonian populism and its partisan nature to Reformed Protestant sources, especially those familiar with the Federalist Party. The shift of Presbyterians like Hodge into the Whig Party ran along several lines. Some simply opposed Jackson's constitutional overreach in vetoing the charter for the Second Bank of the United States. That perspective ran alongside assumptions about the value of a unified national system of trade, manufacturing, and commerce, which Jackson's economic nationalism prevented. Presbyterians contended additionally that public morality was essential to the health of the republic. Here a constellation of controversies and remedies came together to make a generic, establishmentarian Protestantism (Congregationalist, Presbyterian, and Episcopalian) the arbiter of the nation's public piety. Efforts to protect the Sabbath, opposition to secret societies, such as the godless Masons, and promotion of public education that nurtured faith in God and reverence for the Bible were issues that attracted Hodge to the political coalition Whigs assembled. Hodge regarded the Whigs as the inheritors of the Federalist outlook partly because they fused "conservative social and political principles with a faith in economic and technological progress."[8]

A desire for "moral order, benevolence, respectability, and social harmony" eventually landed Hodge in the Republican Party, founded in 1854 during sectional controversies over slavery.[9] The radical (abolitionist) element in the Republican Party would have given Hodge pause even if his views about slavery evolved to the point of recognizing its injustice and deleterious influence on the nation. He also regarded the South's Slave Power and its expansion into the western states a threat to the balanced order that he hoped would characterize the United States as it matured. Hodge's support for the Republicans required him to overlook unsavory elements, such as anti-Catholicism and moralistic temperance legislation. But the party's commitment to the Constitution was another signal—perhaps the last vestige—of the institutional order that most resonated with Hodge's Presbyterian instincts.

Two divisive issues that drove Hodge's political calculations were the Sabbath and the treatment of Native Americans. The controversial nature of the federal government delivering mail on Sundays became an issue as early as 1810 when Congress passed legislation that required postmasters to open their offices on the first day of the week. Congregationalists and Presbyterians opposed the legislation and persisted in coordinated efforts to halt business on the Lord's Day. In reaction to steamboats and stagecoaches transporting passengers and goods on Sundays, in 1828 Presbyterians joined the General Union for the Promotion of the Christian Sabbath. Around the same time, Hodge, recently returned from Berlin, entered debates about politics. In 1831, he wrote an essay in the seminary's journal to correct an anti-Sabbatarian article published in the *American Quarterly Review*. Hodge hearkened back to older Presbyterian ideals about a holy commonwealth when he wrote that observance of the Lord's Day was the "only security for public morals." Setting one day a week aside for worship allowed for Protestants to issue "the great source of information and culture of a moral kind." Because virtue was "essential to the well being of society," turning Sunday into any other day was to destroy "the great source of that knowledge without which virtue cannot exist."[10]

Nonetheless, Hodge did not believe his understanding of public virtue conflicted with civil and religious liberty, in which case his appeal to a godly commonwealth had limits. Observing the Lord's Day "is the means of enlightening the minds of men," and it also "disenthrals them from the yoke of superstition and the bondage of priests."[11] That tinge of anti-Catholicism was not as significant, however, as Hodge's fulsome praise for the benefits of Anglo-American Protestantism. The two nations that showed the highest regard for the Sabbath, Great Britain and the United States, led the world in cultivating "sound religion," "internal stability," and "external respect and power." Their beliefs had contributed directly to their status as the "mothers and guardians of civil and religious liberty." Hodge further worried that Britain and the United States would decline if they abandoned their "regard for the Sabbath."[12]

The Jackson administration's policies on Native Americans drew less directly on Hodge's religious convictions than the Lord's Day had, but the controversy revealed American Presbyterian political alliances at the start of the second party system. Hodge's friendship with Theodore Frelinghuysen, New Jersey's U.S. senator and a prominent figure in the institutions of the American Protestant Benevolent Empire,[13] gave Hodge access to other senators who supported the existing treaties with the Cherokee nation. Many of these politicians had also supported Sabbath legislation. The Jackson administration's Indian Removal Act (1830) was, in Hodge's view, a dire threat to the Christian character of the republic and its long-term prosperity. Hodge, whose political philosophy was inherently cautious, wrote to his brother in response to Jackson's treatment of the Cherokees: "I think I could join a rebellion, with a clear conscience, as I am sure I could with a full heart."[14] He approved heartily John Marshall's ruling in the Supreme Court that deemed unconstitutional Georgia's actions against the Cherokees. When Marshall died in 1835, Hodge regarded it a "great national calamity."[15] Jackson's Native American policies, in turn, were largely responsible for Hodge's support for William Wirt, an Anti-Masonic candidate, in the 1832 presidential election. Wirt had been the attorney who argued against Georgia before the Supreme Court.

A combination of moral and economic issues drove Hodge into the Whig Party, led by U.S. senators Henry Clay (Kentucky) and Daniel Webster (Massachusetts), who opposed Jackson's economic policies. The Whigs also regarded the Democrats as "morally ambiguous demagogues who, remorselessly pursuing the spoils of office and neglecting orthodox Protestant interests, resorted to cheap egalitarianism and the language of social conflict."[16] That many evangelical Protestants, especially Baptists and Methodists, did not find the Whigs a congenial home speaks to the establishmentarian outlook that lingered among Presbyterians and Congregationalists. Whereas Democrats such as Jackson portrayed their political adversaries as advocates of uniting church and state, sanctified meddlers, and moral imperialists, Hodge's Whigs presented themselves as the party of moral order, national unity, economic prosperity, civilization, and public responsibility. For a Presbyterian such as Hodge, in particular, protections on personal property and encouragement of national markets went hand in hand with an emphasis on "discipline, improvement, and moral responsibility in both the individual and society."[17] For Whigs, liberty was not synonymous with freedom from constraint but reflected the Reformation idea of Christian freedom in line with moral truths. It was several steps removed from older associations of freedom from the papacy and the church's independence from the Crown. Even so, the language of liberty from tyranny persisted as a way for American Presbyterians to make sense of society.

England

A contemporary of Hodge in England, William McKerrow (1803–78), provides an odd test for the proposition that Presbyterianism found a political outlet in Whiggery. The son of a wheelwright and turner in Kilmarnock, Scotland, McKerrow attended a congregation in the Burgher branch of the Secession Church. The domestic and ecclesiastical environment of the young McKerrow was antireligious establishment and politically radical. According to Ian J. Shaw, this version of Presbyterianism could include a reformist mélange of "opposition to slavery and the Corn Laws, and support for voluntarism and total abstinence."[18] Any hint of radicalism did not weaken Presbyterian priorities for a learned ministry. McKerrow attended the University of Glasgow, the choice for most Secession pastors. His course of study enabled McKerrow to pass exams in Latin, Greek, logic, moral philosophy, math, and natural philosophy—subjects required for admittance to the United Secession Church Divinity Hall, where in 1821 the student embarked on a five-year course.[19] In 1826, the Presbytery of Kilmarnock licensed McKerrow to preach and soon sent him to Manchester, England, to minister alongside one of the Scottish Presbyterians who had rejuvenated English Presbyterianism (see chapter 6 herein). The senior pastor was Robert Jack, who like McKerrow, though almost forty years older, grew up in the Secession church in Glasgow, attended the university there, and served in two Scottish pulpits before transferring to the Lloyd Street chapel in Manchester. By the time that McKerrow arrived, Jack, who was fifty-six, was not necessarily infirm (though he died ten years later), but had grown the church sufficiently to need an assistant.[20]

Ian J. Shaw summarizes McKerrow as not only "an eminent and honoured minister, but a progressive and formative thinker and activist on social issues."[21] To American Presbyterian ears that description might have sounded odd, but in the English setting the liberalism that Americans took for granted could border on radical. Another factor in accounting for McKerrow's politics was the context of a rapidly industrializing city. The congregation's demographics revealed a large number of Scots who engaged in trades and business enterprises that were solidly middle to upper-middle class. They ranged from domestic servants to cashiers, drapers, manufacturers, printers, and a surgeon.[22] Although McKerrow tried to keep politics out of the pulpit, he also tailored a ministry to encourage moral and social improvement. Whether that pastoral concern reflected middle-class interests or represented an outworking of Reformed Protestant political theology was at times a distinction without a difference. Whatever its inspiration, McKerrow's politics displayed the

Presbyterian expectation for political influence in cultivating a godly society. At the same time, social demands could overwhelm the narrowly Presbyterian aims of a reformed church.

Like most Presbyterians of his time, McKerrow supported education as a means of religious nurture and social improvement. In addition to establishing Sunday school in his congregation, a faith-based effort that initially provided instruction in reading, writing, and math through Protestant materials, McKerrow also encouraged learning for all members of the church. As early as 1839, he started a Young Men's Society that hosted religious, literary, and moral discussions. This initiative became the model for a 1854 program, the Junior Scholar Improvement Society, designed to encourage wholesome reading material and discussions among older Sunday school students. Lyceums, also begun in the late 1830s, were another vehicle for self-improvement—through lectures, scientific demonstrations, and book discussions. McKerrow added a church library to sustain reading habits. It included theology, poetry, science, history, and biography. McKerrow drew the line at novels, which may have hurt the effectiveness of the church library. He believed that wholesome reading could nurture "wise and virtuous, useful and happy" readers, but novels polluted the imagination. Aside from the uplifting quality of books, McKerrow also believed education would not make industrial workers discontent with monotonous jobs but give them tools to rise above humble circumstances and improve family life. To counter conservatives who worried that educating the masses fostered rebellion, McKerrow argued that the uneducated were usually the ones who damaged the smooth operation of mills and factories.[23]

McKerrow's conviction about the importance of education led inevitably to support for public schools. He favored state funding but preferred local management. In 1847, he worked with other Protestants in Manchester to propose a system for "secular" education. Its funds came from local taxes and involved oversight by locally elected administrators. The inclusion of Unitarians and Anglicans raised questions about the religious atmosphere of the schools. McKerrow supported teaching scripture but agreed to limit selections to passages approved by other Protestants. The hope was to avoid sectarian squabbling. But it also reflected a belief that education prepared students for understanding the truths of Christianity. According to the proposal, education had the power to shape "the temporal and eternal welfare of millions of beings, with minds naturally as intelligent and souls as immortal as our own."[24] For explicitly religious content, McKerrow thought local churches should supplement the public schools. The success of his plan was evident in the Education Act of 1870, which gained approval thanks in part to McKerrow's advocacy.[25]

The ideal of the self-reliant, literate, and productive member of society was also evident in McKerrow's understanding of economics. He was a strong advocate of free trade and was active in the Anti-Corn Law campaign. The Corn Law debates revealed different economic theories: the British government's mercantilism (e.g., keeping corn prices high to protect domestic producers) versus Manchester liberal economists (e.g., free trade to lower prices and stimulate market incentives). The contest also reflected different class allegiances, with advocates of the Corn Laws favoring landed gentry and opponents looking out for workers. McKerrow's liberal economics, which almost always favored free trade, was not a sign of the church sidling up to wealthy capitalists. Instead his economic views reflected concern for what changing economic circumstances were having on the middle and working classes in his church and city. In the 1832 elections, McKerrow supported both Whig candidates, mainly on the basis of free trade. Economic reforms, he believed, encouraged peace, justice, benevolence, and the extension of the gospel. Along with advocating free trade came opposition to colonialism and war. "McKerrow's solution to the problem of war," Shaw writes, "was a combination of his unwavering confidence in the power of free trade to reduce potential for conflict, and in arbitration as a means to resolve disputes."[26]

Social and personal improvement went hand in hand in McKerrow's Presbyterian politics, while commerce, the work ethic, and education were the means for lifting the working class out of poverty. His congregation in Manchester encouraged its professional and middle-class members to provide assistance to the poor. Regular collections were part of the church's activities and proceeds went to a soup kitchen, a night asylum, and clothing for the needy. McKerrow was aware of the danger of a culture of dependence and insisted that recipients of relief be "deserving." To be poor simply because someone was idle, wasteful, or intemperate was a sign of flawed character, in the Presbyterian pastor's eyes. "If the cause of poverty was personal indiscipline," Shaw observes, "[McKerrow] offered only discerning assistance, encouraging self-help as his response."[27]

If McKerrow's politics reflected Protestant notions of personal responsibility and self-improvement with a helping of solidarity, his outlook on religious establishments followed the logic of Scotland's Secession Church. Shaw calls McKerrow's commitment to voluntarism a parallel position to his belief in free trade. An established church was a form of monopoly on religious truth, "more unjust and injurious than the commercial."[28] The occasion for McKerrow's defense of voluntarism came in the 1830s amid Anglican calls for a renewed commitment to a religious establishment, a position that became more vociferous after the 1828 repeal of the Test and Corporation Act (1673), which abandoned religious tests for civil office. In a series of letters to the *Manchester Times*, edited by one of McKerrow's church members, the pastor argued that religious establishments were "a most unwarrantable infringement of the rights of conscience." They were also the "offspring of bigotry, the essence of tyranny, and the source of injustice."[29] The proper alternative was for government to promote education so that people could explore scripture for themselves and sort out the competing claims of the Protestant churches.

Shaw observes that McKerrow's Scottish Secession background was partly responsible for a "radical voluntaryist" position that made him an outlier among English Nonconformists.[30] At the same time, his location in Manchester placed him at the forefront of "advanced Liberalism" in ways that showed little antagonism between religious belief and the pursuit of social improvement through free trade, public education, temperance, and self-sufficiency. He gave "Christian legitimacy" to the development of liberalism. In so doing, McKerrow threw in his lot with a shift from England's traditional structures and hierarchies to a commercial society of self-disciplined managers and workers. The new arrangements, he believed, provided better opportunities for evangelism and ministry. A Scottish background may have colored McKerrow's outlook, but it was not unusual, if David Hempton is right, for English Nonconformists in their "campaigns against the remnants of Britain's confessional state" to side with "progressive democracy and assertive individualism." "Free trade, freedom from compulsory church rates and tithes, free access to Oxford and Cambridge, freedom from slavery and freedom from the consequences of state support for Anglican . . . elementary education" were not merely McKerrow's causes in Manchester, the epicenter of English liberalism.[31] They were the causes of English Nonconformists more generally.

Scotland

If McKerrow seemed to freelance in adjusting Presbyterian ministry to industrializing English cites, Thomas Chalmers labored within the constraints of an ecclesiastical establishment that was ambivalent about modernization. Arguably one of the greatest Scottish ministers since John Knox and Andrew Melville, Chalmers (born in 1780) grew up in the small coastal town of Anstruther in the home of a merchant and town provost. He studied math at St. Andrews and at the age of nineteen was ordained by the Presbytery of St. Andrews. His early career reflected the Kirk's privileged place in Scotland. Further study at Edinburgh prepared Chalmers to teach math at the University of St. Andrews, even while he was called as pastor to the nearby parish of Kilmany. His duties were fairly typical when (as in England) clergy were among the best educated and most capable of holding academic positions, even in nontheological subjects. While in Kilmany, the pastor had a change of heart about awakened Protestantism and experienced his own sort of conversion. At the same time, he became frustrated at his inability to secure an appointment in math at the University of Edinburgh. Chalmers's next move was to pastor at the Tron parish in Glasgow, where he gained notice both for his pulpit ministry and among the city's urban population. Part of his work among the urban poor included creating in 1819 a new Glasgow parish, St. John's. Academic ambition never left Chalmers, and four years later he took a post in moral philosophy at the University of St. Andrews. His next move was in 1827 to teach divinity at the University of Edinburgh. The capstone of his rise to prominence was his 1832 election as moderator of the General Assembly. With that office, Chalmers solidified his position as leader of the Evangelical Party (see chapter 6 herein).[32]

The pastor-theologian's doctrinal conservatism, personal holiness, and opposition to patronage followed Presbyterian convictions echoing through the Kirk's history back to Melville and Knox. At the same time, Chalmers was conversant with new ideas and social developments in ways that called, he believed, for adjustments in Presbyterian faith and practice. He was attempting to update the covenantal ideal of a godly covenanted kingdom adapted to an increasingly democratic and middle-class Scotland. Chalmers's particular combination of academic inquiry and piety was responsible for the genius, or oddness (depending on one's perspective), of his modernized Presbyterianism.

Chalmers's significance for the history of Europe (over against his place in Presbyterian history) rests on his accomplishments as a political economist. A. M. C. Waterman observes that Chalmers "was the only internationally recognised public figure in the history of Scotland to achieve distinction as an economist." Waterman adds that Adam Smith and David Hume may have had enjoyed followings in France and England, but "were private men, playing little part if any in great affairs of state." Chalmers, however, experienced "more professional fame" than any other Scottish economist. This status explains why no other nineteenth-century economist, except Karl Marx, has received the attention in English publications that Chalmers has.[33] In fact, in 1827 when he gave his inaugural lectures at the University of Edinburgh, listeners needed tickets for admission and braved snow and sleet for two hours before doors opened under the watchful eye of police to ensure public safety.[34] Chalmers's notoriety had less to do with his views about the Kirk than his ideas about the economy.

Chalmers's academic work as a political economist and moral philosopher distinguished him from his Presbyterian peers in North America and England. Hodge and McKerrow, for instance, dabbled in social thought, compared to Chalmers's immersion in the literature. For that reason, his theories about economics rose above the immediacy of public policy and resisted alignment with a political party. Chalmers's ideas evolved in ways that also made him hard to classify by partisan politics. His first work in political economy, for instance, *Enquiry into the Extent and Stability of National Resources* (1808), addressed Britain's economic challenges thanks to war with France while simultaneously attempting to set the country on a course to meet the new demands of finance and industry. His ideal was a self-sufficient society, largely agrarian, that produced enough food for its population. This outlook placed Chalmers against trade policies that sent industrial goods overseas in exchange for food. It was also Spartan in the sense of favoring taxes on luxury goods and policies that channeled excess economic resources back into the national economy and common good. The moral component of Chalmers's theory meant rejecting the idea of human happiness based on consumption. He proposed instead the elevation of tastes through education and religion that, in turn, would yield work and self-sacrifice for the sake of the wider community.[35]

By the time that Chalmers wrote his second major work, *On Political Economy, in Connexion with the Moral State and Moral Prospects of Society* (1832), he had experienced a religious awakening, worked with Glasgow's urban poor, lectured at the university, and emerged as the leader of the Kirk's Evangelicals. Unlike the earlier work—written in the context of an external threat from Napoleon's France—twenty-five years later the challenge was overpopulation. Chalmers had always relied on Thomas Malthus, who argued that a nation's population would inevitably outrun food production. Liberal economists also took Malthus for granted, but replied that free trade and industrial development would overcome Malthusian worries. Chalmers himself regarded Adam Smith and leaders of the Whig Party as too optimistic. He continued to assess a nation's wealth by agricultural output. If government lowered taxes, landowners would benefit and waste untaxed incomes on luxury goods.[36] For this reason, in addition to opposing liberal economic theories or political reforms as inadequate to address Britain's basic inequalities, Chalmers recommended church assistance and Christian virtues. He urged the British people to understand limits (economic and moral) and develop moral restraint. They needed, as Stewart J. Brown summarized, to be industrious, "develop habits of foresight and saving," and "embrace a communal benevolence, through which each individual would recognize a responsibility for his neighbour's needs."[37]

This economic diagnosis opened two sides of Chalmers's career. On the one hand, it drew upon his past experience with church relief for Glasgow's urban poor. His earlier 1817 plan for the new parish, St. John's, combined efforts to address poverty and to extend the Church of Scotland across the nation. It began with assessing the poor in the Town's Hospital in Glasgow to discover the most needy. The plan extended to funding for parish schools to educate the poor in knowledge that encouraged industry and restraint. It also included evangelizing all who had not made a profession of faith. The system also relied upon a distinction between the deserving poor and those who refused to take responsibility for their conditions. The experiment resulted in a decrease of paupers (from 125 to 94) within the parish, and zero church members sent to the hospital for relief assessment.[38] Though historians and critics have questioned the success of Chalmers's experiment (and his own glowing assessment), his efforts seemed briefly to prove that poor relief might well be managed through a church-based program rather than a government bureau.

Chalmers's economic theories, on the other hand, pointed forward to his case for religious establishment. In the 1830s, as the leader of the Evangelical Party, Chalmers served as Convener of the Committee on Church Extension. In this capacity, he combined zeal for more converts with ideas about urban poverty to revitalize the Church of Scotland. In 1834, for instance, plans for church extension involved creating twenty new parishes that ideally would reach people outside the church and provide the necessary relief for those in the industrial parts of Scottish society.[39] In Chalmers's nineteenth-century version of the godly commonwealth, the church was the most effective institution to negotiate the kingdom's transition through troubled times. What workers especially needed, those with whom the Kirk had the least success, was suffi-

Figure 8.1. *Quitting the Manse* (1847), by George Harvey.

cient moral and religious instruction to learn the virtues that industrial work required. "The moral and economic principle, on which to ground [workers'] determination," he wrote in an 1837 report, was "to humanise a population, and impart such habits as are best for both the comfort and the virtue of families."[40] This was ironically the same period in which Chalmers's commitment to religious establishment frayed thanks to another controversy over patronage and the eventual 1843 Disruption (see chapter 6 herein). Through all that adversity, Chalmers remained firm in his understanding of a godly kingdom with Presbyterianism beating at the heart of economic, educational, and religious life.

Thanks to the Kirk's establishment status, Chalmers's proposals for diaconal work and church extension took place in the setting of Whig-versus-Tory partisanship. Chalmers's natural political alliance was with the Whigs, since Evangelicals in the Kirk saw liberals as allies in seizing control of the Church of Scotland. Part of this affinity owed to political partisanship because the Kirk's Moderate Party looked to the Tories for favor. Still, Tory support for religious establishment made more sense in England than in Scotland, but a similar logic applied. At the same time, the economic interests of Evangelicals, who tended to be middle class and professional, also created affinity for the Whigs. This left Evangelicals such as Chalmers in an awkward position. Thanks to his commitment to religious establishment, Chalmers's call for the state to support the Kirk's moral, educational, and religious mission was functionally Tory. But in debates over patronage and assertions of the church's spiritual independence, Chalmers and his Kirk allies could seem to favor the Whigs, who were inclined to favor disestablishment, especially after repeal of the Test Act (1828). The Disruption of 1843 brought this tension to the surface and sometimes yielded a "voting bloc of considerable weight" against Conservatives.[41] Though formally committed to the establishment principle, the Free Church of Chalmers was in the predicament of dissenting from Conservatives, who were instrumental in sustaining the Church of Scotland.

The ecclesiastical politics of the Kirk were never far from other controversies in nineteenth-century Scottish politics. The reform of the Corn Laws, for instance, had implications for the Kirk and the Free Church. Regulating trade and fixing tariffs on imported goods to favor domestic producers was a mercantilist policy that free traders criticized. This policy became a political football for both Whigs and Conservatives. For Chalmers, an advocate of free trade, the Corn Laws were an impediment to

Scotland's economic health, even while he was skeptical that trading agricultural products for industrial goods would strengthen the Scottish economy.[42] At the same time, these laws had implications for the Church of Scotland since its revenues depended on grain taxes. A drop in prices would reduce the Kirk's revenue. By virtue of leaving the establishment, Free Church members had less to lose in economic reforms.

Echoes of the Scottish Reformation also reverberated in nineteenth-century Scottish politics when the government of Prime Minister Robert Peel approved funding for Maynooth College, an Irish seminary for training Roman Catholic priests. This 1845 decision drew the Free Church into political alliance with other Scottish dissenting Protestants. Indeed, the Scottish Central Board of Dissenters, founded in 1834 by prominent Edinburgh families, proposed that its members support the Free Churchmen and hoped for similar sympathy in return. Scotland's Protestants outside the Kirk might disagree about the principle of an established church, but "all friends of religious liberty" should find a way to pursue "harmonious co-operation."[43] Chalmers was one of seventeen Free Church ministers to sign an 1845 letter to all "evangelical" churches in England, Wales, and Ireland that called for a meeting in London to "concentrate" Protestant opposition to "encroachments of Popery and Puseyism." The letter acknowledged the challenges of such a meeting and suggested ways Protestants "might engage together in devotional exercises" and so avoid obvious points of contention. Perhaps a simple meeting could display a form of "brotherhood highly honoring to [Christian] profession."[44] One political consequence of such Protestant cooperation was the defeat in 1847 and 1852 elections of Whig candidates in Aberdeen, Edinburgh, Stirling, Perth, Paisley, and Dundee who had voted in favor of Peel's funding of Maynooth.[45]

Chalmers's death (May 31, 1847) coincided with several local elections. It also signaled the end to a phase of Presbyterian politics that was more a function of historic tussles both within an ecclesiastical establishment and between Scotland and Westminster than an outworking of Reformed Protestant conviction. Iain Hutchinson observes that Chalmers shaped the views of his fellow ministers along the lines of "laissez-faire," "opposition to any support for able-bodied unemployed," and a preference for "voluntary" giving, rather than compulsory assessment, for poor relief.[46] Beyond these policies, Presbyterian churchmen did not display "any interest in domestic social problems." Some of this was a function of democracy's slow introduction in Scotland. The First Reform Act of 1828 opened the vote to many more Scots than English (an increase of 1,400 percent and 41 percent, respectively), but the ratio of voters to adult males in Scotland (1:8) lagged behind England (1:5).[47] The 1843 Disruption took place in a democratizing Scotland, but was hardly the result of a populist turn. Not until the Second Reform Act of 1868 did the ratio of voters to adult males drop (1:3.5). That was also the time when political parties could worry less about aristocratic classes' hegemony and turn to other issues, such as ecclesiastical disestablishment, temperance, and public health legislation. In other words, nineteenth-century Scottish politics abandoned questions about Christian society in favor of economic policies essential to the nation's well-being.

Chalmers was obviously a major figure in the first round of those economic debates. His own theories and ideal of a godly commonwealth tapped historic expectations for a Christian Scotland (and by extension the United Kingdom). That Christian outlook in the broader society gave Chalmers's ideas currency. Brown writes that Chalmers provided a social direction to the evangelical revival. He sought the conversion of those outside of the church (the working class in cities) and at the same time was an advocate for their "temporal happiness." This had a certain influence among the educated upper and middle classes, especially the younger members of those groups. At the same time, as formidable as Chalmers was in working the levers of church politics, he was "never able to function effectively in secular politics."[48] As such, at the same time that Presbyterians in places like the United States were coming to terms with secularized political parties and using those institutions to sustain Christian expectations for a godly society, the old ideal of the covenanted and Reformed nation hemmed in Scottish Presbyterians. The Free Church's defense of religious establishment was arguably the greatest example of historic Presbyterianism's reluctance to abandon early modern social structures.

Ireland

Irishman Henry Cooke (1788–1868) was a contemporary of Chalmers. Cooke's statue in central Belfast is arguably more prominent than Chalmers's in Edinburgh—the Irishman does have fewer competitors. Cooke's

Presbyterianism was a shadow of Chalmers's: Irish Presbyterianism was a muted version of the Scottish variety. Not only were Irish Presbyterians typically migrants from Scotland, but they invariably thought like Scots about church life even though they were on the outside looking in at the Church of Ireland (Anglican). Scottish Presbyterianism, whether the kind modeled by the Covenanters, the post-1689 settlement, or the Seceders' conservative variety, were examples for their Irish cousins. Cooke himself was generally moderate, despite conflicts with Arians over Reformed orthodoxy. He had the instincts of the religious establishment and was comfortable with nineteenth-century British order.

Born in 1788 to a tenant farmer, Cooke's humble origins and haphazard education were hardly the recipe for an ecclesiastical statesman. The condition of schools in County Down sent him to Glasgow College to complete a basic education, but he finished courses only in arts and divinity. At the age of twenty, the Presbytery of Ballymena licensed Cooke to preach as an assistant pastor. He soon left the congregation in Randalstown. For the next decade he moved between church work and tutoring, even while he was completing his education by taking courses in summers at the University of Glasgow in theology and at Trinity College Dublin in math and sciences. In 1818, he received a call to Killeleagh by Dromore Presbytery where he began his fight against Arianism among Irish Presbyterians. Although unsuccessful at first in opposing the ordination or academic appointments of specific candidates, his willingness to lead the charge against theological liberalism gave Cooke notoriety. It led to his election in 1824 as the moderator of the general synod at Moneymore. For the next fifteen years, Cooke managed an effort to keep Arians out of the church, which included subscription to the Westminster Standards for ordination. In the meantime, in 1829 he opened a congregation on May Street in Belfast, where he drew large crowds. He remained in this pulpit until the end of his career in 1867. From this position Cooke emerged as the leading voice of Irish Presbyterian politics.[49]

Cooke's ascendance in the Irish church coincided with a surge of evangelicalism that colored political alignments, even if Irish Presbyterians did not fit neatly within the British Liberal/Tory divide. In church life, this evangelical wave laid the foundation for the first General Assembly (1840) (see chapter 6 herein) and the significant revival of 1859.

Its religious aspects prompted Thomas Witherow in 1858 to contrast three periods of Irish Presbyterianism. The first was a "battle for existence against Prelacy." The second was a "battle for truth against heresy." In the new period that Witherow outlined, Irish Presbyterians were contending "for the Gospel of Christ against sin and ignorance at home" and "unbelief and heathenism" around the world.[50] This renewed vitality tapped both Presbyterian devotion and the interdenominational awakenings of the era that launched many foreign missions agencies, Bible societies, and Sunday schools in Europe and North America. The hallmarks of Presbyterianism—doctrine, polity, and worship—were now allies of evangelical spiritual zeal and organizational creativity.

In politics, a vigorous Presbyterianism could be either conservative or liberal. Cooke represented the conservative side of the church, and his prominence suggested he was not alone. What drove Cooke to find alliances with conservatives and even the Church of Ireland was the perennial demographic problem of Roman Catholics' numerical majority. Statistics from 1830 show that 81 percent of the Irish people were Roman Catholic, 11 percent Anglican, and 8 percent Presbyterian.[51] The threat of Roman Catholicism, which tapped the mythology of the Reformation, prompted Cooke to calculate Irish Presbyterians' interest along Protestant rather than narrowly Presbyterian lines. As early as 1834, he had already organized a meeting at Hillsborough that formed the basis for an alliance of Irish Protestants.[52]

Cooke's worries about Roman Catholics and Irish politics took shape while countering the appeal of Daniel O'Connell, the "Liberator" of Irish Catholics. A founder in 1823 of the Catholic Association, O'Connell's 1828 election from County Clare forced the question of Roman Catholics holding office in the British government. The Catholic Relief Act of 1829 provided the remedy that both seated O'Connell at Westminster and ended the remaining restrictions of penal laws. To secure reform of the Irish economy and prosperity for Irish Catholics, O'Connell opposed the 1801 Union of Great Britain and Ireland. In 1840, Charles Gavan Duffy, the Roman Catholic editor of the Belfast paper *The Vindicator*, invited O'Connell to visit the city and debate Cooke about Irish independence. Although critics portrayed O'Connell as an Irish nationalist, he was more often than not a pragmatist who worked within the possibilities of British politics. As it happened, the debate never took place, but the two men exchanged a series of fairly personal barbs in newspapers before the proposed meeting. O'Connell did travel to Belfast, but his safety was always a concern. Police tried to prevent riots as protestors threw rocks at O'Connell's train to Belfast. In the city, he could not leave his hotel room to attend Mass. He delivered his side of the debate from the window of his hotel room. Jeering from the crowd prevented most from hearing him. A few days after O'Connell's departure from Belfast, Cooke gave a speech that described his opponent as a "genius of knavery" and "an apostle of rebellion." To O'Connell's charge that Ulster Protestant youth were merely under the sway of Cooke's rhetorical gifts, the Presbyterian shot back; the reason young people supported union was "the Bible and its principles." It was the same influence as the Holy Spirit's on John Knox, "who never feared the face of man."[53]

Cooke's appeal to the Bible and the Reformation may have persuaded Ulster Protestants, but a growing economic gap between Ireland's industrializing north and agrarian south was increasingly overshadowing the island's confessional divide. Cooke was aware of this split but also took pride in his fellow Protestants' industry. In his reply to O'Connell, Cooke recalled the transformation of Belfast during his life. When he was a boy, Belfast was merely a "village." By 1840 it had blossomed into a "glorious sight": "the masted grove within our harbor—our mighty warehouses teeming with the wealth of every clime—our giant manufactures lifting themselves on every side-ur streets marching on, as it were, with such rapidity, that an absence of a few weeks makes us strangers in the outskirts of our towns." All this was the product of "the Union."[54] Liberty, Protestantism, and industry were the genius of modern Ireland, and from Cooke's vantage all Irish Presbyterians agreed. Soon after the failed debate between O'Connell and Cooke, rallies to oppose repeal of the Anglo-Irish union heaped praise on the Protestant for turning the politician's "triumphal progress" into "silent shame and downcast mortification."[55]

Cooke's ability to speak for Irish Presbyterians soon came in for reassessment thanks to historic tensions between Presbyterians and Anglicans. The dispute between Presbyterians and the archbishop of Derry, Archibald Boyd (see chapter 6 herein), over the penal laws fueled Irish Presbyterians' resistance to Cooke's desire for a political alliance with the Church of Ireland. The moderator of the 1843 General Assembly, John Edgar, picked up Cooke's Whiggish interpretation of Presbyterian politics, but used it to assert the validity of his church's ordination entirely apart from Anglican approval. He asked whether Irish Presbyterians still had "the courage and constancy of their fathers," whether they were able and confident still to "assert the principles and maintain the liberty which their fathers bequeathed." Edgar even invoked the tragic aspect of the Scottish Reformation in ways foreign to Cooke. He reminded his communion that Presbyterian convictions were "dyed with their blood, and sanctified by their piety and their prayers."[56] Not very far in the background of this aggressive Presbyterianism was dissatisfaction with the British government's siding with the Church of Scotland at the time of the 1843 Disruption. That same year, the Irish General Assembly recognized the Free Church of Scotland "alone as the legitimate representative of those from whom the Presbyterian Church in Ireland has always regarded it the noblest distinction to be descended."[57] (It took almost forty years for the Presbyterian Church of Ireland to resume relations with the Church of Scotland.)

Changes in Ireland's economy raised additional questions about Cooke's assessment of industrial and urban progress. Ireland's land-lease system was a burden on Presbyterian farmers, who had no reliable political representation in London and in local affairs were subject to governments dominated by Anglicans. Politically liberal Presbyterians defended tenant rights, also known as the Ulster Custom, which gave a departing tenant the discretion to sell the value of improvements he had made to the next tenant. These rights extended to both the rent structure and length of tenure and were part of a set of agricultural reforms in the United Kingdom that culminated in William Gladstone's Land Act of 1881.[58] As much as the livelihoods of people who worked the land were at stake, tenant-rights disputes also revealed the need for representation in government for rural communities. This set of policies earned the name "Presbyterian interest." It circulated during the 1840s in newspapers under the editorial oversight of Presbyterians. These publications also led the challenge to Cooke's understanding of Irish politics. Opposition to Cooke was strong enough to provoke his withdrawal from the General Assembly between 1843 and 1847.[59] If the Presbyterian interest leaned toward liberals in government, the church's authors used faith to diagnose the situation. According to *A Catechism of Tenant-Right* (1850), written by James McKnight, this was not a secular question but one of

"LIFE, MORALS, and RELIGION." Although of vital interest to Presbyterians, McKnight also explained that economic reforms would contribute to the "social happiness of millions" and "safety and prosperity of the British empire."[60]

Economic tensions between an industrializing north and an antiquated land system (which contributed to famine) were not alone responsible for nurturing liberal politics among Irish Presbyterians. Still, political debates at midcentury revealed a set of Presbyterian voices that were not content with Cooke's conservative politics. The need for adequate representation in Parliament eventually prompted demands for opening suffrage to greater numbers of Irish people. In the 1852 general election, Presbyterian editors portrayed suffrage as a "bold, constitutional insurrection of the democratic masses for their own class emancipation."[61] Andrew R. Holmes reads such language as radical. But it did aid in the election of one candidate for an Ulster constituency. By 1855, church leaders had formed the Presbyterian Representation Society whose purpose was to remind church members of their duty to use the franchise. Its issues went well beyond the economy to military chaplaincy, abolishing Anglican ecclesiastical courts, and access to parochial burial grounds. As Presbyterians tried to redress their second-class status in Irish affairs, they used the 1857 elections to send three Presbyterians to Westminster from County Londonderry. The newspaper *Banner of Ulster* interpreted the election as the end to an Anglican monopoly on government in Ireland. These were also signs of Cooke's decline in Irish Presbyterian affairs. He lost more favor when his critics in the church supported Gladstone's Irish Church Bill and disestablishment of the Church of Ireland. One of Cooke's critics put the question this way: "A Tory Presbyterian is a kind of ecclesiastical and political incongruity. . . . A Scotch Whig used to be just another name for a true-blue Presbyterian."[62]

The major hurdle for Presbyterian liberalism came with Gladstone's policy of Home Rule. By then Cooke had been dead for almost two decades. Although the 1886 legislation reflected liberal efforts to increase local representation and reform the economy, it also raised the specter of Irish Protestants' numerical minority. The Presbyterian Church's General Assembly passed two resolutions, one in 1886 and another in 1893, against Home Rule while also supporting economic reforms designed to prevent Irish independence.[63] Presbyterian conservatives and liberals may have been divided politically, but they agreed that Ireland's place in the British union "provided the best framework for promoting liberty and prosperity." Conversely, "Rome Rule" would produce a Roman Catholic ascendancy and end Protestants' religious and civil liberties.[64] According to Thomas Witherow, professor at Magee College, an outpost of anti-Tory sentiment, Irish Presbyterians understood the complaints of Irish Catholics since they too had suffered ill treatment from government and were forced to pay rents that tenants could not afford. But an Irish Parliament and separation from Great Britain would be "the greatest calamity of all."[65]

The question of Home Rule, in Andrew R. Holmes's judgment, vindicated Cooke's "political vision . . . in the long term."[66] But in the short run, the Reformation fusion of civil and religious liberty with antipopery gave Presbyterians a cultural identity distinct from both Anglicans and Roman Catholics. What John Rogers, a pastor in Comber, claimed in 1857 during the debates over tenant rights was an understanding of Presbyterian faith and politics that inspired Irish heirs of the Scottish Reformation. The Covenanters, he reminded fellow church members, "leveled the fabric which prelatic and arbitrary power had been erecting for generations on British soil." In contrast, prelacy was the "implacable foe of civil and religious liberty," the "unmitigated resister of Christ's crown and covenant rights," the "enemy of progress, prosperity, and all righteousness."[67] Whatever self-righteousness came with their politics, Irish Presbyterians supported many aspects of a liberalizing Ireland.

Canada

In Canada, a political tendency among Presbyterians was hard to find if only because Canadian society did not achieve sufficient coherence for specific political platforms until confederation in the 1860s. Curiously enough, the consolidation of Presbyterianism into a communion with national borders developed at the same time as confederation. John Webster Grant writes that "confederation could take place only if the people would accept it, and the opinions of Canadians were moulded in part by the churches to which they belonged."[68] The puzzle of British North America that blossomed into Canada contained several pieces—the

Atlantic provinces, Canada East and West (formerly Lower and Upper, later Quebec and Ontario), the West and the Northwest. The confederation process started in 1841 with the unification of Upper and Lower Canada into one province. But that merger was fraught with tensions between Roman Catholics and Protestants. The Act of Union of 1841 assured equal representation in the legislature, even though Roman Catholics in Lower Canada had a larger population than the less settled Upper Canada.

On top of this political, regional, and demographic diversity, Presbyterians added increased zest to Canada's many parts. All of Scotland's Presbyterian varieties found a home in British North America. The Church of Scotland, Seceders, and Free Church Scots organized congregations, presbyteries, and synods in the different provinces that later became Canada. Each communion accordingly established institutions and set expectations within the distinct geography that extended from the Atlantic to the Gulf of Alaska. Political and denominational unification went hand in hand. As such, Presbyterian political outlooks in Canada were generally nationalistic. This was markedly different from Scotland, where the ideals of church and national reform started among elites and then became the norm for the nation. In Canada, Presbyterian identity matured with the formation of a Canadian nation.

One way to illustrate these ties is to follow the career of George Monro Grant, a pastor of humble origins from Pictou County, Nova Scotia, who culminated his career at Queen's University (Kingston, Ontario) as principal and made the institution a "dynamic national institution."[69] The evolution of Grant's own career ran parallel to the growth of Queen's from a denominational college training Presbyterian pastors into a university that served the nation. Both of those stories underscore Canadian Presbyterianism's transition from a set of communions that echoed Scottish church life into a (somewhat) unified ecclesiastical body in service of a confederation aspiring to be modern and progressive.[70]

Born in 1835, Grant lost his right hand in an accident on the family farm. That incident ironically opened the way for Grant, with support from his parents, to pursue a career that did not depend on manual labor. He went to school at Pictou Academy, the institution established by Thomas McCulloch, a Secession pastor who migrated to Nova Scotia in 1803 and wanted an alternative to the existing academies that were only open to Anglicans. From there, Grant went to the West River Seminary, a training ground for the Seceders' archrivals, the Anti-Burghers, an indication that Scottish antagonisms were still fresh in the New World over a century later.[71] When he was eighteen, Grant's family transferred from an anti-Burgher congregation to one with Church of Scotland affiliations, which made the young man eligible for scholarships for study in Scotland at the University of Glasgow.

His studies between 1853 and 1860 included the arts, sciences, and theology. The biggest influence while in Glasgow, however, was the city's Barony Church, where Grant became active. The pastor, Norman McLeod, took Grant under his wing, and the student repaid the favor by observing that "[McLeod] was the greatest man I have ever known."[72] Under McLeod, who had studied with Thomas Chalmers, Grant's outlook shifted to ministry among the city's laboring classes and political reforms that improved living standards. Despite McLeod's respect for Chalmers, he did not follow the Free Church out of the Kirk at the time of the Disruption. Grant's time at Barony Church also opened doors at another parish in Cathcart, where the pastor, an older member of the Moderate Party, increased the student's interest in urban ministry, specifically through Sunday school.

Exposure to the Church of Scotland softened the hard edges of whatever Seceder conviction Grant had retained. It also made him wary of the Free Church. Although he admired the sacrifice of its ministers, its commitment to missions and ministry to the working class, Grant found the Free Church's rigidity akin to priestcraft. Its doctrinal tenacity bordered on a "fanaticism which is stern and fierce." Meanwhile, Grant grew to appreciate ecclesiastical establishments. They may not have been practical in the colonies but in Scotland the established church "gave a broad sanity to religion."[73]

Grant returned to Nova Scotia in 1861 as a missionary for the Church of Scotland. His task was not so much to evangelize local residents as to organize congregations. His successful efforts at church planting—one congregation in Nova Scotia and two on Prince Edward Island—led to a call in 1863 to St. Matthew's Church in Halifax, one of the province's largest and wealthiest Presbyterian churches. A theological moderate, Grant admired both the American evangelist Dwight L. Moody and Thomas Carlyle's Romantic idealism as alternatives to rigid Reformed theology. In Halifax, Grant instituted several programs designed to improve social conditions among the working classes. These included supporting a School for the Blind, the Halifax Institution for the Deaf and Dumb, the Children's Home and Child Immigration Schemes, the Old Ladies' Home, the Halifax Industrial School, the Halifax Visiting Dispensary, and the Young Men's Christian Association. St. Matthew's under Grant's direction also called a urban missionary, who organized poor relief and established a night refuge for the homeless. His wealthy parishioners supported these causes, even as Grant moved comfortably in their circles. His marriage to Jessie Lawson, a daughter of one of Halifax's wealthy merchants, was one indication of the pastor's status in Halifax society.

Grant's attitude to the ministry and the church's role in society functioned as a way to maintain social prominence without a religious establishment. Strict doctrine would not allow the church to gain broad support. To have a voice in society, Grant became a Presbyterian but held church teachings loosely even while insisting on social norms that reflected a Protestant ethic. William Lawson Grant, his son and biographer, captured this two-pronged aspect of his father's career when he wrote that Grant "had no sympathy with those who arrogated to the ministry priestly or supernatural powers." Yet, when it came to society, "with the fervour of the Old Testament prophets, he denounced the shams and hypocrisies and immoralities of his time, his city and his congregation."[74] This stance involved uplifting the lower classes through education, industriousness, safety in the workplace, and temperance. Through it all, Grant "thundered unceasingly" against "vice, hypocrisy, and meanness."[75]

If Grant fought vice, ignorance, and sloth, he did so with the soothing manner of the British Romantics. In a lecture to the YMCA of Halifax in 1867 titled "Reformers of the Nineteenth Century," Grant made passing references to Thomas Chalmers before recommending the triumvirate of William Wordsworth, Samuel Taylor Coleridge, and Thomas Carlyle. He found their idealism (philosophical) and mysticism a welcome shift from the Enlightenment's empiricism and paved the way for a recovery of confident Christianity. The value of these English writers for politics was to elevate the spiritual above the physical, to see "the divine . . . in every man." This outlook could calm the antagonism between the wealthy and laboring masses and facilitate democratic government.[76] Grant was silent about specific policies that flowed from the English Romantics. But that did not diminish their greatness because they stood opposed to "unbelief, materialism, and falsehood." If Canadians heeded, they could work to cleanse the world of wickedness and error. Simply look, he concluded, in words borrowed from Carlyle, to "the duty that lies nearest you!"[77]

Grant's preaching showed similar themes and haziness. One of his widely circulated sermons, on Galatians 5:1 ("Stand fast, therefore, in the liberty wherewith Christ hath made us free"), explored the nature of true freedom. For Grant, the Apostle Paul was calling for liberation from the narrow constraints of "scholastic subtleties and carefully worded articles."[78] Christianity freed believers for service in the world. Salvation was not confined to a person's relationship with God. It included the consecration of the world. True religion reveled in the "boundless beauty" of nature, "all that robust, cheery, ordinary life that takes pleasure without check of conscience," and "the play of fancy, or song, or art." Christianity was the way to affirm that "all things gathered together in one, even in Christ."[79]

That 1866 sermon coincided with the Canadian debates over confederation and revealed Grant's own position. Joseph Howe, premier of Nova Scotia, whom Grant regarded as "the noblest of our native born men," was the province's chief opponent of union.[80] Howe's objections were economic and cultural. Without rail lines, confederation would marginalize Nova Scotia from greater Canada and the United States. Also it could not overcome Canada's cultural diversity. Grant's aspirations for harmony and unity easily overcame Howe's reservations. Prominent political figures on both sides of the debate were in his Halifax congregation, and Grant avoided the topic from the pulpit. But he did speak in favor of confederation from other venues. Grant argued, on the basis of German unification, that consolidation brought greater efficiency. He acknowledged that plans for confederation had imperfections. The pastor especially feared that the best politicians would seek office in Ottawa and leave local, provincial politics in the hands of "second-class public men."[81]

In Grant's mind, what was good for Canada was also desirable for Canadian Presbyterians. Telling the difference was sometimes difficult since Grant's estimate of the church's work was bound up with serving greater Canada. Indeed, the church was the principal means for overcoming Canada's provincial and cultural diversity. A union of the Presbyterian communions—four at the time of the Confederation in 1867—was necessary for the consolidation of Canada itself.

That it took Presbyterian churches almost a decade to catch up to Canada was not the fault of Grant, whose book *Ocean to Ocean* (1873), a travelogue written while a participant on Sandford Fleming's expedition across the Canadian west, unified the country with a Presbyterian's blessing. An engineer of Scottish heritage, Fleming's task was to find a route for the Canadian railway, a necessary stop in uniting Canada's territories. Promoters of confederation felt a measure of urgency. They feared the United States might poach from Canada's recently formed provinces. Fleming had been a member in Grant's congregation and had cooperated with his pastor on a number of endeavors in Halifax. Grant's presence on this journey, perhaps unusual for a Presbyterian pastor, reflected friendship and a shared commitment to national unity. (Fleming would later serve as chancellor at Queen's University in Kingston, Ontario, from 1877 to 1902, where Grant was then principal.) Grant explained in the introduction to *Ocean to Ocean* that the incorporation of British Columbia into the Canadian confederation (1871) was the triumph of one British America "under the aegis of the Empire" over the control of the northwest in the hands of private interests (e.g., the Hudson Bay Company).[82] It also brought the challenge of accomplishing in one or two years what had taken the United States fifty years to do, namely, the people of a new nation "triumphing over all the obstacles of nature."[83]

Grant's concern for improved working conditions and standards of living was bound up with confidence in the blessings afforded by political consolidation and industrial growth. He viewed the northwest as a "great and fertile" land, capable of sustaining millions of people. The air was "pure and dry," ready to sustain "health and strength of body." It had the potential to be a home for the "stream of emigration that runs from northern and central Europe to America."[84] All it needed was access through "rail and steamboat." Nevertheless, Canada depended on more than material resources. The Dominion also needed a people of character. Here Grant exuded confidence: "We come from a race that never counted the number of its foes, nor the number of its friends, when freedom, loyalty or God was concerned." Canada was for Grant "the last clear field given by a beneficent Creator in which the children of men could have scope, untrammeled by ancient institutions, to work out the best ideas derived from the experience of the past."[85] Grant did not merely have in mind Canadians of Protestant stock. He also lauded Methodist pastors and Roman Catholic missionaries as much as the Presbyterians he met on the journey.

Coordinating Presbyterian ministry to migrants and settlers in the west would require allocating ecclesiastical resources. Such efficiency would also require putting behind the church controversies Presbyterians had brought with them from Scotland. The chief remaining division on the eve of Canada's confederation was between the heirs of the Kirk and the communions that had left (Seceders and Free Church). Presbyterians not affiliated with the Kirk had already begun to unite along Canadian realities. But the synods tied to the Kirk, John S. Moir writes, still "gloried" in their "Scottishness" and preferred aura of establishment. That ethos likely hurt an appeal to Canadians without strong Scots identity. At the same time, Presbyterian heirs to the Kirk did not need to increase their ranks because in Ontario and Quebec they still derived one-third of their income from the Clergy Reserves. In the Maritimes, two-thirds of the Scottish congregations received aid from the Church of Scotland.[86] The benefits of existing arrangements did not, however, slow the momentum of Canadian confederation.

The biggest challenges to uniting Presbyterians in Canada were older debates that had informed the distinct convictions of Reformed Protestants in England and Scotland. One contested point was merely practical. What would come of the various educational institutions that each denomination had established? Attachment to Scotland had its limits. A school in Canada was much more preferable than a student needing to study in Glasgow or Edinburgh. As divisive as college education could be, negotiations proceeded by deferring institutional consolidation until Presbyterians ratified church union. A much more contentious question was the age-old topic of Christ's headship over his church. In the controversies that led to Secession or Disruption, the Church of Scotland had waffled. Consequently, the issue of Christ's headship brought to the surface suspicions from Scottish church history. As a remedy, negotiators devised a compromise that granted "full liberty of opinion" on this particular Presbyterian conviction. The proposed union also avoided differences over worship; during the decade running up to union, the use of organs in services had a mixed reception. Canadian Presbyterians also affirmed the Westminster Standards as the church's doctrinal standard while making provision for a diversity of attachments to those 1640s documents. The breadth required to accommodate the many strands of Presbyterian experience was so great that some refused to join the united communion. For the stricter Canadians, the united church was loose on doctrine, worship, and the headship of Christ.[87]

Moir indicates that Canadian nationalism likely had a bigger influence on Presbyterian union than ecclesiastical union had on political confederation. In the magazine of the Presbyterian Church in the Lower Provinces, one editor asked if it were wise to resist church union when the "people and government of Britain anxiously desire a union of these two colonies." In another magazine, one Presbyterian asserted that "there never was a time when [church union] could be more appropriately brought forward than" at a time when British North America was confederating.[88] George Munro Grant was himself enthusiastic about church and state. Still, for him, the union of Presbyterianism might be the start of forming one church for all of Canada, one that included Presbyterians, Methodists, and Anglicans, he told the Montreal branch of the Evangelical Alliance in 1874. It could even embrace Roman Catholics. "Why not?" he asked. "God can do greater things even than this. And who of us shall say, God forbid?"[89]

Despite Grant's hearty support, negotiations for the church union took the better part of four years. Still, on Sunday, June 13, 1875, as part of the inauguration of the Presbyterian Church in Canada, Sunday school children gathered at Montreal's Victoria Skating Rink with parents and officers from local congregations. Two days later, representatives from each of the four Presbyterian communions marched in procession to Victoria Hall. They proceeded to ratify the proposed union before attending a joint worship service in the afternoon at nearby St. Paul's kirk. In the evening, the new denomination held a reception to celebrate. According to one report, the morning session at Victoria Hall saw the 6,000-seat facility filled to capacity. Decorations included streamers and flags. All assembled sang Psalm 100, then heard a reading of Psalm 133, followed by prayer. Always attentive to order, clerks read the minutes of each communion from the respective synod before repeating the terms of the proposed union. The oldest member of the group then declared that the union was officially consummated. The *Montreal Witness* reported that the "vast audience joined hands in singing the 133rd Psalm with enthusiasm and feeling, probably never equaled in any preceding religious assembly in Canada."[90]

At the very end of the ceremony, Grant spoke. He dispensed with his prepared remarks. Instead, he was brief: "Beloved, let us love one another, for love is of God and everyone loveth is born of God, and knoweth God; he that loveth not knoweth not God for God is Love." A Maritimer in the crowd shouted, "Our Church had a leader."[91] What Donald MacLeod writes of the unions of Secession and Kirk Presbyterians in the early 1860s also characterized the creation of the Presbyterian Church of Canada: it was "genuinely Canadian, reflective of a new identity, and prepared to advance with courage and determination, in a new country, helping to set a new direction in a colony that was, like the church formed that day, coming into new maturity and independence."[92]

Along with Presbyterians in other parts of the Anglophone world, Canadians added nationalism to the political outlook of Knox's and Rutherford's heirs. They had already supported expanded suffrage and democratic participation in government, economic progress through free trade and industrialization, programs of welfare for sectors of society hardest hit by modernization, and voluntarism as the best way to sustain the church's ministry within a liberal social order in which elites had less control of public policy's mechanisms. And now Canadian Presbyterians solidified ties between church and nation.

George Monro Grant's work as principal of Queen's University in Kingston, Ontario, illustrated this facet of Canadian Presbyterianism. Originally Queen's College, a Church of Scotland institution courtesy of Queen Victoria's 1841 royal charter, the school was chiefly a training ground in the arts and sciences for prospective ministers. Its original model was the Scottish university, especially Glasgow and Edinburgh. After confederation, Queen's lost government funding and appeared to be headed for absorption within the University of Toronto. Grant became principal in 1878 and arguably saved Queen's existence. He had gained experience with higher education administration through service on the board of Dalhousie College in Halifax, which he helped to become an institution that served all Presbyterian branches.

At Queen's, Grant's immediate challenge was fundraising, and his magnanimous ways were well suited. The reluctance of Presbyterians to support the university prompted a turn to the government. Queen's ties to the church made secular funding difficult. Grant's solution was to channel government funds through an independent School of Mining and Agriculture, established in 1893, and to dissolve ties between Queen's and the church except for the college of theology. To increase Queen's identity as a state institution, Grant reduced the number of Presbyterians on the board of trustees, raised matriculation standards, and recruited faculty based not on church ties but academic training. Grant remained convinced that the university, the church, and Canada were equal parts of his work as principal: "The work of the Church in our day is to reconcile itself with all that is best in modern thought. There is no institution where that can be done so as to reach the whole Church but Queen's."[93]

Grant was not alone in blending faith, the academy, and national service. The Progressive Era in the West witnessed theological and political adjustments that reinforced each other under a broad heading of social uplift and civilizational advance. This outlook also tapped the older Presbyterian sense of the church as an agent in creating a godly commonwealth. To bring Presbyterianism into a modern, liberal society required sanding down sharp edges of theology and strict adherence to Presbyterian order.[94] Still, the old aim of carrying on the reform of the whole church for the good of the people inspired Grant and his fellow nineteenth-century Presbyterians. The modern version of the Presbyterian political vision—now politically, economically, and religiously diversified—still carried the torch for God's kingdom and social righteousness. The following description of Queen's University in Grant's era captures the devices by which the old ideal of a covenanted kingdom had resurfaced in the guise of a modern Christian nation:

> Christianity being involved in the whole of life, it was important to break down artificial sacred and secular distinctions. From there it was a natural step to break down a distinction between secular and sacred teaching, and even between secular and sacred writings. . . . There was a tendency also to break down the sharp distinction between the "Christian" and the "non-Christian" and therefore to challenge the traditional concepts of "conversion" and "the new birth." There was an inclination to shift from the assumption of man's inherent wickedness to the assumption of the Enlightenment that most men wish to be good and that the task of the church was to get them

> more and more involved in doing good. There was a shift away from the assumption that the kingdom of heaven must come through spiritual change in the individual, to the suggestion that the millennium could be approached, at least, by voluntary social work and also by legislation promoted by men of goodwill.[95]

Presbyterian Modern

The variety of nineteenth-century Presbyterian adaptations to political and economic liberalism may well have come together with the 1868 appointment of James McCosh as president of the College of New Jersey (soon to be Princeton University). That McCosh's tenure began on the centennial of another Scot's administration at the college was at least symbolic if not also indicative of American Presbyterians' debt to their British heritage. The new president came with international Presbyterian credentials. One of the original pastors in the 1843 Disruption, McCosh was steeped in Scottish Presbyterianism. He grew up in a Covenanting stronghold in southwest Scotland (Ayrshire), studied at Glasgow and Edinburgh, and in 1834 became a minister in the Kirk. At Edinburgh he had studied with Thomas Chalmers. The professor's influence was evident in McCosh's identification with the Evangelical Party and their subsequent decision to leave for the Free Church. There he remained until 1851 when he accepted an appointment in logic and metaphysics at Queen's College, Belfast, where he taught for sixteen years. When he left Belfast for Princeton, McCosh won the trifecta of international Presbyterianism—from Scotland, to Ireland, to the United States.[96]

To say that McCosh synthesized Presbyterianism for modern society is an overstatement. But his seemingly easy transition among churches in Scotland, Ireland, and the United States does suggest that he stood within an international consensus on the place of Presbyterian convictions in a political world long removed from the social realities that had given life to church reform on behalf of a reformed nation. His first book, *The Method of Divine Government, Moral and Physical* (1850), reads like a disquisition on God's law as the basis for a holy commonwealth with reference to Old Testament Israel. But it was actually a reflection on the social conventions and explicitly religious influences that cultivated personal virtue and public order. In one section, McCosh observed the ways that extreme wealth and poverty nurtured disregard for morality, because people were either above ordinary social constraints or had no place lower to fall.[97] Outside his study, McCosh's participation in public affairs was generally low key. Based on his experience with the Free Church, McCosh encouraged Irish Presbyterians to embrace voluntarism and abandon the establishmentarian elements of the *regium donum*. Some Irish thought he was guilty of "intermeddling in what he as a foreigner could not understand."[98] He was, in contrast, on solid ground among the Irish on temperance. McCosh's opposition to the saloon echoed Chalmers's diagnosis of the ills of industrial society, but it also drew on his own experience as a pastor among the working class where alcohol was a threat to healthy families. Like other Presbyterians, McCosh did not press for legislation to the exclusion of informal mechanisms that addressed social problems. He cooperated with other Presbyterians in Belfast to establish a room for workingmen to socialize without the lure of alcoholic beverages. Like other Presbyterians in the Anglo-American world, McCosh also sought to make education accessible to the lower orders of society.[99]

In the United States, McCosh again worked quietly in various civil spheres. In New Jersey politics, he sought and supported the leadership of able and responsible officials as a "staunch Republican."[100] McCosh continued to support temperance, oppose saloons, and implemented campus policies to prevent students from acquiring alcohol.[101] He lent his status at the college to persuade New Jersey's legislature to open public schools for the state's residents. In an 1871 speech, McCosh could not avoid Scottish pride by contrasting the provision of education in his homeland for all classes, compared to England where schooling was reserved for elites. His argument for public schools was of a piece with a gospel of upward mobility and cultural uplift. In each district, he said, the state should ensure that a "boy may be led by training in literature, science and art to acquire higher tastes, and thus be saved from low indulgences, and induced to enter and to follow the higher professions of life and to spread . . . a refining influence."[102] Although minor, civil service reform was another of McCosh's political interventions. His 1880 letter to Rutherford B. Hayes, printed in the *New York Times*, recounted the favorable effects of such reform in Britain. McCosh praised Democrats for supporting the policy and thought Republicans should not doubt their political adversaries' sincerity.[103]

Arguably the most political of McCosh's essays or addresses came before the Evangelical Alliance of 1887. The occasion was notable in several respects. Aside from his subject, the relations between capital and labor, the Alliance resonated with McCosh's own efforts to create a Presbyterian equivalent of a pan-Protestant fraternity of communions. He envisioned a federation of international Presbyterian churches (chiefly transatlantic), modeled on the U.S. system of federalism, to conduct missions, evangelism, and education on a scale beyond the capacity of any single denomination. Such breadth of endeavor was also on McCosh's mind as he reflected on economic conditions that were creating great wealth and improving standards of living, even as they sowed antagonism between rich and poor.

He began by appealing to Presbyterian teaching on the two kingdoms. God had established two kingdoms, one temporal and one spiritual, and though they "may form an alliance to promote common ends," such as education or morality, and the church and civil government "must retain . . . independence." With this distinction came the reality of Christ as "the sole head and king of his church," a Presbyterian doctrine that, if affirmed by all of Christendom, could have saved the church from "worldly minded pastors." McCosh explained these starting points by reminding his audience of his own background in the Free Church, where ministers gave up their livings—"mine was one of the most enviable." Still, despite the church's spiritual calling, it was also responsible for being "the great peacemaker of the universe," which extended to finding harmony between rich and poor. As a negotiator, the church should not attack either capital or labor. Rivalries and jealousies were sure to surface as each class "seeks its own interest."[104] As an independent authority, the church needed to "nurse the wounded" and "comfort the . . . bankrupt and the poor." Although the church must be impartial, McCosh did wonder why American churches had so few working-class church members. As a college president, McCosh did not presume to know the answer. But he went back to lessons he learned from Chalmers and recommended pastoral visitation in the homes of workingmen: "A minister will not be able to reach the hearts of his people unless he visits among them." McCosh admitted that he "never learned to preach till I visited among my people."[105]

McCosh showed the extent to which Presbyterians were capable of adapting historic convictions to modern realities while retaining the church as a gatekeeper of national norms. Even without an established church or the ideal of a covenanted nation, Presbyterians adjusted to economic and political developments partly to retain influence in modern society. Some of Presbyterianism's political adaptability grew out of pragmatic considerations rather than ideals about the best or most godly society. As long as the church had a place in public debates, Presbyterians like McCosh appeared to be content with modern social and economic circumstances.

At the same time, McCosh revealed a progressive tendency in Presbyterianism that was present at its origins. Because Presbyterianism began as a force of opposition to rule by bishops and continued as a form of checks upon elites in both government and the church, Presbyterians saw overcoming injustices of the past with improvements that led to a fairer future. Such a disposition almost always placed Presbyterians on the side of freedom and limited government, whether in the form of freedom of conscience or ecclesiastical autonomy from meddling magistrates. This cast of mind nurtured in Presbyterians at least sympathy if not outright support for political and economic reforms that reduced the authority and wealth of the few and expanded society's benefits as broadly as possible. Such an outlook, as in the case of the United States, could lend support for small government and reliance on voluntary associations for improving social conditions. But even where the state's footprint in managing the forces of modernization was larger than the American form of government, Presbyterians generally supported those "good" governments whose rule extended the blessings of modern society as widely as possible. For this reason, increase in suffrage, more extensive representation in government, free trade and better distribution of goods for more affordable prices, higher rates of literacy and advanced learning, and greater suppression of vices, not to mention the separation of church and state, were all policies on Presbyterians' horizon within their specific national contexts.

This constellation of political and economic positions was a long way from the godly commonwealth of the Scottish Reformation or England's Second Reformation. But after the Glorious Revolution, Presbyterians learned by experience and reflection that the same political arrangements that lightened the church's burden from an overreaching magistrate were also among the tools by which modern nations could fashion a generically Christian society.

CHAPTER 9

Presbyterian Nationalisms

James Anthony Froude (1818–94) was an unlikely candidate to underscore the centrality of Presbyterianism in British history. As a young man, he had written fiction that trafficked in the sordid subjects of adultery, atheism, and sexual impotence. But Froude also had a pious side, at least for a time. A student at Oriel College, Oxford, at the height of the Oxford Movement, and a brother of Richard Hurrell Froude, an Anglo-Catholic polemicist, James Anthony was on a path that could easily take him, as it had John Henry Newman, from the Church of England's High Church party into the Roman Catholic Church. But Froude became frustrated with the Oxford Movement. By the late 1840s, officials at Oriel asked him to resign his fellowship. In turn, Froude turned to editing *Fraser's Magazine* and began his career as a historian.

His twelve-volume history of England, published between 1856 and 1870, was well received. According to one biographer, Froude was "known all over the world as the most brilliant of living English historians."[1] This reputation earned him an appointment in 1868 as rector of the University of St. Andrews. This post at Scotland's oldest university made some sense in the light of Froude's interpretation of the English Reformation as "the root and source of the expansive force which has spread the Anglo-Saxon race over the globe."[2] Even if Froude regarded Scottish Presbyterianism as a mere extension of English Protestantism and whitewashed the Scottish Reformers' rigidity, his celebration of such Presbyterian virtues as thrift, sobriety, and moral rigor undoubtedly endeared him to university officials and the wider Scottish public.

In 1871, Froude made explicit his high regard for the Scots' historic faith in a public address before the St. Andrews community, entitled, simply enough, "Calvinism." To those who taught at the university's theological colleges, the Englishman's understanding of Calvin's doctrines may have sounded superficial. Even so, Froude's brief for Calvinism was an elixir for any Presbyterian weary with charges of rigidity, dogmatism, and intolerance. He conceded that Calvin's teaching on free will could appear to undermine morality. In point of fact, Calvinism possessed "singular attractions" for some of the "greatest men that ever lived," for Martin Luther, John Calvin, John Knox, Andrew Melville, Oliver Cromwell, John Milton, and John Bunyan. Each man's "life was as upright as their intellect was commanding and their public aims untainted with selfishness . . . frank, true, cheerful, humorous, as unlike sour fanatics as it is possible to imagine any one, and able in some way to sound the key-note to which every brave and faithful heart in Europe instinctively vibrated."[3] If Calvinism could produce worthies such as these, Froude deduced, then its genius could not be reasonably denied. Calvinists, Froude added, "abhorred as no body of men ever more abhorred all conscious mendacity, all impurity, all moral wrong of every kind." For this reason, any trace of national righteousness in England and Scotland stemmed from "convictions which were branded by the Calvinists into the people's hearts."[4]

Scottish Presbyterians may or may not have wanted Froude's help, but they did not have to spend time with him, since his appointment as rector was an honorary title. At the same time, Froude's appropriation of the Reformation and its influence on British society was telling. It was of a piece with the narratives Presbyterians constructed to write their churches into their nation's respective histories. For instance, Froude turned Knox into a freedom fighter of the sixteenth century's emerging Protestant nationalism. The Reformer represented "all that was best in Scotland." He was "no narrow fanatic," but a "large, noble, generous man, with a shrewd perception of actual fact, who found himself face to face with actual iniquity."[5] Froude understood that Knox made some missteps with Queen Elizabeth and overreached on the dangers of female rulers. But the Reformer's objections to episcopacy were plausible since Froude thought bishops were little more than proxies for the Crown. If bishops could have served in the church merely "as an elder among elders," Presbyterians would have been wrong to object. But Elizabeth and her advisors wanted a church that was not "too genuine" or independent. For an institution with a divine commission, sincerity "might be dangerously powerful."[6]

Whether he intended it or not, Froude was vindicating those "hot" Protestants of the sixteenth and seventeenth centuries whose desire for thorough church reform in England and Scotland had been an unsettling factor in the nations' politics. Of course, the rise of nation-states and the system of territorial sovereignty that emerged with the Peace of Westphalia (1648) was not the product of the Reformation in any simple sense. But church reform was a significant factor during the rise of Europe's system of nation-states. This was especially true for England and Scotland, where Presbyterians constantly spoke—and often organized—to attain a truly Christian nation. Because of Presbyterianism's place in debates and the actual creation of modern Scotland, it established a firm place in the histories of the nations in the current or former orbit of the British Crown—England, Scotland, Ireland, the United States, and Canada. Froude's own narrative of the rise of a Protestant England and the British Empire echoed Presbyterians on both sides of the Atlantic. For these writers who dabbled in history, the story of national greatness started with the sixteenth-century Reformations in the British Isles and picked up momentum with the contribution of Presbyterians. These heirs of Knox and Samuel Rutherford may have abandoned Scotland's National Covenants, but the desire for a godly nation inspired historical interpretations that showed Presbyterianism to be a chief, if not essential, element in national formation.

Scotland's History of Presbyterian Liberty

Presbyterianism was never a welcoming presence in British politics. Advocates of further reform had challenged the episcopal structures used by the church at least since the fourth century. Presbyterians wrote and circulated theories of permissible political resistance, not unique to Western Christians. Yet, they were still a thorn in the side potentially for monarchs who did not live up to biblical ideals. For at least these reasons, Presbyterianism took almost a century and a half to find a secure footing. William III's recognition in 1690 of the General Assembly for the Church of Scotland culminated a long struggle, in both England and Scotland, for a church reformed in doctrine and polity. Even if the Kirk, so constituted, had to abandon some of the Presbyterian rigor that had prompted political disruptions in both seventeenth-century England and Scotland, the Church of Scotland was a vindication of the efforts of Knox, Melville, and the first General Assembly (1560). The 1707 Union of Scotland and England only added to the delicate status of the Church of Scotland—how to show proper deference to London and the Crown, and coexist with a fellow established church overseen by bishops, the long-acknowledged foe of Presbyterians.

Finding a version of Presbyterianism that was acceptable for British society taxed the historical imagination. Was Knox's trumpet blast too bellicose?[7] Was Cartwright's admonishment too strident?[8] Might Rutherford's affirmation of two separate spheres for church and state have violated rules of propriety?[9] The French Revolution had compounded the problem of how to remember Presbyterianism since its leaders and positions had clear affinities with England's 1640s civil wars and regicide. Could Presbyterians on the other side of 1789 celebrate their past without drawing too much attention to parts of their destabilizing, if not radical, past?

Among the first appropriations of the Scottish Reformation came in 1838 with Scottish bicentenary commemorations of the National Covenant. Two separate events took place. One in Edinburgh, organized by a mix of what James J. Coleman calls the "moderate Whig-Evangelical Party" and the "Wild Party" (the vigorous opponents of patronage who led the Disruption of 1843), featured an identification of Presbyterian church government with the "restoration of civil and religious liberty."[10] David Dickson, minister at St. Cuthbert's, used the occasion to raise questions about Scotland's loss of spiritual zeal. Nevertheless, he fully endorsed the Church of Scotland as the vindication of Presbyterianism over the errors of episcopal (whether English or Roman) tyranny. For him, the General Assembly of 1638 set into motion the civil liberties that the Glorious Revolution sealed.[11] Presbyterian polity had not simply reformed the church but then the entire nation. "Have we not, then, done well in meeting together this day," Dickson asked, to honor "those illustrious master-builders who repaired, and beautified, and strengthened, and completed this glorious edifice in 1638, pulling down, with unsparing hand, the gorgeous and glaring ornaments with which Popery had disfigured it, and which Prelacy scrupled to remove?" Dickson reminded his audience that Presbyterian polity may have been biblical but it was also Scottish, suitably "adapted to the tastes, to the habits, to the wants, and to the feelings of the Scottish people." Presbyterianism had become part of the Scots' "business" and entered "into their bosoms."[12]

The other bicentennial commemoration, this one in Glasgow, included representatives from the Kirk, Reformed Presbyterians, and Seceders, but the Church of Scotland was very much in charge. The moderator of its General Assembly, William Muir, minister at St. Stephen's Church, Edinburgh, preached a sermon that set the tone. His text, from Psalm 68, allowed a comparison between Presbyterianism and the glories of King David's Jerusalem. The Scots may have lacked the "splendour of ritual, for attracting the senses." But Presbyterianism compensated with a "beautiful gradation of courts" that distinguished it from the "tyrannizing of despotical ecclesiastics" and the "confusion of wild democracy." Muir also paid tribute to the Westminster Confession, which, though a product of an English assembly, was the culmination of a "movement" begun at Scotland's 1638 General Assembly.[13] The challenge for the nineteenth-century Kirk, Muir explained in his conclusion, was the same as that for the early generations of Presbyterians—namely, that the presence of God would be prepared "in every parish, in every house, in every heart in Scotland": "To copy our venerated fathers is to keep and guard with unceasing anxiety and jealousy our Protestantism—well assured that this is the very ark of our country's safety—assured that hitherto every betrayal of the sacred interests of Protestantism has drawn down a withering blight on our country's prosperity . . ." The only way to ensure "the gracious presence of God" in Scotland's Zion, was to "follow the example of our fathers in preserving our allegiance to Jehovah, free from unhallowed tamperings with Jehovah's enemies."[14]

Ongoing Scottish excavations of Presbyterian history displayed a surprising ecumenicity that even the Disruption of 1843 could not dampen. The formation of the Free Church was a reminder of Presbyterian zeal over against the Kirk's hard-won moderation. The cure was to return to levels set by sixteenth-century Reformers, who were both earnest and discerning. Commemorations of John Knox provided an occasion to highlight a proper Presbyterian combination of both religious zeal and national spirit. The Free Church's statue of Knox, installed in 1896, was for the Assembly's moderator a "signal testimony" that "in spite of their divisions, their troubles, their difficulties, and their contentions, all the branches of [the Scottish Church] are one." This sentiment echoed an earlier report from the Kirk's General Assembly that the tercentenary of the Scottish Reformation should be celebrated by all the churches and characterized by "a spirit of union."[15] Critics from the Episcopal Church in Scotland did not agree. Some decided to rain on the commemorative parade by contending that Presbyterianism was an unconstitutional rebellion, full of a "persecuting and excommunicating spirit," that undermined basic civil and religious liberties. Presbyterians responded by observing the English origins of the Westminster Confession. In which case, the Church of Scotland used doctrinal standards commissioned by English officials at a time when the Crown itself was threatening civil and religious liberty in both kingdoms.[16]

Appeals to London did not become obstacles to Scottish pride, however. At a tercentenary of Knox's death (1872), one Glasgow minister proclaimed that "neither in Germany nor in England," where the "bitter fruits" of Rationalism and Ritualism were ripening, "had the work of the Reformation been as thoroughly done as in Scotland."[17] For the Free Church's William Cunningham, the Church of England had never been the proper instrument of bringing the gospel to the "mass of the population" because it lacked "the vigor, the energy and the courage of Knox."[18] According to Alexander Duff, Scottish Presbyterians' first foreign missionary, Scotland not only bested England in the church reform sweepstakes but the Scots had actually prodded the English to embrace civil liberty. Knox and fellow Presbyterians had awakened England's "long dormant energies," given birth to the Glorious Revolution, and "at once placed Great Britain in the van of civilized nations."[19]

Scottish Episcopalians, nevertheless, rejected the Presbyterian narrative. They reminded those with ears to hear that Presbyterianism was often a source of political instability both in England and Scotland. Defenders of bishops added that religious and civil liberty were hardly the fruit of Presbyterian reforms.[20] By the nineteenth century, Presbyterian defenders were less inclined to answer episcopal critics. Unlike ancestors prone to polemic, these Presbyterians were content to place the Kirk within the mainstream of Scottish history. This was especially true for members of the Free Church who needed to prove that the Disruption had not severed the new communion from Scotland's general lines of national development. Neil Forsyth explains that the Free Church more than any Presbyterian body drew upon a Whig interpretation of Scottish history to prove its legitimacy.[21] Free Church pastor James Dodds, for instance, wrote *The Fifty Years' Struggle of the Scottish Covenanters 1638 to 1688* (1868) to show that those most zealous of Presbyterians were crucial to the development of British liberties. The region where Covenanters were strongest, the western hills of the Scottish Lowlands, were also "the ramparts of British freedom."[22] In a moment of generosity, Dodds also insisted that British liberty was the joint product of the English Parliament and the Scottish Kirk. Dodds had help from Aitken Wylie, another Free Church pastor (ordained first in the Secession church), who wrote *The Story of the Covenant and the Services of the Covenanters to the Reformation in Christendom and the Liberties of Great Britain* (1880). For Wylie, Presbyterians were at the forefront of creating "presbyterian democracy—a genuine priesthood of all believers," which broke "the shackles of feudalism and set Britain as a whole on the road to the civil and political liberties."[23]

The history that nineteenth-century Presbyterians taught included two lessons for English-speaking fellow travelers outside Scotland. One was Scottish exceptionalism. Presbyterian historians who commemorated Knox, the first General Assembly, or the National Covenants promoted the Scots as the most important ingredient in the recipe of British liberties. The great issue of the seventeenth century was how to confine the "exercise of royal authority within the boundaries of law," Thomas M'Crie wrote in his biography of Knox (1818). As much as the English establishment hammered out the constitutional arrangements that restrained the monarchy, "it cannot be denied, and it ought not to be forgotten, that the ministers of Scotland were the first to avow this rational doctrine." Presbyterians, thereby, "set an example to the friends of civil liberty in England."[24]

The other lesson was the greatness of the British constitution mediated through the Glorious Revolution, the political glue that held together Protestants in the Anglophone world. Scottish historians argued that Presbyterians had been "equal partners" in the creation of Great Britain. In this context, Covenanters emerged as "senior partners" with the English in the creation of the British constitution.[25] And though this logic restrained the Scots' sense of inferiority to the English within the Union, it was also responsible for instilling in Presbyterians outside Scotland a positive estimate of British history and the empire's presence in world affairs.

Scotland Once Removed

Writing Presbyterianism into the history of Scotland made sense because the Scottish Reformation took up many chapters in the kingdom's modern development. But what about settings where Knox and Melville were not political actors but merely reliable authors? In Ireland, that question was poignant since Presbyterians were a minority demographically and took a back seat to the Church of Ireland. Yet, Irish Presbyterians also used the Scottish Reformation as their historical North Star almost as much as the Scots had. According to Richard Smyth, a Presbyterian theologian teaching at Magee College, Londonderry, "nowhere in the world, either in Scotland or out of it, is the memory of those, who in the seventeenth century, contended for faith and liberty, more sacredly cherished than among their descendants in Ulster."[26] Smyth had a wide canvass on which to paint—from the first General Assembly (1560) to William III. But his 1872 commemorative essay on Henry Cooke made clear that the most important part of Scotland was its "Covenanter and Puritan" heritage.[27] Ireland's ties to Scotland were especially important in Smyth's placement of Irish history fully within British developments. Smyth, like his Irish peers, used their favorite source on Scottish history, Thomas McCrie, the Scottish Secessionist minister, who wrote biographies of John Knox (1811) and Andrew Melville (1819). Although he wrote to remind the Scots of their heritage, McCrie was the favorite author of Irish Presbyterians. At the time of his death in 1835, the Synod of Ulster passed a resolution to honor McCrie for his historical writings.[28]

Irish Presbyterians were not entirely dependent on the Scots for understanding the past. James Seaton Reid, a minister in the Synod of Ulster before teaching church history and government from 1837 to 1841 at the Royal Belfast Academical Institution, wrote a three-volume history of Presbyterianism in Ireland, published between 1834 and 1851. The first two volumes (1834 and 1837) were likely responsible for Reid's subsequent appointment at the University of Glasgow (1841–51). His Scotophilic outlook was not simply designed to tickle Scottish ears but it also benefited Presbyterians in need of legitimacy within Ireland. Reid's scholarship was, as Andrew R. Holmes argues, a "vindication" of those evangelical Irish Presbyterians who claimed to "be direct descendants" of the original Scottish settlers in Ulster.[29]

Reid's history also wove Presbyterian faith into "the well-established pattern of British Whig historiography."[30] The piece of history that proved the constitutional bona fides of Irish Presbyterians was their role in the Williamite Revolution of 1691 and the siege of Londonderry. During the war between William III's and James II's supporters, according to Reid, "the cause of constitutional freedom" was indebted to the "noble efforts" of Presbyterians in Ireland. Their aid to William linked Presbyterians "intimately" to the most "important changes in the civil affairs of Great Britain during the last two centuries."[31] In addition to their military and political service, Reid reminded readers, Presbyterians displayed "probity, peaceableness, and industry, as well as an enlightened attachment to the principles of civil and religious liberty." In effect, the fruit of the "successful resistance to the arbitrary government of James II" ripened "on the plains of Ulster."[32]

Reid went so far as to single out the Covenanters for praise. His version of the Scottish National Covenants became another stanza in his paean to Presbyterian politics. The Covenanters were forerunners of civil and religious liberty by opposing papal tyranny and episcopal authoritarianism. To turn Covenanters into Whigs, Reid needed to generalize from the sometime illiberal antics of the Reformed Presbyterians. For him, the Covenanters became the Scots responsible for ascertaining and uniting "the friends of civil and religious liberty."[33] The Irish Unitarian

Henry Montgomery tried to keep Reid within the bounds of responsible commemoration. Montgomery countered that "it would be very difficult to find any thing in human Records, more blood-thirsty and intolerant than this *Solemn League*."[34] Whether or not this counterpunch landed with Reid's readers, the link he forged between his own communion and British liberties reinforced Ulster Presbyterians' identification with Great Britain and its political institutions.

Reid's successor at the General Assembly's college in Belfast, W. D. Killen, extended the narrative that placed Irish Presbyterianism firmly within British history. A minister for roughly a decade before the church appointed him to teach church history, Killen also inherited the administrative work of Henry Cooke when he became president of the Belfast college. He literally expanded Reid's work by bringing the third volume of the history of the Presbyterian Church in Ireland to completion soon after the older historian's 1851 death. The *History of the Presbyterian Church in Ireland . . . Continued to the Present Time* (1853) covered the period between the Glorious Revolution and the 1871 Irish Church Act (synonymous with disestablishment). The book began with the intrigue of William's arrival in Ireland and covered the delicate subject of the 1798 Rising. In the case of the United Irishmen, Killen rejected formal connections between Presbyterianism and the rebels. Those Presbyterians who participated were in "opposition to the authority" of their church.[35] Furthermore, the ministers involved were from "New Light" backgrounds, a detail that further separated the rebels from genuine Presbyterians. The only spiritual significance of 1798 came when Presbyterians witnessed the "melancholy scenes of the Rebellion," understood the limits of "carnal security," and turned "with increasing seriousness" to "the interests of eternity."[36]

When the story reached 1875, Killen's narrative took a sectarian and nationalist turn. In the context of debates over Home Rule, the Belfast professor determined that the best prospects for Presbyterians came from a united Protestantism rather than merely Presbyterian leadership. To exclude Roman Catholicism from Irish history, Killen separated the Gaelic churches from Rome's influence in the medieval period. Patrick's missionary efforts had produced a Hibernian clergy that only later succumbed to the papacy's English ambassadors. In addition to failing to promote godliness, "the Bishop of Rome has been the deadly foe of the civil and religious liberties of Irishmen." Worse, the church of Rome represented "a perfect specimen of spiritual despotism."[37] For this reason, Presbyterians and Episcopalians together possessed the opportunity to usher in the "most glorious" day ever to "dawn on the Isle of Saints."[38] Killen still reserved a special status for Presbyterians. They had "saved their country by their noble defence of Londonderry" only to receive as their thanks harassment from bishops and have their children "branded, with impunity, as bastards."[39] Still, Killen hoped that with still further church reform Ireland's Protestant bishops might unite the island's "various [Protestant] fragments" into the plan once sketched "by the immortal Ussher."[40]

In contrast to Killen's sectarian Ireland, Thomas Witherow, a pastor and historian unnoticed by Scotland's churches and universities, rendered a somewhat less polemical reading of Irish Presbyterianism. A native of Londonderry, Witherow's humble origins forced him to study exclusively in Belfast. He prepared for the ministry and eventually pastored for twenty years in Maghera. When the Maggee Presbyterian College opened its doors in 1865, Witherow became the first full-time faculty member with responsibility for teaching church history and pastoral theology. The bulk of his literary output took place after his academic appointment. His interests ranged between military history (especially the Irish battles of 1689) and Irish Presbyterianism. Like other writers, Witherow not only featured Presbyterianism's positive contribution to Ulster but also Presbyterian ties between Scotland and Ireland.

Witherow's two volumes of biographical sketches and excerpts of Irish primary sources wove together the political and religious history of Ulster. In the first, *Historical and Literary Memorials of Presbyterianism in Ireland (1623–1731)* (1879), the author wrote that separating the literary from the historical material was impossible. The "writings of our ministers," he explained, "reflect and perpetuate the feeling of the time when they were produced." Although he did not describe that feeling, Witherow's readers had a sense of it when he listed the turning points of Irish history: "the Plantation Settlement," "the civil wars of the Commonwealth," the Restoration, "the Revolution," "the Penal Acts of the eighteenth century," the "descent of the Pretender on the Scottish shores," the Volunteer movement, the "Rebellion of 1798," and the "advent of the milder and more beneficial legislation of the nineteenth century."[41] By the end of the second volume, *Historical and Literary Memorials of Presbyterianism in Ireland (1731–1800)* (1880), Witherow turned to church history. His overview of Irish Presbyterianism began with Scottish transplants in Ulster. Scottish ministers, driven out by the Stuarts, who had subscribed the Confession of Faith, followed John Knox's form of government, and sowed "the good seed that had already taken root in Scottish soil."[42] Irish dependence on Scotland's Presbyterianism had forced ministers to train at the University of Glasgow, exposing them to rationalism rather than sound doctrine, which in turn caused the Irish church to suffer from the evil effects of such training.[43] The infusion of Seceders challenged Irish complacency and provided sound ministry to many in need of good churches. Still, Witherow was ambivalent about the Seceders' influence. By adopting a posture that "constantly frowns upon vice and condemns it," the church lost skeptics and wayward persons who chose their own associations instead of the company of the saints. Yet, by turning Irish Presbyterians toward creedal subscription, the Seceders successfully taught the lesson that a doctrinal standard was "essential to our orthodoxy, to our prosperity, and to our usefulness in the world."[44]

Witherow managed to meld Presbyterian pride with Christian generosity, a combination not always popular among Irish Protestants. In 1858, he wrote lines that were as redolent of Whiggish Presbyterianism as any of his nineteenth-century peers produced. History had clarified that Ireland was a better place thanks to Presbyterianism: "It is Presbyterian industry that has made the desert smile: it is Presbyterian teaching that has given a high tone of morality to the sober and industrious peasantry of the province: it is Presbyterian principles permeating the population that have every where infused the feelings of self-respect and independence, and which make it so difficult for any man who bears the Presbyterian name to bend his neck to any yoke of bondage."[45]

But more often than not, Witherow cast Ireland's Protestant heritage not as proof of superiority but as the condition for the civil liberties for all Irishmen, Roman Catholics included. Witherow eschewed sectarianism in his 1873 book on the 1689 battles of Londonderry and Enniskillen, crucial moments in the Williamite Wars. Two centuries later, Ireland had emerged out of a state of dependency and conflict and become a "constituent portion of a great empire, whose subjects reside in every clime, and whose flag waves on every sea."[46] Modern Ireland had relegated to the past its tribal "local wars," which were "more characteristic of savage than civilized life." Under the British constitution, "where government is simply the reflection of popular opinion," the Irish people no longer needed to live in resentment or resort to violence."[47] Witherow put a royal point on this brief for modern tolerance when he reminded readers what William III had said: the king's objective was to "deliver the Protestants, not to persecute the Papists."[48] Honoring Ireland's history and the battles of 1689 required never insulting the vanquished. If Irish Protestants attributed to Roman Catholics all the "crimes of his great-grandfather," fairness also required crediting him "for any little virtues that the old gentleman must have possessed." The same applied to Presbyterians trying to "plume ourselves in . . . the merits and services of our own great-grandfather" while denying the "faults and follies of which it is whispered he was guilty." "The truth is," Witherow wrote, "no man has the right to tax his neighbor with the sins of his progenitors, and to credit himself with nothing but the virtues of his own."[49]

Scottish North America

If Presbyterians in Scotland and Ireland tended to write their churches' histories into the glories of British politics, for their cousins in North America ecclesiastical exceptionalism depended on national success. Since Presbyterians had to share religious life with other Christians in Canada and the United States, the history of their respective nations became the norm for understanding the contributions of their denominations. To show their importance and value in the North American setting, churches needed to demonstrate support for and harmony with the emerging nation.

One negative indicator of this New World trend was resistance to church union in Canada by churches that had been transplants from the Church of Scotland. At the same time, Brian J. Fraser observes, the leading demographic within Canadian Presbyterianism was its ethnic (Scottish) "commercial middle class." In fact, the major force behind the creation of a Canadian Presbyterian ecclesiastical body as distinct from a communion in the shadow of the Kirk was "the aggressive Presbyterianism of urbanized, industrialized, expansionist central Canada." Fraser also contends that in a British colonial setting where Presbyterianism had to coexist with other Anglophone Protestants, the model for church organization was the denomination. Even the ideal of one church for the entire nation, never realized even in Scotland, needed to be reformulated for Presbyterians from "a particular constituency," such as the Seceders, Free Church, or Church of Scotland.[50] Meanwhile, those Presbyterians who idealized a Scottish Christendom were reluctant to place their ecclesiastical fortunes in a specifically Canadian church. An additional factor in the creation of Canadian Presbyterianism was openness to settling in western lands. Those Presbyterian bodies who had less history with the Clergy Reserves funding (see chapter 7 herein), such as the Seceders and Free Church, were often the first to jump at planting churches in a newly settled territory. To do so was to identify with Canada's westward expansion and unification. John S. Moir shows how those ministers with Kirk backgrounds "gloried" in their Scottishness. Canadian characteristics could not measure up.[51]

This flexible identity gave churches from Seceder and Free Church backgrounds the upper hand in church union deliberations. Of the four communions in 1875 to form the Canada Presbyterian Church, 344 came from the first version of a Canadian Presbyterian communion: the 1861 union of Free Church and Secession Synods of Upper and Lower Canada, which had 49,315 members. Next in membership (18,082) was the Presbyterian Church in the Lower Provinces (formed in 1860 from Free and Seceder synods in Nova Scotia), which had 124 ministers. The Church of Scotland in Canada (which emerged in Upper and Lower Canada during the 1830s and 1840s) had 141 ministers and 17,247 members. Its sister body, the Church of Scotland in the Maritimes (a polity formed between 1830 and 1850), had 31 ministers and 4,622 members. Of the thirty-one ministers who refused to participate in the 1875 union, they were mostly from the Maritime Provinces.[52] In Ontario and Quebec, the number of ministers loyal to the Kirk who rejected the union was a handful, and within twenty-five years they accounted for two congregations.[53]

The highest hurdle to clear in forming a Canadian church was the exact doctrinal meaning of Christ's headship over both church and state (see chapter 8 herein). Even as Presbyterians reckoned with the ambiguities of their political theology, they had few reservations about the new confederation itself. Canada was full of possibilities, and Presbyterians did not want to be left behind in a parochial part of the emerging Canadian society. Unlike Scotland or Ireland where Presbyterians might draw attention to their own churches' involvement in pivotal moments of national history, in Canada a united denomination was playing catch-up to the 1867 confederation of British North America. For that reason, advocates for church union invariably looked to geography as much as church polity for Canadian Presbyterianism's distinct identity.

One obscure window into the minds of Canadian Presbyterians on the benefits of a united church came from an 1871 essay competition, co-sponsored by church and civil agencies. The $200 award went to Robert Campbell, of Montreal, who wrote a fifty-page essay on the challenges and possibilities for a united Presbyterian church. In his preface, Campbell invoked the great tradition of Presbyterianism started by John Knox, in hopes of finding a platform "anterior" to three centuries of divisions. Such a plan required all parties to avoid "everything offensive."[54] In his estimate, the greatest difficulties had little to do with theology per se, for example, how to reconcile different systems of government, finances, educational institutions. The main obstacles included seemingly minor ones, such as using hymns and organs in worship, to the larger question of the church's relationship to civil authorities. Here Campbell rather fancifully tried to transport Canadian Presbyterians to a historical blank slate, a time when Presbyterian politics sat comfortably within the liberal structures of nineteenth-century British societies. He combined the ideals of the apostolic church with the freedoms that enabled modern Presbyterians to choose a congregation based on personal preferences. Union, Campbell also argued, would turn Presbyterians into a large denomination with sufficient prestige to attract the best candidates for ministry.[55] Instead of being divided into different corporate entities, a united church would allow Presbyterians "to assert and maintain their principles and rights against the encroachments of other churches."[56] This did not mean that other churches should fear a Presbyterian establishment, since political liberty was the unique contribution of the Scots and its Presbyterian churches. "Episcopacy, Methodism, and Congregationalism," Campbell wrote, "are the products of another country and people," different from the Scots and their cousins in Northern Ireland.[57] A union of Canadian Presbyterians became a means toward preserving the Dominion's debt to its Scottish character.

The appeal of Scotland's heritage did draw attention implicitly to tensions among Canadian Presbyterians that came directly from Scottish controversies. The wounds from the Free Church's disruption (1843) were still fresh. Campbell himself could not forget the claims by those leaving the Kirk who spoke of seeing "the Shekinah remove, and the Spirit of God depart from the desecrated sanctuary."[58] This was not remote history, because the author also reminded readers that the Disruption had also split Canadian Presbyterians.[59] Campbell was nevertheless optimistic and observed that "days of darkness" were but a "prelude to a great glorious future."[60] The divisions that Campbell noticed, even as late as 1871, were not sufficient to prevent union. After three years of meetings, a majority of the Church of Scotland representatives approved a plan. The one major proviso was the continued administration of the Temporalities Fund by an existing board composed of its pre-union membership.[61] Otherwise, despite Canadian Presbyterians' "affection toward the whole Church of God" and desiring to have "fraternal interactions with . . . its several branches," those entering this union affirmed their "Ecclesiastical relations to Churches holding the same doctrine, government and discipline."[62] With that understanding, the unification of Canada overcame centuries of church conflict. A political Canada had given birth to a Canadian Presbyterianism.

A sermon preached in Montreal by Robert F. Burns on the Sunday after the union was indicative of national and Presbyterian dynamics. The need to put aside the specific arguments over Presbyterianism's place in Scottish society and government yielded a generic brief that stressed place, size, and international relations. Burns himself embodied Canadian Presbyterianism's codependence with Scotland. Born in Paisley, Scotland, the son of Robert Burns, a close ally of Thomas Chalmers in the Disruption that produced the Free Church, who became a prominent pastor, administrator, and missionary among Canadian Presbyterians, the junior Burns matured in Canada and took his bearings from church life there. Educated in Scotland, the younger Burns eventually ministered in Toronto, Montreal, St. Catherine's, Chicago (Illinois), and, at the end of his career, Halifax.

That eastern city was his home when in Montreal he preached the sermon "Our United Church," based on the phrase from Colossians 3:15, "Be ye thankful." Burns's reasons for gratitude owed almost everything to Canadian Presbyterians catching up to fellow Protestants in other parts of the world and, consequently, achieving a kind of stature that a prolonged attachment to Scotland had hindered. Burns encouraged Canadians to rejoice that they were joining an international trend among Reformed churches. His survey of global developments included the welcome subtraction—"cutting the cancer"—of Unitarianism from Irish Presbyterianism and the subsequent union of the Ulster Synod with Seceders, "causing our fair Hibernian sister to 'prosper and be in health' as never before."[63] Canadians were now enlisting in a worldwide Presbyterianism that included 146 synods, 1,180 presbyteries, 20,133 congregations, 18,774 pastors, and a total church membership of 34,351,877.[64] Was Burns showing a lack of confidence when he added 20,579,768 Lutherans to his count? With Lutherans in the group, the combined Lutheran-Presbyterian presence throughout the world numbered more than half the world's 107 million Protestants. As ecumenical as Burns's math was, it also indicated Protestants were worried about Roman Catholicism's size and scope.

The best reason for gratitude was place—the territory that constituted the Canadian Confederation. Burns opened the Psalter to remind his audience that "the lines have fallen to us in pleasant places" (Ps. 16:6). First, Canada was part of the British Empire, which "embraced one sixth of the area of the globe" and included "over one sixth of the world's population." Queen Victoria herself, whose "gentle sway" proved her "the best of sovereigns," was further reason to celebrate Canada's place in the British Empire. Second, the confederation occupied a "good land." Canada was larger than the United States and larger than all of Europe. It supplied "field and sustenance for teeming millions."[65] Burns likened the new united church to the Israelites entering the promised land. "These limitless prairies, piercing mountain ranges and peaceful valleys; those fields and forests unexplored where men will yet be 'famous according as they have lifted up axes on the tall trees,'" Burns enthused, "will bye and bye, be swarming hives and crowded marts, echoing the hum and hurry of an intelligent and industrious population." Of course, Presbyterians had to share a Christian Canada with other Protestants, even Episcopalians. But the words of Joshua were just as applicable: "There remaineth yet very much land to be possessed, go ye up to possess the land" (Joshua 13:1).[66]

After three centuries, Canadian Presbyterians had rallied around a national identity that did not need a national covenant or established church. To find their greatness, they looked to the resources—natural and spiritual—available in the creation of Canada.

America's Independent Presbyterians

Burns's comparison of Canada with the United States was apt because American Presbyterians were simultaneously marshaling their church's resources to aid national consolidation. At almost the same time as the formation of a united Canadian church, American Presbyterians were also patching up differences that had resulted in four separate communions in the largest branch of Presbyterianism, the Presbyterian Church in the U.S.A. (PCUSA). In 1837, American Presbyterians had divided into the Old and New School branches thanks to disagreements about doctrine, church government, and ecclesiastical support for political activism (such as antislavery and temperance). As the sectional crisis of the 1850s inched the United States to war, Presbyterians divided along regional lines. In 1857, the New School, the communion friendlier to activism and less strict about doctrine, split between northern and southern synods. Four years later, Old School Presbyterians did the same when some ministers called upon the church to pledge its loyalty to the U.S. federal government (after declarations of secession by southern states). After the Civil War, Presbyterians made plans to reunite. In 1867, Old and New School communions in the South put aside differences to form the Presbyterian Church in the United States. In 1869, the northern wings of Old and New School also reunited to reconstitute the PCUSA. (The northern [PCUSA] and southern [PCUS] denominations remained separated until 1983.)[67]

Although reunion of Old and New School Presbyterians in the North set Americans up as leaders in the worldwide cooperation of Reformed and Presbyterian communions, it also established the framework for understanding Presbyterianism in the history of the United States. From the advantage of hindsight, the logic of reunion was the ecclesiastical equivalent of preserving the political union of the American nation. In the Plan of Union's preamble, authors could not help but draw inspiration from the U.S. Civil War. That conflict demonstrated "the ease with which diversities of sentiment may be harmonized and combined in one purpose to maintain national life."[68] The situation in the United States was clearly analogous to Canada, even if the Americans were not following developments in British North America. Presbyterian architects of union called attention to the expansion of the territory of the United States, that is, the doubling of states admitted to the Union since 1837. The nation's population had also increased dramatically, thanks to 6 million immigrants and 4 million emancipated slaves. Growth in the United States also had a dark side, including threats to Christianity from Romanism and rationalism to infidelity and paganism. All of these changes required both groups of Presbyterians to put aside differences and unite in a "magnanimous purpose, inspired both by patriotism and religion, to Christianize the whole country."[69] When the plan added that a united church in the United States might be a model for healing ecclesiastical divisions in Europe, Presbyterians were laying seeds for the sort of American exceptionalism that characterized their twentieth-century descendants,[70] some of whom were architects of the post–World War II international order.[71]

This rationale for union disappointed strict Presbyterians, who insisted on fidelity to their Reformation heritage, but the 1869 Reunion did pave the way for an alignment between the church and the United States. Even Charles Hodge, who opposed merger on doctrinal grounds (e.g., the debates of 1837 had not been settled), had conceived of Presbyterianism in standard Whiggish terms. In an 1855 address on the nature of Presbyterianism, Hodge tackled the question of church power. He followed the Presbyterian convention of contrasting his own communion with Rome, prelacy, and independency. Three convictions set Presbyterianism apart: (1) the people have a right to a "substantive part" of church government, (2) presbyters are the "highest permanent office" in the church, and (3) smaller parts of the church are subject to larger bodies, which are in turn obligated to the whole church.[72]

From that definition, Hodge had an easy time showing the benefits of Presbyterianism for civil politics. Presbyterians' affirmation of spiritual liberty was crucial to political liberalism because civil liberties followed directly from "religious liberty." This was the opposite of a system that vested church power in a "divinely constituted hierarchy" and fostered claims by kings and nobles of "divine right" supremacy.[73] Although Hodge did not mention the United States in his hour-long lecture, his American audience likely heard his remarks as a blessing upon the U.S. political system. At the end of his talk, Hodge likened Presbyterianism to republicanism: both systems depended on "people enlightened and virtuous." For good measure, he observed that Presbyterianism's balance of order and liberty, civil liberties and subjection to legitimate authority, made Presbyterian church government "the parent and guardian of civil liberty in every part of the world." Thanks to Hodge's theological conservatism, he was quick to mention that the political advantages of Presbyterianism were secondary to its unparalleled capacity to extend and establish "the gospel."[74] But for anyone in the audience who departed from the speaker's strict theology, Hodge's discussion of Presbyterianism reinforced a sense that the church was vital to the health of the United States.

If ties between Presbyterianism and the U.S. government were only implicit for Hodge, in the case of Thomas Smyth those links were overt. Born in 1808 in Belfast, the son of a grocer and Presbyterian elder, Smyth attended Belfast College before training to be a pastor at Princeton Seminary (he graduated in 1831). Ordained by the Presbytery of Newark to conduct missions in Florida, Smyth's trip south included a stop in Charleston, South Carolina. His skills prompted a call from Second Presbyterian Church, whose pulpit was then vacant. He remained in Charleston for the next forty years (he died in 1873). Known for his library and long sermons (during one service a church member threw his hat on the floor to indicate that Smyth should "put a lid on it"), the Charleston pastor also wrote extensively. A collection of his essays and books filled a ten-volume set when published posthumously in the early twentieth century. Smyth was also a pronounced defender of both Presbyterianism and republicanism. That combination produced a case that the United States owed a debt to the church government of Calvin and Knox.

Smyth's 1843 book, *Ecclesiastical Republicanism, or the Republicanism, Liberality and Catholicity of Presbytery in Contrast with Prelacy or Popery*, did not obscure the author's argument with a vague title. It was a companion piece, at least chronologically, to another 1843 book, *Presbytery and Not Prelacy the Primitive and Scriptural Polity*, a work in three long sections that extended to 500 pages, and whose main point was the antiquity of Presbyterian church government. Both books came with a rejuvenated Anglicanism thanks to the Oxford Movement in the background. Smyth's intention was not simply to clarify the biblical pattern of church government; his larger purpose was to explain the influence of church government on republicanism. He believed that Presbyterianism (by which he meant all church polities without a bishop) went hand in hand with republicanism.[75] To do this, Smyth repeated the Presbyterian hallmark of the church's spiritual independence and Christ as its sole head. He also affirmed adamantly that Presbyterianism did not depend on any form of civil authority. Its churches could function in any sort of political environment, from democracy to monarchy. Still, Presbyterianism and republicanism were "best adapted to secure the greatest amount of personal liberty, social enjoyment, and political prosperity."[76] The reason was that Presbyterianism embodied the "principle of representation," posed barriers to the "ambition and encroachments of the clergy," secured the rights of clergy and people, and united "believers into one body."[77] Smyth even implied that the United States was the fulfillment of Presbyterianism. Presbyterians wanted a church "with unlimited freedom and spiritual independence," where there was "no king but Christ," where believers cringed "to no priestly mediators," or licked the dust of "wooden crucifixes": "Our government is the government of written laws, and it is administered by the people themselves, without hindrance or tyranny." The harmony of church and civil polity elevated the United States above Scotland. The Church of Scotland, alas, had become a mere vassal of "state establishment" while American Presbyterians were free from "interference of man" and "earthly laws."[78] "We alone can sit under our vine and fig tree," Smyth wrote, "none daring to molest or make us afraid." In the United States, Presbyterianism was "the religious strength of the country, the grand bulwark" against "Popery and Puseyism," the best way to secure "national greatness and prosperity."[79]

Glue Britannia

Despite obvious differences between the United States and other parts of the Anglophone world, Hodge and Smyth echoed the case for Presbyterianism that their cousins made in England, Scotland, Ireland, and Canada. Although Scotland was the source of inspiration for many, the

British Empire more generally provided a congenial environment for Presbyterians to assert their national significance. However much the Irish and Canadians needed to calibrate their work according to Scotland's history, the English, Scots, Irish, Canadians, and Americans all justified a Presbyterian contribution to national life, in different stages and degrees, by tying the legacy of the Reformation to the achievement of British liberties.

That blend of church reform and political advance prompted nineteenth-century Presbyterians to identify with British political traditions in ways that diminished attachments to the original sixteenth-century arguments for Presbyterian reform. Linda Colley argues in *Britons* that despite antagonisms between Presbyterians and Episcopalians, or Dissenters and established churches, after 1700 Protestantism functioned as the umbrella under which English, Scottish, and Welsh Protestants clustered. The rationale behind Protestant identity was the British rejection of Roman Catholicism, a legal reality until Catholic Emancipation in 1829. Colley explains that even if the religious establishments in England and Scotland created hardships for Nonconformists, the Protestant cast of British government also made allowances for Protestants outside the Church of England or Church of Scotland. Britain also held holidays that united various communions around a shared Protestant identity. May 29 became a day of jubilee to commemorate the restoration of the monarchy. So, too, August 1 was a day for the British to celebrate the Hanoverian monarchy and securing the Protestant Succession. November 5 was another day of national significance that honored both William III's arrival in 1688 to battle James II and the rescue of James I in 1605 from the Gunpowder Plot.[80] Meanwhile, the popularity and repeated printings of Fox's *Book of Martyrs* and John Bunyan's *Pilgrim's Progress* were further signs of a generic Protestantism among the British people.[81] Colley admits that Britain was no confessional state. Still, for all the obvious chauvinism, British Protestantism gave the people a sense of pride, courage to face hardship, and an "identity."[82]

The Glorious Revolution, Tony Claydon and Ian McBride add, was especially important for harnessing almost all Presbyterians in the transatlantic world within the paddock of British Protestantism. After the Restoration, when demands for further reformation by zealous Presbyterians appeared as disruptive to the new government as Roman Catholicism, the last Stuart monarchs were incapable of finding a religious settlement that could pacify all the kingdoms' strains of Christianity. But with the victories of William III between 1689 and 1691, and with Scotland and Ireland as the sites for the decisive battles, the Glorious Revolution consolidated potentially divisive Irish and Scottish Protestants within London's orbit.[83] The Union of 1707 and the Irish Declaratory Act of 1720 functioned as formal expressions of the bonds that the Glorious Revolution had created. This was the same period when the mainstream of Presbyterianism in Scotland and Ireland abandoned the older ideals of a covenanted nation and Kirk in favor of British liberties, the Hanoverian succession, and the advantages of a moderately reformed church. The result was an "anglo-centric view of history and politics" that left most Presbyterians in Scotland, England, and Ireland (minus some Covenanters and Seceders) on the side of the British constitution as the "fountainhead of civil and religious liberty, freedom of the press, diffusion of knowledge and religious toleration."[84]

As fluid and at times arbitrary as British Protestant identity might seem, the overlap between the two continued on both sides of the Atlantic well into the nineteenth century. What forged the character of this Anglo-American Protestantism, Claydon and McBride argue, was not law or policy, but aspiration. Presbyterians, along with other Anglo-American Protestants, continued to promote the ideal of an "elect, godly nation," even as they could not achieve it in practice. For Claydon and McBride, Protestant Britishness nurtured an "anxious aspiration." Anglo-American Protestants conceived of themselves as "special objects" of divine providence. Instead of taking comfort from this attention, God's favor more often than not produced "lamentation and alarm" for the many ways in which British society (and North America) had departed from God's laws. The result was a form of Protestant nationalism that was more prescriptive than descriptive. It even found as a precedent, as it had for the Presbyterians at the time of the National Covenant, the experience of the Israelites. "The lesson of the analogy with Israel was not that God loved his faithful nation," Claydon and McBride assert. Instead, Protestant nationalists understood that "election had never been secured," and that an elect people "could be scattered by divine wrath if they did not make constant exertions to re-earn their special status."[85] The drive among British Protestants of the eighteenth and nineteenth centuries, whether in the Old World or the New, was to deliver a Protestant society. Despite divisions and debates among denominations, or even among strict and moderate Presbyterians, the British Protestant aspiration forged a Protestant nationalist ideal.[86]

This Protestant British identity was in the background of Anthony Froude's own twelve-volume history of England (and echoed nineteenth-century Presbyterians across the transatlantic world). The main figure in Froude's history was Elizabeth I, the original royal nemesis of Presbyterians. The author sided with her Presbyterian challengers when he asserted that her religious policies were duplicitous and merely fig leaves to cover her quest for a secure throne. He concluded the same about her use of the English bishops to enforce her policy.[87] For all the queen's faults, Froude credited Elizabeth for statecraft and foreign policy that gave Protestantism a foothold that no other European government could have secured. The defeat of the Spanish Armada in particular, for Froude, determined the fate of the Reformation. It "decided" that the Dutch provinces "should never be reannexed to the Spanish Crown." In France, it "assured the ultimate succession of the King of Navarre." These French and Spanish developments, in turn, "determined the fate of the Reformation in Germany." England's victory also gave JamesVI/I of Scotland "conclusive reasons for remaining Protestant." The battle with Spain was also "the sermon which completed the conversion of the English nation, and transformed the Catholics into Anglicans."[88] In Froude's estimate, the entire fate of the Reformation hung in the balance of Elizabeth's reign: "Either Protestantism would have been trampled out altogether, or expelled from Europe to find a home in a new continent." No Protestant church would have survived to "hold the balance between atheism and superstition."[89]

American Protestants confirmed Froude's assessment of English Protestantism's significance. George Barrell Cheever, a pastor in New York City, who had grown up in Maine and been a classmate of Nathaniel Hawthorne and Henry W. Longfellow at Bowdoin, moved easily between Congregationalist and Presbyterian pulpits. He first served in Salem among Congregationalists, then at Allen St. Presbyterian in New York, and finally at the Congregational Church of the Puritans, also in New York. A three-year trip (1836–39), with much of 1837 spent in England and Scotland, alerted Cheever to the dangers of national churches. Even so, Cheever launched into a faith-based activism back home in the United States, where he defended capital punishment and fought slavery. He also wrote about the United States the way Froude did about England three decades earlier.

In his 1841 book, *God's Hand in America*, Cheever employed standard Anglo-American Protestant rhetoric to describe the United States as the place most benefiting from divine providence. In chapter 1 on reasons for gratitude, Cheever listed in order the advantages of the United States: free access to scripture in "our own language," the "Christian Sabbath," "holy and enlightened" ministers, and the work of the Holy Spirit, especially in the vitality of revivals.[90] These were the most blessed benefits, but a "wise and good" government, "freedom of opinion," and good common schools were no less noteworthy.[91] What stood out in this depiction of the United States was its generically Protestant and anti-Catholic character. The United States was the opposite of Rome—it was enlightened, nonsectarian, democratic, and free. In a word, the United States was the culmination of a society in which the church was no longer dependent on the state. Churches were free to operate through a host of unencumbered agencies. The state's independence from the church was also liberating. Without a meddling church, government could operate in a responsible manner (i.e., republicanism). Cheever later described in *The Hierarchical Despotism* (1844) how through "A CHURCH WITHOUT A BISHOP, AND A STATE WITHOUT A KING," the United States pointed the way for the "liberty of all mankind."[92]

British and American exceptionalism expressed by Froude and Cheever, respectively, were likely as incoherent as they were debatable, as John Wolfe argues. But the generic Protestant nationalism on display in England, the United States, Scotland, Ireland, and Canada enabled Presbyterians to maintain their place in national affairs, even as they moved to a status as one denomination among others. The Presbyterian contribution to Protestant national identities was by no means decisive in the Anglophone world thanks to the pluriformity of Protestant denominations. The peculiarly Presbyterian aspect of such nationalism was the way assertions of national identity tapped the original sixteenth-century Presbyterian claim, namely, that church reform was essential to a godly nation. In the seventeenth century, Presbyterians learned what could come of insisting too strongly on a covenanted nation. After 1660, with minor exceptions, Presbyterians distanced themselves from the older claims and settled for moderate versions of Presbyterian nationalism. The Protestant nationalism of the nineteenth century was one more stage in that moderating shift, perhaps even more tepid than the restraint that characterized the eighteenth-century Kirk. Even so, by 1850 Presbyterians had found remarkably similar ways in different political settings to affirm continuity with their founding fathers and assert their importance to the nations where they ministered.

Conclusion

Presbyterian Modern

The relationship twenty-first-century Scottish Presbyterians have with the British Crown is almost the opposite of what John Knox wanted. It is also potentially a source of jealousy among their denominational cousins. Where else in the Anglophone world do Presbyterian communions, with a reputation for political agitation, receive visits from royal delegates with warm wishes from the sovereign? In 2015, for example, Queen Elizabeth II followed royal protocol and appointed Lord Hope of Craighead (David Hope) lord high commissioner to the General Assembly of the Free Church of Scotland. Hope, who had served as deputy president of the Supreme Court of the United Kingdom, functioned in a similar capacity before the General Assembly of the Church of Scotland. In his remarks to the Free Church, Hope told a story about his father's affection for Thomas Chalmers and the Free Church.[1] The General Assembly returned the favor by issuing a "Loyal and Dutiful Address" to the queen. These Presbyterians expressed "continued loyalty to Your Majesty's Person and Throne and to the Constitutional Monarchy of which you are the honoured Head and Representative." The Free Church also expressed gratitude "for Your Majesty's continued recognition of the work and ministry throughout the United Kingdom of the Free Church of Scotland" and pledged to "uphold your Majesty's person, family and governments, before the throne of grace."[2]

Exchanges like these between the British Crown and Presbyterian assemblies are not the norm for Presbyterians in England, Northern Ireland, or North America. The British monarch does not send a commissioner to the General Assembly of the Presbyterian Church in Ireland or to the Presbyterian Church of Canada. Nor do the governments of Canada or the United States display formal regard to their respective Presbyterian bodies—mainline or sectarian. Leaders of the largest denominations in Canada and the United States could well wonder why the Crown pays any attention to the Free Church, a tiny communion that at its founding rejected oversight from the British government. Yet, in Scotland where for at least 150 years Presbyterians were contentious participants in national politics, the sovereign sends representatives to greet a small Presbyterian communion?

These church–state courtesies were hardly the point of the original plan to reform the English and Scottish churches with a Presbyterian government. The first advocates of Presbyterianism wanted to replace episcopal governance with the oversight of assemblies of pastors and elders, the way Calvin had organized the churches of Geneva. The long European history of monarchs and emperors appointing bishops was so much the accepted way of running the church that the introduction of Presbyterianism was a threat to political order and stability. Even more aggravating was Presbyterianism's challenge to the British Crown's status as the head of the (English) church. Presbyterians who wanted to defend the crown rights of Christ were clearly upsetting a church–state relationship that was only two generations old in England. Once the English monarchy passed to the Stuarts, who inherited the awkward responsibility of managing religious affairs in both England and Scotland, the political potency of Presbyterianism exploded.

Negotiating English Presbyterianism was relatively easy compared to in Scotland, where changes in church structures took hold (as they did not in England) at least three decades before James VI of Scotland became James I of England. A 1581 covenant with James VI inserted Presbyterian demands for a reformed church and godly commonwealth smack dab into the politics of a minor European power that was on its way, very gradually, to becoming a global hegemon. If Presbyterians have occupied a large place in the history of the modern West, especially compared to Reformed Protestants and Lutherans, one reason is their standing, no matter how welcome, within the British Empire. In fact, without their long and contentious relationship with English and Scottish authorities, Presbyterians might matter as much as Baptists or Quakers in histories of Anglo-American politics.

Aside from replacing bishops with assemblies, Presbyterians also claimed the spiritual independence of the church. This was a doctrine that gave Presbyterianism a Janus-faced quality, even if it was implicit in Christ's own words to skeptical interlocutors: "Render unto Caesar the things that are Caesar's and to God the things that are God's." Those words were in scripture, so Christians needed to account for a strange duality in their understanding of civil and ecclesiastical governments. Because the English Crown by virtue of its supremacy over the Church of England was both a spiritual and temporal authority (not unlike the pope's temporal power over the Papal States), Presbyterian assertions of the church's spiritual independence inherently challenged existing political arrangements. Monarchs typically found bishops to be easier to manage than the preferred Presbyterian form of church councils. Still, however unruly General Assemblies could be, the Presbyterian insistence on the spiritual independence of the church undermined royal supremacy in ecclesiastical matters. For Presbyterians, Christ was head of the church (and the state). The part that Presbyterians did not say out loud was that even with Christ as head, the General Assembly was the highest ecclesiastical authority.

Even as Presbyterians challenged episcopal oversight and royal supremacy, they remained loyal to the Christendom ideal of a godly kingdom. They also relied on a theological tradition that drew upon continuities between Old Testament Israel and the church. Presbyterians took inspiration from Hebrew monarchs and the ideal of a covenanted nation bound to follow God's laws. The spiritual independence of the church notwithstanding, Presbyterians in Scotland pressed for a reform of church, Parliament, the Crown, and the people that culminated in the National Covenant (1638). This may have been the most successful of later Protestant movements that resulted from the so-called Second Reformation (to which most notably the Dutch, German, and French Reformed churches also belonged).[3]

The political consequences of the Scottish Reformation gave Presbyterians a level of significance not attained by Protestants on the European continent. The specific issue that emerged in several contexts was the power of excommunication. Calvin stood as the font for Reformed

Protestants who affirmed the autonomy of the church in spiritual matters and so opposed Erastianism—the idea that the state should have the power of discipline within the church—but Presbyterians took the autonomy of the church at least one step further. The reason had as much to do with the place of British magistrates in church–state relations as with the logic of establishmentarian Presbyterianism. For Presbyterians, the ideal of the church's spiritual independence and sovereignty came with specific political and national obligations summarized in the National Covenant of 1638 and the Solemn League and Covenant of 1643. This political history made Presbyterianism exceptional. Among other confessional Protestants—Lutherans and Reformed—Presbyterianism is the only communion (minus Anglicanism) where church history was bound up with the politics of some of the most powerful and wealthy nations in the modern world. No other confessional Protestant church had as much invested in the fortunes of particular national governments as did Presbyterians.

No Presbyterian before 1700 could have imagined transforming a church government bound up with political forms of late medieval Europe into the forerunner of limited government, constitutionalism, popular sovereignty, and religious liberty. Later Presbyterians might tell the histories of John Knox, Samuel Rutherford, and even the Covenanters as harbingers of liberal democracy, but the 1649 execution of a king (for which Presbyterians had virtually no responsibility) was a long way from a declaration of independence 125 years later from the British monarch. The original Presbyterians inhabited a world still part of medieval Europe's Christendom. The thought of a Presbyterian communion as a voluntary association within a religiously diverse democratic society was at best a fantasy, at worst a nightmarish return to the chaos of Cromwell's Commonwealth. Because Presbyterianism originated at a time when throne and altar arrangements were still the norm, with Hebrew monarchs adding a pious sheen, the eventual association of Presbyterianism with the American Revolution was a marvelous bait and switch. By calling the American War for Independence a "Presbyterian rebellion," George III gave the successors to Calvin and Knox permission to rebrand themselves as heralds of religious and civil liberty.

Arthur Herman's *How the Scots Invented the Modern World* (2001) reveals how difficult reconciling old and modern Presbyterian politics is.

He finds traces of democratic ideals in the exploits of Knox, George Buchanan, and the National Covenant, where "government of the people and for the people" took root.[4] Even so, Herman admits that Presbyterians such as the Covenanters were "inspired less by their love of democracy than by their hatred of Satan." "The things we associate with a democratic society today meant nothing to them."[5] For that reason, Herman turns to David Hume and Adam Smith, who were on good terms with Moderates in the Kirk, to find the Scottish inventors of the modern world. Also in the orbit of the Scottish Enlightenment, Herman argues, were Scottish and Scotch-Irish colonists in North America who supported American independence vigorously but appropriated their Presbyterianism cautiously. Some, primarily from the Highlands, opposed the war and maintained loyalty to the Crown. Herman estimates that 20,000 Scottish immigrants left the emerging United States for the Canadian provinces and another 35,000 went to Nova Scotia. But among the Ulster Scots, a hatred of the English turned them patriotic.[6] Of the fifty-six signers of the Declaration of Independence, nineteen (one-third) were either Scottish or Scotch-Irish. Presbyterianism itself was less likely to have influenced American patriots than education at Scottish universities or a Scottish curriculum mediated through colonial institutions, such as the College of New Jersey where John Witherspoon presided.

In the end, Witherspoon emerges as the Rosetta Stone for understanding Presbyterianism's place in the transition from divine-right monarchy and constitutional monarchy to British and American versions of liberal democracy. His own use of Scottish history was instructive for his importance to modern Presbyterianism. In 1758, he could highlight the British government's treatment of the Covenanters to argue for the importance of protecting constitutional liberties.[7] Two decades later, on the eve of the revolution in America, Witherspoon stressed economic advantages of trade within the British Empire to counter the government's tax policies and to argue for American independence.[8] Here was the patriot Presbyterian, Witherspoon, linking the American cause far more to the insights of Scottish moral philosophy and political economy than to lessons learned from Presbyterians' political history. The "Presbyterian rebellion" did not rely on language of resisting tyranny or restoring the "crown rights" of Jesus. Instead, Witherspoon argued from the emerging liberal political and economic world. The American Revolution, then, was not the work of strict Presbyterians praying for a godly society. On the contrary, Presbyterians had become spokesmen for social improvement and moral reform.

A contemporary of Witherspoon's (and an ecclesiastical belligerent) in the Church of Scotland was William Robertson. He was the Presbyterian minister who served as principal of the University of Edinburgh between 1762 and 1793. Like Witherspoon, Robertson was also reconfiguring Presbyterianism for modern society. He did not try to connect Presbyterians to a "libertarian tradition in Scottish politics."[9] For Robertson, the liberalization of Scottish politics owed mostly to the "post-Union Anglicanisation" of Scottish society. Robertson saw a similar dynamic in North America. In his two volumes on colonial America (which stopped before the War for Independence), Robertson regarded the Puritans as the Anglo-American equivalent of the Scots' Covenanters. The Puritans, like the Covenanters, "united together . . . by a solemn covenant with God, and with one another" which they believed was "in strict conformity" to scripture. The genuine source of liberal politics in North America, Robertson argued, was Roger Williams in Rhode Island. His colony "was mild and tolerating," where "the exercise of private judgment was a natural and sacred right" and "the civil magistrate ha[d] no compulsive jurisdiction in the concerns of religion" and government was "purely democratical."[10]

As different as Robertson was from Witherspoon on doctrine and piety, both eighteenth-century Presbyterians recognized that the national aspirations of the first generation of Presbyterians provided little basis for a political order based on civil liberties and restrained government. Robertson and Witherspoon expressed implicitly what the majority of all Presbyterians after 1750 knew—expectations for a godly monarch working harmoniously with a Reformed church to nurture a holy commonwealth was impossible and also likely misguided in the past. Conservatives such as Witherspoon, and Moderates such as Robertson, understood that modern societies called for religious toleration, a church with a reduced set of responsibilities within a broader set of civil institutions, and a political system that secured freedom of speech, thought, worship, and assembly for all legitimate members.

Some Presbyterians did not know what Witherspoon and Robertson knew. These Protestants maintained original Presbyterian politics and rejected liberal ideas about religion and government. Georgetown

University political theorist Jerome E. Copulsky calls these Presbyterian resisters "heretics," that is, "adversaries of liberal order." Presbyterians are not alone in Copulsky's list of outsiders, but he does devote significant attention to Reformed Presbyterians in the United States. These were (and are) the Protestants who used the Scottish National Covenants as the North Star of church–state relations. Samuel B. Wylie, an Irish American pastor of prominence among Reformed Presbyterians, is one heretic whom Copulsky cites to illustrate Protestant ill-liberalism. Wylie's 1803 book, *Two Sons of Oil* . . ., not only dissented from the government of the United States but also reiterated seventeenth-century Scottish political theology. Church and state were the two divinely ordained governments in the world, and the civil magistrate had a duty to maintain and protect the true church. By these metrics, according to Wylie, the U.S. government was neither moral nor legal. Wylie complained that the Constitution "does not even recognize the existence of God, the King of nations." For that reason, true Christians were duty-bound to reject what "was opposed to the moral law of God."[11] Even if Wylie conceded that the U.S. government was "the best now existing in the Christian world," Christians were obligated to engage in political dissent, including refusing oaths of allegiance to the Constitution, voting in elections, and civil or military service. For Copulsky, Wylie was not merely complaining about U.S. government but more profoundly about "the displacement of religion from its long-standing dominant position" in Western society. As a Covenanter, Wylie was trying to recover "politics suffused with deep spiritual meaning" the way Presbyterianism had 150 years earlier.[12]

As much as Copulsky provides further proof of the seismic differences between early modern and modern Presbyterianism (e.g., between Wylie and Witherspoon), he misses the degree to which Presbyterian heresy was a necessary stimulant for the orthodoxy of liberal democracy. Presbyterians began church life thinking they could have a reformed church and a godly magistrate. They assumed that the Christian ruler would necessarily support the true church. It took 150 years (from 1560 to 1710) for many Presbyterians to understand that they could not have it both ways. A godly magistrate might turn out to be an Anglican or at least a Christian who did not recognize Presbyterianism as "the true" faith. This Presbyterian blind spot also came with the assertion of the church's independence and sovereignty in spiritual matters. Presbyterians' assertion that Christ was the true head of church and state produced the controversies for which political liberalism was the best solution. What Copulsky calls liberal heresy was also a necessary stage in arriving at a liberal orthodoxy in Anglo-American politics.

Interpreting Presbyterian politics is especially challenging at a time when postliberalism finds expression in Christian and secular contexts. Some may want to celebrate Presbyterians as the most awesome patriots who supplied the religious justification for the American Revolution. This book shows the weakness of that interpretation. Another possibility is the one that Copulsky adopts: Presbyterianism should be seen, at least in its covenanting form, as political heresy. This book confirms that judgment in many respects. Presbyterian support for either the American Revolution or the 1798 Rising in Ireland was not the same as the convictions that Presbyterians used against Charles I. By the early nineteenth century, Samuel Wylie was outside the United States' liberal political consensus. He also occupied a minority position among Presbyterians not only in the United States but also Scotland, England, and Ireland. This book dissents from verdicts like Copulsky's, however, by drawing attention to the way even Presbyterian political heresy (the seventeenth-century version) contributed to liberal democracy. The Presbyterian assertion of the church's spiritual independence and its elaborate and sometimes baffling explanation of the spiritual and temporal spheres of Christ's rule were necessary features in building liberal politics.

In sum, this book provides an account of Presbyterian politics that recognizes both its liberal and illiberal characteristics from the start, and insists that both must be acknowledged. Copulsky is correct to draw attention to the heretical side of Presbyterianism. Yet, when he lists the achievements of political liberalism—"uncoupling a profession of faith from political belonging," "protecting liberty of conscience," "liberating churches from government favor," constructing a "polity on the basis of human reason [instead of] revelation," shifting political horizons to include "expansion of knowledge, economic growth, and human welfare"[13]—he misses that Presbyterian heretics also desired these social goods. To be sure, Presbyterian liberals were not always intellectually consistent. But remarkably, the effort to implement John Calvin's novel form of church government in England and Scotland contributed both directly and unintentionally to the arrival of liberal democratic political order.

BIBLIOGRAPHIC ESSAY

This book is long, and a lengthy bibliography will only make it longer. For the sake of modest brevity, the following overview of secondary works on Presbyterianism and relevant political works on British and North American politics includes only books. Many of the articles that are often as instructive as longer studies are featured in the notes for each chapter, which readers should consult for episodes in Presbyterian churches and the political history of England, Scotland, Ireland, the British Empire, the United States, and Canada.

Many historians have told pieces of the narrative proposed here, but few have synthesized the political trajectory of Presbyterian calls for reform from initial sixteenth-century complaints about bishops and royal supremacy to the nineteenth-century Presbyterian denominations in lockstep with nation-states. The best scholarship remains largely confined to a specific period, communion, or nation. From the perspective of three centuries of developments and five transatlantic contexts (England, Scotland, Ireland, United States, and Canada), interpretations of Presbyterianism need to account for a shift from quasi-theocratic to liberal views on religion and politics. Such accounts also need to situate Presbyterian involvement in political rebellion or revolution in that transition. The best existing literature for assessing Presbyterianism and politics divides somewhat logically into six categories: (1) theology and political resistance, (2) John Calvin and Geneva's churches, (3) political history (including relevant revolutions), (4) national histories, (5) denominational history, and (6) biographies of Presbyterians with national significance.

Political Theology and Political Theory

The literature on religion and political theory is extensive. The works most helpful for situating British and American Presbyterians in the intellectual history of modern politics, including resistance theory, are the following: Quentin Skinner, *The Foundations of Modern Political Thought*, 2 vols. (Cambridge: Cambridge University Press, 1978); J. H. Burns, ed., *The Cambridge History of Political Thought, 1450–1700* (Cambridge: Cambridge University Press, 1991); W. J. Torrance Kirby, *The Zurich Connection and Tudor Political Theory* (Leiden: Brill, 2007); John Witte Jr., *The Reformation of Rights: Law, Religion, and Human Rights in Early Modern Calvinism* (Cambridge: Cambridge University Press, 2007); Glenn Burgess, *British Political Thought, 1500–1660* (New York: Palgrave Macmillan, 2009); John Coffey, *Exodus and Liberation: Deliverance Politics from John Calvin to Martin Luther King, Jr.* (New York: Oxford University Press, 2014); Daniel L. Dreisbach and Mark David Hall, eds., *Faith and the Founders of the American Republic* (New York: Oxford University Press, 2014); Mark Valeri, *The Opening of the Protestant Mind: How Anglo-American Protestants Embraced Religious Liberty* (New York: Oxford University Press, 2023); and Jerome E. Copulsky, *American Heretics: Religious Adversaries of Liberal Order* (New Haven, CT: Yale University Press, 2024).

John Calvin and Geneva's Churches

Scholarship on Calvin and Geneva in English is only a fraction of the studies in French, Dutch, and German. The works most valuable for *Protestants and Patriots* include the following: William G. Naphy, *Calvin and the Consolidation of the Genevan Reformation* (Madison: University of Wisconsin Press, 1967); Robert M. Kingdon, *Adultery and Divorce in Calvin's Geneva* (Cambridge, MA: Harvard University Press, 1995); Philip Benedict, *Christ's Churches Purely Reformed: A Social History of Calvinism* (New Haven, CT: Yale University Press, 2002); Bruce Gordon, *Calvin* (New Haven, CT: Yale University Press, 2009); and Scott M.

Manetsch, *Calvin's Company of Pastors: Pastoral Care and the Emerging Reformed Church, 1536–1609* (New York: Oxford University Press, 2012).

Presbyterians and Politics (Especially Revolutions)

Scholarship on the conflicts leading to the English Civil War is vast, and to chart the Presbyterian aspects of it, these following works are among the most useful: Hugh Trevor-Roper, *The Crisis of the Seventeenth Century: Religion, the Reformation, and Social Change* (New York: Harper & Row, 1967); Robert S. Paul, *The Assembly of the Lord: Politics and Religion in the Westminster Assembly and the "Grand Debate"* (Edinburgh: T&T Clark, 1985); John Morrill, ed., *The Scottish National Covenant in Its British Context* (Edinburgh: Edinburgh University Press, 1991); Laura A. M. Stewart, *Re-Thinking the Scottish Revolution: Covenanted Scotland, 1637–1651* (New York: Oxford University Press, 2016); Kirsteen M. Mackenzie, *The Solemn League and Covenant of the Three Kingdoms and the Cromwellian Union, 1643–1663* (Oxford: Routledge, 2017); David R. Como, *Radical Parliamentarians and the English Civil War* (New York: Oxford University Press, 2018); Chris R. Langley, ed., *The National Covenant in Scotland, 1638–1689* (Rochester, NY: Boydell, 2020); Eliot Vernon, *London Presbyterians and the British Revolutions, 1638–64* (Manchester: Manchester University Press, 2021); and Anthony Milton, *England's Second Reformation* (New York: Cambridge University Press, 2021).

On Presbyterians and the American Revolution, the following provide a sample of the assessments: Howard Miller, *The Revolutionary College: American Presbyterian Higher Education, 1707–1837* (New York: New York University Press, 1976); Elizabeth I. Nybakken, ed., *The "Centinel": Warnings of a Revolution* (Newark: University of Delaware Press, 1980); Kevin P. Phillips, *The Cousins' Wars: Religion, Politics, Civil Warfare, and the Triumph of Anglo-America* (New York: Basic Books, 1999); Arthur Herman, *How the Scots Invented the Modern World* (New York: Crown Publishers, 2001); James Webb, *Born Fighting: How the Scots-Irish Shaped America* (New York: Broadway Books, 2004); Eric Nelson, *The Royalist Revolution: Monarchy and the American Founding* (Cambridge, MA: Harvard University Press, 2014); William Harrison Taylor, *Unity in Christ and Country: American Presbyterians in the Revolutionary Era, 1758–1801*

(Tuscaloosa: University of Alabama Press, 2017); and Peter C. Messer and William Harrison Taylor, eds., *Revolution as Reformation: Protestant Faith in the Age of Revolutions, 1688–1832* (Tuscaloosa: University of Alabama Press, 2021).

The topic of Presbyterians and the Irish Rising of 1798 has attracted a number of important studies that negotiate the theme agilely, even if religion is not always at the center of attention. These include the following: David Dickson, Dáire Keogh, and Kevin Whelan, *The United Irishmen: Republicanism, Radicalism, and Rebellion* (Dublin: Lilliput Press, 1993); Nancy J. Curtin, *The United Irishmen: Popular Politics in Ulster and Dublin, 1791–1798* (New York: Oxford University Press, 1994); I. M. McBride, *Scripture Politics: Irish Presbyterians and Irish Radicalism in the Late Eighteenth Century* (Oxford: Clarendon, 1998); David Wilson, *United Irishmen, United States: Immigrant Radicals in the Early Republic* (Ithaca, NY: Cornell University Press, 1998); and Guy Beiner, *Forgetful Remembrance: Social Forgetting and Vernacular Historiography of a Rebellion in Ulster* (New York: Oxford University Press, 2018).

Presbyterians and National Politics

The influence of Presbyterianism in the formation of nations is bound up with the place of Presbyterians within wider Protestant support for British politics and cultural norms. The following works cover Britain and North America: Brian J. Fraser, *The Social Uplifters: Presbyterian Progressives and the Social Gospel in Canada, 1875–1915* (Waterloo, ON: Wilfrid Laurier University Press, 1988); Mark A. Noll, *Princeton and the Republic, 1768–1822: The Search for a Christian Enlightenment in the Era of Samuel Stanhope Smith* (Princeton, NJ: Princeton University Press, 1989); John Wolffe, *The Protestant Crusade in Great Britain, 1829–1860* (Oxford: Clarendon, 1991); Linda Colley, *Britons: Forging the Nation, 1707–1837* (New Haven, CT: Yale University Press, 1992); Colin Kidd, *Subverting Scotland's Past: Scottish Whig Historians and the Creation of an Anglo-British Identity, 1689–1830* (New York: Cambridge University Press, 1993); Roger A. Mason, ed., *Scots and Britons: Scottish Political Thought and the Union of 1603* (New York: Cambridge University Press, 1994); Conor Morrisey, *Protestant Nationalists in Ireland, 1900–1923* (New York: Cambridge University Press, 1996); Nancy Christie and Michael

Gauvreau, *A Full-Orbed Christianity: The Protestant Churches and Social Welfare in Canada, 1900–1940* (Toronto: McGill-Queen's University Press, 1996); Paul K. Conkin, *The Uneasy Center: Reformed Christianity in Antebellum America* (Chapel Hill: University of North Carolina Press, 1995); Tony Claydon and Ian McBride, eds., *Protestantism and National Identity: Britain and Ireland, c.1650–c.1850* (New York: Cambridge University Press, 1999); Ian McBride, *History and Memory in Modern Ireland* (New York: Cambridge University Press, 2001); and Hugh Trevor-Roper, *The Invention of Scotland: Myth and History* (New Haven, CT: Yale University Press, 2008).

Presbyterian (and Related) Denominations

The literature on Presbyterianism as a Christian tradition is arguably the most extensive and parochial, but even here church historians have looked at denominations in their social and political context. In the case of Scotland, the overlap of civil and ecclesiastical influence naturally receives more attention than in those societies where Presbyterians were one or more of a wider collection of Protestant denominations.

The study of Presbyterianism should not be isolated from the literature on Puritanism, because both developed at the same time and were concerned to implement further reform in the national churches of England and Scotland. For that reason, the following are useful for understanding both groups of Protestants: Horton Davies, *The English Free Churches* (London: Oxford University Press, 1952); R. Tudor Jones, *Congregationalism in England, 1662–1962* (London: Independent Press, 1962); Patrick Collinson, *The Elizabethan Puritan Movement* (Berkeley: University of California Press, 1967); St. John Drelincourt Seymore, *The Puritans in Ireland, 1647–1661* (Oxford: Clarendon, 1969); Robert T. Kendall, *Calvin and English Calvinism to 1649* (Oxford: Oxford University Press, 1979); K. L. Sprunger, *Dutch Puritanism: A History of the English and Scottish Churches in the Netherlands* (Leiden: Brill, 1982); Andrew Pettegree, *Marian Protestantism: Six Studies* (Aldershot: Scolar Press, 1996); Diarmaid MacCulloch, *Thomas Cranmer: A Life* (New Haven, CT: Yale University Press, 1996); Crawford Gribben, *God's Irishmen: Theological Debates in Cromwellian Ireland* (New York: Oxford University Press, 1997); Michael P. Winship, *Hot Protestants: A History of Puritanism in*

England and America (New Haven, CT: Yale University Press, 2018); David D. Hall, *The Puritans: A Transatlantic History* (Princeton, NJ: Princeton University Press, 2019); and John G. Turner, *They Knew They Were Pilgrims: Plymouth Colony and the Contest for American Liberty* (New Haven, CT: Yale University Press, 2020).

For Presbyterianism specifically in England, Scotland, and Ireland, the following are among the most useful: A. H. Drysdale, *History of the Presbyterians in England: Their Rise, Decline, and Revival* (London: Publication Committee of the Presbyterian Church of England, 1889); J. D. Douglass, *Light in the North: The Story of the Scottish Covenanters* (Grand Rapids, MI: Eerdmans, 1964); Andrew Drummond and J. Bulloch, *The Scottish Church, 1688–1843: The Age of Moderates* (Edinburgh: Saint Andrews Press, 1973); Andrew Drummond, *The Church in Victorian Scotland, 1843–1879* (Edinburgh: Saint Andrews Press, 1975); John S. Moir, *Enduring Witness: A History of the Presbyterian Church in Canada* (Montreal: Presbyterian Church of Canada, 1987); Peter Brooke, *Ulster Presbyterianism: The Historical Perspective, 1610–1970*, 2nd ed.(Belfast: Athol Books, 1994); David N. Livingstone and Ronald A. Wells, *Ulster-American Religion: Episodes in the History of a Cultural Connection* (Notre Dame, IN: University of Notre Dame Press, 1999); James Lachlan McLeod, *The Second Disruption: The Free Church in Victorian Scotland and the Origins of the Free Presbyterian Church* (East Linton: Tuckwell Press, 2000); Margo Todd, *The Culture of Protestantism in Modern Scotland* (New Haven, CT: Yale University Press, 2002); Andrew R. Holmes, *The Shaping of Ulster Presbyterian Belief and Practice, 1770–1840* (New York: Oxford University Press, 2006); Jane E. A. Dawson, *Scotland Re-Formed, 1488–1587* (Edinburgh: Edinburgh University Press, 2007); and Polly Ha, *English Presbyterianism, 1590–1640* (Stanford, CA: Stanford University Press, 2010).

On Presbyterianism in North America, readers should consult the following: John T. McNeill, *The Presbyterian Church in Canada, 1875–1925* (Toronto: General Board, 1925); Leonard J. Trinterud, *The Forming of an American Tradition: A Re-Examination of Colonial Presbyterianism* (Philadelphia: Westminster Press, 1949); Ernest Trice Thompson, *Presbyterians in the South*, 3 vols. (Richmond, VA: John Knox Press, 1963–1973); George M. Marsden, *The Evangelical Mind and the New School Presbyterian Experience: A Case Study of Thought and Theology in Nineteenth-Century America* (New Haven, CT: Yale University Press, 1970); Keith N.

Clifford, *Resistance to Church Union in Canada, 1904–1939* (Vancouver: University of British Columbia Press, 1985); Richard Vaudry, *The Free Church in Victorian Canada, 1844–1861* (Waterloo, ON: Wilfrid Laurier University Press, 1989); Michael Gauvreau, *The Evangelical Century: College and Creed in English Canada from the Great Revival to the Great Depression* (Montreal: McGill-Queen's University Press, 1991); David B. Marshall, *Secularizing the Faith: Canadian Protestant Clergy and the Crisis of Belief, 1850–1940* (Toronto: University of Toronto Press, 1992); James H. Smylie, *A Brief History of the Presbyterians* (Louisville, KY: Geneva Press, 1997); and Valerie Wallace, *Scottish Presbyterianism and Settler Colonial Politics: Empire of Dissent* (New York: Cambridge University Press, 2018).

Presbyterian Biographies

Prominent Presbyterian leaders, both pastors and laity, played outsize roles in crucial episodes of national life in Britain and North America, and scholars have produced biographies that cover both ecclesiastical and civil aspects of these figures' careers. Among the notable figures whose biographies exemplify historians' treatments of Presbyterians' involvement in national affairs are the following: J. L. Porter, *The Life and Times of Henry Cooke* (London: John Murray, 1871); William Lawson Grant and Frederick Hamilton, *George Monro Grant* (Toronto: Morang & Co., 1905); Robert S. Paul, *The Lord Protector: Religion and Politics in the Life of Oliver Cromwell* (London: Lutterworth Press, 1955); Boyd S. Schlenther, *The Life and Writings of Francis Makemie* (Philadelphia: Presbyterian Historical Society, 1971); W. S. Reid, *Trumpeter of God: A Biography of John Knox* (New York: Scribner, 1974); Stewart J. Brown, *Thomas Chalmers and the Godly Commonwealth in Scotland* (New York: Oxford University Press, 1983); John Coffey, *Politics, Religion, and the British Revolutions: The Mind of Samuel Rutherford* (New York: Cambridge University Press, 1997); W. B. Patterson, *William Perkins and the Making of Protestant England* (Oxford: Oxford University Press, 2014); L. Charles Jackson, *Riots, Revolutions, and the Scottish Covenanters: The Work of Alexander Henderson* (Grand Rapids, MI: Reformation Heritage Books, 2015); Jane Dawson, *John Knox* (New Haven, CT: Yale University Press, 2016); and Gideon Mailer, *John Witherspoon's American Revolution* (Chapel Hill: University of North Carolina Press, 2016).

NOTES

Introduction

1. One early source for this quotation is John Milton, *Of Reformation Touching Church-Discipline in England* (1641), ed. Will Talliaferro Hale (New Haven, CT: Yale University Press, 1916), 154.

2. These quotations come from Richard Gardiner, "The Presbyterian Rebellion?," *Journal of the American Revolution*, September 5, 2013, https://allthingsliberty.com/2013/09/presbyterian-rebellion/.

3. James Webb, *Born Fighting: How the Scots-Irish Shaped America* (New York: Broadway Books, 2004), 137, 136.

4. See Richard Gardiner, "The Presbyterian Rebellion: An Analysis of the Perception That the American Revolution Was a Presbyterian War" (PhD diss., Marquette University, 2005).

5. Quotations from Joseph S. Tiedemann, "Presbyterianism and the American Revolution in the Middle Colonies," *Church History* 74, no. 2 (2005): 313.

6. Tiedemann, "Presbyterianism and the American Revolution," 313.

7. Miller, quoted in Tiedemann, "Presbyterianism and the American Revolution," 308.

8. J. C. D. Clark, "The American Revolution: A War of Religion?," *History Today*, December 1989, 13.

9. Roger A. Mason, "History and Identity in Reformation Scotland," in *Kingship and Commonweal: Political Thought in Renaissance and Reformation Scotland* (Edinburgh: Tuckwell Press, 1998), 172.

10. Thomas Kidd, *Subverting Scotland's Past: Scottish Whig Historians and the Creation of an Anglo-British Identity, 1689–1830* (Cambridge: Cambridge University Press, 2003), 57.

11. David Allan, "Protestantism, Presbyterianism and National Identity in Eighteenth-Century Scotland," in *Protestantism and National Identity: Britain and Ireland, c.1650–c.1850*, ed. Tony Claydon and Ian McBride (Cambridge: Cambridge University Press, 1998), 185–86, quotation at 186.

12. See, for instance, Gideon Mailer, "Presbyterian Confederal Ideology from the Imperial British Constitution to the New United States," in *Revolution as Reformation: Protestant Faith in the Age of Revolutions, 1688–1832*, ed. Peter C. Messer and William Harrison Taylor (Tuscaloosa: University of Alabama Press, 2021), chap. 3.

13. On Calvin's reforms of church government, see Jeffrey R. Watt, "Consistories and Discipline," in *Calvin in Context*, ed. R. Ward Holder (Cambridge: Cambridge University Press, 2019), chap. 12; and Watt, *The Consistory and Social Discipline in Calvin's Geneva* (Rochester, NY: University of Rochester Press, 2020).

14. These figures come from Philip Benedict, *Christ's Churches Purely Reformed: A Social History of Calvinism* (New Haven, CT: Yale University Press, 2002), 97, 72.

15. The phrase from Knox is widely quoted but seldom attributed to its original instance. See, for example, Roger A. Mason, ed., *Knox: On Rebellion* (Cambridge: Cambridge University Press, 1994), xxxviii.

16. Quentin Skinner, *The Foundations of Modern Political Thought*, Vol. 2, *The Age of Reformation* (Cambridge: Cambridge University Press, 1978), 302–48. See also Robert M. Kingdon, "Calvinism and Resistance Theory," in *The Cambridge History of Political Thought, 1450–1700*, ed. J. H. Burns (Cambridge: Cambridge University Press, 1991), 193–218; and John Witte Jr., *The Reformation of Rights: Law, Religion, and Human Rights in Early Modern Calvinism* (Cambridge: Cambridge University Press, 2007).

17. In addition to the works cited above in note 14, for starters see Roger A. Mason, *Empire, Union and Reform* (Edinburgh: Edinburgh University Press, 2007); Eliot Vernon, *London Presbyterians and the British Revolutions, 1638–64* (Manchester: Manchester University Press, 2021); David VanDrunen, *Natural Law and the Two Kingdoms: A Study in the Development of Reformed Social Thought* (Grand Rapids, MI: Eerdmans, 2010); Matthew J. Tuininga, *Calvin's Political Theology and the Public Engagement of the Church: Christ's Two Kingdoms* (Cambridge: Cambridge University Press, 2017); Ian McBride, *Scripture Politics: Ulster Presbyterians and Irish Radicalism in the Late Eighteenth Century* (Oxford: Clarendon, 1998); Glenn Burgess, *British Political Thought, 1500–1660: The Politics of the Post-Reformation* (New York: Palgrave Macmillan, 2009); W. Bradford Littlejohn, *The Peril and Promise of Christian Liberty: Richard Hooker, the Puritans, and Protestant Political Theology* (Grand Rapids, MI: Eerdmans, 2017); Kirsteen M. MacKenzie, *The Solemn League and Covenant of the Three Kingdoms and the Cromwellian Union, 1643–1663* (London: Routledge, 2017); and John

Coffey, *Politics, Religion and the British Revolutions: The Mind of Samuel Rutherford* (Cambridge: Cambridge University Press, 2002).

18. Benedict, *Christ's Churches Purely Reformed*, 135.

19. On the variety of political contexts among Reformed Protestants, see D. G. Hart, *Calvinism: A History* (New Haven, CT: Yale University Press, 2013), chaps. 1–4.

20. See, for instance, Daniel J. Elazer, *Covenant and Commonwealth: From Christian Separation Through the Protestant Reformation*, Vol. 2 (New Brunswick, NJ: Transaction Publishers, 1996).

21. According to Rick Phillips, that "the words of the Confession strike us as strange is precisely because we see so few people faithfully keeping either oaths or vows. . . . Why would a Christian confession of faith include a seven-paragraph chapter regarding oaths and vows?"; see Phillips, "Through the Westminster Confession: Chapter 22," reformation21, https://www.reformation21.org/confession/2013/06/chapter-22-1.php.

22. For the text of the Solemn League and Covenant, see https://thewestminsterstandard.org/the-solemn-league-and-covenant/.

One The French Connection

1. On Calvin's contests with Geneva's civil government and elites, see William G. Naphy, *Calvin and the Consolidation of the Genevan Reformation* (Louisville, KY: Westminster John Knox, 2003 [1994]), chaps. 3, 6.

2. The line appears regularly in writing about Knox, but for one example, see Carter Lindberg, *The European Reformations* (Malden, MA: Wiley, 2010), 317.

3. Jane Dawson, *John Knox* (New Haven, CT: Yale University Press, 2015), 204.

4. Quoted in David D. Hall, *The Puritans: A Transatlantic History* (Princeton, NJ: Princeton University Press, 2019), 52. Hall supplies useful biographical material on Cartwright.

5. See Hall, *The Puritans*, chap. 2.

6. For a short overview, see D. G. Hart, *Calvinism: A History* (New Haven, CT: Yale University Press, 2013), 35–41.

7. Hall, *The Puritans*, 48–49.

8. Donaldson, "The Relation between the English and Scottish Presbyterian Movements to 1604" (PhD diss., University of London, 1938), 108–9.

9. Donaldson, *Relation between the English and Scottish Presbyterian Movements*, 111.

10. Donaldson, *Relation between the English and Scottish Presbyterian Movements*, 118.

11. John Whitgift, *An answere to a certen Libel intituled, An admonition to the Parliament* (London: Henrie Bynneman, 1572), 5.

12. Whitgift, *An answere to a certen Libel*, 191.

13. Whitgift, *An answere to a certen Libel*, 183–84.

14. Quoted in Whitgift, *An answere to a certen Libel*, 71.

15. Whitgift, *An answere to a certen Libel*, 77.

16. Whitgift, *An answere to a certen Libel*, 132.

17. Quoted in Whitgift, *An answere to a certen Libel*, 136.

18. Whitgift, *An answere to a certen Libel*, 137.

19. Thomas Cartwright, *A replye to an ansvvere made of M. Doctor VVhitgifte Against the admonition to the Parliament* (Hemel Hempstead: John Stroud, 1573), 13.

20. Cartwright, *A replye to an ansvvere made*, 14.

21. Cartwright, *A replye to an ansvvere made*, 123–26.

22. Cartwright, *A replye to an ansvvere made*, quoted in Benjamin Brooke, *Memoir of the Life and Writings of Thomas Cartwright* (London: John Snow, 1845), 121.

23. Whitgift, quoted in Brooke, *Memoir*, 185.

24. Cartwright, quoted in Brooke, *Memoir*, 187.

25. Cartwright, quoted in Brooke, *Memoir*, 188.

26. Cartwright, quoted in Brooke, *Memoir*, 120.

27. Whitgift, quoted in Brooke, *Memoir*, 169.

28. Cartwright, quoted in Brooke, *Memoir*, 171, 172.

29. See, for instance, Norman Sykes, *Old Priest and New Presbytery: The Anglican Attitude to Episcopacy, Presbyterianism, and the Papacy since the Reformation* (Cambridge: Cambridge University Press, 1956).

30. Hall, *The Puritans*, 62–63.

31. See Jane Dawson, *John Knox* (New Haven, CT: Yale University Press, 2015), chaps. 9 and 17.

32. Margo Todd, "Practicing the Books of Discipline: The Problem of Equality before the Law in Scottish Parish Consistories," in *Calvin and the Book: The Evolution of the Printed Word in Reformed Protestantism*, ed. Karen E. Spierling (Goetttingen: Vandenhoeck & Ruprecht, 2015), 33.

33. Philip Benedict, *Christ's Churches Purely Reformed: A Social History of Calvinism* (New Haven, CT: Yale University Press, 2002), 162.

34. The First Book of Discipline of the Church of Scotland: https://www.fpchurch.org.uk/about-us/important-documents/the-first-book-of-discipline-1560/.

35. "The Fourth Head—Concerning Ministers and Their Lawful Election," in First Book of Discipline.

36. "The Fifth Head—Concerning the Provision for the Ministers, and for the Distribution of the Rents and Possessions Justly Appertaining to the Kirk," in First Book of Discipline.

37. "The Eighth Head—Touching the Election of Elders and Deacons, etc.," in First Book of Discipline.

38. Benedict, *Christ's Churches*, 163.

39. "The Fifth Head," in First Book of Discipline.

40. Benedict, *Christ's Churches*, 164.

41. Benedict, *Christ's Churches*, 164–65.

42. Benedict, *Christ's Churches*, 164–65.

43. "Chapter Four: Of the Office-Bearers in Particular, and First of the Pastors or Ministers," in the Second Book of Discipline, https://www.fpchurch.org.uk/about-us/important-documents/the-second-book-of-discipline-1578/.

44. "Chapter Eleven: Of the Present Abuses Remaining in the Kirk Which We Desire to be Reformed," in Second Book of Discipline.

45. "Chapter Seven: Of the Elderships, and Assemblies, and Discipline," in Second Book of Discipline.

46. "Chapter Three: How the Persons that Bear Ecclesiastical Functions are to be Admitted to Their Office," in Second Book of Discipline.

47. "Chapter Seven," in Second Book of Discipline.

48. "Chapter One: Of the Kirk and Policy Thereof in General, and Wherein it is Different from the Civil Policy," in Second Book of Discipline.

49. "Chapter Ten: Of the Office of a Christian Magistrate in the Kirk," in Second Book of Discipline.

50. Hugh Trevor-Roper, *The Invention of Scotland: Myth and History* (New Haven, CT: Yale University Press, 2008), 33.

51. Quoted in J. H. Burns, "George Buchanan and the Anti-Monarchomachs," in *Scots and Britons: Scottish Political Thought and the Union of 1603*, ed. Roger A. Mason (Cambridge: Cambridge University Press, 1994), 115.

52. Burns, "George Buchanan," 116–18.

53. Hall, *The Puritans*, 97.

54. S. J. Reid, "Of Bairns and Bearded Men: James VI and the Ruthven Raid," in *James VI and Noble Power in Scotland 1578–1603*, ed. S. J. Reid and M. Kerr-Peterson (London: Routledge, 2017), 32–56.

55. Roger A. Mason, "George Buchanan, James VI and the Presbyterians," in Mason, ed., *Scots and Britons*, 129.

56. Mason, "George Buchanan, James VI and the Presbyterians," 130.

57. From a sermon by Richard Bancroft, archbishop of Canterbury, quoted in Mason, "George Buchanan, James VI and the Presbyterians," 132.

58. Mullan, quoted in Mason, "George Buchanan, James VI and the Presbyterians," 134.

59. Hall, *The Puritans*, 102.

60. Elizabeth, quoted in Hall, *The Puritans*, 102.

61. Melville, quoted in Hall, *The Puritans*, 102.

62. Hall, *The Puritans*, 107.

Two The Problem with Scottish Kings

1. A good brief overview of English Bibles is in Mark A. Noll, *In the Beginning Was the Word: The Bible in American Public Life, 1492–1783* (New York: Oxford University Press, 2015), chap. 2.

2. See W. B. Patterson, "King James I and the Protestant Cause in the Crisis of 1618–1622," *Studies in Church History* 18 (1982): 319–34.

3. John G. Turner, *They Knew They Were Pilgrims: Plymouth Colony and the Contest for American Liberty* (New Haven, CT: Yale University Press, 2020), 40, 57.

4. Melville, quoted in Agnes Mure MacKenzie, *The Scotland of Queen Mary and the Religious Wars, 1513–1638* (London: A. Maclehose, 1936), 282–83.

5. King James VI, *The Trew Law of Free Monarchies*, ed. Johann P. Sommerville (Cambridge: Cambridge University Press, 1996).

6. Quoted in W. B. Patterson, *James VI and I and the Reunion of Christendom* (Cambridge: Cambridge University Press, 1997), 26.

7. Patterson, *James VI and I and the Reunion*, 27.

8. See Patterson, *James VI and I and the Reunion*, 85–86.

9. MacKenzie, *Scotland of Queen Mary*, 323.

10. See Polly Ha, *English Presbyterianism, 1590–1640* (Stanford, CA: Stanford University Press, 2011), 126–36.

11. Robert S. Paul, *The Assembly of the Lord: Politics and Religion in the Westminster Assembly and the "Grand Debate"* (Edinburgh: T&T Clark, 1985), 112.

12. See David R. Como, *Radical Parliamentarians and the English Civil War* (New York: Cambridge University Press, 2018).

13. See Ha, *English Presbyterianism*, 36–43.

14. Quoted in David D. Hall, *The Puritans: A Transatlantic History* (Princeton, NJ: Princeton University Press, 2019), 192.

15. See Hall, *The Puritans*, 191–94.

16. On Henderson's life, see L. Charles Jackson, *Riots, Revolutions, and the Scottish Covenanters: The Work of Alexander Henderson* (Grand Rapids, MI: Reformation Heritage Books, 2015), chaps. 1–2.

17. John Morrill, "The Scottish National Covenant of 1638 in its British Context," in *The Nature of the English Revolution* (London: Longman, 1993), 93.

18. Morrill, "The Scottish National Covenant of 1638," 94.

19. Morrill, "The Scottish National Covenant of 1638," 97.

20. Stevenson, *Scottish Revolution*, 20.

21. Stevenson, *Scottish Revolution*, 33.

22. Hall, *The Puritans*, 245.

23. Quoted in Hall, *The Puritans*, 246.

24. Hall, *The Puritans*, 247.

25. Hall, *The Puritans*, 248.

26. Jackson, *Riots, Revolutions*, 149–50.

27. Alexander D. Campbell, "Episcopacy in the Mind of Robert Ballie, 1637–62," *Scottish Historical Review* 93, no. 236 (2014): 29–55, quotation on 38.

28. Alexia Grosjean and Steve Murdoch, *Alexander Leslie and the Scottish Generals of the Thirty Years' War, 1618–1648* (New York: Routledge, 2015), 2.

29. Leslie, quoted in Grosjean and Murdoch, *Alexander Leslie and the Scottish Generals*, 97.

30. Grosjean and Murdoch, *Alexander Leslie and the Scottish Generals*, 94.

31. Grosjean and Murdoch, *Alexander Leslie and the Scottish Generals*, 101.

32. "The Bishops Wars and Wars of the Three Kingdoms (1639–1646)," https://www.thereformation.info/bishopswars/.

33. For details of this summary, see Mark Charles Fissel, *The Bishops' Wars: Charles I's Campaigns against Scotland, 1638–1640* (New York: Cambridge University Press, 1994), chaps. 1–2.

34. See "Act Sess. XV. 7. Aug. 1641. *Overtures anent Bursars, and Expectants*," in Church of Scotland, General Assembly, *The principall acts of foure Generall Assemblies, of the Kirk of Scotland holden [brace] at Edinburgh 1639, at Aberdene 1640, at S. Andrews and Edinburgh 1641, at S. Andrews 1642* (Edinburgh: Evan Tyler, 1642), https://quod.lib.umich.edu/e/eebo2/B20345.0001.001/1:4?.

35. Paul, *The Assembly of the Lord*, 114.

36. Quoted in Jackson, *Riots, Revolutions*, 217.

37. Jackson, *Riots, Revolutions*, 219.

38. Benedict, *Christ's Churches*, 400.

39. Quoted in Jackson, *Riots, Revolutions*, 215.

40. Jackson, *Riots, Revolutions*, 221–22.

41. Quoted in Glenn Burgess, *British Political Thought, 1500–1660: The Politics of the Post-Reformation* (London: Bloomsbury, 2009), 192.

42. John Coffey, *Politics, Religion and the British Revolutions: The Mind of Samuel Rutherford* (New York: Cambridge University Press, 1997), 168.

43. Quoted in Benedict, *Christ's Churches*, 401.

44. Charles I, quoted in Hall, *The Puritans*, 291.

45. Jackson, *Riots, Revolutions*, 248, 249.

46. Quoted in Hall, *The Puritans*, 291.

47. Hall, *The Puritans*, 293.

48. Hall, *The Puritans*, 293.

49. Benedict, *Christ's Churches*, 408–9.

50. Hall, *The Puritans*, 296.

51. Paul, *Assembly of the Lord*, 536, 537.

52. Paul, *Assembly of the Lord*, 513–16.

53. Sundry Ministers of Christ within the City of London, *Jus divinum regiminis ecclesiastici: or, the Divine right of Church-government . . .* (London: R. W., 1654 [1646]), 126–27, quotation from 129.

54. *Jus divinum regiminis ecclesiastici*, 233–34.

55. *Jus divinum regiminis ecclesiastici*, 93.

56. Samuel Rutherford, *THE DIVINE RIGHT OF Church-Government AND Excommunication: OR A peaceable DISPUTE for the perfection of the holy Scripture in point of Ceremonies and Church-Government* (London: John Field, 1646), 544.

57. Rutherford, *THE DIVINE RIGHT OF Church-Government*, 546.

58. Rutherford, *THE DIVINE RIGHT OF Church-Government*, 547.

Three Presbyterianism (Finally) Established

1. Philip Benedict, *Christ's Churches Purely Reformed: A Social History of Calvinism* (New Haven, CT: Yale University Press, 2008), 408.

2. Benedict, *Christ's Churches*, 408.

3. Hyde, quoted in Benedict, *Christ's Churches*, 408.

4. Benedict, *Christ's Churches*, 409.

5. See Benedict, *Christ's Churches*, 410.

6. Quoted in Benedict, *Christ's Churches*, 412.

7. Benedict, *Christ's Churches*, 412.

8. Benedict, *Christ's Churches*, 413.

9. Tim Cooper, "Richard Baxter and the Savoy Conference (1661)," *Journal of Ecclesiastical History* 68, no. 2 (2017): 326n1.

10. See Cooper, "Richard Baxter and the Savoy Conference," 332–33.

11. Reprinted in Gerald Lewis Bray, *Documents of the English Reformation* (Cambridge: James Clark, & Co., 2004), 545.

12. Austin Woolrych, *Britain in Revolution: 1625–1660* (New York: Oxford University Press, 2004), 775.

13. Barry Till, "The Worcester House Declaration and the Restoration of the Church of England," *Historical Research* 70, no. 172 (1997): 206.

14. See Till, "The Worcester House Declaration," 207.

15. Quoted in Till, "The Worcester House Declaration," 208.

16. Edward Stillingfleet, *Proposals Tender'd to the Consideration of Both Houses of Parliament, For Uniting the Protestant Interest for the Present; And preventing Divisions for the Future . . .* (London: Henry Clark, 1689), 16–17, https://quod.lib.umich.edu/e/eebo/A61586.0001.001?view=toc.

17. Stillingfleet, *Proposals Tender'd*, 18.

18. Stillingfleet, *Proposals Tender'd*, 21.

19. Stillingfleet, *Proposals Tender'd*, 22.

20. David Fuller, *English Church and State: A Short Study of Erastianism* (Raleigh, NC: Lula, 2016), 56.

21. See Till, "The Worcester House Declaration," 224–25.

22. C. G. Boling et al., eds., *English Presbyterians: From Elizabethan Puritanism to Modern Unitarianism* (London: George Allen & Unwin, 1968), 78–79.

23. Boling et al., *English Presbyterians*, 79.

24. Cooper, "Richard Baxter," 339.

25. Mark Goldie, *Roger Morrice and the Puritan Whigs*, and Michael Winship, "Defining Puritanism in Restoration England," quoted in Cooper, "Richard Baxter," 339.

26. Sharp, quoted in Cooper, "Richard Baxter, 339.

27. Jeffrey R. Collins, "The Restoration Bishops and the Royal Supremacy," *Church History* 68, no. 3 (1999): 549–80.

28. John Gauden, quoted in Collins, "The Restoration Bishops," 560.

29. See Gerald R. Cragg, *Puritanism in the Period of the Great Persecution, 1660–1688* (New York: Cambridge University Press, 1957), 13–15.

30. Cragg, *Puritanism in the Period of the Great Persecution*, 17.

31. Johnston and Row, quoted in Godfrey Davies, *The Restoration of Charles II, 1658–1660* (New York: Oxford University Press, 1969 [1955]), 32.

32. Wodrow, quoted in Davies, *Restoration of Charles II*, 32.

33. Davies, *Restoration of Charles II*, 33.

34. Davies, *Restoration of Charles II*, 38.

35. See Davies, *Restoration of Charles II*, 38–39.

36. See R. S. Spurlock, "The Tradition of Intolerance in the Church of Scotland," in *Reformed Majorities in Early Modern Europe*, ed. H. J. Selderhuis and J. Marius J. Lange van Ravenswaay (Goettingen: Vandenhoeck & Ruprecht, 2015), 303–12.

37. See Mark Linden Mirabello, "Dissent and the Church of Scotland, 1660–1690" (PhD diss., Glasgow University, 1988), 30–38.

38. Mirabello, "Dissent and the Church of Scotland," 31.

39. Davies, *Restoration of Charles II*, 49.

40. Quoted in Davies, *Restoration of Charles II*, 49.

41. See Mirabello, "Dissent and the Church of Scotland," 45.

42. James Rankin, *A Handbook of the Church of Scotland* (Edinburgh: William Blackwood and Sons, 1879), 29.

43. See Mirabello, "Dissent and the Church of Scotland," 49–50.

44. Clare Jackson, *Restoration Scotland, 1660–1690: Royalist Politics, Religion and Ideas* (Suffolk, NY: Boydell Press, 2003), 115–16.

45. Mirabello, "Dissent and the Church of Scotland," 173.
46. Mirabello, "Dissent and the Church of Scotland," 177nn23 and 24.
47. Mirabello, "Dissent and the Church of Scotland," 178n25.
48. Mirabello, "Dissent and the Church of Scotland," 178n25.
49. Mirabello, "Dissent and the Church of Scotland," 185–86.
50. Mirabello, "Dissent and the Church of Scotland," 194.
51. Quoted in Mirabello, "Dissent and the Church of Scotland," 193.
52. Mirabello, "Dissent and the Church of Scotland," 194.
53. Mirabello, "Dissent and the Church of Scotland," 199–202.
54. Gillian H. MacIntosh, *The Scottish Parliament under Charles II* (Edinburgh: University of Edinburgh Press, 2007), 183–84.
55. Mirabello, "Dissent and the Church of Scotland," 215.
56. See Mirabello, "Dissent and the Church of Scotland," 220–25.
57. Mirabello, "Dissent and the Church of Scotland," 221.
58. Mirabello, "Dissent and the Church of Scotland," 223–25.
59. Quoted in Mirabello, "Dissent and the Church of Scotland," 297.
60. The point about a diminished commitment to a national church comes from Mirabello, "Dissent and the Church of Scotland," 308n24.
61. See Mirabello, "Dissent and the Church of Scotland," 299.
62. See Mirabello, "Dissent and the Church of Scotland," 304.
63. Quoted in Mirabello, "Dissent and the Church of Scotland," 305.
64. See Rankin, *Handbook of the Church of Scotland*, 39; William Maxwell Hetherington, *History of the Church of Scotland: From the Introduction of Christianity to the Period of Disruption*, 3rd ed. (Edinburgh: John Johnstone, 1843), 177.
65. "Claim of Right Act (1689)," https://www.legislation.gov.uk/aosp/1689/28.
66. See Alasdair Raffe, *The Culture of Controversy: Religious Arguments in Scotland, 1660–1714* (Rochester, NY: Boydell Press, 2012), chap. 7.
67. Hetherington, *History of the Church of Scotland*, 181–82.
68. Alasdair Raffe, "Presbyterianism, Secularization, and Scottish Politics after the Revolution of 1688–1690," *The Historical Journal* 53, no. 2 (2010): 328–33.
69. See Raffe, "Presbyterianism, Secularization, and Scottish Politics," 328.
70. *Heads of Agreement Assented to by the United Ministers in and about London: Formerly Called Presbyterian and Congregational* (London: Thomas Cockerill, 1691), 6–7.
71. *Heads of Agreement Assented to by the United Ministers*, 6–7.
72. See Alasdair Raffe, "Presbyterians," in *The Long Eighteenth Century, c. 1689–c. 1828*, Vol. 2 of *The Oxford History of Protestant Dissenting Traditions*, ed. Andrew Thompson (New York: Oxford University Press, 2018), 17.
73. Timothy Larsen and Mark A. Noll, "Series Introduction," in Thompson, ed., *The Long Eighteenth Century*, xv.

Four No King, No Creed

1. Littleton Purnell Bowen, *The Days of Makemie: Or The Vine Planted, A.D. 1680–1708* (Philadelphia: Presbyterian Board of Publication, 1885), 471–72.

2. On Makemie's life and significance, see James H. Smylie, "Francis Makemie: Tradition and Challenge," *Journal of Presbyterian History* 61, no. 2 (1983): 197–209.

3. Van Dyke, quoted in Smylie, "Francis Makemie," 199.

4. Quoted in Smylie, "Francis Makemie," 200, 201.

5. Charles Scott Sealy, "Church Authority and Non-Subscription Controversies in Early 18th Century Presbyterianism" (PhD diss., University of Glasgow, 2010), 66–67.

6. Sealy, "Church Authority and Non-Subscription," 67–68.

7. Quoted in Sealy, "Church Authority and Non-Subscription," 68.

8. Wodrow, quoted in Sealy, "Church Authority and Non-Subscription," 68.

9. Cooper, quoted in Sealy, "Church Authority and Non-Subscription," 69 (emphasis Cooper's).

10. See D. G. Hart, *Calvinism: A History* (New Haven, CT: Yale University Press, 2013), 147–48.

11. See Sealy, "Church Authority and Non-Subscription," 70.

12. Ryan K. Frace, "Religious Toleration in the Wake of Revolution: Scotland on the Eve of the Enlightenment (1688–1710s)," *History* 93, no. 3 (2008): 359.

13. Frace, "Religious Toleration in the Wake of Revolution," 361.

14. Calamy, quoted in Frace, "Religious Toleration in the Wake of Revolution," 364.

15. Frace, "Religious Toleration in the Wake of Revolution," 368.

16. Boston, quoted in Jeffrey Stephen, *Scottish Presbyterians and the Act of Union (1707)* (Edinburgh: Edinburgh University Press, 2007), 232.

17. See Jeffrey Stephen, "Defending the Revolution: The Church of Scotland and the Scottish Parliament, 1689–1695," *Scottish Historical Review* 89, no. 227 (2010): 19–53.

18. Christopher A. Whatley, "Reformed Religion, Regime Change, Scottish Whigs and the Struggle for the 'Soul' of Scotland, c. 1688–c. 1788," *Scottish Historical Review* 92, no. 1 (2013): 93.

19. Alasdair Raffe, "The Hanoverian Succession and the Fragmentation of Scottish Protestantism," in *Negotiating Toleration: Dissent and the Hanoverian Succession, 1714–1760*, ed. Nigel Aston and Benjamin Bankhurst (New York: Oxford University Press, 2019), 160.

20. See Raffe, "The Hanoverian Succession," 155–60.

21. See Raffe, "The Hanoverian Succession," 157–59.

22. Raffe, "The Hanoverian Succession," 163.

23. See Stewart J. Brown, "Protestant Dissent in Scotland," in *The Long Eighteenth Century, c. 1689–c. 1828*, Vol. 2 of *The Oxford History of Protestant Dissenting Traditions*, ed. Andrew C. Thompson (New York: Oxford University Press, 2018), 145–46.

24. See Donald Fraser, *The Life and Diary of the Reverend Ebenezer Erskine, A.M.: Of Stirling, Father of the Secession Church, to which is Prefixed a Memoir of His Father, the Rev. Henry Erskine, of Chirnside* (Edinburgh: W. Oliphint, 1831), 7.

25. Ebenezer Erskine, "The Stone Rejected by the Builders," in *The Select Writings of the Rev. Ebenezer Erskine: Doctrinal Sermons*, Vol. 1, ed. David Smith (Edinburgh: Fullarton and Co., 1851), 314–15, 329.

26. Brown, "Protestant Dissent," 147.

27. Brown, "Protestant Dissent," 148.

28. Brown, "Protestant Dissent," 148.

29. Brown, "Protestant Dissent," 151.

30. Brown, "Protestant Dissent," 151.

31. Alexander Gordon, *The Story of Salter's Hall, Address* (Nottingham: H. B. Saxton, 1902), 7.

32. See Gordon, *Story of Salter's Hall*, 8.

33. Geoffrey Holmes, "The Sacheverell Riots: The Crowd and the Church in Early Eighteenth-Century London," *Past & Present* 72 (August 1976): 63–64.

34. Humfrey, quoted in James C. Spalding, "The Demise of English Presbyterianism: 1660–1760," *Church History* 69, no. 1 (1959): 76.

35. See Spalding, "The Demise of English Presbyterianism," 76, quotation at 77.

36. Quoted in Spalding, "The Demise of English Presbyterianism," 78.

37. Spalding, "The Demise of English Presbyterianism," 78.

38. See Spalding, "The Demise of English Presbyterianism," 79.

39. See Andrew C. Thompson, "Toleration, Dissent, and the State in Britain," in Thompson, ed., *The Long Eighteenth Century*, 270–71.

40. Mark Burden, "Dissent and Education," in Thompson, ed., *The Long Eighteenth Century*, 386.

41. Quoted in Burden, "Dissent and Education," 387.

42. Christopher Dudley, "The Decline of Religion in British Politics, 1710–1734," *British Scholar* 3, no. 1 (2010): 49.

43. Dudley, "The Decline of Religion in British Politics," 53–54.

44. See Allan Brockett, *Nonconformity in Exeter, 1650–1875* (Manchester: Manchester University Press, 1962), 99.

45. Quoted in Brockett, *Nonconformity in Exeter*, 108.

46. Brockett, *Nonconformity in Exeter*, 108.

47. See Clarke Huston Irwin, *A History of Presbyterianism in Dublin and the South and West of Ireland* (London: Hodder and Stoughton, 1890), chap. 1.

48. See Andrew R. Holmes, "Protestant Dissent in Ireland," in Thompson, ed., *The Long Eighteenth Century*, 119–22.

49. See Holmes, "Protestant Dissent in Ireland," 119–20.

50. Ian McBride, "Ulster Presbyterians and the Confessional State, c. 1688–1733," in *Political Discourse and Seventeenth- and Eighteenth-Century Ireland*, ed. D. George Boyce et al. (New York: Palgrave Macmillan, 2001), 175.

51. McBride, "Ulster Presbyterians and the Confessional State," 176–77.

52. McBride, "Ulster Presbyterians and the Confessional State," 177.

53. McBride, "Ulster Presbyterians and the Confessional State," 178.

54. McBride, "Ulster Presbyterians and the Confessional State," 181.

55. McBride, "Ulster Presbyterians and the Confessional State," 182–83.

56. McBride, "Ulster Presbyterians and the Confessional State," 184.

57. Abernethy, quoted in Sealy, "Church Authority," 102.

58. Francoise Deconinck-Brossard, "Sermons," in Thompson, ed., *The Long Eighteenth Century*, 342–43.

59. See Sealy, "Church Authority," 132–38.

60. Brown, "Protestant Dissent," 128–29.

61. McBride, "Ulster Presbyterians," 186.

62. Holmes, "Protestant Dissent," 129.

63. See Holmes, "Protestant Dissent," 129–31.

64. See Sealy, "Church Authority and Non-Subscription," 171–72.

65. Hoadly, *The Nature of the Kingdom, or Church, of Christ: A Sermon Preach'd before the King, at the Royal chapel at St. James's, on Sunday March 31, 1717* (London: James Knapton, 1717), 16, https://quod.lib.umich.edu/e/ecco/004809919.0001.000?rgn=main;view=fulltext.

66. Sealy, "Church Authority and Non-Subscription," 176.

67. See Sealy, "Church Authority and Non-Subscription," 181–83.

68. Quoted in Sealy, "Church Authority and Non-Subscription," 184.

69. Quotation from Sealy, "Church Authority and Non-Subscription," 134–35.

70. On the American Presbyterian controversy over the eighteenth-century awakenings, see Leonard J. Trinterud, *The Forming of an American Tradition: A Re-Examination of Colonial Presbyterianism* (Philadelphia: Westminster Press, 1949), 140–43.

Five Liberal Presbyterian Rebellions

1. Mark A. Noll, *Princeton and the Republic, 1768–1822: The Search for a Christian Enlightenment in the Era of Samuel Stanhope Smith* (Princeton, NJ: Princeton University Press, 1989), 58.

2. Noll, *Princeton and the Republic*, 28.

3. Noll, *Princeton and the Republic*, 73.

4. Kevin Phillips, *The Cousins' Wars: Religion, Politics and the Triumph of Anglo-America* (New York: Basic Books, 1999), 92, 177.

5. On the religious background of the American Founders, see David L. Holmes, *The Faiths of the Founding Fathers* (New York: Oxford University Press, 2006).

6. See Noll, *Princeton and the Republic*, 25–27, on negotiations between the College of New Jersey and Witherspoon.

7. On colonial Presbyterianism, see Leonard J. Trinterud, *The Forming of an American Tradition: A Re-Examination of Colonial Presbyterianism* (Philadelphia: Westminster Press, 1949).

8. Ned Landsman, *Scotland and Its First American Colony, 1683–1765* (Princeton, NJ: Princeton University Press, 2014), 251.

9. On Simm and Witherspoon, see Landsman, *Scotland and Its First American Colony*, 254–56.

10. Witherspoon, quoted in Noll, *Princeton and the Republic*, 51.

11. Witherspoon quoted in Noll, *Princeton and the Republic*, 48.

12. Gideon Mailer, *John Witherspoon's American Revolution* (Chapel Hill: University of North Carolina Press, 2017), 219.

13. Mailer, *John Witherspoon's American Revolution*, 231.

14. Many of the Presbyterians who approved the Union later objected to the 1711 Scottish Episcopalians Act, which granted a place for episcopacy and the English Book of Common Prayer in Scotland.

15. John Witherspoon, *The Dominion of Providence Over the Passions of Men: A Sermon [on Ps. Lxxvi. 10]* (Philadelphia: R. Aitken, 1776), 41.

16. John Witherspoon, "On Conducting the American Controversy," in *The Works of the Rev. John Witherspoon*, Vol. 4 (Philadelphia: William W. Woodward, 1802), 307.

17. Witherspoon, "On Conducting the American Controversy," 306.

18. John Witherspoon, *Address to the Natives of Scotland Residing in America*, in *The Works of the Rev. John Witherspoon*, Vol. 3 (Philadelphia: William W. Woodward, 1802), 51, 57, 54.

19. Quoted in James L. McAllister Jr., "Francis Alison and John Witherspoon: Political Philosophers and Revolutionaries," *Journal of Presbyterian History* 54, no. 1 (1976): 50.

20. The full letter is reprinted in Benjamin Hait, Francis Allison, James Sprout, George Duffield, and Robert Davidson, "The Resolve to Resist, 1775–1776," *Journal of Presbyterian History* 52, no. 4 (1974): 377–400, quotation on 390.

21. Hait et al., "The Resolve to Resist, 1775–1776," 391.

22. See Mailer, *John Witherspoon's American Revolution*, 243.

23. Eric Nelson, *The Royalist Revolution: Monarchy and the American Founding* (Cambridge, MA: Harvard University Press, 2014), 2.

24. McAllister, "Francis Alison and John Witherspoon," 53.

25. James B. Bell, *A War of Religion: Dissenters, Anglicans, and the American Revolution* (New York: Palgrave Macmillan, 2008), 215.

26. Bell, *A War of Religion*, 211–14.

27. Quoted in Elizabeth I. Nybakken, *The "Centinel": Warnings of a Revolution* (Newark: University of Delaware Press, 1980), 20.

28. Nybakken, *The "Centinel,"* 22.

29. See Andrew R. Holmes, "Protestant Dissent in Ireland," in *The Long Eighteenth Century, c. 1689–c. 1828*, Vol. 2 of *The Oxford History of Protestant Dissenting Traditions*, ed. Andrew C. Thompson (New York: Oxford University Press, 2018), chap. 6.

30. Richard Robert Madden, *Antrim and Down in '98: The Lives of Henry Joy M'Cracken, James Hope, William Putnam M'Cabe, Rev. James Porter, Henry Munro* (London: Burns Oates & Washburne, n.d.), 8.

31. For the context of the United Irishmen, see I. R. McBride, *Scripture Politics: Ulster Presbyterians and Irish Radicalism in the Late Eighteenth Century* (Oxford: Clarendon, 1998), chaps. 7–8.

32. See Nancy J. Curtin, *The United Irishmen: Popular Politics in Ulster and Dublin, 1791–1798* (New York: Oxford University Press, 1998), 32–36.

33. Madden, *Antrim and Down*, 39.

34. Madden, *Antrim and Down*, 39.

35. Curtin, *United Irishmen*, 265.

36. Madden, *Antrim and Down*, 245.

37. Madden, *Antrim and Down*, 76.

38. McBride, *Scripture Politics*, 19.

39. William Molyneux, quoted in McBride, *Scripture Politics*, 18.

40. McBride, *Scripture Politics*, 17.

41. Burke, quoted in McBride, *Scripture Politics*, 19.

42. McBride, *Scripture Politics*, 29.

43. Ultán Gillen, "Ascendency Ireland, 1660–1800," in *The Princeton History of Modern Ireland*, ed. Richard Bourke and Ian McBride (Princeton, NJ: Princeton University Press, 2016), 64.

44. See Madden, *Antrim and Down*, 54–57.

45. See McBride, *Scripture Politics*, 87–91.

46. McBride, *Scripture Politics*, 95.

47. McBride, *Scripture Politics*, 106–7.

48. McBride, *Scripture Politics*, 108.

49. McBride, *Scripture Politics*, 109.

50. Andrew R. Holmes, *The Shaping of Ulster Presbyterian Belief and Practice, 1770–1840* (New York: Oxford University Press, 2006), 116.

51. Holmes, *The Shaping of Ulster Presbyterian Belief and Practice*, 138.

52. Holmes, *The Shaping of Ulster Presbyterian Belief and Practice*, 141.

53. A. T. Q. Stewart, "The Transformation of Presbyterian Radicalism in the North of Ireland, 1792–1825" (MA thesis, Queen's University Belfast, 1956), 10.

54. Quoted in Madden, *Antrim and Down*, 80.

55. Madden, *Antrim and Down*, 69.

56. Quoted in Michael Durey, *Transatlantic Radicals and the Early American Republic* (Lawrence: University of Kansas Press, 1997), 147.

57. David Wilson, *United Irishmen, United States: Immigrant Radicals in the Early Republic* (Ithaca, NY: Cornell University Press, 1998), 126.

58. Wilson, *United Irishmen, United States*, 128.

59. Wilson, *United Irishmen, United States*, 131.

Six Presbyterianism after Establishment

1. Quoted in Dalphy I. Fagerstrom, "Scottish Opinion and the American Revolution," *William & Mary Quarterly* 11, no. 2 (1954): 264.

2. See Fagerstrom, "Scottish Opinion," 265.

3. Quoted in Fagerstrom, "Scottish Opinion," 266.

4. Quoted in Fagerstrom, "Scottish Opinion," 268.

5. Quoted in Fagerstrom, "Scottish Opinion," 268n47.

6. James H. Smylie, "Charles Nisbet: Second Thoughts on a Revolutionary Generation," *American Presbyterians* 73, no. 3 (1995): 147.

7. Quoted in Smylie, "Charles Nisbet," 151.

8. Quoted in Emma Vincent, "The Responses of Scottish Churchmen to the French Revolution, 1789–1802," *Scottish Historical Review* 73, no. 196 (1994): 191.

9. Quoted in Vincent, "The Responses of Scottish Churchmen," 191–92.

10. Vincent, "The Responses of Scottish Churchmen," 197, 198.

11. Vincent, "The Responses of Scottish Churchmen," 196.

12. Quoted in Vincent, "The Responses of Scottish Churchmen," 204.

13. *Annals of the General Assembly of the Church of Scotland from the Final Secession in 1739 to the Origin of the Relief in 1752* (Edinburgh: John Johnstone, 1838), 231, 232.

14. Stewart J. Brown, "Moderate Theology and Preaching, c. 1750–1800," in *The History of Scottish Theology*, Vol. 2, ed. David Fergusson and Mark W. Elliott (New York: Oxford University Press, 2019), 69.

15. Brown, "Moderate Theology and Preaching," 70.

16. *Annals of the General Assembly*, 232.

17. *Annals of the General Assembly*, 233.

18. *Annals of the General Assembly*, 239.

19. George Hill, *A View of the Constitution of the Church of Scotland*, 3rd ed. (Edinburgh: John Waugh, 1835[1817]), 26.

20. Hill, *A View of the Constitution*, 28.

21. Hill, *A View of the Constitution*, 29.

22. Hill, *A View of the Constitution*, 31.

23. Hill, *A View of the Constitution*, 32.

24. Quoted in Andrew L. Drummond and James Bulloch, *The Scottish Church, 1688–1843: The Age of the Moderates* (Edinburgh: Saint Andrew Press, 1973), 104, 105.

25. David J. Brown, "The Government of Scotland under Henry Dundas and William Pitt," *History* 83, no. 270 (1998): 226–27.

26. Drummond and Bulloch, *Scottish Church*, 222.

27. See D. G. Hart, *Calvinism: A History* (New Haven, CT: Yale University Press, 2013), 177–91.

28. Drummond and Bulloch, *Scottish Church*, 153.

29. Drummond and Bulloch, *Scottish Church*, 153.

30. George Hill, "Nature and Extent of Power Implied in Church Government," in *Lectures in Divinity*, Vol. 2, 3rd ed. (Edinburgh: Waugh and Innes, 1833), 499. Writing from the perspective of the conservative Free Church of Scotland, Peter Bayne judged Hill's lectures on church government to have "no difficulty in realising the Church as apart from and independent of the State"; see Bayne, *The Free Church of Scotland: Her Origins, Founders, and Testimony*, 2nd ed. (Edinburgh: T&T Clark, 1894), 14.

31. For an overview of the episode, see J. B. Morrell, "The Leslie Affair: Careers, Kirk and Politics in Edinburgh in 1805," *The Scottish Historical Review* 54 (April 1975): 63–82.

32. Drummond and Bulloch, *Scottish Church*, 155, 156.

33. Morrell, "Leslie Affair," 81.

34. Stewart J. Brown, "Religion and the Rise of Liberalism: The First Disestablishment Campaign in Scotland, 1829–1843," *Journal of Ecclesiastical History* 48, no. 4 (1997): 682.

35. Brown, "Religion and the Rise of Liberalism," 687–88.

36. Brown, "Religion and the Rise of Liberalism," 691.

37. Brown, "Religion and the Rise of Liberalism," 693.

38. Brown, "Religion and the Rise of Liberalism," 694.

39. Brown, "Religion and the Rise of Liberalism," 696–97.

40. Quotation from Arvel B. Erickson, "The Non-Intrusion Controversy in Scotland, 1832–1943," *Church History* 11, no. 4 (1942): 310.

41. Erickson, "The Non-Intrusion Controversy," 313.

42. "Solemn Engagement in Defence of the Liberties of the Church and People of Scotland," reprinted in James Bryce, *Ten Years of the Church of Scotland: From 1833 to 1843, with Historical Retrospect from 1560*, Vol. 2 (Edinburgh: Blackwell and Sons, 1850), 429.

43. "Solemn Engagement in Defence of the Liberties," 431.

44. "Solemn Engagement in Defence of the Liberties," 435–36.

45. "Solemn Engagement in Defence of the Liberties," 436.

46. Erickson, "Non-Intrusion Controversy," 321.

47. "Solemn Engagement in Defence of the Liberties," 437–38.

48. "Solemn Engagement in Defence of the Liberties," 317–18, 382.

49. Brown, "Religion and the Rise of Liberalism," 703.

50. Michael Ledger-Lomas, "Unitarians and Presbyterians," in *The Nineteenth Century*, Vol. 3 of *The Oxford History of Protestant Dissenting Traditions*, ed. Timothy Larsen and Michael Ledger-Lomas (New York: Oxford University Press, 2017), 101.

51. Ledger-Lomas, "Unitarians and Presbyterians," 101.

52. See R. Buick Knox, "The Relationship between English and Scottish Presbyterianism, 1836–1876," *Records of the Scottish Church Historical Society* (1981), 43; and David M. Thompson, "Nonconformists and Polity," in *T&T Clark Companion to Nonconformity*, ed. Robert Pope (Edinburgh: T&T Clark, 2013), 106.

53. Ledger-Lomas, "Unitarians and Presbyterians," 102.

54. Lorimer, "Sketch of Old English Presbyterianism," in Synod of the English Presbyterian Church, *The Presbyterian Church of England: A Memorial of the Union* (London: James Nisbet and Co., 1876), 21.

55. Alexander Hutton Drysdale, *The History of the Presbyterians in England: Their Rise, Decline and Revival* (London: Publication Committee of the Presbyterian Church of England, 1889), 62–73, 287–303, 545–60.

56. Synod of the Presbyterian Church of England, *Digest of the Actings and Proceedings of the Synod of the Presbyterian Church in England, 1836–1876* (Synod's Publication Committee, 1877), 28.

57. *Digest of the Actings and Proceedings*, 29.

58. "The Polity of the Presbyterian Church," in *The Presbyterian Church of England*, 16.

59. "The Polity of the Presbyterian Church," 16.

60. *Digest of the Acts and Proceedings*, 29.

61. *Digest of the Acts and Proceedings*, 28.

62. *Digest of the Acts and Proceedings*, 29.

63. *Digest of the Acts and Proceedings*, 31.

64. Archibald Alexander, "The Established Church of Scotland, with an Account of the Secession of the Same," *Biblical Repertory and Princeton Review* 7, no. 1 (1835): 2.

65. Alexander, "The Established Church of Scotland," 30.

66. Alexander, "The Established Church of Scotland," 41.

67. Archibald Alexander, "The Scottish Seceders," *Biblical Repertory and Princeton Review* 7, no. 2 (1835): 224.

68. The Old School versus New School controversy of the 1830s and the subsequent split, which lasted until 1869, was the result of controversies over church polity, creedal subscription, and interdenominational cooperation.

69. Archibald Alexander, review of *The Present Conflict between the Civil and Ecclesiastical Courts Examined, with Historical and Statutory Evidence for the Jurisdiction of the Church of Scotland et al.*, *Biblical Repertory and Princeton Review* 11, no. 4 (1839): 510, 526.

70. Joseph Addison Alexander and Charles Hodge, "Proceedings of the General Assembly of the Free Church of Scotland, May 1843: with a Sketch of the proceedings of the Residuary Assembly," *Biblical Repertory and Princeton Review* 16, no. 1 (1844): 87.

71. Alexander and Hodge, "Proceedings of the General Assembly of the Free Church of Scotland," 102.

72. Charles Hodge, "The Claims of the Free Church of Scotland," *Biblical Repertory and Princeton Review* 16, no. 2 (1844): 245.

73. Joseph Addison Alexander, "History of the Church of Scotland, from the Introduction of Christianity to the period of the Disruption," *Biblical Repertory and Princeton Review* 16, no. 3 (1844): 417, 418.

74. Alexander and Hodge, "Proceedings of the General Assembly of the Free Church of Scotland," 103, 105.

75. Alexander and Hodge, "Proceedings of the General Assembly of the Free Church of Scotland," 117, 118.

76. Alexander and Hodge, "Proceedings of the General Assembly of the Free Church of Scotland," 112, 113.

77. Alexander and Hodge, "Proceedings of the General Assembly of the Free Church of Scotland," 114, 115.

78. Samuel Miller, *Letters concerning the Constitution and Order of the Christian Ministry: As Deduced from Scripture and Primitive Usage* (New York: Hopkins and Seymour, 1807), 8–10.

79. Miller, *Letters concerning the Constitution and Order*, 10–12.

80. Miller, *Letters concerning the Constitution and Order*, 18.

81. Miller, *Letters concerning the Constitution and Order*, 340.

82. Miller, *Letters concerning the Constitution and Order*, 346.

83. Miller, *Letters concerning the Constitution and Order*, 347.

84. Stuart Robinson, *The Church of God as an Essential Element of the Gospel: And the Idea, Structure, and Functions Thereof* (Philadelphia: Joseph M. Wilson, 1858), 11.

85. Robinson, *The Church of God*, part II.
86. Robinson, *The Church of God*, 117, 118.
87. Robinson, *The Church of God*, 120, 121.
88. Robinson, *The Church of God*, 127.
89. Robinson, *The Church of God*, 128.
90. Robinson, *The Church of God*, 126.

Seven Divine-Right Stipends

1. William Gregg, *History of the Presbyterian Church in the Dominion of Canada* (Toronto: Presbyterian Publishing and Printing Company, 1885), 55–56.
2. Gregg, *History of the Presbyterian Church*, 58–59.
3. Hodge, quoted in Gregg, *History of the Presbyterian Church*, 61.
4. Quoted in Gregg, *History of the Presbyterian Church*, 73.
5. Gregg, *History of the Presbyterian Church*, 74.
6. Gregg, *History of the Presbyterian Church*, 74.
7. See D. G. Hart, "In the Shadow of Calvin and Watts: Twentieth-Century American Presbyterians and Their Hymnals," in *Singing the Lord's Song in a Strange Land: Hymnody in the History of North American Protestantism*, ed. Edith L. Blumhofer and Mark A. Noll (Tuscaloosa: University of Alabama Press, 2004), chap. 4.
8. Watts and Enty, quoted in G. M. Ditchfield, "Changed in Dissenting Perceptions of the Hanoverian Succession, 1714–c.1765," in *Negotiating Toleration: Dissent and the Hanoverian Succession, 1714–1760*, ed. Nigel Aston and Benjamin Bankhurst (New York: Oxford University Press, 2019), 61.
9. K. R. M. Short, "The English Regium Donum," *The English Historical Review* 84 (January 1969): 59–60.
10. Short, "The English Regium Donum," 64.
11. Short, "The English Regium Donum," 69.
12. Quoted in Short, "The English Regium Donum," 69n2.
13. Short, "The English Regium Donum," 70.
14. Short, "The English Regium Donum," 71.
15. Short, "The English Regium Donum," 70.
16. Short, "The English Regium Donum," 73.
17. Quoted in Short, "The English Regium Donum," 75.
18. Quoted in Short, "The English Regium Donum," 74.
19. See Charles Ivar McGrath, "The Penal Laws: Origins, Purpose, Enforcement and Impact," in *Law and Religion in Ireland, 1700–1970*, ed. Kevin Costello and Niamh Howlin (New York: Palgrave Macmillan, 2021), chap. 2.

20. See *Irish* Regium Donum*: Its History, Character, and Effects* (London: Arthur Miall, 1865), 3–17.

21. See Peter Brooke, *Controversies in Ulster Presbyterianism, 1790–1836*, chap. 3, https://doi.org/10.17863/CAM.19194.

22. See John M. Barkley, *Short History of the Presbyterian Church in Ireland*, chap. 3, http://lisburn.com/books/history-presbyterian/history-presbyterian-2.html.

23. See Brooke, *Controversies in Ulster Presbyterianism*, chap. 5.

24. Archibald Boyd, *Sermons on the Church; or The Episcopacy, Liturgy and Ceremonies of the Church of England Considered in Four Discourses* (Dublin: W. Curry and Co., 1838), 88.

25. W. D. Killen, "Discourse I," in *Presbyterianism Defended and the Arguments of Modern Advocates of Prelacy Examined and Refuted* (Glasgow: William Collins, 1839), 60.

26. William McClure, "Discourse II," in *Presbyterianism Defended*, 112.

27. James Denhman, "Discourse III," in *Presbyterianism Defended*, 189.

28. Alexander Porter Goudy, "Discourse IV," in *Presbyterianism Defended*, 282.

29. Henry Wallace, "Introductory Essay," in *Presbyterianism Defended*, ix.

30. Wallace, "Introductory Essay," x.

31. Wallace, "Introductory Essay," viii.

32. Wallace, "Introductory Essay," vi.

33. Wallace, "Introductory Essay," vii.

34. Wallace, "Introductory Essay," viii.

35. Wallace, "Introductory Essay," ix.

36. Andrew R. Holmes, *The Irish Presbyterian Mind: Conservative Theology, Evangelical Experience, and Modern Criticism, 1830–1930* (New York: Oxford University Press, 2018), 94.

37. Andrew R. Holmes, *The Shaping of Ulster Presbyterian Belief and Practice, 1770–1840* (New York: Oxford University Press, 2006), 216.

38. A Voluntary, *The Irish* Regium Donum, 29.

39. A Voluntary, *The Irish* Regium Donum, 30.

40. A Voluntary, *The Irish* Regium Donum, 34.

41. Report quoted in A Voluntary, *The Irish* Regium Donum, 39.

42. A Voluntary, *The Irish* Regium Donum, 44–45.

43. A Voluntary, *The Irish* Regium Donum, 46.

44. A Voluntary, *The Irish* Regium Donum, 47.

45. Quoted in Stephen J. Peterson, *Gladstone's Influence in America: Reactions in the Press to Modern Religion and Politics* (New York: Palgrave Macmillan, 2018), 42.

46. Peterson, *Gladstone's Influence in America*, 45.

47. "Disestablishment: Free to Shape Our Future," https://www.churchofireland.org/about/disestablishment-150.

48. Thomas Hamilton, *History of the Irish Presbyterian Church* (Edinburgh: T&T Clark, 1886), 183.

49. Hamilton, *History of the Irish Presbyterian Church*, 184.

50. James Begg, *The Proposed Disestablishment of Protestantism in Ireland: Its Bearings upon the Religion and Liberties of the Empire* (Edinburgh: James Nichol, 1868), 9.

51. Begg, *The Proposed Disestablishment of Protestantism in Ireland*, 19.

52. Robert Elder, *The Irish Church Question: Considered with Special Reference to Free Church Principles, and the Present Duty of the Members of the Free Church* (Glasgow: David Bryce & Co., 1868), 7.

53. Elder, *The Irish Church Question*, 10.

54. Elder, *The Irish Church Question*, 8.

55. Elder, *The Irish Church Question*, 11.

56. Elder, *The Irish Church Question*, 6.

57. On the rise of Presbyterianism in eastern Canada, see Charles H. H. Scobie and George Rawlyk, *The Contribution of Presbyterianism to the Maritime Provinces of Canada* (Montreal: McGill-Queen's University Press, 1997).

58. See John S. Moir, *Enduring Witness: A History of the Presbyterian Church in Canada* (Don Mills, ON: Presbyterian Publications, 1987), chap. 5.

59. William Gregg, *Short History of the Presbyterian Church in the Dominion of Canada, from the Earliest to the Present Time* (Toronto[?]: privately printed, 1892), 24.

60. Gregg, *Short History of the Presbyterian Church*, 50–51.

61. Gregg, *Short History of the Presbyterian Church*, 51.

62. Gregg, *Short History of the Presbyterian Church*, 52.

63. Gregg, *Short History of the Presbyterian Church*, 53.

64. Formed in 1761, the Relief Church was the result of another contest in which the wishes of wealthy patrons prevailed over those of the parish in the selection of a pastor. Although this was also a factor in the Seceders' origins, the Relief Church was a broader church and welcomed Episcopalians and Independents. See chapter 4 herein.

65. Quoted in Oliver R. Osmond, "The Churchmanship of John Strachan," *Journal of the Canadian Church Historical Society* 16 (September 1974): 46.

66. Osmond, "The Churchmanship of John Strachan," 57.

67. Osmond, "The Churchmanship of John Strachan," 51.

68. Quoted in Curtis Fahey, *In His Name: The Anglican Experience in Upper Canada, 1791–1854* (Montreal: McGill-Queen's University Press, 1991), 128.

69. Fahey, *In His Name*, 130.

70. See Osmond, "Churchmanship," 50.

71. See Osmond, "Churchmanship," 50.

72. Quoted in John S. Moir, *Early Presbyterianism in Canada* (Gravelbourg, SK: Gravelbooks, 2003), 97.

73. See Moir, *Early Presbyterianism in Canada*, 98.

74. Moir, *Early Presbyterianism in Canada*, 100–101.

75. On the Free Church in Canada, see Richard W. Vaudry, *The Free Church in Victorian Canada, 1844–1861* (Waterloo, ON: Wilfred Laurier University Press, 1989).

76. Neil G. Smith, Allan L. Farris, and H. Keith Markell, *A Short History of the Presbyterian Church in Canada* (Toronto: Committee on History, Presbyterian Church in Canada, 1966), 46.

77. Smith, Farris, and Markell, *A Short History of the Presbyterian Church in Canada*, 46.

78. For these developments, see Moir, *Enduring Witness*, 101–3.

79. See Moir, *Enduring Witness*, chap. 6.

80. Moir, *Enduring Witness*, 106.

81. William Kilbourne, *The Firebrand: William Lyon Mackenzie and the Rebellion in Upper Canada* (Toronto: Clark, Irwin, and Co., 1956), 36.

82. Allan Greer, "1837–1838: Rebellion Reconsidered," *Canadian Historical Review* 76, no. 1 (1995): 8.

83. *The Report of the Earl of Durham: Her Majesty's High Commissioner and Governor-General of British North America*, 3rd ed., ed. John George Lambton et al. (London: Methuen and Co., 1922), 98.

84. *Report of the Earl of Durham*, 116.

85. *Report of the Earl of Durham*, 124.

86. *Report of the Earl of Durham*, 148.

87. *Report of the Earl of Durham*, 157.

88. *Report of the Earl of Durham*, 157.

EIGHT Presbyterian Politics after Establishment

1. David Hempton, *Religion and Political Culture in Britain and Ireland: From the Glorious Revolution to the Decline of Empire* (New York: Cambridge University Press, 1996), 168–69.

2. Daniel Walker Howe, *The Political Culture of American Whigs* (Chicago: University of Chicago Press, 1979), 21.

3. Richard Carwardine, "Religion and Politics in Nineteenth-Century Britain: The Case against American Exceptionalism," in *Religion and American Politics: From the Colonial Period to the 1980s*, ed. Mark A. Noll (New York: Oxford University Press, 1990), 241.

4. See Paul C. Gutjahr, *Charles Hodge: American Guardian of Orthodoxy* (New York: Oxford University Press, 2011).

5. Richard Carwardine, "The Politics of Charles Hodge," in *Charles Hodge Revisited: A Critical Appraisal of His Life and Work*, ed. John W. Stewart and James H. Moorhead (Grand Rapids, MI: Eerdmans, 2002), 278.

6. Carwardine, "The Politics of Charles Hodge," 258.

7. Hodge, quoted in Carwardine, "The Politics of Charles Hodge," 259.

8. Carwardine, "The Politics of Charles Hodge," 264.

9. Carwardine, "The Politics of Charles Hodge," 268.

10. Charles Hodge, "The American Quarterly Review on Sunday Mails," *Biblical Repertory and Princeton Review* 3, no. 1 (1831): 104.

11. Hodge, "The American Quarterly Review on Sunday Mails," 106.

12. Hodge, "The American Quarterly Review on Sunday Mails," 108.

13. This refers to the voluntary associations such as Sunday schools and Bible societies that Congregationalists and Presbyterians formed in the 1820s and beyond to promote religion and civilization. It drew much energy from the revivals of the so-called Second Great Awakening (1820–40).

14. Hodge, quoted in Carwardine, "Politics of Charles Hodge," 264.

15. Carwardine, "Politics of Charles Hodge," 264.

16. Carwardine, "Politics of Charles Hodge," 269.

17. Carwardine, "Politics of Charles Hodge," 266.

18. Ian J. Shaw, *High Calvinists in Action: Calvinism and the City, Manchester and London, 1810–1860* (New York: Oxford University Press, 2003), 155.

19. Shaw, *High Calvinists*, 156.

20. John M'Kerrow, *The History of the Secession Church*, rev. ed. (Glasgow: A. Fullarton and Co., 1841[1939]), 919–20.

21. Shaw, *High Calvinists*, 157.

22. Shaw, *High Calvinists*, 167.

23. Shaw, *High Calvinists*, 180–81.

24. Quoted in Shaw, *High Calvinists*, 182.

25. Shaw, *High Calvinists*, 184.

26. Shaw, *High Calvinists*, 189.

27. Shaw, *High Calvinists*, 195.

28. Shaw, *High Calvinists*, 185.

29. Quoted in Shaw, *High Calvinists*, 185.

30. Shaw, *High Calvinists*, 197.

31. Hempton, *Religion and Political Culture*, 169.

32. See Stewart J. Brown, *Thomas Chalmers and the Godly Commonwealth in Scotland* (New York: Oxford University Press, 1983).

33. A. M. C. Waterman, "The Place of Thomas Chalmers in Scottish Political Economy," in *A History of Scottish Economic Thought*, ed. Alexander Dow and Sheila Dow (London: Routledge, 2006), 193.

34. Waterman, "The Place of Thomas Chalmers," 187.

35. See Waterman, "The Place of Thomas Chalmers," 190–92.

36. See Brown, *Thomas Chalmers*, 197–98.

37. Brown, *Thomas Chalmers*, 198.

38. Brown, *Thomas Chalmers*, 131–34.

39. Brown, *Thomas Chalmers*, 236.

40. Quoted in Robert I. Mochrie, "Thomas Chalmers and the Civic Virtues," paper presented at the Association of Christian Ethicists, July 2008, 25, https://img1.wsimg.com/blobby/go/1bd725fe-b962-45d0-a959-d70afb527618/downloads/1cfm2lpob_503719.pdf?ver=1601157947818.

41. I. G. C. Hutchinson, *Industry, Reform and Empire: Scotland, 1790–1880* (Edinburgh: Edinburgh University Press, 2020), 245–47.

42. Brown, *Thomas Chalmers*, 196.

43. Hutchinson, *Industry*, 255.

44. A. S. Thalwell, *Proceedings of the Anti-Maynooth Conference of 1845: With an Historical Introduction, and an Appendix* (London: Seeley, Burnside, and Seeley, 1845), clxxxvi.

45. Hutchinson, *Industry*, 255.

46. Hutchinson, *Industry*, 145.

47. Hutchinson, *Industry*, 237, 239.

48. Brown, *Thomas Chalmers*, 372, 374.

49. See Andrew R. Holmes, *The Irish Presbyterian Mind: Conservative Theology, Evangelical Experience, and Modern Criticism, 1830–1930* (New York: Oxford University Press, 2018), 12–15.

50. Witherow, quoted in Andrew R. Holmes, "Presbyterian Religion, Historiography, and Ulster Scots Identity, c. 1800 to 1914," *The Historical Journal* 52, no. 5 (2009): 612.

51. Richard W. Vaudry, *Anglicans and the Atlantic World: High Churchmen, Evangelicals, and the Quebec Connection* (Montreal: McGill-Queen's University Press, 2003), 48.

52. See Christine Kinealy, ed., *Lives of Victorian Figures*, Part II, Vol. 1, *Daniel O'Connell* (London: Routledge, 2007), 119.

53. Josias Leslie Porter, *The Life and Times of Henry Cooke* (London: John Murray, 1871), 412.

54. Porter, *The Life and Times of Henry Cooke*, 412–13.

55. Report from the *Dublin Evening Mail*, quoted in Porter, *The Life and Times of Henry Cooke*, 415.

56. Edgar, quoted in Holmes, *Irish Presbyterian Mind*, 350.

57. General Assembly statement, quoted in Holmes, *Irish Presbyterian Mind*, 350.

58. Holmes, *Irish Presbyterian Mind*, 353.

59. Holmes, *Irish Presbyterian Mind*, 352.

60. *A Catechism of Tenant-Right*, quoted in Holmes, *Irish Presbyterian Mind*, 353.

61. Quoted in Holmes, *Irish Presbyterian Mind*, 356.

62. Quoted in Holmes, *Irish Presbyterian Mind*, 364.

63. Holmes, *Irish Presbyterian Mind*, 366.

64. Holmes, *Irish Presbyterian Mind*, 368.

65. Witherow, quoted in Holmes, *Irish Presbyterian Mind*, 368.

66. Holmes, *Irish Presbyterian Mind*, 368.

67. Quoted in Holmes, *Irish Presbyterian Mind*, 358.

68. John Webster Grant, *The Church in the Canadian Era* (Vancouver: Regent College Publishing, 1998[1972]), 24.

69. "Grant, The Rev George Monro (1835–1902)," Queen's Encyclopedia, https://www.queensu.ca/encyclopedia/g/grant-rev-george-monro.

70. An important study of Grant comes from Barry Mack, "George Monro Grant: Evangelical Prophet" (PhD diss., Queen's University, 1992).

71. William Lawson Grant and Frederick Hamilton, *George Monro Grant* (Toronto: Morang and Co., 1905), 18–19.

72. Grant, quoted in Grant and Hamilton, *George Monro Grant*, 32.

73. Grant, quoted in Grant and Hamilton, *George Monro Grant*, 37, 36.

74. Grant and Hamilton, *George Monro Grant*, 107.

75. Grant and Hamilton, *George Monro Grant*, 116.

76. George Monro Grant, *Reformers of the Nineteenth Century: A Lecture* (Halifax: James Bowes and Sons, 1867), 27.

77. Grant, *Reformers of the Nineteenth Century*, 31, 32.

78. George Monro Grant, *Sermon Preached at the National Scotch Church, St. Matthew's, Halifax, On the Morning of the First Sunday of 1866* (Halifax: James Bowes and Sons, 1866), 13.

79. Grant, *Sermon Preached at the National Scotch Church*, 11, 13.

80. Quoted in Grant, *George Munro Grant*, 92.

81. Grant, *George Munro Grant*, 95.

82. George Monro Grant, *Ocean to Ocean: Sandford Fleming's Expedition through Canada in 1872* (Toronto: James Campbell and Son, 1872), 20.

83. Grant, *Ocean to Ocean*, 20.

84. Quoted in Grant, *George Munro Grant*, 133.

85. Grant, *George Munro Grant*, 134, 135.

86. John S. Moir, *Enduring Witness: A History of the Presbyterian Church in Canada* (Montreal: Presbyterian Church of Canada, 1987[1974]), 134–36.

87. See Moir, *Enduring Witness*, 136–39.

88. Editorials, quoted in Moir, *Enduring Witness*, 134, 135.

89. Grant, quoted in Moir, *Enduring Witness*, 135.

90. Grant, *George Munro Grant*, 145–47.

91. Grant, quoted in Grant, *George Munro Grant*, 150.

92. A. Donald MacLeod, "The Union of 1861: Establishing an Authentic Canadian Identity for Colonial Presbyterians," http://adonaldmacleod.com/papers/the-union-of-1861-establishing-an-authentic-canadian-identity-for-colonial-presbyterians/.

93. Grant, quoted in Hilda Neatby et al., *Queen's University*, Vol. 1, *1841–1917: And Not to Yield* (Montreal: McGill-Queen's University Press, 1978), 225.

94. On Grant's legacy at Queen's, see George Rawlyk and Kevin Quinn, *The Redeemed of the Lord Say So: A History of Queen's Theological College, 1812–1912* (Kingston, ON: The College, 1980).

95. Rawlyk and Quinn, *The Redeemed of the Lord Say So*, 234.

96. J. David Hoeveler Jr., *James McCosh and the Scottish Intellectual Tradition* (Princeton, NJ: Princeton University Press, 1981), remains a reliable examination of the Presbyterian's thought.

97. See James McCosh, *The Life of James McCosh: A Record Chiefly Autobiographical* (New York: Scribner, 1896), 254–57.

98. McCosh, *The Life of James McCosh*, 121.

99. McCosh, *The Life of James McCosh*, 127–31.

100. McCosh, *The Life of James McCosh*, 258.

101. McCosh, *The Life of James McCosh*, 256–57.

102. *Addresses Delivered in Reference Free High School before the Legislature of New Jersey, March 1st, 1871* (Trenton, NJ: Murphy and Bechtel, 1871), 8.

103. "Civil Service Reform: Dr. M'Cosh's Experience in Great Britain," *New York Times*, December 13, 1880.

104. James McCosh, "The Relation of the Church to the Capital and Labor Question," in Evangelical Alliance, *National Perils and Opportunities* (New York: Baker and Taylor, Co., 1887), 215–17.

105. McCosh, "The Relation of the Church," 223.

Nine Presbyterian Nationalisms

1. Ciaran Brady, *James Anthony Froude: An Intellectual Biography of a Victorian Prophet* (New York: Oxford University Press, 2013), 2.

2. James Anthony Froude, *Calvinism: An Address Delivered at St. Andrews, March 17, 1871* (New York: Scribner, 1871), 7.

3. Froude, *Calvinism*, 7–8.

4. Froude, *Calvinism*, 7–8.

5. James Anthony Froude, *The History of England from the Fall of Wolsey to the Death of Elizabeth*, Vol. 1 (New York: Charles Scribner and Co., 1870), 104–5.

6. Froude, *The History of England from the Fall of Wolsey*, 578, 579.

7. In 1558, John Knox wrote *The First Blast of the Trumpet Against the Monstrous Regiment of Women* against female monarchs.

8. In 1572, Thomas Cartwright wrote *A Second Admonition to Parliament* against episcopal government in the Church of England.

9. In 1644, Samuel Rutherford wrote *Lex Rex* in defense of Presbyterian calls for the independence of the church from meddling civil officials.

10. James Joseph Coleman, "The Double-Life of the Scottish Past: Discourses of Commemoration in Nineteenth-Century Scotland" (PhD diss., University of Glasgow, 2005), 91.

11. Dickson's remarks in *Report of the Great Public Meeting Held in the Assembly Rooms, Edinburgh . . .* (Edinburgh: The Edinburgh Printing and Publishing Co., 1838), 8.

12. *Report of the Great Public Meeting*, 13.

13. William Muir, "The Whole Services, as Conducted in the High Church of Glasgow, at the Commemoration of the General Assembly of 1638," in Church of Scotland, *Review of Pamphlets on the Commemoration of the General Assembly 1638* (Edinburgh: Balfour & Jack), 15, 18.

14. Muir, "The Whole Services," 23, 24.

15. Quoted in Coleman, "Double-Life of the Scottish Past," 106, 109.

16. Both sides, quoted in Coleman, "Double-Life of the Scottish Past," 112.

17. Glasgow minister, quoted in Coleman, "Double-Life of the Scottish Past," 100.

18. Cunningham, quoted in Coleman, "Double-Life of the Scottish Past," 101.

19. Duff, quoted in Coleman, "Double-Life of the Scottish Past," 97.

20. See Colin Kidd, *Subverting Scotland's Past: Scottish Whig Historians and the Creation of an Anglo-British Identity, 1689–1830* (New York: Cambridge University Press, 2003), chap. 4.

21. Neil Forsyth, "Presbyterian Historians and the Scottish Invention of British Liberty," *Scottish Church History* 34, no. 1 (2004): 107.

22. Dodds, quoted in Colin Kidd, *Union and Unionisms: Political Thought in Scotland, 1500–2000* (New York: Cambridge University Press, 2008), 142.

23. Wylie, quoted in Kidd, *Union and Unionisms*, 143.

24. M'Crie, quoted in Forsyth, "Presbyterian Historians," 96.

25. Forsyth, "Presbyterian Historians," 108.

26. Smyth, quoted in Andrew R. Holmes, "The Scottish Reformations and the Origins of Civil Liberty in Britain and Ireland: Presbyterian Interpretations, c. 1800–1860," *Bulletin of the John Rylands Library* 90, no. 1 (2014): 2.

27. Holmes, "The Scottish Reformations," 4.

28. Andrew R. Holmes, "Presbyterian Religion, Historiography, and Ulster Scots Identity, c. 1800 to 1914," *The Historical Journal* 52, no. 3 (2009): 626.

29. Holmes, "Presbyterian Religion, Historiography," 625.

30. Holmes, "Presbyterian Religion, Historiography," 626.

31. Quoted in Holmes, "Presbyterian Religion, Historiography," 627.

32. Holmes, "Presbyterian Religion, Historiography," 627.

33. James Seaton Reid, quoted in Holmes, "Presbyterian Religion, Historiography," 628.

34. Montgomery, quoted in Holmes, "Presbyterian Religion, Historiography," 628.

35. James Seaton Reid, *History of the Presbyterian Church in Ireland: Comprising the Civil History of the Province of Ulster, from the Accession of James the First . . . Volume 3* (Belfast: William Mullan, 1867), 494.

36. Reid, *History of the Presbyterian Church in Ireland*, 507, 509.

37. W. D. Killen, *The Ecclesiastical History of Ireland: From the Earliest Period to the Present Times*, Vol. 2 (London: Macmillan, 1875), 548, 549, 550.

38. Killen, *The Ecclesiastical History of Ireland*, 553.

39. Killen, *The Ecclesiastical History of Ireland*, 547.

40. Killen, *The Ecclesiastical History of Ireland*, 552, 553.

41. Thomas Witherow, *Historical and Literary Memorials of Presbyterianism in Ireland (1623–1731)* (Belfast: William Mullan and Son, 1879), 2–3.

42. Thomas Witherow, *Historical and Literary Memorials of Presbyterianism in Ireland (1731–1800): Second Series* (Belfast: William Mullan and Son, 1880), 341.

43. Witherow, *Historical and Literary Memorials of Presbyterianism in Ireland (1731–1800)*, 344.

44. Witherow, *Historical and Literary Memorials of Presbyterianism in Ireland (1731–1800)*, 348–49.

45. Witherow, quoted in Holmes, "Presbyterian Religion, Historiography," 632.

46. Thomas Witherow, *Derry and Enniskillen in the Year 1689: The Story of Some Famous Battlefields in Ulster* (Belfast: William Mullan, 1873), 322.

47. Witherow, *Derry and Enniskillen*, 323.

48. Witherow, *Derry and Enniskillen*, 324, 325.

49. Witherow, *Derry and Enniskillen*, 327.

50. Brian J. Fraser, *The Social Uplifters: Presbyterian Progressives and the Social Gospel in Canada, 1876–1915* (Waterloo, ON: Wilfred Laurier University Press, 1988), 51, 53.

51. John Moir, *Enduring Witness: A History of the Presbyterian Church in Canada* (Montreal: Presbyterian Church of Canada, 1987[1974]), 136.

52. Fraser, *Social Uplifters*, 57.

53. John A. Johnston, "'No Slippery Undertaking': The Presbyterian Union of 1875," paper presented at the 1975 meeting of the Canadian Society of Presbyterian History (1875), 99–100, https://csph.ca/papers/.

54. Robert Campbell, *On the Union of Presbyterians in Canada* (Montreal: F. Grafton, 1871), 6, 7.

55. Campbell, *On the Union of Presbyterians in Canada*, 23.

56. Campbell, *On the Union of Presbyterians in Canada*, 38.

57. Campbell, *On the Union of Presbyterians in Canada*, 46–47.

58. Campbell, *On the Union of Presbyterians in Canada*, 6.

59. Campbell, *On the Union of Presbyterians in Canada*, 16–18.

60. Campbell, *On the Union of Presbyterians in Canada*, 28–29.

61. Joint Committee of the Presbyterian Churches in the Provinces of British North America, *Minutes of the Joint Committee of the Presbyterian Churches in the Provinces of British North America, on the Subject of Union* (Toronto, 1873), April 1873 minutes, 9.

62. *Minutes of the Joint Committee of the Presbyterian Churches*, 6.

63. R. F. Burns, *Our United Church: A Discourse Preached in Coté Street Presbyterian Church, Montreal, on the Evening of Sabbath the 20th June, 1875* (Montreal: A. A. Stevenson, 1875), 7.

64. Burns, *Our United Church*, 14.

65. Burns, *Our United Church*, 6.

66. Burns, *Our United Church*, 7 .

67. See D. G. Hart and John R. Muether, *Seeking a Better Country: 300 Years of American Presbyterianism* (Phillipsburg, NJ: P&R Books, 2007), chaps. 7–8.

68. "Report on the Reunion of the Presbyterian Church," in *The Presbyterian Digest: A Compend of the Acts and Deliverances of the General Assembly of the Presbyterian Church in the United States of America*, ed. George E. Moore (Philadelphia: Presbyterian Board of Education, 1873), 69.

69. "Report on the Reunion of the Presbyterian Church," 69.

70. "Report on the Reunion of the Presbyterian Church," 70.

71. See John D. Wilsey, *God's Cold Warrior: The Life and Faith of John Foster Dulles* (Grand Rapids, MI: Eerdmans, 2021).

72. Charles Hodge, *What Is Presbyterianism?: An Address Delivered before the Presbyterian Historical Society* (Philadelphia: Presbyterian Board of Publication, 1855), 6–7.

73. Hodge, *What Is Presbyterianism?*, 11.

74. Hodge, *What Is Presbyterianism?*, 79.

75. Thomas Smyth, *Ecclesiastical Republicanism, or the Republicanism, Liberality and Catholicity of Presbytery in Contrast with Prelacy or Popery* (Boston: Crocker and Brewster, 1843), 1.

76. Smyth, *Ecclesiastical Republicanism*, 3–4.

77. Smyth, *Ecclesiastical Republicanism*, 204.

78. Smyth, *Ecclesiastical Republicanism*, 206.

79. Smyth, *Ecclesiastical Republicanism*, 207.

80. Linda Colley, *Britons: Forging the Nation, 1707–1837* (New Haven, CT: Yale University Press, 1992), 19, 20.

81. Colley, *Britons*, 27–28.

82. Colley, *Britons*, 53.

83. Tony Claydon and Ian McBride, "The Trials of the Chosen Peoples: Recent Interpretation of Protestantism and National Identity in Britain and Ireland," in *Protestantism and National Identity: Britain and Ireland, c.1650–c.1850*, ed. Tony Claydon and Ian McBride (New York: Cambridge University Press, 1998), 17–18.

84. Claydon and McBride, "The Trials of the Chosen Peoples," 20.

85. Claydon and McBride, "The Trials of the Chosen Peoples," 27.

86. Claydon and McBride, "The Trials of the Chosen Peoples," 28.

87. James Anthony Froude, *History of England from the Fall of Wolsey to the Death of Elizabeth*, Vol. 12 (New York: Scribner, Armstrong, and Co., 1873), 569–70, 556, 562.

88. Froude, *History of England from the Fall of Wolsey*, 556.

89. Froude, *History of England from the Fall of Wolsey*, 562.

90. George Barrell Cheever, *God's Hand in America* (New York: M. W. Dodd, Brick Church Chapel, 1841), 66, 68.

91. Cheever, *God's Hand in America*, 69, 71, 73.

92. Cheever, quoted in John Wolfe, "A Transatlantic Perspective: Protestantism and National Identities in Mid-Nineteenth-Century Britain and the United States," in Claydon and McBride, eds., *Protestantism and National Identity*, 308.

Conclusion

1. "Visit of the Lord High Commissioner—Free Church General Assembly 2015," https://www.youtube.com/watch?v=Y-6HxDJzMeE.

2. "Loyal and Dutiful Address," in *Principal Acts of the General Assembly of the Free Church of Scotland* (2015), 35.

3. See D. G. Hart, *Calvinism: A History* (New Haven, CT: Yale University Press, 2013), chap. 3.

4. Arthur Herman, *How the Scots Invented the Modern World: The True Story of How Western Europe's Poorest Nation Created Our World and Everything in It* (New York: Three Rivers Press, 2001), 16.

5. Herman, *How the Scots Invented the Modern World*, 18.

6. Herman, *How the Scots Invented the Modern World*, 212.

7. Quoted in Gideon Mailer, *John Witherspoon's American Revolution* (Chapel Hill: University of North Carolina Press, 2016), 74.

8. John Witherspoon, "Address to the Natives of Scotland," quoted in Mailer, *John Witherspoon's American Revolution*, 73–74.

9. Colin Kidd, *Subverting Scotland's Past: Scottish Whig Historians and the Creation of an Anglo-British Identity, 1689–1830* (New York: Cambridge University Press, 2003), 193.

10. William Robertson, *The Works of William Robertson*, Vol. 8, *The History of America*, bk. 9, https://oll.libertyfund.org/titles/the-works-of-william-robertson-vol-8-the-history-of-america-books-9-10-an-historical-disquisition-concerning-ancient-india.

11. Wylie, quoted in Jerome E. Copulsky, *American Heretics: Religious Adversaries of Liberal Order* (New Haven, CT: Yale University Press, 2024), 57, 59.

12. Copulsky, *American Heretics*, 285.

13. Copulsky, *American Heretics*, 287, 286.

INDEX

D. G. HART is professor of history at Hillsdale College. He is the author of many books, including, most recently, *Benjamin Franklin: Cultural Protestant.*

www.ingramcontent.com/pod-product-compliance
Lightning Source LLC
Chambersburg PA
CBHW070403100426
42812CB00005B/1621

* 9 7 8 0 2 6 8 2 1 0 8 2 3 *